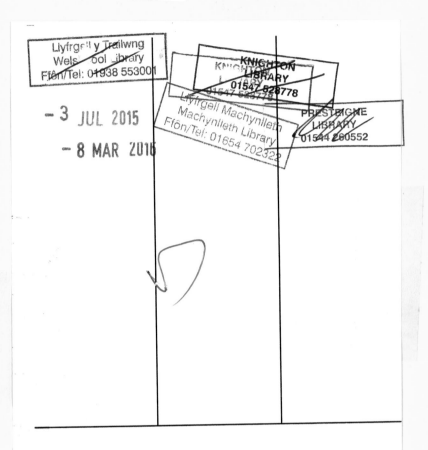

AN EYE FOR AN EYE

AN EYE
FOR AN EYE

A GLOBAL HISTORY OF
CRIME AND PUNISHMENT

MITCHEL P. ROTH

REAKTION BOOKS

This book is dedicated to all who have been wrongfully accused,
convicted and punished over the millennia

Published by
Reaktion Books Ltd
33 Great Sutton Street
London EC1V 0DX, UK

www.reaktionbooks.co.uk

First published 2014

Printed and bound by TJ International, Padstow, Cornwall

A catalogue record for this book is available from the British Library

ISBN 978 1 78023 359 8

Contents

Introduction

The past is never dead. It's not even past.

William Faulkner, *Requiem for a Nun*, Act 1, Scene 3 (1951)

The past is a foreign country; they do things differently there.

Leslie Poles Hartley, *The Go-Between* (1953)

In 2006 the international media was once again abuzz with the goings-on in several prison systems. Usually one would expect what follows to be a sad story of deprivation and despair. Has one ever heard of a 'feel-good' prison story? In most instances the first reaction would be appropriate, since there is little disagreement that prisons past and present are too often associated with poor food and hygiene, overcrowding and riots, violence and degradation, gangs and other bad actors. But this time it was a relatively anomalous episode revolving around three Israelis locked up in Sweden. In most cases, prisoners, particularly Israeli prisoners locked up abroad, jump at the chance to be transferred home from foreign jails. But this was not the case here. When offered this arrangement all three prisoners rejected the offer citing the more favourable conditions of the Scandinavian prison, where they could enjoy 'steaks, sex and private television airing World Cup games for free'. If this does not sound enticing enough, read about the other perks available in these jails-cum-'five-star hotels'. For starters, the aforementioned steaks, free cable TV and three-day conjugal visits in a luxury apartment provided on the prison grounds. Add to this the fact that not only does each prisoner have his own cell but along with numerous other amenities, twice a year he gets to traverse the streets of Stockholm (accompanied by a police car).[1]

This story was selected because it demonstrates on a micro level the diversity of just one form of punishment in two very different countries during the same time period. Both are at the higher end of the developed world. The point is that if there is this much discrepancy between penal sanctions at this level and time, one would expect the distinctions to be even more glaring when contrasting crime and punishment across a temporal and global perspective. The birth of the penitentiary and the introduction of incarceration during the eighteenth-century Age of Reason was a landmark in the global history of crime and punishment. While the infliction of pain on the human body had its limits, the notion of imprisonment continues to evolve and experimentation in various forms of detention continues around the world, limited only by financing, technology and the imagination. The examples of twenty-first-century Swedish and Israeli prison decorum offer just a fleeting glance into the global story of crime and punishment. But we are getting ahead of our story.

An Eye for an Eye takes the reader on a sometimes uncomfortable tour through the continuum of crime and punishment. It is not the type of tour a time traveller would probably sign up for, what with all of the beheadings, hangings, stonings and other gruesome accounts of penal sanctions of times past and present. There are a number of fine books examining the history of crime and punishment in specific countries, religions, regions and continents, but as of yet, except for multi-volume reference books, none have attempted to tackle this topic from a global perspective. The historical narrative that follows surveys the wide range of crimes and punishments that have developed over the millennia.

For the purposes of this book, punishment is defined (in the historical/written record) as a penalty imposed, usually by a state, on an offender who has violated a law. Historically, the concept of crime developed along the same lines as sin. The Bible, the Quran and the Torah were among the watershed developments contributing to the rationalization of crime through notions of sin and moral propriety. What distinguished crime from sin (breach of moral law), both of which deemed unacceptable behaviours, was that crime is generally understood to violate a written law. As the responsibility for handling crime passed from theological authorities to the state, and as clergies were replaced by police officers, 'sin has seemed to disappear by having been given it a new name and new monitor'.[2]

There is no definitive answer to the question, 'What is crime?' Popular conceptions equate crime with bad behaviour, or what one might today refer to as anti-social behaviour. But for the purposes of this book and to offer coherence to its structure, crime will be regarded as a legal concept, that is, what is or is not against the law. Readers will find that a society's criminal laws give vast insight into what a society and its rulers regard as its core values, morals and principles. In fact, for some cultures their earliest writings or literature come to us in the form of rules of behaviour and codes of conduct, often along with an accompanying set of punishments. It is pretty much accepted that the criminalization of behaviour is a gradual process and it is only in relatively sophisticated societies that we can apply the category of crime or distinguish between interpersonal transgressions and state violence. In prehistoric societies offenders were judged and punished by the community, due to the belief that their actions had endangered the entire community. From a global perspective crimes have differed as widely as the societies that defined them and continue to do so today. This work benefits from the amount of attention given to the history of crime and punishment over the past twenty years and therefore should be considered a synthesis and survey of this topic over the millennia, rather than a comprehensive reference work, which would be beyond the scope of a single volume.

One can only hypothesize about the prehistory of crime and punishment in the earliest stages of the development of human communities. Some disciplines have attempted to bridge this divide by interpreting the dark past by drawing inferences from observations of traditional cultures just before European contact and basing their assumptions on these observations. Prior to fourteenth-century England, there is little in the way of data about murders and other interpersonal crimes in the rest of the world. By most accounts, it was only with the advent of England's twelfth-century eyres, which brought periodic visitations by king's justices into the shires to record the minutiae of criminal activities, that a systematic study of homicide and other crimes can begin.[3] Naturally, the history of crime and punishment becomes easier to write with the accretion of more written documentation. It is then that the historian needs to winnow the deluge of material, in contrast to the mining of whatever scant sources are available.

Societies tend to develop methods of punishment that fall in line with their cultural beliefs. For example, Asian society often used exhibitory public punishments, which were considered a 'humiliation worse than death'. No form of death was more feared than one that interfered with the somatic integrity of the body. Thus the ultimate punishment consisted of beheading (often along with other physical mutilations), since it was believed that the body needed to be buried intact for the soul to make the proper passage.

Contrary to media sensationalism and popular culture's fixation on legions of serial killers and mass-murderers, long-term evidence suggests that the world is actually becoming a safer place.[4] Since the dawn of civilization, humans seem to have demonstrated a remarkable predisposition for committing mayhem against one another, as well as coming up with novel sanctions to punish those who transgressed community standards of propriety. Every culture has developed its own understanding of crimes and punishments, and human behaviour has been remarkably consistent over the millennia in its response to bad behaviour, limited only by technology and the imagination. Long before the creation of written law, societies developed rules and customs for keeping order and developed sanctions to protect the community from malefactors who violated them. Researchers refer to this early period with a variety of monikers, all seeking to avoid the pejorative 'primitive'. More neutral in spirit and much less judgmental, scholars prefer more seemly descriptors, such as 'prehistoric', 'tribal', 'preliterate', 'pre-colonial' and so forth. Examining how societies define crimes and come up with punishments for each is at the crux of what follows. Temporal and global variations in attitudes towards crime and punishment offer an excellent prism from which to view the march of mankind.

The history of crime and punishment is a work in progress as new discoveries periodically turn accepted notions on their heads. Picture the understanding of Babylonian law prior to the discovery of the Code of Hammurabi in 1901, or Egyptology before the Rosetta Stone was found in 1799, allowing a major breakthrough in deciphering hieroglyphics. Writing any type of 'global history' has to take into account the fact that for most of the human record there is no written documentation. Even in the twenty-first century, it is a challenge to acquire meaningful data on crime and punishment from vast heavily populated swathes of the world. So, if it is almost impossible to gather meaningful crime-related data in such nations as China, Vietnam, North Korea, Saudi Arabia, Sudan and Cuba, consider the challenges in finding sources for constructing a historical record from the preliterate past. Like the primordial past, the present is sometimes 'a foreign country', a daunting cipher when measuring patterns of crime and punishment in furtive societies and authoritarian regimes. So, researchers are often left to inference, deduction, anecdotes and speculation when chronicling global history of any subject over long periods of time. However this can sometimes be overcome by turning to folklore, oral history, anecdotes, mythology and classical literature, archaeological and anthropological evidence that can sometimes yield unexpected results to fill in the missing gaps in the historical and prehistorical record.

When one speaks of prisons and fines, the gallows and guillotine, beheading or whipping with the knout, it is obvious we are referring to various forms of punishment. However, when it comes to crime it is much more complicated since not every culture considers the same activities crimes. Theological regimes have been known to discipline adultery, fornication, blasphemy, citing the Lord's name in vain, apostasy and other acts as forms of criminal activity. But if the overwhelming majority of secular countries do not subscribe to these proscriptions, what is one to make of the fact that adultery is still a crime in 24 American states?

A number of fundamental axioms concerning global crime and punishment hold true over time. For example, as societies develop there is a tendency for them to shift sanctions from physical punishment to financial compensation and imprisonment. But no premise is more universal than the fact that over the historical record the status of victim and perpetrator was the main deciding factor over the outcome of a criminal case and the main determinant for punishment. From antiquity through the feudal era and into the present, it always helped to have been born into the privileged classes if one needs to appear before the justice system. From the first written legal code, law became a rich man's preserve. Hammurabi's Code clearly stated that punishment falls heaviest on the lower classes, repudiating any notion of equal favour under the law. For most common crimes wealthy malefactors could expect to suffer less pain and lower fines if the victim was a commoner or of a lower caste, as in the case of India. Punishment by status can be found in India's ancient *Laws of Manu*, among the Ifugao of the Philippines, and in Tang era China. But there are always curious anomalies, such as in the case of the Aztecs, who expected better behaviour from the nobility; thus the reverse was true, and members of the elite could expect more punitive sanctions than were meted out to commoners. Other constants include the fact that perpetrators of crime, particularly violent crime, have overwhelmingly been young males over the centuries. It would also follow that the most punitive punishments were directed at them as well. For example, there are no cases of women being hanged, drawn and quartered in the English experience.

Another pattern that has existed throughout the recorded history is the incessant search for more humane forms of execution. From Athenian use of the poison hemlock and simple beheading, to the technological marvels of the guillotine, the electric chair, and gas chamber and finally (for now) lethal injection, penal reformers have played an important role in determining how we execute the supposedly worst among us. The modern world has even intruded into some of the most primitive penal sanctions in use today. While in times past prisoners went to the headsmen with little in the way of preparation, in places such as modern Saudi Arabia they are often tranquillized before being beheaded in a public square and those facing hand and foot amputations in Sharia-dominated countries are soothed prior to the process with a healthy dose of anaesthesia.

Taking a global historical approach demonstrates not just the universality of certain crimes and punishments, but also beggars the notion that primitive sanctions were more brutal than modern ones. Yes, penalties were harsh and unforgiving, and rarely all but certain, but in most cases ancient tribal sanctions paled in comparison with Western penalties of being broken on the wheel, burned alive or disembowelled while alive just several centuries ago.

All works of history, especially those intended to be global in scope, are subject to limitations of content and length, inclusion and exclusion. This work is no exception. A deliberate decision was made to focus on certain crimes and punishments over others. Selection of what is and is not covered is predicated on whether there are specific criminal statutes directed at the offence. While global histories could be devoted to such topics as prisoner-of-war and death camps, genocide, terrorism, internecine conflict between religious sects, ethnic and political groups, and the Spanish Inquisition and other religious crusades against misbehaviour, it is beyond the scope of this historical survey.

When it comes to the historical record, children and women are frequently missing when it comes to crime and punishment. As mentioned earlier, most crimes have long been the purview of young adult males. When women enter the discussion, the farther back in history we go, they tend to be linked to 'gender-specific' crimes of witchcraft, fornication and infanticide. Children for the most part are even less obvious in historical chronicles since they are typically treated informally by justice systems, leaving few records in their stead. The crimes and punishments that follow are culled from those that have had the most continuity over time in many different cultures. For example, crime such as kidnapping is excluded from the coverage, although there are several fine books specifically devoted to it. But for a global history of crime and punishment the conceptual underpinnings of the act are rather new. In America, for example, kidnapping did not become 'a fully constructed public issue' until the Charley Ross case in 1874.[5]

Another topic that would be worthy of an entire book would be the history of financial crime. Probably the signature crime (thus far) of the twenty-first century, economic crimes have been with us since the first coins were cast, the first taxes invoked and the first financial crimes promulgated. For most of the historical record, financial crimes have consisted of counterfeiting, smuggling, tax evasion, bribery and so forth. Today, when the topic is broached it typically hinges on discussions of billion-dollar frauds perpetrated by the likes of Bernard L. Madoff. New technologies have facilitated frauds that were once unimaginable. Large-scale frauds have occurred with seeming regularity since the rapid expansion of commerce in the seventeenth century, but they are far from a universal pox on mankind, and thus have been mostly omitted from this work.

In order to weave a broad and interesting tapestry featuring the twin themes of crime and punishment, the author has delved into the dark corners of a number of diverse national historiographies. In most related books on the topic, the subject-matter is typically Western-centric, due in no small part to the greater number of sources available. This book attempts to broaden the discussion by shedding light on lesser known and less chronicled portions of the world, which have heretofore been missing from the historical discussion of crime and punishment. In order to accomplish this I have selected what I consider are a number of illuminating themes, events and stories in order to offer some type of chronological momentum and consistency.

Chapter One takes the reader from prehistory into the ancient world of criminal codes and punishments. Before the jury, the prison and the court system, preliterate cultures relied on unwritten customs more rigid than the written law. This chapter will examine what is known about some of these cultures before venturing into the earliest written codes of the Near East, Egypt, India, China and elsewhere.

Chapter Two examines the development of various influential legal traditions. More than a dozen legal traditions have come and gone over the historical record, leaving perhaps four legal traditions for the modern era. Some systems have survived, as in the case of Islamic, common, civil and socialist legal traditions, while many more have either disappeared or survived as hybrid systems. Most attention is focused on the common and civil legal traditions, probably due to the fact that European colonial powers spread them across the globe through conquest and colonization.

Chapter Three examines developments in crime and punishment in a variety of societies as they progressed towards state building. This chapter covers the way feudal societies were organized and how they implemented justice, before the rise of centralized bureaucracies and the creation of authorities for collecting taxes, creating laws and keeping the peace. Feudal societies flourished in regions as disparate as Japan and Western Europe, and the system remained an important organizing force for societies well into the nineteenth century.

Chapter Four chronicles the transformation of punishment and the development of the modern penitentiary. It is crucial to the story since a society's penal regime tells us much about a state and how far it has progressed towards reaching higher standards of civilization. As countries unevenly adopted the penitentiary there was a tendency for them to move beyond public capital and corporal punishments as they made the radical departure towards the use of imprisonment sanctions.

Chapter Five surveys the development of more organized forms of criminality prior to the globalization of crime. Until the nineteenth century, crime was mostly a local concern. Early bands of criminals appeared where governments were weak, policing ineffective and the population stratified. There was an amazing diversity of outlaw bands, popping up in virtually every society. Some of the earliest accounts come from Asia. Thirteenth-century Japan's shogunate featured the *akuto,* or 'evil bands'. Various permutations of the outlaw stereotype have ranged from India's dacoits, Scottish reivers to Mexican *plateados,* Brazilian *cangaceiros* and other variations. There were even Jewish and gypsy bandits in Europe. But what they all had in common was that they prevailed only in vicinities where they had some type of popular support, usually in rural districts. Moreover, their days were typically numbered once governments became better organized and policing more adequate. It was with the rise of more organized criminal organizations, such as slave traders, maritime pirates and drug traffickers that criminal activities began to transcend national boundaries concomitantly with advances in transportation and communication and the opportunities made possible by various global prohibition regimes.

Chapter Six tracks the roots of international criminal gangs and takes off from the previous chapter which highlighted local and regional organized criminal activity. The rise of globalization, made possible with improved transportation and communication developments, along with the passage of poorly conceived commerce prohibitions stimulated the rise of transnational criminal gangs that continue to blight the modern world.

Chapter Seven explores the history of murder, focusing on forms of multiple murder and related sex crimes. A similar chapter could have been devoted to robbery, rape, bribery and other crimes that have had staying power over the centuries. But no crime serves as a template for measuring crime better than murder, which continues to be probably the most reported of all types. Murder has been a subject of interest in the world's literature from the ancient Greeks and the Bible to Shakespeare and to the current popularity of the true crime genre. Despite all of the scientific and cultural advancements of our species, we still kill each other at alarming rates. By one estimate, more than 1 million Americans were murdered in the twentieth century (not including victims of war). As old as mankind, murder plays a recurring role in this survey. Over a century ago, Frederic William Maitland remarked that 'if a fairy were to offer him the opportunity of personally witnessing the same type of scene across societies, he would choose a murder trial, because it reveals so many matters of the first importance'.[6] One crime historian even suggests that the very word 'murder' has the advantage of belonging to everyday language. Unlike such crimes as blasphemy, manslaughter, parricide and paedophilia, it is doubtful that anyone hearing the word 'murder' would misidentify it as anything other than taking a life. As historian Roger Lane put it, 'Murder is in fact the easiest of crimes to track through time: always taken seriously, almost always subject to law, never common enough to be completely tolerated or overlooked.'[7] Perhaps no form of murder is studied more than serial murder. Contrary to popular notions that serial murder is a modern phenomenon, there is evidence that serial killers have always been part of the human experience. One needs look no further than fairy tales, stories of witchcraft and the purported existence of werewolves and vampires over the centuries. From Africa to western Europe, shapeshifting stories of leopard men, wolfmen and the like were probably inspired by actual mutilation murders in a time of superstition before the birth of modern policing and forensic investigation.

Chapter Eight examines the role played by colonialism and other state building processes in the spreading of penal sanctions across the globe. Societies in close proximity to one another tend to develop similar philosophies about crime and punishment. However, societies that evolve in relative isolation, such as China and Egypt, often produce vastly different conceptual models of crime and punishment. But one of the most powerful vehicles for the transmission of notions related to crime and punishment has been the process of European colonialism. For centuries world powers have established colonies in the far-flung reaches of the world, in the process transmitting their penal philosophies and sometimes borrowing from indigenous traditions as well. Later, as these colonies, territories and protectorates made the transition to statehood, much of their penal philosophy was grounded in the hybridization of colonial and indigenous penal practices.

Chapter Nine completes the saga of crime and punishment, demonstrating the cyclical nature of crime and punishment as well as the remarkable continuity between ancient and modern criminal behaviours. This chapter shows that at the same time that high-tech crimes are evolving and increasing, ancient misbehaviours such as blasphemy, heresy, adultery, piracy and witchcraft continue to flourish alongside the age old punishments of executions, shaming and banishment. This chapter also demonstrates a willingness of societies to go back to the historical record when it comes to crime and punishment, adapting crime control strategies from the past, while calling into questions former penal regimes heavily predicated on capital punishment and imprisonment.

A global history of crime and punishment reveals that despite amazing advances on every level of the human experience, there is a remarkable continuity in what crimes are committed as well as the sanctions used to punish them. Although the means for committing crimes are quite different in the digital post-industrial world, the goals and motivations of criminals and criminal justice systems have not strayed too far from their antecedents. Ultimately, *An Eye for an Eye* demonstrates that the history of crime and punishment remains an inconsistent chronicle of experimentation – borrowing, adapting and finding new alternatives – often finding penal officials going back to history books to retool ancient sanctions for a new world. Although empirical evidence regarding their success is meagre if not suspect, the past decades have seen the return of shaming, chain gangs and exhibitory punishment, sanctions once thought relics of a penal past.

I

Crime and Punishment: In the Beginning

Over the past two centuries, thanks to the preservative qualities of northern European peat bogs, uncannily preserved corpses of men, women and children dating back to the early Iron Age have been un-covered virtually intact. Some of the bodies bore the marks of executions – cut throats, strangulation marks, bone fractures and other wounds – made prior to being tossed into the bogs. One of the most famous of these, Lindow Man, dating back to 350 BC, was uncovered in 1984 in a Cheshire peat bog, and is now on display in the British Museum. Modern technology has allowed scientists to reveal his last moments and identify numerous injuries as well as the ropes still fastened around his bound limbs; these were just the preliminaries to having his throat slit. With numerous fractures of the face and skull it would seem he had been murdered and unceremoniously tossed into the water. Other bodies bear the marks of hanging, strangulation and decapitation, leading one archaeologist to surmise that these could represent 'the beginnings of a sense of justice and punishment', at least in northern Europe.[1] In any case, the actual circumstances of Lindow Man's death will never be known for sure since it is all but impossible to distinguish between a murder and a ritual killing.[2]

Writing in the first century AD, the Roman historian Tacitus offers some of the earliest insights into the penal practices of preliterate Northern European cultures. Tacitus claimed that the bog deaths (he called the bog bodies *corpores infames*, or infamous bodies) were ordered for various sexual transgressions such as adultery and that,

> The mode of execution varies according to the offence. Traitors and deserters are hung on trees; cowards, shirkers and sodomites

are pressed down under a wicker hurdle into the slimy mud of the bog. The distinction in punishment is based on the idea that offenders against the State should be made example of; deeds of shame should be buried out of men's sight.

But the operative word here is still 'probably' because despite all we think we know about the unwritten past and the words of ancient historians there is still no consensus as to whether the bog bodies were the result of punishment, sacrifices to the gods, or a combination of both.[3] What is beyond conjecture is the fact that they did not die natural deaths.

Since time immemorial, humans seem to have had a natural predisposition for committing mayhem and coming up with novel sanctions to punish those who perpetrated the acts. In fact it often seems that we are as hardwired for violence as we are for empathy. The earliest written testimony to such behaviour dates back more than 4,000 years to the ancient Near East. Mankind, however, has been around much longer than that.

Some sense of order has underpinned every human society, as did the recognition that individual impulses had to be restrained somehow for the good of the wider community. Various authorities argue that law only exists where there is a system of courts and law codes supported by a fully politically organized state; but very few pre-state societies had law in this sense. However, rules protecting community members from malicious actions of other members are found everywhere, and in this sense law does exist in most preliterate societies. But these laws differ widely. Early societies came in all manner of incarnations, as did their customs and belief systems. As one anthropologist put it, there is 'no one "primitive law", any more than there is one primitive society'.[4] Nonetheless, every society has developed rules for governing and regulating behaviour.

Before the advent of writing, societies equated what we regard as 'crimes' or 'sins' with acts that were most likely to bring the wrath of gods onto the community; acts that were considered a danger to the whole community. For example, African Ashanti tribal members equated crime with sin, or *oman akyiwadie*, acts that were 'hateful to the tribe', or actions that were not only offensive to tribal ancestral spirits but were most likely to bring the wrath of the gods on the entire tribe. It was thus up to the chief to see that the malefactor was punished, otherwise the tribe would be punished through the wrath of its ancestors.[5]

Much of what is known, or what we think we know about crime and punishment in the preliterate era is speculative, based in large part on anthropological, ethnographic and archaeological research. But without a written record, any findings must remain purely approximate, based on oral histories and the observation of extant nomadic and hunter-gatherer groups. When the British anthropologist Robert Sutherland Rattray studied the African Ashanti society at the turn of the twentieth century he concluded that they were 'peaceful', with no trace of vendetta, and with the penal system resting in the hands of high-ranking leaders such as judges, chiefs and kings. He was confident in his assumption that as the Ashanti rose in power it was accompanied with an increase in the severity of punishments, 'probably the antithesis of early justice'.[6] The word 'probably' is the operative term here since much of unrecorded history is not much more than an educated guess. The closest Rattray could come to interpreting the past was to examine Ashanti culture prior to European contact. One of his most startling claims was that the strongest sanction seemed to be 'the power of ridicule'. Through his research and examination of the oral tradition he found that the fear of ridicule was always present, suggesting that 'it is doubtful if even the worst of humanly inflicted punishments was more dreaded than this subtle weapon which came in laughing guise to rob a man of his own self-respect and the respect of his associates'. There is an Ashanti proverb that gives credence to his theory, stating, 'If it be a choice between disgrace and death, then death is preferable.' This is best illustrated by a story about a village elder who bent down in obeisance to a visiting dignitary but 'inadvertently broke wind'; within an hour he had gone home and hanged himself. His tribal brothers, when queried about his drastic reaction were of one mind, agreed he had done the appropriate thing under the circumstances.[7]

Thanks to oral traditions and the research by ethnographers and anthropologists such as Rattray, we do have some foundation for interpreting early Ashanti traditions of crime and punishment. The most common form of capital punishment was beheading with a small knife. Executioners were expected to grab the individual and begin cutting from the front of the neck to the back. (You might get some idea of this from videos of recent beheadings of American hostages by Al Qaeda in Iraq.) But the ever pragmatic Ashanti allowed the executioner, 'if he did not want to look him in the face', to hold the head down and 'slice and saw through the neck commencing from the back'. Other methods included strangling with a leather thong or manually, and bludgeoning with a club.[8] In other cases some type of mutilation would suffice for execution. In cases where subjects were considered impertinent they might have the right ear (or part of it) severed. This is illustrated in a popular story told about a man ordered to pay a sheep as compensation for some offence; he responded that a cow would be more appropriate, despite knowing full well that this animal was anathema to the group. In response he had both ears cut off. In other cases, those accused of bearing false witness or verbal abuse would have their lips cut off; the nose might be amputated in cases where individuals were either disrespectful or had a reputation for preening and overbearing conduct.[9] Castration was reserved for attendants in the chief's harem who happened to catch a glimpse of a naked wife; therefore the attendants usually entered the harem announcing their arrival, shouting: 'So ho, so ho!' There were certainly other punishments, but it was also evident that prior to the arrival of Europeans one could avoid execution in certain cases through the process of 'buying one's head' (paying one's way out), except in cases of murder. Pregnant women sentenced to death were fastened to logs until they gave birth; both were then executed. By contrast, the British, who would later colonize the Ashanti region, demonstrated their civility by allowing a condemned female prisoner to give birth before being executed, the only difference being that the child was put up for adoption.

There are few worldwide norms when it comes to crime and punishment. Indeed, 'the absolutely uniform human conscience does not seem to exist', at least according to the historian Jacques Barzun.[10] However, incest is one crime that seems to be almost universally recognized as abhorrent behaviour. Blood kinship was the strongest binding force in prehistoric societies suggesting the existence of the incest taboo in almost every society dating back to an origin in prehistory. Incest was among the capital cases of a sexual nature. The Ashanti considered incest a capital crime and referred to it as *mogyadie*, or 'the eating of one's own blood'. However, the meaning of incest was much broader than its modern context, since it included having sexual intercourse with anyone belonging to the same blood or clan, no matter how distant the links; just sharing the same clan name was enough to have both parties put to death. By most accounts no other sin was regarded with more revulsion.

When it comes to adultery there is much less universality, although it typically became a matter to be punished only when the woman was the guilty party. The earliest written codes exact punitive sanctions for adultery. Adulterous women would be accorded the death penalty under Hammurabi, the Hebrews and later in classical Greece. It should also be understood that the inhabitants of Babylonia in the time of Hammurabi (c. 1792–1750 BC) probably practised some form of ancestor worship, and adulterous behaviour could harm or weaken bloodlines and would be considered sacrilegious. In the earliest preserved Near Eastern adultery laws, brutal punishments were aimed at regulating relationships between family members. When it came to adultery the husband was permitted to decide between executing both the wife and lover or mutilating them; the wife could expect to have her nose cut off, while the lover faced castration and some type of facial mutilation. Adulterous women of the Tupuri tribe in modern-day Cameroon had to wear a brass ring around the neck for life; Native American Blackfoot women had to instantly submit to nose amputation if caught in the act by their husband.

In some tribal cultures all forms of homicide were considered criminal, whether accidental or planned, since it deprived the ruler of a subject.[11] According to Uganda's Sebei tribal law, unlike Western law, killing a close relative was not viewed as murder; this can only be rendered comprehensible when considering the fact that the clan was the legal entity with respect to killing. In cases such as this, the leader of the clan can be practical. One anthropologist who has studied the Sebei people remembers an account where the chief concluded, 'One life has been destroyed. We cannot lose two men from the clan. The deceased was a bad man and deserved to be killed.' Some African tribal societies such as the Bantu in the southwest of the continent drew distinctions between accidental manslaughter and accidental injury of property, while the Ifugao of the Philippines took remarkable care in discriminating between voluntary and careless and accidental deeds. Among some Native American Plains cultures the penalty for murder was four years' banishment. During this period the murderer was required to remain on the edge of the camp and hold no relations with anyone but immediate family members who were permitted to provide him with sustenance. The duration of the punishment depended on the perspective of the victim's family, since he could return from exile as soon as they allowed it.[12] Tribes such as the Pawnee rarely took life for life, while members of the Powhatan Confederacy in Virginia treated murder as an offence against society, requiring the execution of the offender in the name of the chief.

Honour Killings, Vendettas, Compensation and Blood Money

Crimes committed in the name of honour are still common in many parts of the world. Nowhere does this tradition have a stronger legacy than in the Mediterranean region, where husbands have been legally killing their wives (and lovers) for acts of infidelity since at least 400 BC. Fast-forward 2,400 years to the twentieth century, where Article 587 of the Italian Penal Code allowed a cuckolded husband (or outraged father or brother) to punish the errant wife (daughter or sister or lover) and expect to serve only between three and seven years behind bars. In similar fashion, Article 562 of the Lebanese Penal Code allowed a man to slay a female relative whose sexual conduct 'dishonours the family'. A women's group attempted to have this rule overturned in the 1970s, but the Christian president Suleiman Frangieh responded: 'Don't touch honour'. He backed up his words by pardoning a man only nine months after he strangled his daughter for flirting. The honour defence has been acknowledged in at least three American states, including Texas into the twentieth century. Outlawed in 1991, 722 men used the honour defence in São Paulo, Brazil, in the 1980s alone. It should be noted here that in Latin America crimes of honour defences were just one of many notions imported to the New World by colonial cultures centuries earlier.

The earliest societies recognized the importance of maintaining order by prohibiting the escalation of blood feuds. One way in which this was accomplished was by requiring that the only permissible retaliatory act would be either the death or mutilation of the offender by a member of the aggrieved party's family, and that the cycle of revenge would go no farther after this. It was at this point that a family was considered to be off the hook and to have paid its debt to the victim's family. One of the most common constructs of early law systems is the substitution of blood money or restitution in lieu of retaliation. The Code of Hammurabi and other Mesopotamian laws as well as the Old Testament (especially in Exodus and Deuteronomy) contain provisions for compensation (as does later Islamic law). Blood money was well known in Germanic law where agnatic relatives were liable for the blood money. It played an important part in the Anglo-Saxon justice system. The Laws of Ethelbert, dating back almost 1,500 years, contain a detailed list of payments for various injuries.

Blood money was a tradition enshrined by Islamic law (see chapter Two). Disputes over killings, even in modern-day Pakistan, are still

CRIME AND PUNISHMENT: IN THE BEGINNING

resolved out of court through an agreement between the victim's heirs and the perpetrators. The former must forgive; the latter must pay *diyat,* or compensation. This was illustrated in the case of CIA operative Raymond Davis, who claimed to have killed two Pakistanis in self-defence, but was arrested nonetheless. Senior Pakistani officials suggested that the case could be resolved with the payment of money to the families to drop the case.[13]

Over the centuries, wherever blood feuds were an accepted part of the extra-legal process, there were often strict rules that had to be followed. As late as the twentieth century an Albanian assassin was expected to warn his victim before killing him; the act itself can never be perpetrated from behind. Once killed, the corpse was then to be laid face up; and no one was permitted to rob the corpse. Other rules prohibit the targeting of shepherds or committing murders in a marketplace or on a busy road. In Albania, blood feuds could be temporarily interrupted by mutual consent whenever either faction wanted to work their fields, give a party or conduct business. The bereaved family was permitted to exact vengeance on the killer or any of his kin within 24 hours; after 24 hours only the killer could be targeted.

Over the past several thousand years there is ample proof that many societies accepted some type of material compensation to avert retaliation from a victim's aggrieved family or kinship group. There is just as much documentation recognizing that societies differed regarding which crimes could be resolved through compensation. Ifugao customary law (from Luzon in the Philippines), for example, allowed payment for virtually all offences, except for wilful homicide, which could be satisfied only through the shedding of blood.

In other cultures where collective responsibility is recognized (meaning the perpetrator's kin group is responsible), the murder of a family member may lead to a vendetta. Aboriginal Australians in Queensland have avoided this by replacing it with a 'legalized encounter' involving the criminal, armed with a shield, and the kin or local group of the slain. The members of the kin group are permitted to throw spears at the killer, who blocks them as best he can. Once he has been wounded and some blood has been shed by the target, the proceedings (and future conflict between both sides) are considered concluded, whether he dies or not. Lest this be confused by the later trial by ordeal to determine guilt or innocence, in this case the perpetrator was known to be guilty at the very beginning.

Still other cultures, such as the Eskimo of Greenland, responded to injury, theft, destruction of property or abduction of wives with a form of shaming in which they create satirical songs mocking the perpetrator of the crime, 'exaggerating and deriding them and even rattling the family skeletons as well'. The accused was allowed to respond in kind, but the kicker here is that no overt physical action took place. When it came to murder, however, the stakes were raised for the culprit, with the closest relative of the victim expected to respond in similar fashion against the assailant or his closest family member. The notion of collective responsibility can have the unintended consequence of handing down the feud to the next generation, leading to the loss of many innocent lives. According to one anthropologist, 'Years may pass before punishment for the misdeed is attempted, and in the meantime the murderer may visit his victim's family, be welcomed and entertained by them, and live in peace for the longest period. Then he may suddenly be dispatched by his companions on a hunting party or challenged to a wrestling match and put to death if vanquished.'[14]

Another curious aspect of tribal criminal law comes to us from the tribes of South Africa, such as the Zulu and Xhosa. Justice was in the hands of the chief, since by tradition all persons belonged to him. Therefore he was to be compensated for any loss of a subject. A male was worth seven head of cattle, and a woman ten head (the difference is due to the dowry obtained at marriage). While prior to 1820 a husband could kill an adulterer with impunity, for the most part, fines constituted the main criminal penalty.

Revenge has been the driving force behind penal systems from antiquity to the present. Recent cases in Latin America, the Middle East and elsewhere continue to demonstrate the propensity of agricultural societies to take the law into their own hands in the name of justice. On 11 June 2003 the village leader of La Candelaria, Mexico, was buried after having been abducted and murdered. Villagers quickly rounded up four suspects, lynching two of them and leaving another for dead. Infuriated by a legacy of systemic corruption and repression, local residents administered their own brand of extra-legal justice without government interference, leading one observer to suggest 'The rule of law has never existed in Chiapas', adding that 'When people don't have access to justice, they are in a whole different environment [and] justice is defined by those who carry it out.' Lynchings were common in the more indigenous parts of Mexico in 2002, long before the current internecine bloodshed between the drug cartels. Many of the killings were the result of personal vendettas and feuds. Police, however, were of the impression that 'Indians killing Indians [was] almost a natural state of affairs' and worried about intervening lest they 'upset the delicate power balances inside and between the villages that maintain at least a semblance of order in the region'.[15]

Two years later the mayor of a Bolivian town was strung up unceremoniously from a lamppost and set on fire. He had already been beaten to death by the time the rope was fastened around his neck. Local residents had unsuccessfully taken a legal course of action prior to the lynching. They had brought their accusations of embezzling hundreds of thousands of dollars of government funds meant for the poor villagers to the Bolivian finance ministry, the Senate and the courts – all failed to act. The death of the mayor of the downtrodden village of Ayo Ayo was widely viewed as an 'act of communal justice', part of what was accepted as a 'time-honoured tradition' in small mountain communities an hour south of La Paz. As one observer put it, he was killed 'because he was part of an unjust system that has kept Bolivian Indians in poverty and out of power'. In the words of one peasant, the white and mestizo elite that run the country 'should be finished in the same way, if not burned, then drowned or strangled or pulled apart by four tractors'. This perspective was supported by one sociologist who saw the lynching 'as a rejection of a justice system widely perceived as serving the interests of the rich and the powerful'. In any case, the death penalty was only used in extreme cases when entire communities saw no other alternatives.[16]

The Code of Hammurabi

In 1901, French archaeologists excavating in what was formerly Mesopotamia (present-day Iraq) unearthed the Code of Hammurabi, an 8-foot-high basalt slab of black stone inscribed with 4,000 lines of cuneiform.[17] It was here between the Tigris and Euphrates rivers that conditions favourable for the development of complex social organization took shape some 5,000 years ago. The code would go on to influence penal procedures throughout the growing civilized world, but its rules would only reach ancient Greece and Rome following contacts with the Near East.

There is enough fragmentary evidence of earlier law codes from the region of the fertile crescent to recognize that a system of fines and compensation had been developed some 300 years before Hammurabi, dating back to the founder of the Third Dynasty of Ur, Ur-Nammu (r. c. 2111–2095 BC); some of the verbiage from this code is replicated in the Code of Hammurabi. But what distinguishes Hammurabi's Code is the first appearance of the principle of the notion of 'an eye for an eye'. The Code diverges from earlier law codes that relied on fines and various forms of compensation, by introducing the *talio* (Latin, retaliation), considered the first attempt to control private vengeance. This law of retaliation took such a literal view of accountability, that if a house collapsed and killed the son of the owner, the son of the responsible builder was killed instead of the builder himself. However, if a slave was killed in the collapse, all that was required was to compensate the loss with another slave (ll. 229–31). In another clause, 'If a man strikes a free-born woman so that she loses her unborn child, he shall pay ten shekels for her loss' (ll. 209–10). But, if the woman dies, the assailant's daughter would be put to death. Likewise, individuals caught looting during fires could be tossed into the flames. The influence of these laws is readily discernible in Near Eastern history. In a later Assyrian law code inscribed on a set of clay tablets and uncovered during an archaeological excavation in 1903, the same cuneiform literary pattern continued: 'If during a fight with a citizen, a woman ruptures one of his testicles, then the sentence is amputation of one finger, if after medical treatment the other testicle ruptures, sentence is blinding in both eyes.' As recently as 1999, under Pakistani law, family members were allowed to kill a convicted killer in the same manner their relative was killed (or show mercy). This was demonstrated after a serial killer convicted of strangling, dismembering and dissolving the remains of 100 children was sentenced to be killed in the same manner.

In essence, the Code of Hammurabi is divided into 282 sections, each representing innovations launched by the king; not a fully formed set of laws, the Code introduced a set of punishments each distinct for the three classes of people recognized in Babylonian society. What it did not do, though, was codify any new body of laws to neither guide legal proceedings nor inform citizens of their rights and duties.[18]

Penalties were very harsh, but paled in comparison to being broken on the wheel or being boiled or disembowelled by European executioners just several centuries ago. Under Hammurabi's Code, the death penalty was mentioned some 30 times, and non-capital physical punishments included amputations of tongues, eyes and breasts as well as floggings. Execution by drowning was reserved for adultery, incest with a daughter-in-law, and cheating customers at a tavern by watering down alcoholic drinks. Impalement was the penalty for women who procured an abortion.

Hammurabi claimed authorship of the Code, and its provisions are secular proof of the power of the state. The state's reaction to deviant behaviour was essentially one of vengeance: death for death. The notion of revenge is integral to most criminal justice systems. It also introduced the principle of 'expressive' or 'sympathetic' punishment, a reference to the use of corporal punishment on a part of the body that had committed a crime, usually requiring amputation or some mutilation. For example if a man stole something from another, he would be expected either to pay a fine or have his hand cut off; a repetition of the act would require the amputation of the other hand. If a man kissed a married woman, he could have his lower lip cut off. Likewise in cases of indecent assault, fingers would be removed and rapists emasculated, while those with calumnious tongues could expect their amputation in like fashion.

Hammurabi's Code also introduced perhaps the first law directed at financial crime. The code mentions penalties for theft, but it also refers to fraud as in the case of 'tavern keepers', usually of the female persuasion, who violate the law if they do not 'accept corn according to gross weight in payment of drink, but takes the money, and the price of the drink is less than that of the corn',[19] wherein she 'shall be convicted and thrown into the water', shorthand for drowning.

Status, Crime and Punishment

In Hammurabi's Babylonia, social classes became more differentiated; as a result, his eponymous code became a rich man's law, establishing that an offender's and victim's standing in society determined what punishment was warranted. Punishment for crimes depended on which of three classes the victim and the perpetrator belonged to. For example, 'If a noble has broken another's bone, they shall break his bone. If he has destroyed the eye of a commoner or has broken the bone of a commoner, he shall pay one mina of silver. If he has destroyed the eye of a noble's slave or broken the bone of a noble's slave, he shall pay one half his value.' This system of graduated punishments depended on the seriousness of the offence committed and the position of the criminal. While ordinary women were permitted to visit a wine shop, if a priestess did, she was burned to death. A female wine seller caught cheating on weights might be thrown into a river; but if she allowed her wine shop to be used as a meeting place for robbers she would be executed.

Babylonia was not alone in determining punishment according to the status of victim and offender. India's ancient *Laws of Manu* (*Manava*

Dharmasastra or *Manusmriti*) punished criminal acts according to the caste of those involved. Upper-caste Brahmins typically were fined or escaped punishment altogether. The harshest penal measure they might expect was banishment, even for murder. At the other extreme were the lower-caste Shudra, who could receive corporal punishment for even the most minor offences. According to the *Laws of Manu*, 'He who raises his hand or a stick, shall have his hand cut off; He who in anger kicks with his foot, shall have his foot cut off.' Murdering a Brahmin was a capital crime, and the assault or defamation of a member of the upper caste by the more lowly was punished with sympathetic punishments. For example, if a Brahmin was injured by a Shudra, the limb that was used in the assault was to be severed, and spitting on a superior called for the cutting off of the assailant's lips. Similarly, if he urinated on him his penis would be severed and 'if he breaks wind against him, the anus' (viii:279–80, 282–3). Acts of defamation required the amputation of the tongue, and mentioning the names and castes of the twice-born with insulting language required 'an iron nail, ten fingers long' and 'red-hot' to be thrust into the malefactor's mouth (viii:270–72).

Throughout the era of the Tang dynasty (618–907), the Chinese followed the practice of punishment according to rank. High-ranking offenders could expect lighter punishments or escape it altogether; servants and bondsmen, on the other hand, found guilty of a crime received punishment one degree more severe, for slaves two degrees more severe. A slave, for example, who assaulted a commoner so as to break limb or eye, was executed; conversely, a master who killed his slave (without cause) could at worst receive a year of penal servitude. We know from various sources that in early Aztec culture in Mexico, the Aztecs used sanctions along class lines as well, but in a slightly different way. For example, they were more punitive for nobles than for commoners when it came to issues such as public drunkenness, behaviour that demeans their status, but were more compassionate in cases of adultery.[20]

Until the twentieth century many African countries adjudicated offences and punishments through customary laws. In Nigeria, for example, the personal characteristics of the offenders often decided the sanction. A chief or rich man would not be executed for murder, but was permitted to compensate the victim's family with a slave, whether as compensation or to be executed in his place. In like circumstances those of higher status could pay fines that would have led to enslavement for someone in a lower position.[21]

The Ifugao of the Philippines, as late as the twentieth century, recognized a class system based on wealth; fines were dispensed according to one's social status, not unlike Hammurabi's ancient code. It has been documented that following a homicide (that does not require the shedding of tribal blood), a wealthy killer is expected to provide 'elabourate feasts and supply a variety of articles to be distributed among the dead man's heirs' unless the victim was of lower status. In the case of a mid-ranking family or the lower caste, the compensation would be much lower. However, if the homicide was committed by a member of the lower two castes the fine could not be 'materially commuted' and he would have this debt weighing over him for the rest of his life and his children would inherit the debt.[22]

Mosaic Law and the Near Eastern Tradition

The Code of Hammurabi exerted a tremendous influence on the development of Hebrew law. In fact a number of words found in Hebrew law are derived from Sumerian and Babylonian legal traditions. For example, modern Orthodox Jews utilize a Sumerian expression in terms of divorce: it has been suggested that the Hebrew term *keritut*, for divorce or severance, may derive from the ancient Sumerian practice by which a husband '[cuts] the corner of his wife's garment to symbolize the severance of the marriage bond'.[23] Better yet, when reading the Torah at synagogue, the Orthodox Jew still touches the applicable place in the scroll with the fringes of his prayer shawl, blissfully unaware that he is repeating an ancient Mesopotamian tradition that requires one to impress the hem of his garment on a clay tablet signifying obeisance to the requirements of the legal record.[24] Nonetheless, the first five books of the Bible, known to the Greeks as the Pentateuch and the Jews as the Torah, contain the Ten Commandments, credited with providing the foundation for legal systems throughout much of the Western world.

The traditional family represented in the Bible was akin to an extended household or family headed by a father, imbued with the power to pass judgement in life and death issues. In ancient Hebrew villages the reins of power were held by household fathers who also filled in as leaders of the community, thus reflecting a judicial system dominated by men. Households often comprised numerous sets of child-bearing adults and their offspring; enough to protect and feed the group. In cases where a son or other family member was assaulted and injured by another family member it was up to the father to determine how much restitution should be made, which was typically determined on 'basis of work days lost' while the son was on the mend (Exodus 21:18–19). It would be counterproductive to insist on maiming the perpetrator since this would deprive the family of two workers. When it came to restitution for injury to a woman it was computed by its impact on her ability to have children after the attack. In cases of homicide, if the killer was from the same household as the victim the offence was fratricide; if the killer came from another household it was murder. In such cases the village would use sanctions that conformed to the norms of reciprocity which required a life be given for a life. It was up to the village assembly to either sentence the actual murderer to death, or another member of the household in their place. On the other hand, the assembly might allow the killer's household to pay the victim's household compensation. But, when it came to issuing a death sentence it was determined in terms of what was in the best interests of the village. Compensation was acceptable when it was decided the village would be better off by not compounding the murder by taking away another person from the village.[25] In turn, the killer contributed land and children to the family of the bereaved. Similar to the Hebrews, some African villages commute death sentences in lieu of a fine of cattle or providing the victim's household with a human being physically comparable to the victim, or with a woman capable of bearing a child for the victim's family.

Although the Mosaic Law does not stand in the forefront of the world's great legal systems, its Decalogue, better known as the Ten Commandments, is probably history's best-known list of behavioural prohibitions; but the difference is that the Commandments do not include specific punishments for each offence, and therefore should not be mistaken for a legal code. Hebrew law utilized *sympathetic punishment* (punishment the same as the victim's). No adage is more prominent in the annals of crime and punishment as 'an eye for an eye, a life for a life'. This very literal view of accountability can be found in Exodus 21:23, where it is stated: 'Life for life, eye for eye, tooth for tooth, hand for hand, foot for foot, burning for burning, wound for wound, stripe for stripe'. It was only in post-biblical times that commentators began to interpret these words allegorically, as setting a limit to punishment, as in 'up to an eye' or 'up to a tooth'. Preferences had clearly shifted by then to some form of financial compensation for physical harm.

There were several important areas where Babylonian and Jewish law diverged. In biblical Israel, property crimes in biblical Israel were never punished by death, instead opting for fines. Since human life was considered sacrosanct, considering that man was made in God's image, the Mosaic code is far more forgiving in many respects compared to previous Near Eastern codes, by according the body with respect and avoiding the shedding of tribal blood. Conversely, when it came to homicide in Mesopotamia, victims were permitted to accept financial compensation; whereas in Jewish law a convicted murderer was expected to be executed. According to the Hebrew Bible the taking of a human life, or homicide, was permissible only in cases of self defence, war and the application of the death penalty. Ancient Hebrews acknowledged 36 capital crimes, which included murder, certain sexual offences, idolatry, blasphemy, desecration of the Sabbath and witchcraft; all of these would have future reverberations in western Europe as tens of thousands of accused witches went to their deaths between the medieval era and the seventeenth century.

Non-capital crimes were punished through a variety of non-lethal sanctions, including a form of imprisonment, banishment, fines and sympathetic punishments. If one committed an unintentional homicide or manslaughter the perpetrator could be sentenced to be banished to one of six designated cities of refuge; exile to a non-Jewish land was out of the question since the individual would probably be forced to worship foreign deities. Likewise, while in the city of refuge you were protected from lynching at the hands of your victim's kin. As mentioned previously, sympathetic punishment would involve the same injury as that received by the victim. Banishment lasted until the death of the city's high priest. Hopefully, the banished individual would arrive shortly before the death of an elderly priest, since if the priest was youthful the captivity could last a lifetime. While in the city of refuge, since you were living there against your free will, the high priest's family was expected to clothe, house and feed you.

There were a number of forms of execution mentioned in the Bible, including burning, stoning and decapitation. Of these the most frequently cited was lapidation, better known as stoning. This penalty involved the participation of members of the entire community and was typically utilized for offences thought to bring the greatest threat to the entire community. It was up to prosecuting witnesses in this case to cast the first stones. This was intended to deter false accusations. Stoning is among the oldest forms of capital punishment. For more than two millennia this punishment has been used in more than a handful of countries. First used under Mosaic Law, it is probably more firmly linked to Islam in the popular imagination due to its occasional contemporary use.

Among its more recent occurrences was its use in the Kurdish Yazidi community in Iraq in 2007 and in northern Afghanistan in 2010, when a young couple was stoned to death as they planned to run away and get married. Stoning typically follows a certain protocol that requires males to be buried up to the waist and women to their neck prior to the stoning. Religious courts today expect stones to be small enough so that death will not occur quickly after only several blows; on the other hand they must be able to inflict physical harm. A stoning can last between ten and twenty minutes. In a 2009 study by Pew Research Center, 83 per cent of Pakistanis believed adulterers should die in this fashion. According to Amnesty International, as recently as 2008, more than 1,000 spectators witnessed the execution in Somalia of a thirteen-year-old girl by this method.[26]

Decapitation was seen as the quickest and most humane form of execution and was reserved for those who committed wilful murder and communal apostasy (renunciation of religion). From a twenty-first-century perspective, it would seem that ancient forms of execution such as beheading had been relegated to the grim past. However, over the past decade Islamic extremists have adopted the method to punish selected Westerners. By some account this method had its roots in the ancient Middle East and was adopted by all of the major religions at one time or another. In AD 627, the prophet Muhammad ordered the beheading of 600 members of a Jewish tribe near Medina. His explanation was that he believed they had committed treason by consorting with his enemies. In similar fashion his favourite grandson, Hussein bin Ali, was beheaded in Karbala in 680 and his head delivered on a silver platter to Cairo by way of Damascus. Beheading is still an official sanction in Iran and Saudi Arabia. In 2003 alone 52 men and one woman were beheaded in Saudi Arabia for crimes, ranging from murder and robbery to homosexuality and drug trafficking. In the modern era, prisoners are often tranquillized prior to being led into a public square. Blindfolded, with their feet shackled and hands cuffed behind their backs, they are then beheaded. Despite calls from human rights groups such as Amnesty International, Saudis maintain a strict observation of Islamic law that mandates the death penalty for a range of crimes. In reality, most Saudi nationals stand little chance of being executed, with mostly poor migrant workers more likely to face the wrath of the sword. But in 1977 the great-granddaughter of the country's founding king was executed with her lover. He was beheaded, she was shot.[27] When it comes to the use of beheading as a sanction most clerics would criticize its use by terrorists, not because it is un-Islamic, but because of its improper utilization.

However, it would be a mistake to identify the punishment of beheading specifically with Islam since it has been used by numerous cultures that considered it a humane alternative to such methods as hanging, crucifixion or disembowelling (as part of being hanged, drawn and quartered). Whether it was humane or not, it depended on the sobriety of the headsman. When Mary Queen of Scots was executed in 1587 it took three tries to sever her head, perhaps due to a drunken headsman. The English had adopted beheading by law in 1076 and offered it to those of high rank. Five hundred years later, Sir Thomas More had his sentence for treason commuted to simple beheading, instead of being hanged until 'half dead', then cut down alive, having his 'privy parts cut off, his belly ripped, his bowels burnt, his four quarters set up over four gates of the City, and his head upon London Bridge'.

In the biblical era, death by burning was the penalty for nine categories of incest and one of adultery. Burning, more significantly, was probably used for such moral offences due to the symbolic purification aspect of the sanction. Since there were prohibitions against shedding tribal blood, physical punishments were intended to be less sanguinary than other codes, but no less severe. By the post-biblical era those condemned for crimes such as incest and adultery were condemned to strangulation, apparently using a rope held at each end by two witnesses; the rope was covered in non-abrasive material to avoid scratching the neck. As the condemned opened his mouth, molten lead was poured down his throat scalding his inner organs.

Among the more painful corporal punishments used by the Israelites was flogging, which was the preferred penalty for 168 offences, including seven types of incest, eight violations of dietary laws, three violations of marital laws by priests, marrying a bastard or descendant of the Gideonites, and having sex with a menstruating woman. In the post-biblical era the maximum number of lashes or stripes was 40; gradually the concept was developed that a man should be flogged according to his strength – in other words only the amount that the court surmised he could bear. Prohibiting no more than 40 stripes suggests a more humane spirit at work (Deuteronomy 126).

Egypt

Egyptian civilization developed about the same time as the Sumerians, but was very different in no small part due to its proximity to vast stretches of desert that served as a shield against potential invaders. Egypt's millennia-long continuity outlasted Sumeria's by most accounts due to the latter's location on a vast open plain, offering hospitable geographical conditions for almost constant warfare. Egypt, on the other hand was isolated and more homogeneous; so instead of fighting among themselves, like the myriad cultures of the ancient Near East, the Egyptian tribes learned to coexist along the Nile and cooperate to battle annual floods, perhaps explaining why it lasted 27 centuries.[28]

What is known about early Egyptian crime and punishment survives in what one Egyptologist described as a 'random mixture of court documents, civil contracts, private writings, observed behaviour, fictional tales and some royal decrees'.[29] From these we know that offences varied widely, from borrowing donkeys without permission to more modern sounding offences such as burglary, violent robbery, fraud and tax evasion, murder and the supreme crime of regicide. By modern Western standards, punishment for those found guilty was swift and severe. Those convicted for a litany of crimes could expect, at best, exile on work gangs, beatings and various mutilations; at worst impalement on a post, a slow and painful death referred to literally as 'giving on top of the stake'. Presaging the power of the state as the chief law enforcer, the Egyptian pharaohs were the final dispensers of the law, who had the prerogative to introduce new laws and punishments.

According to some of the best preserved testimony dating back to the Nineteenth Dynasty of Seti I, penalties included 'beatings with 200 blows and five open wounds' for stealing from the gods. But, painful beatings, cuttings, mutilations, amputations and executions were meant to make the victim suffer both pain and humiliation and 'satisfy the state's need to reassert its power as a warning to others'.[30] Beginning in the Eighteenth Dynasty, corporal punishments and/or monetary penalties became the norm for criminal actions, with capital punishment playing an increasingly important role in the list of state sanctioned penalties. At this point in history, a virtually cashless economy meant that compensation was mostly limited to 'metal and man hours'. It was in this era that the 'tax defaulter Mery has the dubious honour of becoming the first named Egyptian known to have been sentenced to be flogged', receiving 100 blows for 'false litigation'.[31]

By the end of the Eighteenth Dynasty (thirteenth century BC) attitudes towards crime with more punitive sanctions were becoming the norm. Severe penalties were introduced to curb official corruption. If an individual was found guilty of preventing free traffic on the Nile he would have his nose amputated and be exiled to a community in the Sinai Desert. Assortments of new mutilations were introduced to mark the convicts (and thus identify their crime). Ears and noses were the preferred targets for amputation. This was followed by hard labour; facial mutilation would not prevent their ability to work. One expert has suggested that it was probably common to see many deformed members of the community who had been marked by disease or were the victims of poor medical skills and terrible accidents, thus facial and other mutilations would probably not have had as horrific an impact on the public as they would in the modern era. The amputation of the nose and the outer parts of the ears, while painful, rarely resulted in death or physical complications. Since both were essentially made of cartilage or gristle, there was little in the way of blood supply, with little risk of bleeding out; while the victim might suffer breathing or hearing problems, it was far less physically threatening than amputating hands and limbs.[32]

Although the death penalty was used chiefly for crimes against the state (the king and the divine order he represented), death sentences seem to have been relatively rare compared to other ancient societies. Human history's oldest extant written death sentence dates back to sixteenth-century BC Egypt, when a criminal was condemned to death for practising magic and ordered to commit suicide. Executions, while not quite the spectacle they would become in the later Roman Colosseum, were often conducted in public as a warning from the state to potential law breakers. This was especially so when it came to treason, rebellion and adultery, which were sometimes punished with burning at the stake. In other cases the preferred form of civilian execution was being impaled on a wooden stake,[33] while murderers were beheaded. Egypt, like most ancient peoples, considered parricide the most serious crime and a more loathsome punishment was reserved for it. One would be rolled naked in thorns and then burned, or in the case of a mother killing her child, forced to wear the corpse around her neck until it rotted away.

Officials used three methods for obtaining confessions including beating the back, legs and arms; threatening to expel one to Nubia (Sudan); or having body parts severed. The most common form of physical punishment seemed to have been flogging, while mutilation was reserved for more serious infractions. Parricides were mangled and then burned alive on thorns. Adultery could result in 1,000 lashes for a man and the loss of a woman's nose. Rapists were castrated and traitors had their tongues severed.

Theoretically the same law applied to all members of society equally, with even the richest nobility not out of reach of the law. Crimes such as high treason were treated harshly among any social class. Egyptian records are rife with accounts of robbery, theft and fencing stolen goods and other criminal offences, including gangs breaking into tombs and looting them dating back to the reign of Ramses IX.

The Egyptians believed that everyone had both a physical and a spiritual nature, regarding physical death as simply an interruption, rather than the complete cessation of life. Furthermore, they believed that following death one would face judgement before the god Osiris and 42 Judges in the Hall of Judgement. The most serious penalty was a death sentence followed by a loss of burial privileges. Being burned to death had an especially deleterious effect on an eternal afterlife, since without a body the deceased could not pass the tests that would allow him to achieve this. The Egyptian *Book of the Dead* contains a series of laws that if broken would affect one's afterlife, one in which you were either tortured for posterity or received a pleasant fate.

Ancient China

More than 3,000 years ago, the *I Ching* referred to the punishment of *shih ho*, or 'biting through', in a rather understated fashion: 'His neck is locked in the wooden cangue; His ears are gone. Great Misfortune.' The cangue was a heavy wooden collar measuring about 3 or 4 feet square, with a hole in the centre for the head. It would be locked in position on the wearer's neck. Its width, however, was such that it was impossible for one to reach the mouth and face with the hands. Depending on the circumstances, malefactors could be sentenced to wear one from one to two months. Typically, shaming was part of the lesson, and the wearer would be forced to sit in the vicinity of where he committed his criminal act. At night he would be led away by an official and would spend the night in custody. If he was lucky enough he might be permitted to take it off until the next day. He was also forced to beg for food if he did not have a support network to provide the essentials.

Imperial China's penal system was one of the longest lasting in human history, using the same methods of punishment for more than 2,000 years. What makes the study of the Chinese penal system so perplexing is its acceptance of harsh punishments for so long in light of changing attitudes in other parts of the world. It contrasted sharply with similar institutions and traditions that developed in the West and Near East, in no small part due to its gestation in such natural and man-made isolation; insuring its legal system would develop independently of Middle Eastern and European legal codes, which in one way or another shared common roots in Mesopotamian law.

By the twenty-second century BC, a more complex society had emerged in China. In many cases early societies developed similar pro-cedures for punishing bad behaviours; in China punishments were quite distinct even at this early period, with procedures ranging from fines and tattooing to the more physical, including beatings, amputation of ears, noses and feet, and castration. One distinguishing characteristic was the types of dress prescribed as parts of penalties. In the case of a malefactor being tattooed to mark his crime, he could only wear a cloth head covering, but not a hat, which was thought would shield his face from view. Those sentenced to foot amputation were allowed to wear hemp, but not silk or sandals. Victims of castration could not wear a full-length gown, but only one that extended to the knee; indicating he had been physically shortened (reflected in the shortened garment). In similar fashion, a man facing decapitation was only permitted to wear a cloth tunic without a collar. But these punishments were apparently used only in the worst cases, due to the availability of various leniency provisions in the laws. As in future societies, exile was often accepted in lieu of punishment whenever possible.

Flogging was a common penal practice during the Song dynasty (AD 960–1270). By law, only 40 blows from a bamboo cane could be inflicted. Protocol required the criminal to lie on the ground face down. The clothes around his buttocks were unfastened and the beating took place. In the case of a woman, she would be allowed to kneel and only her outer garb would be removed; then she would be beaten about her body and legs. The differences in severity of punishment depended on the strength of the blows rather than the numbers, and there were surely attempts to bribe the attendant to go easy on the blows. Another corporal punishment involved slapping the face with a foot-long leather flap (2–3 inches wide). The convict was then forced to kneel down, with the official holding his hair with one hand while striking his face with the leather flap. Strokes were limited to twenty or thirty; but this did not prevent, by some accounts, the lips being beaten 'into a jelly'.[34] While there were also illegal tortures that defied the imagination of everyone except for the torturer, in most cases penalties ranged from banishment and imprisonment to beheading.

Athenian Greece

Ancient Greece was a welter of hundreds of independent and semi-independent states, rather than a united country. Of these, Athens looms largest, making it almost synonymous with Greece in the ancient world. The Greek law codes that developed in the seventh century BC differed from earlier Near Eastern and Mosaic laws in a number of respects. Unlike the laws of the omnipotent King Hammurabi, and God's law that dominated Mosaic Law, Athenian law was based on the popular consent of the people. By most accounts the Greeks absorbed aspects of Mesopotamian law and Eastern legal ideas and channelled them westwards. However, unlike the ancient Hebrews they had no direct contact with that culture. There was a sharp contrast between the two civilizations, with the Mesopotamian kings operating as absolute monarchs, while the Greeks, at least in the city-state of Athens, maintained a basic respect for the rights of people. In any case, Greek law was surely influenced indirectly by Mesopotamian and Hebrew laws.

There is ample evidence that ancient Athenians had significant fear of being victims of violence or being robbed of their possessions in streets or public places.[35] Likewise, Athenians such as Aristotle, Socrates, Protagoras and others early on were able to make causal links between poverty and crime created by the juxtaposition of wealth and poverty. Nonetheless, this did not necessarily protect the indigent from the most punitive penalties for crimes such as theft and robbery. Robbers and burglars caught in the act could be legally dispatched if they could not provide any defence under interrogation. These executions would often include some type of public humiliation in the process of being nailed to a plank and left to die by exposure to the elements or being strangled in public. In case of the imposition of a fine, some type of shaming might be imposed including a five-day stint pinioned in the stocks.

The first major strides towards a real criminal law took place in the so-called Homeric Age (eighth century BC), when the cogs of justice revolved around an informal process between the victim and the perpetrator. In the case of adultery, seduction and rape it was up to the cuckolded husband or his closest relative, in the case of a free woman, to seek justice; in the case of a slave, the master filled this position. Certain crimes such as cattle theft, robbery and piracy were apparently common and threatened the entire community; thus the community sought group retaliation. In cases of homicide between family members, the perpetrator was banished. If the assailant was not related, the killer would typically try and escape or pay blood money to avoid succumbing to the wrath of the victim's family.

The first written law code of the ancient Greeks is attributed to the statesman Draco, who in the seventh century BC was commissioned to write a new law code, in an attempt to stem blood feuds and control civil disorder. The term 'draconian' commemorates his supposedly ruthless use of the death penalty for almost every offence in the code. We mostly know of Draco's code through the works of later Greek historians. According to Plutarch, 'even those who stole salad or fruit received the same punishment as those who committed sacrilege or murder . . . Draco's laws were written not in ink, but blood.'[36] But, it is only in the realm of homicide that we can more than speculate about crime and punishment in such an early period in Greek history. The most important justice innovation of this era was the establishment of the Court of Areopagus for murder cases, arson and other serious offences. We do know that a victim, with his dying breath, had the power to forgive his killer, thus making him immune from punishment. Demosthenes would later attest to this, writing, 'If the victim himself before he dies absolves the doer from the homicide, no other member of the family may proceed against him, but those for whom, if convicted; the laws ordain expulsion and exile and death, if they are once absolved, are freed from all utterance by this utterance.'[37]

To avoid cycles of revenge killings, Draconian law gave murderers three choices. They could acknowledge guilt and immediately go into exile; submit to trial but remain free and obey the rules while free, which meant avoiding sacred and public places; or they could decide to take their chances by ignoring the first two choices, whereby the offender could be immediately killed or arrested by an Athenian if he entered a public or sacred place (an early example of citizen's arrest). Under Draco we see distinctions being made between justifiable and unjustifiable homicides; each required different sanctions. It was only in cases of premeditated or voluntary homicide that the state was imbued with the power to kill; it could also allow the victim's family to accept compensation in place of state sanctions.

When it came to homicide, unlike other offences, there was no time limit for prosecution, or for the family members to legally take action against the offender. What is known is that it would bring shame on a family if they did not follow up on the matter. What's more, Athenians were anxious that a guilty man never escape justice because he was not detected soon enough. This reverberates in modern justice where murder is still one of the few crimes in the u.s. without a statute of limitations. It is only in the case of homicide that we have any fragmentary evidence of crime and punishment at this early era. We know that perpetrators of unpremeditated murder would be banished for an undetermined period. And it was only when the relatives of the victim agreed to it that the exile could be terminated. One contemporary passage, reportedly the words of one sentenced to permanent exile, lamented, 'If I am convicted and put to death, I shall leave behind for my children the disgrace of an unholy deed; of if I go into exile, I shall be an old man without a city, a beggar in a foreign land.'[38] While a banished offender was in exile he was expected to be protected from violence or blackmail, and if he was harmed the assailant would be punished. However, returning early from exile removed his cloak of protection, making him easy prey for anyone that sought to exact revenge.

Deliberate homicides and bodily injuries, as well as cases of arson and poisoning, were tried at the Court of Areopagus (unintentional homicide was not punished). Over time executions made the transition from pieces of heavy wood to the sword. There is some debate as to what this wood looked like, but it probably resembled a club. Archaeological evidence suggests another execution protocol in which the condemned was fastened to a piece of wood standing in an upright position. Attached to the board by five iron bands around his neck, wrists and ankles, he was either left to die of exposure and starvation or, as others have suggested, was strangled by means of an iron collar tightened around the neck like a garrotte.

It can be inferred that the Greeks utilized lapidation as an established custom, referring to the practice 'to put on a tunic of stones'. Early Greek crime and punishment accepted compensation in most cases; preferring death for murderers and traitors, who could expect stoning or hemlock. During the Heroic era, precipitation – the tossing of the convicted off a precipice – was adopted. It typically involved hurling someone from a high rock plateau or down into a chasm. The Barathron ensured death since the chasm was fitted with spikes and hooks designed to lacerate the body. By the fifth century bc, hemlock replaced the Barathron; meanwhile, hanging, crucifixion and beating to death with a cudgel were also used. The introduction of hemlock, like beheading, the guillotine, the modern gas chamber, electric chair and lethal injection, marked an early attempt at introducing more humane forms of capital punishment. The most famous use of this poison, made from juice pounded from its seeds and leaves in a mortar, was in the case of the 70-year-old vagabond and philosopher Socrates, who in 399 BC was sentenced to death for corrupting the youth of Athens and refusing to accept divinities of the city. Death by hemlock was no doubt unpleasant, with death typically accompanied by spasms and convulsions, but it was still recognized as a civilized alternative to shedding blood.

Theft of certain vegetables and fruit, sacrilege, idleness and homicide were all capital crimes. In reality, Draco's code was probably no more punitive than customary law, but received its bad rap from an Athenian populace that was disappointed that he had not implemented any radical changes in the legal system. Draco's code represented a transition from a preliterate era of customary law to one that was written. Its importance lies in the fact that it required observance of certain fixed procedures and meted out predetermined punishments. His laws were published for all to see on pillars of wood for religious matters and on bronze for other laws.

By the fifth and fourth centuries BC, Athenians had a very enigmatic attitude towards homicide. Like other cultures at such an early date, it was the duty of the family of the victim to seek retribution or vengeance. However, it was more complicated than simply 'an eye for an eye'. In addition to vengeance it was essential to expiate the crime, in other words freeing the state from the contamination incurred by the homicide. Killers were viewed as having unclean hands – as being contaminated by the crime – and it was believed that they would pass this on to all others they came into contact with as well as the entire state where the crime had been committed. In order to purify the state it was left to the victim's family to either obtain vengeance against the perpetrator or to come to some type of reconciliation that would result in the victim's family essentially pardoning the malefactor.[39]

Athenians were indeed a patriotic lot, and any manifestation of disloyalty or treason was regarded as a most supreme transgression, re-quiring death and the confiscation of property by the state. But for many offenders the worst part was not being allowed to be buried in Athens. This is made most clear by the historian Thucydides who reported that after Themistocles was executed for treason his friends smuggled his bones back into Athens for burial. When it came to sanctions, impiety, in the form of robbing temples, practising magic or vandalizing statues of the gods, ranked almost as high as treason. Compared to previous (and future) civilizations, when it came to moral infractions the Greeks were notably less harsh in their response. In most cases the worst one might expect would be to have the pubic hair plucked out or a radish thrust up the anus.[40] But, when it came to adultery an aggrieved husband was empowered to kill the participants when he caught them in the act. This can be traced back to Draco's code which proclaimed, 'If one man kills another after catching him with his wife . . . he shall not go into exile for homicide on such account.' Likewise, he could decide to accept monetary compensation instead of personal vengeance.

'The Ancient Black Art of Money Forgery'

There are numerous similarities between forms of crime from antiquity to the present. Most ancient crimes made the transition to modern statute books in one form or another. Just take murder, robbery and theft for starters. All were defined as criminal or sinful behaviours in earlier eras, although definitions have evolved over the historical continuum. This is especially true regarding financial crimes. As life became more complicated and various legal codes evolved, some form of record keeping was needed to track such essential tasks as what goods were in the temple warehouses and whether citizens had made their required contributions to the community pot. In Mesopotamia, for example, everyone was expected to give their fair share to the gods. Human nature being what it is, many surely tried to avoid payment (as they do with taxes today) by simply asserting they 'paid' or contributed already. Keeping records through cuneiform or Egyptian hieroglyphics gave civilizations the means and potential for achieving higher forms of government but also ensuring that certain duties were followed.

As early as the third millennium bc the invention of money took its place next to the other harbingers of civilization in Egypt and Mesopotamia – writing and organized farming. However, early money consisted of bullion rather than coins, thus value was determined by weight of metals used in transactions. Again, we find human nature demonstrating an almost preternatural affinity for criminal behaviour. There are numerous accounts suggesting that at very early stages counterfeiters were at work attempting to duplicate the metal tokens and later coinage of royal mints. As he built on Draco's accomplishments, Solon in the seventh century bc became a zealous proponent of the rule of law, insisting that only by punishing crimes such as theft or the embezzlement of public funds could the rule of law advance.

Compared to other legal codes, the Bible was less interested in property crimes, which never garnered the corporal or capital punishments dictated elsewhere in the ancient world. Instead they were adjudicated by the payment of fines and restitution.

By the time of the Roman Empire, counterfeiters had learned their craft well, able to replicate techniques used in the casting of clay moulds for the melted metals in use. Over the historical record counterfeiters would be subject to some of the most brutal punishments. Emperor Constantine had them burned alive. Others who clipped precious metals from coins and then melted it down had their ears 'clipped or cut off'. Others had their citizenship revoked. As the Empire flourished counterfeiters lost their noses when they were not being castrated or being tossed into lion pits. Nonetheless, as the empire began to decline counterfeiting became a popular trade among the patricians.

Harsh punishment for counterfeiters extended to other cultures as well. As Islam continued to spread in the eighth century AD, counterfeiters had their hands amputated and in seventh-century China they were punished with facial tattooing and later the death penalty. By the fourteenth century Chinese banknotes were emblazoned by the warning, 'To counterfeit is death'.[41]

Slavery and Imprisonment

Slavery has existed throughout history. Over the centuries a wide range of cultures have embraced the use of slavery, including the Greeks, Koreans, Hindus, Native Americans, Romans, Vikings, Turks, British and Anglo-Americans. By most accounts, it 'was regarded as a natural and legitimate social institution in all ancient civilizations'.[42] Prospects for a long life never boded well for slaves; Egyptians killed them to accompany royalty to the afterlife. Indeed, many cultures actually bought slaves with the main purpose of sacrificing them. However, in many cases slavery, better understood as forced or compulsory labour, was also a penal sanction. The Greek historian Herodotus noted that in the eleventh century BC, the Ethiopian king Sabacos, then ruler of Egypt, substituted forced labour, 'presumably accompanied with detention', for the death penalty. Unlike nineteenth-century race-based slavery, race was not a deciding factor whether someone would be enslaved or not. In reality penal systems in antiquity were much more likely to use fines or banishment than slavery as punishment, unless labour was required for tasks and projects that were beyond the capacity of societies at early stages. Prior to the appearance of capable technologies, enslaving workers was one of the only ways of obtaining labour on a large scale. It is at this point, when there is a major need to mobilize labour to mine precious metals, and build pyramids, roads and monuments that compulsory labour finds its way into a culture's penal sanctions.[43]

From the scant evidence that exists, penal sanctions were of lesser significance when it came to raising slaves. This process was considered rather minor in the ancient Near East and Greece. In Egypt, on the other hand, the main crime source for slaves was debt to the state. In ancient Korea, families of persons convicted of treason, robbers and killers of valuable domestic animals were enslaved. Prior to the Han era, those convicted in China were typically executed and the family enslaved. Following this era, penal enslavement became the main source of slaves; indeed the only recognized source of slaves were families of condemned persons. Therefore, slavery in China became identified with the penal system. Anyone who committed a crime and was enslaved usually bore some type of tattoo or disfiguring mutilation that would distinguish them from freemen. This mark of the criminal was the most important basis for the sale of a human being. In China, with penal and social traditions quite distinct from the Near East and the West, familial ties and responsibility were accorded such importance that an individual's family members and extended kinsmen were held liable for the actions of related malefactors.[44]

Early societies that did not use slavery as a penal sanction surely used some type of confinement to make debtors pay up or to hold criminals waiting for trial or punishment. What differentiates the ancient incarnation of the prison from its modern counterpart is that the early precursors were not purpose-built. Most historical accounts of ancient crime and punishment overlook the fact that like so many other components of modern criminal justice systems, prisons date back to early antiquity. How far back, of course, is anyone's guess; but tombs, execution chambers and holding places for slaves captured in war, date back thousands of years. Information about the earliest ones is scarce; although they are given more than a passing notice in Egyptian hieroglyphics, Greek myths and the Book of Genesis. The notion of locking someone up and throwing away the key is extremely old.

Throughout history early societies required quick and sure penal sanctions, whether mutilation, fines, banishment or death. There is enough evidence to add imprisonment to this list. The earliest accounts can be traced to ancient Egypt, where the largest known structure in human history, the Great Pyramid at Cheops (2650 BC), housed a subterranean pit, referred to as the 'prison-house of the lost'. Likewise, several hundred years later, Egyptians referred to the pyramid at Saqqara, built in the Sixth Dynasty under Teti (2345–2333 BC), as the 'prison pyramid'. East of this complex is another pyramid whose local Arabic name means 'Joseph's Prison'. In the Valley of the Kings and other locations there are many graphic portrayals of imprisonment as it was practised in antiquity. There are even references to prisons in the Rosetta Stone (196 BC), unearthed in 1799. The oldest Egyptian tombs date back over 5,000 years (located on the Nile opposite ruins of Memphis), while the earliest symbol for prison has been traced back to ancient Egyptian hieroglyphics combining the terms 'house' and 'darkness', although we know little else. There is also plenty of speculation that the pyramids were constructed with prison labour.[45] Imprisonment is mentioned in the Book of Genesis (39:20–40:5), while Babylonia employed the *bit kili* (3000 BC–400 BC) for debtors and petty criminals, and during the Assyrian Empire used the *bit asiri* (746–539 BC). The Old Testament reports the use of imprisonment by Egyptians, Assyrians and Israelites. Jerusalem had at least three prisons at the time of Nebuchadnezzar, including Beth ha-keli, or house of detention; Beth haasourim, literally 'house of chains'; and Bor, which was little more than an underground reservoir.

Prisons are mentioned in the historical records of China and Japan, including the *Shangshu* or *Shujing*, which noted the building of a prison by Emperor Fuen VIII (2000 BC). Athenians recognized a variety of punishments in various stages of their history, including fines and the confiscation of property, public shaming and the destruction of the homes of condemned offenders.[46] Free citizens of Athens were rarely imprisoned except in the case of high treason or to coerce debtors to pay their debts to the state. Those awaiting torture or execution were incarcerated, providing an opportunity to showcase prisoners prior to the infliction of serious penalties. In Athens there was even a structure, probably not purpose-built as a prison, the *desmoterion*, or 'place of chains'. Plato wrote extensively (*c.* 300 BC) about imprisonment and slavery, both considered essential for good government. One of the most famous prison stories revolves around the death of Socrates as he proposed and rejected imprisonment as punishment. In *Laws*, Plato had proposed that the state should have three prisons: a public one near the marketplace for the ordinary offender; one called the 'reform centre' near where the Nocturnal Council would meet, and another in the countryside in a solitary spot and with a name that would convey the notion of punishment. Plato recommended a range of incarcerative sanctions up to life in prison, all dependent on the seriousness of the crime, the 'nature' of the criminal and the circumstances surrounding the crime. Despite his theoretical pronouncements, there is no proof that Plato's vision of the model prison system was ever put into practice during his lifetime.[47]

In 1860 the novelist Nathaniel Hawthorne visited Mamertine Prison in Rome.[48] It was here in AD 68 that Paul was taken to be tried by Nero. This particular edifice was located in the Agora marketplace where it functioned as a death house, holding those awaiting legal execution. Initially referred to as the *carcer* (prison), whence the term incarcerated, from medieval times it has been called Mamertine Prison. Both classical Greece and Rome sporadically used a private prison, or *carcer privatus*, to detain debtors and individuals awaiting trial or execution. Rome's first written law code (see chapter Two), the Twelve Tables, mentions a place of forced detention known as the *ergastalum*. But no term conjures up the worst aspects of confinement more than *dungeon*. Derived from the Latin term *dominium*, referring to the precipice where a castle or fortress is built, the French later adopted the term *donjon*, from which the more familiar English word emerged. Over time it became synonymous with inner sanctums and sinister places of confinement.

Summary

Prior to the development of complex systems of law, courts and the penitentiary, early cultures relied on customs, magic and religion to maintain order; customary law could be at times more rigid than any written modern law. In pre-state societies, laws were often attributed either to gods or tribal leaders. Making law through decree or legislation came later. For most of human history it was accepted that laws were the by-product of edicts delivered directly from the gods. The oldest complete legal code yet discovered depicts the sun god (and god of justice) Shamash enthroned and handing down edicts to a deferential King Hammurabi of Sumeria.[49] Likewise, centuries later, Jehovah carved the Ten Commandments into two tablets with his own finger as Moses stood atop Mt Sinai. No decalogue has been discovered prior to that of the Hebrews, although individual provisions can be found in the Code of Hammurabi. Scholars have suggested that the earliest analogue to the Ten Commandments is contained in chapter 125 of the Egyptian *Book of the Dead*, which mentions the declamations of the dead entering the abodes of righteous-ness: 'I have not slighted God. I have not slain. I have not commanded to slay. I have not committed fornication or impurity. I have not stolen. I have not spoken falsehood.' What's more, it is no coincidence that Crete's King Minos was depicted climbing Mt Olympus every nine years to get legal advice from Zeus.

Mesopotamian legal procedures influenced many of its contemporaries including Egypt, Persia and India; but these influences were not as long lasting as they would be in the West, where 'its seed took deepest root'.[50] While Hammurabi's Code would go on to influence penal procedure throughout much of the civilized world, Greece and Rome would be influenced only after its contacts with the Near East; and Islam acquired a legal code only after it conquered the region that is now Iraq. The early Greeks and Romans introduced lawgiving by identifying certain legal principles which people took for granted. However, civilizations in China and Egypt, developing in more isolated regions of the world, offered vastly different conceptual models relating to crime and punishment.

The earliest legal codes consisted almost entirely of sanctions devoted to punishing what were considered the most serious offences, such as murder and physical injuries. As societies reached similar levels of economic progress, in many cases there was less variation in sanctions compared with what would come later. Most reverted to either death for death or some other talionic (punishment in kind or degree) compensation. Some of the world's most familiar crimes and their pun-ishments can be traced back to antiquity, including stoning, hanging, beheading and crucifixion. Crucifixion, credited as the brainchild of either the Persians or the early Phoenicians, was widely used by a broad swath of civilizations, including Assyria, Egypt, Greece, India, Carthage, the Celts and Rome, until it fell out of favour following Constantine's conversion to Christianity in AD 315.[51] It was used in Japan as recently as the nineteenth century. Crucifixion was traditionally used as a political or military punishment, with the Carthaginians and the Persians utilizing it for the execution of military commanders and high officials. The Romans, on the other hand, preferred it for the lower classes, slaves and violent criminals. Targeting the masses with more punitive punishments cemented the notion that punishment was dispensed according to one's class, a theme that continued to resonate over the ensuing centuries, with the onus of pain and suffering felt most heavily by the impoverished and marginalized populations.

2

The Rise of Legal Traditions

While most modern scholars focus on the four major contemporary legal traditions, at least sixteen different traditions have flourished at various points in history. In 1928 John Henry Wigmore identified these systems as: Egyptian, Mesopotamian, Chinese, Hindu, Hebrew, Greek, Roman, Maritime, Japanese, Mohammedan, Celtic, Germanic Slavic, Ecclesiastical, Romanesque and Anglican. Eight years later, Wigmore concluded that six of these traditions had completely disappeared,[1] five had survived as hybrid systems, and Chinese, Hindu and Mohammedan systems remained essentially unmixed. In 1936, thirteen years before the Communist Revolution in China adopted the socialist system, Wigmore identified the Chinese legal system as the world's oldest continuing legal system. But the earlier Chinese tradition, like other previous codes, persists only in a borrowed format.

Except for a handful of states that subscribe to permutations of the socialist legal tradition (Cuba, China, Vietnam, North Korea), the overwhelming majority of the world's nations today base their legal systems in some part on either civil, common or Islamic legal traditions. Of these the civil and common-law systems have received the most attention, due in no small part to the colonial powers that spread these legal traditions across the planet. Thanks to the British Empire, common-law traditions predominate in its English-speaking former colonies in the Caribbean, North America, Canada, Australia, New Zealand and parts of Africa, India and other areas. The socialist legal system, on the other hand, is the newest and probably least utilized major legal tradition, particularly after the demise of the Soviet Union. This system, as it developed in the tumult and chaos following the 1917 Bolshevik Revolution, borrowed extensively from the civil law code and Russian customs. With little in the way of a legal structure, a vast amount of discretion was placed in the hands of tribunal judges (without legal training). Russian Civil Code was influenced by earlier Russian, German, French and Swiss civil codes. Cuba, North Korea, Vietnam and China represent the last vestiges of socialist legal traditions, but in too disparate a pattern to make any generalizations regarding crime and punishment.

Over the centuries these legal traditions were transported to the far corners of the globe, either by conquest or colonialization, where they were subsequently modified in one way or another due to the often diverse conditions of their new homes (see chapter Eight). When common law was brought to the New World, it had to be adapted and modified for alien conditions ranging from wilderness conditions to interacting with numerous highly developed indigenous societies. Likewise, when the English created colonies in Africa, India and Asia they were forced to contend with complex societies that already had developed their own systems of crime and punishment. By the end of the 1940s, the British Empire was vastly diminished, yet examples of common-law-influenced penal codes remained in former colonies, from Zimbabwe and Nigeria to Oceania and North America.

Introduced in the 1820s, caning would outlast British imperialism and be adopted for such offences as begging, distributing pornography, treason and robbery with violence. After independence in 1965 Singapore retained corporal punishment in its legal code and even increased the number of offences punishable by it in 1965, to 30 mandatory offences. One recent case underscores the evolution of older legal traditions once transplanted to a totally different environment. Flagellation with a birch rod has been a feature of British colonial judicial systems for almost 200 years. The British became so identified with this form of corporal punishment that the French referred to it as 'The English Vice'.[2] But in March 1998, British MPs voted to abolish it, joining such former colonies as New Zealand (1990), South Africa (1996) and Scotland (2000). Yet, caning still persists in far corners of the former Empire. The 1994 caning of eighteen-year-old expatriate American Michael Fay in Singapore aroused international condemnation, emanating mostly from the West. Originally charged with 53 counts of vandalism-related offences, Fay pleaded guilty and plea bargained to two counts of vandalism, two of mischief and one charge of possessing stolen property. But what outraged human rights watchers the most was his sentence of four months in jail, a u.s.$2,500 fine and six strokes of a cane (reduced to four under appeal). The country was roundly excoriated by the Western world, but stood its ground. On 4 May 1994 Fay joined nine other prisoners who faced a similar sanction in the prison's caning room. Stripped naked, the prisoner was bent with his arms and legs fastened to an H-shaped trestle by straps. His kidneys were shielded for protection. The only witnesses were a medical officer and the caner. As one journalist described it, 'The caner wound up and, using his full body weight, struck with the 13-mm-thick rattan rod, which has been soaked overnight to prevent splitting. Each stroke on Fay's exposed buttocks came about half a minute apart.'[3] It took at most ten minutes. Once the punishment was concluded caner and prisoner shook hands and Fay returned to his cell without any aid.

Although Singapore's legal system is rooted in English common law, it has developed its own legal traditions and brand of philosophy since independence. A number of observers have noted the influence of British predilection for corporal punishment in their schools and its adoption by many former colonies. By most accounts Singapore has departed from its British roots in fundamental ways, including the elimination of jury trials years ago (regarded as error-prone). This city-state is almost 80 per cent Chinese; although diverse it also has a cohesive value system that emphasizes Confucian virtues such as respect for authority. There is a broad dichotomy between these two world views, best expressed by the Western notion that it is better for a guilty person to be set free than to convict an innocent person, clearly upholding the importance of the individual. By contrast, the Asian perspective subscribes to an ethos that it is better that an innocent person be convicted if the common welfare is protected, than for a guilty person to be set free to inflict further harm on society. Taking into account the convergence of common law and Confucian principles, it should also be added that there is a considerable Muslim presence and that more than 16 per cent of the population follows Malay Muslim customary law. Here British common law is complemented by a separate system of religious courts for Muslims only. What this case (and many others) suggests is that legal traditions are continuously evolving, morphing into hybrids of various traditions to meet the changing demands of demographics, geopolitics and globalization. What's more, it is becoming as difficult to draw clear distinctions between different legal traditions as it is to categorize a country's legal procedures as a specific type.

Roman Civil Legal Tradition

Considered the oldest extant legal tradition, Roman law developed over many centuries: from its founding as a small republic in central Italy in the sixth century BC to the first century BC, when it became the law of everyone that resided within Italian borders; to the third century AD, when it reached all freemen within an empire stretching from the Atlantic ocean in the west to the Euphrates River in the east, thence north to England and Scotland and south to the edge of the Sahara Desert. As the Roman Empire stretched to the far corners of the ancient world it adopted a number of new laws while integrating diverse cultures and traditions into the Empire.

The Romans were ardent students of the Greeks in many endeavours, but when it came to law, they were the masters, making one of the greatest contributions to the development of modern law. Similar to most other civilizations, Roman law was grounded in the unwritten customary laws of the previous centuries, when lawmaking was the purview of the upper or patrician class. Sometime in the fifth century BC, opposition from the lower classes, or *plebeians*, forced lawmakers to codify society's rules in writing, to satisfy their main complaints, that since law was the preserve of the upper classes, crimes and punishments had remained an enigmatic mystery to ordinary Romans. The resulting Law of the Twelve Tables became the first written law code of the Romans. Unfortunately the originals, which were exhibited in the Roman Forum, were destroyed by the Gauls during their sack of Rome in 390 BC. We do know that the legislation was recorded on ten inscribed bronze tablets and set up in the marketplace for all to see and to know. Since only fragments of it remain, the law code has been reconstructed from numerous quotations from works published at a later date. Early Roman law was more concerned with procedure than strictly substantive law, and was first and foremost a codification of existing customs.

The Law of the Twelve Tables prescribed crimes and their penalties, offering insights into the state of Roman civilization at this early date. Crimes committed under the veil of nightfall were of special concern to the justice system. In fact, the word for theft was *furtum*, a derivation of the word *furvus*, 'black', indicating that most thefts took place under cover of darkness. The penalty of hanging was the punishment for clandestinely pasturing animals on another farmer's crops at night; while the sanction for burning a barn or stacks of grain was being burned alive. One high-ranking leader was punished for treachery by being torn apart by three chariots, each heading in a different direction. The king reportedly proclaimed this was 'a warning to all mankind'.[4]

Banishment was a punishment reserved almost exclusively for high-ranking members of society; their inferiors by contrast for similar crimes could expect forced labour or varying severities of death. Banishment was doled out in a variety of incarnations. Relegation, for instance, was confined to mere exclusion from certain territory, while deportation meant not only perpetual exile but loss of citizenship and the confiscation of all property. When it did come to homicide, using a weapon to commit a crime, offering false testimony resulting in death or utilizing poison to murder, patricians in the first century AD would be punished by some of the aforementioned penalties; those on the lower rungs of society could not expect such compassion, and instead were crucified or thrown to wild animals.[5]

Romans applied the same ingenuity to inflicting pain as they did to creating laws. One of their most famous punishments was 'the penalty of the sack', or *culleus*, dating back to 100 BC, when it was contrived to punish individuals who had killed their parents. This method traditionally involved sewing a bleeding malefactor into a leather sack, along with a dog, a monkey, a snake and a rooster, or some other variation. The sack was then hurled into either a river or large body of water. The rest is left to the imagination. Later in the first century BC, Pompeian law replaced the *culleus* with either burning alive or tearing to shreds by wild beasts.[6] In other cases, Roman citizens who allowed their slaves or selves to be circumcised under 'Jewish rites' were deprived of all property and relegated to an island for life. The physicians who performed the surgery were executed.

In the earlier eras, the execution of women was accomplished in private since it first required stripping off all of their garments. Since executioners were forbidden from strangling virgins, they were expected to deflower them first.[7] Other criminals could expect to be publicly executed by any variety of methods, ranging from being burned alive, torn apart by wild animals to being tossed off the Tarpein rock (not unlike the use of the Barathron by the Greeks).

During the first two centuries of the Common Era, the Roman gladiatorial games were a part of everyday life. No edifice represented the glories of Rome more than the majestic Colosseum, where slaves, prisoners and professional warriors engaged each other in life and death struggles in front of huge crowds. When not pitted against each other they were faced off with exotic carnivorous animals brought in from the far corners of the Empire. What is less well known and typically avoided by tour guides was its central role as a place of execution for 200 years. The Roman philosopher Seneca described the executions as 'massacres without any artistry'. For Roman emperors it was an opportunity to reinforce in the minds of their constituents the authority Rome's rulers held over life and death. Prisoners were typically carted in the night before the executions and kept in fetid quarters under the arena until the next day. Knowing full well what lay ahead, it was not uncommon for some to attempt suicide. According to one account by Seneca, a slave ingeniously killed himself by thrusting his head between the wheels of a cart, crushing his head in the process.[8]

Prisoners were brought up to the arena floor around lunchtime and separated into two groups, distinguishing Roman citizens from non-citizens and slaves. The citizens were typically dealt with first and due to their status were accorded relatively quick deaths. Some were killed with a single blow from the headsman. There are accounts of two citizens being sent into the arena together, one armed, the other not; the man with the sword was expected to chase down the other garbed in a loin-cloth and stab him to death. Once this is completed the survivor hands over the sword and is similarly chased down by another prisoner. This process is repeated until there is only one survivor, and he is rewarded by being executed. Humiliation was as much part of the penal process as it was for the non-citizens and in some cases citizens were humiliated by being crucified with slaves.

Following the executions of their superiors, non-citizens and slaves faced the most sadistic deaths and their slow executions usually took up most of the lunchtime break. They were crucified, burned alive and fed to wild animals. Many of those who were about to die had violated sacred laws, having committed murders, arson and desecrated temples. Christian writers chronicled a number of executions by wild animals. There was no end to the imaginative killings. Sometimes, different forms of capital punishment were combined. For example, a slave might be nailed to the cross and then immolated; in other cases they might be tied in a position where animals could eat their limbs. Mythology was an important component of the Roman belief system and to break the monotony of the traditional forms of execution versions of fatal myths would be acted out with the condemned in the role of the victim.

At this point, it is worth examining the penalty of crucifixion in more detail, due in no small part to its iconic significance and the many misperceptions that surround this form of death. Most accounts credit the Phoenicians for introducing crucifixion to the world, while others make a good case for the Persians.[9] It would later be imported to the Greeks, Assyrians, Egyptians and the Romans, who were estimated to have crucified tens of thousands. On one day alone in Rome, Emperor Crassius had 6,000 people crucified to celebrate a recent victory.

Originally crucifixion (the origin for the word 'excruciating'[10]) was meant to be a humiliating form of death and was typically meted out to slaves and serious offenders. Prior to the cross formation, the male-factor was simply tied to a stake in the ground and left to the elements to perish. Once crosses were adopted, they existed in several different configurations – sometimes with four or three arms, others with a simple X-construction. Usually the victim, stripped down to a loincloth, would be scourged or lashed before the execution and forced to carry the main beam of the cross to the place of death (the entire cross would have been unsupportable).

Recent research confirms that this execution was actually a 'slow form of asphyxiation', whether nailed or tied to the cross. In fact there is still some debate as to how the offender was connected to the cross. In 1952 a French physician found it impossible to crucify an adult through the hands. After experimenting with a number cadavers, he found that the maximum weight the body can support is 40 kg if nailed through the hands, anything over that and they would just rip out. Through a process of elimination the only other methods must have been either nailing through the wrist bones (which can support the body) or tying with ropes to the cross. The goal was to make the body hang from the cross in order to slowly asphyxiate the malefactor. As the body hangs, over a period time the diaphragm and intercostal muscles come under such stress that the victim can only inhale (but not exhale), thus forcing the chest to get bigger and bigger until he chokes to death. This ordeal has been estimated to take anywhere between three to four hours and four days.

In January 1971, Israeli archaeologists announced they had identified the remains of a young Judean named Yehohanan (Hebrew for John), who had been first unearthed in 1968, and who most probably had been executed by crucifixion in the first century AD. This discovery provided the first firm evidence of an actual crucifixion in the ancient Mediterranean world. Most records indicate it was used by the Romans until the fourth century when Emperor Constantine outlawed it. However, previous evidence was considered speculative at best, mostly because no trace of nails had ever been discovered in proximity to the body despite holes in forearms and heels (sites excavated in Italy and Romania). Yehohanan's remains were discovered in an ossuary along with the bones of a handful of others. His name was barely legible in Aramaic letters on the exterior. What was so exciting for the archaeologists was the penetration of a man's heel bone by the rusty remains of 7-inch-long nail. According to investigators, the single nail was probably preserved because it came into contact with a hard knot in the olive wood of the cross, thus the nail was slightly bent to the side as it was hammered into place. According to an article by the anatomist and anthropologist Nicu Haas, following tradition, the sequence of events leading to Yehohanan's death probably ended with a *coup de grâce* to his lower extremities with a blow that broke both legs and would have then hastened death by causing haemorrhage and shock. Subsequent attempts to remove the crooked nail from the cross to remove the body probably went awry, making it too difficult to remove the body from the stubbornly embedded nail that held the body to the cross. The anthropologist Haas suggested that the only practical way to separate the victim from the cross would have been to cut the feet off and then remove altogether the nail, a plaque of wood (which helped keep feet in position) and feet from the cross. Jewish custom requiring immediate burial then prevailed, preventing long exposure to the elements after death. It was this perfect convergence of events that led to this groundbreaking find.[11]

When it came to judicial excesses and draconian punishments there were few Roman tyrants that could match the first-century leader Gaius Caesar, better known as *Caligula*, a name that has since become a byword for sadistic cruelty. He reportedly enjoyed torture held in his presence while having dinner or was otherwise relaxing. At one public dinner he ordered executioners to lop off the hands of a slave who had been accused of stealing a strip of silver from a couch. Once this was done, the hands were tied around his neck and he was taken on a tour of the dining hall, bearing a placard explaining his punishment. Caligula developed a reputation for creative sanctions, the more macabre the better. Before signing the execution list form he would often mutter, 'I am clearing my accounts'. He favoured burning alive (vivicombustion), a holdover from the Republican period, and utilized the Colosseum as the venue for the spectacle. During one of the shows featuring wild animals he turned down the butcher's meat as too expensive, and since he had plenty of prisoners to go around ordered criminals to be fed to the animals instead. Standing up on the colonnade he looked down on the prisoners lined before him and reportedly ordered, 'Kill every man between that bald head and the other one over there!'[12] In other cases Caligula forced parents to attend the executions of their sons; on one occasion, a father who claimed he was too ill to watch in person was even provided with a stretcher. Caligula's sadism knew few bounds, as instanced by the execution of a soldier who proclaimed his innocence prior to being tossed to wild beasts. Caligula seemed to relent and brought the condemned back out and had his tongue torn out before completing the sentence. When it came to the multiplicity of execution formats, one of Caligula's biographers claimed he preferred the method that inflicted numerous small wounds, as made clear by his remark, 'Make him feel that he is dying.' Answering the critics of his bloodlust he responded: 'Let them hate me as long as they fear me.'[13]

Under Emperor Tiberius, every crime became a capital one and the words of informers were always accepted as gospel. Some of the accused, confident that they would be found guilty if they went to court, short-circuited the process by killing themselves to avoid the humiliation and painful punishment that would surely follow.

When Constantine converted to Christianity, making it the state religion in the fourth century AD, punishments for sexual and moral offences became more punitive than ever. Infractions that had formerly been considered private wrongs became public offences and were often treated with merciless severity. During former times, adulterers might be deported to separate islands; by the time of the Christian emperors the sanction for all forms of sexual immorality, including adultery, bestiality, incest and homosexuality, became capital crimes. On the other hand, there are some observers who have suggested that rather than purely an impulse toward ancient biblical sanctions, this shift from less cruel punishments for sexual offences might have been a reaction to a wave of rape and kidnapping taking place as some more ambitious Romans sought to engineer their marriages to rich women in this manner.[14] In any case, this was a clear departure from the past, when such crimes as adultery and fornication were sub-capital offences. In the earliest Roman era adultery was defined as having sexual relations with a 'respectable married woman or widow' or an 'unmarried free woman who was not registered as a prostitute'.[15] Punishment usually consisted of the married woman losing half her dowry as well as a third of other property and being banished to an island. Her lover, meanwhile, was sent to a different island and lost half of his property. The father had the right to kill his daughter and her lover, but the catch was finding them in flagrante delicto in his son-in-law's house as well as killing both actors in the drama. Otherwise, if he killed only the lover, the father would be charged with murder. In essence, this caveat was designed to prevent vengeance by the cuckolded husband and his family, instead leaving it as a matter for the courts.

In the early third century AD Emperor Macrinus, who held power only from 217 to 218, perhaps anticipated the later Christian punishments, when two soldiers were convicted of having sexual relations with a maidservant. Due to her position as a prostitute, they should have been shielded from adultery laws, but the two men were put on trial nonetheless. As punishment, he directed two large oxen to be slit open while still alive and to put one of the men into each, with only their heads protruding so they could converse with each other. According to one historian, since they had not violated any laws and had committed a 'non-crime', they had 'earned a unique punishment' that could be found nowhere on the books.[16]

The Twelve Tables remained the foundation of Roman law until it was superseded by Justinian's *Corpus Juris Civilis* almost ten centuries later. Under the direction of the Emperor Julian, the development of Roman law reached its apogee. It brought both simplicity and equity to Roman law by taking almost 1,000 years of juristic experimentation and organizing it into a coherent and organized form. This law code was the foundation for most subsequent European civil codes (as well as their colonies). However, as one legal historian put it, its criminal laws would 'reach modern Europe only in a highly warped form'.[17] In any case Justinian's reign between 518 and 565 marks the transition from antiquity to medievalism, ushering in an era that would culminate in the development of modern Europe.[18] But Roman culture would disintegrate long before the nations of medieval Europe materialized.

Following the fall of the western Roman Empire in the fifth century AD, Germanic tribes, or *barbarians* as the Romans referred to those who had lived outside the Roman Empire, entered world politics as state-forming peoples. Germanic tribes were an important catalyst for the codification of early European law. On the Continent the Franks established themselves in northern Gaul, the Visigoths in Spain, the Ostrogoths in Italy, the Burgundians in southeast Gaul (soon to be conquered by the Franks) and the Vandals in North Africa. Of these the Visigoths, Burgundians and Franks produced the most substantive legal materials, each heavily influencing the other. To date, the most important documentation of late Germanic law is found in Frankish sources. Indeed, except for the Anglo-Saxon law codes, it is considered the most Germanic of all barbarian legislation.[19] Of these the most famous was the *Lex Salica*, or Salic Code, compiled in the first decade of the sixth century. This was introduced as the Franks established in northern Gaul one of the longest lasting barbarian kingdoms. Frankish law is considered the least Romanized and most Germanic tribal code. Unlike Roman law, it does not emphasize marriage, family, inheritance, gifts and contracts, opting instead to establishing fixed monetary and other penalties for a wide variety of damaging acts, such as killing women and children, 'striking a man on the head so the brain shows' or 'skinning a dead horse without consent of owner'. A substantial portion of the Salic Code covers crimes of violence, homicide and theft. If one issue was clear, it was that a man's property and person were considered final collateral for payment, while fines were utilized for stealing 'swarms of bees, dogs, cattle, birds, goats, sheep, and slaves'. Freemen were usually permitted to pay fines, while thieving slaves could expect up to 120 lashes and even castration.

One of the things that stand out about Salic law is its absolute reliance on *wergild*, a system of fines determined by status of victim and perpetrator – a system that would be brought to Britain by German invaders during the fifth and sixth centuries. Accordingly, everyone had a 'man-price', or *wergild*. For example, if anyone killed a man who was in the service of the king he was sentenced to 24,000 denars, while one who killed a free Frank or barbarian living under the Salic law was sentenced to 8,000 denars. When it came to assault, punishment was based on degree of assault and those involved. In Salic law, 'If any person strikes another on the head so that the brain appears, and the three bones which lie above the brain shall project, he shall be sentenced to 1,200 denars.' If someone was struck through the ribs 'so that the wound appears and reaches the entrails', the penalty was 1,200; if shedding only blood that 'falls to the floor', the fine was 600 denars. When it came to slaves, punishments were ratcheted up in severity. Slaves caught stealing anything worth 2 denars were required to pay restitution and could receive 120 blows while stretched out on ground; if a slave stole something worth 40 denars, he would be castrated or ordered to pay 6 shillings.[20]

English Common-law Tradition

Between the mid-fifth and mid-sixth centuries Britain was invaded by Germanic and Scandinavian settlers from across the North Sea. Over time such tribes as the Angles, Saxons and Jutes would coalesce to form

Anglo-Saxon culture. Indeed, the name England is a derivation of 'Land of the Angles'. Here, on the northern fringes of what was once part of the Roman Empire, they encountered a region with few memories of the unsuccessful 400-year Roman attempts to Christianize the indigenous population. By the time Rome withdrew its army in 410, few remnants of their legal code remained in their wake. Germanic traditions would have the most impact on crime and punishment in Britain in the years leading up to the Norman invasion of 1066. One of the underlying codes of Anglo-Saxon life in Britain, like counterparts on the Continent, was that everyone had a price, or *wergild*. More than 100 laws enumerated the various fines, ranging from murder to the smallest breaches of the peace. Each body part had a value; loss of an eye was worth half the price of a man. The loss of a tooth causing disfigurement was worth 16 shillings, but a back tooth only half that. A blow with a closed fist was valued at 3 shillings, half the price of being slapped with an open hand. By most accounts a slap was a double whammy, being both an insult and an injury.

By the seventh century, Christianity was solidly entrenched here as Britain developed into a hodgepodge of modest principalities led by an elite made up of warrior noblemen. Petty kingdoms would rise and fall until the 800s, when several stable kingdoms rose to prominence. Throughout this period murders were compensated with expiatory payments, which had to be paid to a victim's family to avoid cycles of violence and blood feud.

In their classic work on the history of English law, Maitland and Pollock make the point that the Germanic invaders 'were no great penmen', and there is much that is still unclear about the so-called Anglo-Saxon era.[21] Writing around the sixth century AD, Ethelbert of Kent's laws, or *dooms* as they were called then, offer the first written Germanic laws, most of which are related to violent crimes and cattle and horse theft. Besides the *wergild*, the Germanic law codes of Anglo-Saxon England utilized some form of imprisonment for such crimes as theft and witchcraft, but the most common sanctions reflected penalties found in Continental Europe, such as mutilation, death or exile. Hanging had been the principal form of capital punishment in Anglo-Saxon England dating back to the fifth century. Despite a respite in its use during the early Norman period, it would be used as the main form of execution into the twentieth century. For most of the Norman period hanging was accomplished with little scientific technique, allowing the condemned to slowly strangle, rather than having his neck broken through the use of the weighted drop and the placement of the hang-man's knot in a position that brought instant death. It would take centuries for hangmen to make the humane transition from slow strangu-lation to breaking the neck with a knot placed strategically at the base of the neck.

Prior to the advent of the modern criminal justice system there were few procedures for deciding guilt or innocence. The Germanic kingdoms of Europe contributed a number of elements that would influence formal practices such as trial by ordeal and compurgators, better known as oath helpers (individuals willing to swear you were of good character). Both derived their value from the belief that God would intervene on the side of justice. The various Germanic tribes would bring these practices rooted in the judgement of God to England from the Continent. It remained a straightforward system for deciding guilt and innocence until the Norman invasion of 1066.

As demonstrated in the previous chapter, some form of trial by ordeal can be discerned in one shape or another throughout history and in divergent cultures. Trials of fire or water were most common in England, and were accomplished with the assistance of a priest. Considered God's judgement, the ordeal was compulsory for individuals caught in the act, who were formerly guilty of perjury, or unable to pro-vide the requisite number of oath helpers. The ordeal was based on the notion that God would protect the innocent, and it was used continuously into the thirteenth century. In reality the ordeal was the court of last resort, with a community hoping individuals would confess before undergoing this ritual. Trial by fire came in various incarnations. In some cases the accused walked blindfolded across hot coals or heated metal. In others, such as the 'caldron dip', they would place their hand in a cauldron of boiling water and take out a stone or some other object usually weighing about 1 pound. If the hand or feet still showed sup-puration three days after their ordeals they were judged guilty. In other cases individuals were immersed in water; if they sank they were inno-cent, since the guilty would float. Typically crimes ranging from murder, forgery, witchcraft and heresy were treated in this fashion.

The second major method for determining guilt or innocence was through the use of oath helpers. In such instances both the defendant and the accuser in the case provided oath helpers to swear to the truthfulness of each party. The number of oath helpers depended on rank and seriousness of offence. Those who refused to take part in the compurgation or ordeals, or just show up at court on four consecutive days would be pronounced an outlaw, which meant they would be placed outside the protection of the law and could be hunted down and killed. So outlawry was used to punish those who evaded the machinery of justice, refused to pay fines or appear in court or simply fled; on top of this they forfeited all chattels and lost all civil rights. Maitland and Pollock referred to outlawry as 'capital punishment of a rude age'.[22] Once outlawed, an individual was deemed to have gone to war with his community; thus the community went to war against him. It became the right and duty of every man to pursue him, burn his house and ravage his lands, hunt down and slay outlaws before the thirteenth century.

Some crimes, such as treason or clandestine homicide, were considered unatonable, unless one could clear oneself with the adequate number of oath helpers, or pass a more vexing form of ordeal, which required the accused to pluck out a 3-lb weight from boiling water (instead of the typical 1 lb). Likewise, rather than plunge the arm wrist-deep, this heightened form of ordeal required the arm to be dipped up to the elbow. Failure to pass the ordeal would mean execution. In less serious cases such as false accusation, habitual criminality and for individuals who failed the ordeals, punishments consisted of mutilation and corporal punishment.

Germanic tribes favoured 'characteristic' punishments such as tongue amputation for false accusation and the loss of the right hand for perjurers. By the eve of the Norman Conquest the main catalogue of Anglo-Saxon punishment included hanging, burning, drowning, stoning, precipitation, the amputation of ears, noses, upper lips, hands and feet, castration, flogging and being sold into slavery. What is curiously missing here is much mention of purpose-built structures for imprisonment. Perhaps, Pollock and Maitland put it best, noting that, 'The one punishment that can easily be inflicted by a state which has no apparatus of prisons and penitentiaries is death.'[23]

According to the sixth-century Laws of Ethelbert, fugitives from the law could be accorded sanctuary at a church under certain conditions, which included confessing to a crime to a member of the clergy, giving up all weapons, paying a fee to the church, and divulging the specifics of the offences. The perpetrator could expect sanctuary for 40 days, after which he was required to appear before the coroner and promise an oath to abjure, or leave, the realm. The procedure for leaving the country gave safe conduct and directed individuals to the nearest seaport. An alternative to outlawry, abjuration allowed the abjurer to don a white robe and carry a wooden cross to safely avoid consequences of many crimes. But, they were prohibited from staying more than two nights at any stop along the way. By the sixteenth century Henry VIII insisted they were also branded so they could be easily recognized in case they returned to England without pardon. This protocol would continue throughout the Norman era until its abolition under King James I in 1623.

In the ninth century, Scandinavian settlers following in the wake of brutal Danish Viking raids settled in an area known as the Danelaw (and introduced the word 'law' to the English lexicon), which stretched from the Thames river to Liverpool. They would introduce traditions steeped in Scandinavian religious rituals, such as the strangling of criminals on long wooden beams as they were stabbed repeatedly until they died. This ritual in honour of Odin was known as *galgatra*, or the gallows tree. Over the next century they would merge with their Anglo-Saxon neighbours, contributing their own variations of legal codes and institutions as the groups morphed into what became English culture.

One of the pivotal events in British history and the development of the common-law tradition was the invasion of Anglo-Saxon England by the Normans of northern France. The conquest was sealed after the victory of forces under William I, Duke of Normandy, at the Battle of Hastings in 1066. In order to the win the support of his new subjects William adopted most extant Anglo-Saxon laws while introducing Norman customs from the Continent. Following the dictates of that era that often allowed conquered peoples to keep their legal systems, William followed suit, adopting much of the Anglo-Saxon justice system. Among his most notable innovations was eschewing capital punishment in favour of mutilations; as a result no criminal would be dispatched by hanging for the next 40 years. However, this did not prevent scores of malefactors from perishing after having their eyes put out or testicles severed.

The Normans introduced many of the precursors to what would become familiar components of the criminal justice systems that would influence British common-law traditions, including constables, coroners, bailiffs, justices of the peace and the marshal. The coroner for example, beginning in 1194, was introduced at the county level, to conduct investigations into suspicious deaths and house break-ins. Curfews, which had been around for centuries, find their origins in Latin and French history and were traditionally used by the upper class to limit the movements of their inferiors. William used the curfew in a more surreptitious fashion, as a procedure that supposedly protected against the ever-present risks of fire. In a world made of wood, this was a natural precaution. In reality it was most probably designed to keep subversive Anglo-Saxons from meeting during the cold hours of darkness. So, when the curfew bell tolled at eight o'clock each night, all fires were expected to be extinguished or face harsh sanctions.

The Normans also added another judgement of God, trial by battle, to the methods used by the Anglo-Saxons for determining guilt or innocence. The duel, from the Latin *duellum* ('war between two'), had been an accepted tradition of the Germanic Burgundians more than five centuries before the Norman Conquest. In the words of one early king, 'it being just that every man should be ready to defend with his sword the truth which he attests and to submit to the judgement of heaven'. Protocol allowed clergymen, women, and the disabled to use proxies, or champions, after they swore an oath not to use magical spells or potions. In most cases those of high standing fought on horseback, while their inferiors went at it on foot. If the accused could stand his ground between sunrise and sunset he was found innocent and the accuser was hanged instead. In one famous example of trial by battle in 1096, an individual accused the Count d'Eu of conspiring against King William II, who joined the assembled crowd to watch. The count lost the battle and was castrated and had his eyes poked out. Trial by combat was rather practical and allowances were made that negated the use of proxies by levelling the playing field. If a woman was defending her case against a man, he had to stand waist-deep in a pit while she circled him with a stone inside a leather sling. He in turn flailed at her with a club; missing her three times meant she was innocent.[24]

One hundred years after the Norman Conquest, England was threatened with a growing crime problem. In response, Henry II issued the Assize of Clarendon in 1166, which established trial by grand jury. These juries would submit the names of all known criminals in the district for trial by ordeal. Once guilt was determined, harsh punishments were instituted to deter the growing crime problem. Anyone who failed the ordeal was sentenced to either be hanged or have a foot amputated, followed by exile from the realm for 40 days. Ten years later, in 1176, the Assize of Northampton introduced even more punitive sanctions including amputation of the right hand and foot (following conviction by ordeal).

The Assize of Clarendon also introduced major advances in prison development. William I had initially made some strides in this direction by setting into motion the construction of the vaunted Tower of London as the country's first royal prison. But it was mostly designed to hold enemies of the king. Several other purpose-built places of custody would also be constructed. But, with the Assize of Clarendon, Henry II ordered sheriffs to build jails in every county to hold all accused felons until they could be tried by the travelling royal justices. From the late thirteenth century onward, as prisons increased, so did the number of offences requiring incarceration.

Considered the 'Father of Common Law', Henry II introduced travelling judges, who made regular visits to all regions of England, a plan that would eventually lead to a 'common law' throughout the kingdom, characterized by common procedures for handling cases in court. Like most pre-modern legal traditions, custom had previously played an essential part in local court decisions throughout Britain, but this often created confusion for the judges, since customs varied widely according to geography and one's social standing. In years to come, a body of laws developed based on the judges of the King's Court. These laws, or common law, gradually became distinct from the rules and laws that existed in each local region, where formerly Danish and Germanic law prevailed. As new cases arose, the judges relied on similar cases as authority for their decisions. This established the importance of precedent in deciding cases which gradually led to a set of rules uniform throughout not just the kingdom, but also countries that later became colonies of Britain.

Islamic Legal Tradition

Coinciding with, but unrelated to the development of Anglo-Saxon Britain in the wake of the Teutonic barbarian invasions, the Islamic religion emerged out of the Arabian Peninsula in the second half of the seventh century. A latecomer to the story of crime and punishment, the Islamic legal tradition over the following centuries would expand into North Africa and Central Asia and other parts of the world over the next 1,400 years. By most accounts punishment in pre-Islamic Arabia was based mainly on talionic principles, 'well suited to needs of public security and social order in a nomadic setting'. But with no legal system and no concept of the state, kinship solidarity functioned as society's strongest bond. The Prophet Muhammad was born in AD 570, only beginning his mission about 610; but Islamic jurisprudence did not begin to evolve until the eighth century.[25] Early Islamic law was largely adapted from the inherited Arabian culture. The Islamic legal tradition, not unlike Mosaic Law, developed as a theocratic legal system based on the notion of a divine law revealed to a prophet in a scripture. However, Jewish law never developed to the extent of its Islamic counterpart, due in no small part to the many periods of their captivity and dispersion.

According to Islamic Law, a crime is 'the commission of a prohibited act or the omission of a duty that is commanded'.[26] This is not that different from Western positive law that defines it as 'voluntary conduct that violates a public law and for which punishment may be imposed in the name of the state'.[27] Islamic justice has always stressed the dual protection of both the rights of the accused and the protection of society. From a modern perspective, in the days leading up to 11 September 2001, a Somalian warlord recounted ordering a soldier who had accidentally killed a civilian to be sent to the victim's family, 'which promptly shot him in the head'. The warlord casually noted to the interviewer, 'It's Islamic law. That's what makes the community feel happy.'[28]

The two most important sources for the Islamic legal tradition are the Sharia, found in the Quran, and the Sunna. The 'extra-Quranic' Sunna is made up of Arab customs and examples from the life of the Prophet. The Sharia, by contrast, is considered sacred and inviolable law. From a Western perspective it seems less comprehensive than a law code and less tightly organized. One of its major weaknesses as a legal code is that since it is God's work, it requires no changes or supplements. In addition, since the penal law as enshrined in the Quran was developed long before the modern era it is difficult if not impossible to apply it to many contemporary criminal justice issues.

The task of interpreting the legacy of the Prophet fell to the *ulama*, or legal experts, who have since the medieval period occupied a place in society not unlike the Christian clergy. In AD 900 the *ulama* decided that no further interpretations would be needed and that the Sharia should be regarded as complete. One of the reasons why it is difficult to generalize about Islamic legal development is that in the centuries following Muhammad's death four major schools of Islamic law emerged, each with different interpretations of the law. Each named for a founding scholar, they ranged from liberal to fundamentalist. The most flexible was the Hanafi, which recognizes the fact that as society changes so do the circumstances that created various laws, and therefore the 'legal rule is *not* unchangeable'. Originating in Iraq, it became the established interpretation during the long reign of the Ottomans and is today the official school in most of India, Pakistan, and excluding the Arabian Peninsula, several other Mid-eastern nations. The most fundamentalist and least flexible interpretation is the Hanbali, which has worked against any innovation suggested by the other three. Today, Saudi Arabia is its stronghold.

Under Muslim penal law, offences are divided into three classes; each distinguished by whether punishment is predetermined in the Quran or is at the discretion of judges. The most serious crimes, which are considered unforgivable and therefore demand mandatory punishment, fall under the heading of *hudud* crimes, which encompass the most serious and gravest crimes. These crimes brook no pardon, intercession or exculpatory evidence. Punishment is therefore imposed exactly as prescribed in the Quran and Sunna. Punishments are distinguished by the corporal harm to a condemned individual. But, unlike lifetime imprisonment and other penal procedures featured in Western countries, Sharia sanctions are carried out quickly,[29] publicly and inflict only temporary pain to criminals. For example, when hands are amputated for theft, they are typically anaesthetized by a doctor first before being cut off with a sharp lance. There is no unanimous consensus over which crimes fall into the *hudud* category, but the vast majority of sources indicate that the most major crimes consist of adultery, theft, banditry and defamation. Adultery, or having illicit sexual relations, is best understood as having voluntary sexual intercourse with anyone other than one's spouse (no matter if married or not). However, more recently distinctions have been made according to whether one of the adulterers was married or not. In cases where there is less sexual contact than physical penetration of the male organ into the female organ the punishment falls under Ta'azir crimes with different sanctions. As mentioned in the previous chapter, societies pay much attention to the protection and preservation of a clear and honourable bloodline among the community of believers. Adultery carries different penalties according to the status of the guilty party. If married, the penalty is stoning; if unmarried 100 lashes.

A word about stoning in this tradition is necessary here. Like much of Islamic law, it is based on previous customs, particularly the Old Testament, in which Moses set into motion the stoning of a man for violating the Sabbath. Beginning in the first century AD, Rabbinic law authorized stoning as the punishment for a number of offences and provided elaborate instructions on carrying it out. However, we can only speculate on how commonly it was used.

Stoning is not prescribed by the Quran, but is rooted in Islamic legal traditions known as *hadiths*, which designate it as the penalty for adultery. As recently as 2007 a stoning took place in Iraqi Kurdistan's Yazidi community. From a historical perspective it seems savage to Westerners, but scholars insist that it was consistent with the values of Arabian society at the time of Muhammad. Throughout history there has often been more bark than bite in penal sanctions, where punishments were prescribed as 'a symbolic warning' rather than as literal punishment.

Taking away another's movable property without consent and with the intent of adding it to the perpetrator's possessions is regarded as theft. The seriousness of the event often depends on the value and method of stealing. Nonetheless, the Sharia states, 'As for the thief, both male and female, cut off their hands.' To serve as a deterrent this is expected to be done in public. However, no hand amputation is required for stealing property that is not valued in Islam, such as alcohol and pork; and the goods stolen should have a minimum value.

Banditry, is better understood as armed or highway robbery, and is considered a more serious offence because of the implied use of force and lying in wait. In this case the punishment per the Quran is 'execution or crucifixion, or cutting off hands and feet from opposite sides (cross amputation), or exile from the land'. According to one interpretation of the law, judges have some flexibility for dealing with this, using the severity of the act to determine the sanction. But the majority considers penalties ranked according to seriousness with no discretion left to the judge. If someone is killed he will be executed by sword; if he steals money, hands and feet will be severed from opposite sides (right hand and left foot); if he uses threat of violence but does not kill or steal he will be expelled from the land (or imprisoned); and if he steals and kills at the same time he will be crucified (*hiraba*). Amputation, like beheading, is performed with a sword or scimitar. While there is still some debate over the crucifixion protocol, by most accounts the bandit would be crucified alive and then dispatched with a javelin thrust. Others believe the condemned is first executed before being crucified and left to the elements over the following three days as a warning and deterrent to others. Bandits who murdered while stealing were beheaded; then the body was displayed in a crucified-like form. If the bandit *only* murdered and did not steal, it would be solely beheading. In any case, interfering with commerce and travel was not taken lightly, probably explaining why this was so harshly and publicly punished.

The fourth major *hudud* category is defamation, which is better understood as a false accusation of unchastity. As an evidentiary safeguard to prove a case of adultery or fornication, four male witnesses must explicitly relate the same account of what they witnessed. If three testify against the accused, but the remaining witness fails to corroborate the act, the other three are punished, such as in the case of accusing a woman of adultery without providing the four witnesses as required by law. The penalty for this infraction is limited to eighty lashes.

The category of *qisas*, or 'bloody' crimes, is typically committed against bodily integrity, intentionally or not. These would be considered 'crimes against persons' in modern parlance and include murder, voluntary or involuntary killing, intentional or unintentional physical injury or maiming. There are two alternative sanctions for these crimes. *Qisas* penalties are only applicable to intentional crimes against the body, proven with conclusive evidence. *Qisas* is ingrained in the Sharia to satisfy the general tendency toward vindictiveness on the part of the victim and family, and to avoid excess in talion (retaliation), which could result in feuds and even more violence. In this case, equivalent retaliation is permissible, similar in nature to the sympathetic and expressive penalties of Hammurabi and later the Hebrews. But, unlike Hammurabic law, if someone sets fire to another's house, victims cannot retaliate in kind; if one did he would be punished. An alternative punishment of *diyya*, paying compensation to a victim or family, is applied in cases of unintentional crimes against bodily integrity, consisting of such offences as involuntary killing and unintended physical harm. Originally, there was a uniform amount of *diyya* with no distinction between socio-economic groups. Most scholars suggest that *diyya* for a woman was equal to half of that of a male. According to the evidentiary protections required before applying *qisas* sanctions it must be demonstrated that the accused was of sound mind and had committed the act intentionally. Therefore the individual inflicting the talion must have the knowledge and competence to inflict it properly. If not, a professional executioner must be assigned the task on behalf of the victim and his family. Boundaries include not inflicting greater pain than what has been inflicted on the victim. And, if conclusive evidence is lacking, *diyya* suffices.

The third and least serious category of offences is *tazir* crime, which means chastisement, and basically includes offensive behaviour for which the Quran or the Sunna does not prescribe penalties. One Arabist has suggested that *tazir* penalties are more severe than *hudud* or *qisas*, which offer specifically prescribed and limited punishment, while it is left to the judges to decide in this category. In this way 'a man may be flogged again and again until he performs the necessary prayer or duties'.[30] *Tazir* crimes include petty theft, attempted adultery, homosexuality, lesbianism and rape, as well as other behaviours prohibited by the Sharia, but are lacking specific punishments; so sanctions can vary for those charged with eating pork, false testimony, usury, drinking wine and tampering with scales. Since it is left up to the judge or ruler to decide which punishments are due, they first must consider the gravity of the offence, and then the perpetrator himself, considering his personality, criminal record, lifestyle and ultimately the damage caused to society. The death penalty is rarely used for these crimes, but flagellation is highly recommended on the grounds it is in the best interests of the criminal and society. Whippings are preferred since they can be performed quickly, allowing the condemned individual, usually a family's sole wage earner, to get back to work and support his family. By eschewing imprisonment, the family does not become a financial burden on the state, and the individual will not face the corrupting influence of criminals he might come under the influence of in jail. The minimum amount of lashes one could expect is three. No maximum has been agreed to, but typically it is somewhere between 39 and 75 strokes. One story perhaps exemplifies the pragmatic discretion that a judge can use to punish a *tazir* offence. In this version the first governor of Yemen offered wine to his guests, and then prosecuted those who became inebriated. When guests protested he explained, 'The punishment is not for drinking, it is for being drunk.' The Hanafi school only prohibits drinking wine, since that was all that was available at the time of the Prophet; other forms of alcohol (or drugs) are not necessarily prohibited, unless their use leads to intoxication.

In many respects the *tazir* category seems more modern. Since there are no specified punishments for these acts, although they are considered un-Islamic, it enables the Sharia 'to evolve and cope with new requirements of modern life' while still meeting the needs of developing Muslim society. The conundrum of reconciling medieval values with the modern world is exemplified by the recent case of a Saudi woman sentenced to ten lashes for defying the country's ban on female drivers. As the only country in the world that prohibits women from driving, families are forced to hire live-in drivers. It is beyond the reach of most families to pay an extra $300 or more each month, so women have to rely on male relatives for school, doctor's appointments and shopping. Here is a situation, then, where there are no written laws prohibiting women from driving, but according to traditions and religion, this ban is necessary to prevent freedom of movement, thereby making women vulnerable to sin. Activists have chided the authorities for flogging women for driving, while the maximum penalty for traffic violation is a mere fine, leading one to comment, 'Even the prophet's wives were riding camels and horses because these were the only means of transportation.' In defence of the police it should be noted that although they indeed stop women drivers, they usually question them and let them go after signing a pledge not to do this again. It so happens that the woman sentenced to be flogged was taking part in an organized protest, and that the flogging was probably part of a retaliation from religious hardliners.[31]

Sharia in a Modern World

From a modern perspective rigid Islamic law is often considered anachronistic and draconian. This is mostly due to modern regimes departing from the evidentiary safeguards implicit in Islamic law, operating unencumbered by the actual teachings and spirit of Islam. Unfortunately, the less humane aspects of Sharia law have been reinforced by developments in Iran, Pakistan, Saudi Arabia, Sudan, Nigeria and Afghanistan, countries where Islamic law has replaced the more positive attributes of secular law in one way or another. This is particularly true when considering some of the punishments meted out by Sharia-based penal systems. Stoning is among the punishments most often mentioned but its rationalization least understood. In its infancy, Islamic law and other cultures desired to protect the male bloodlines, family, honour and property. In a tribal society it was paramount to know whose children belonged to whom. The relationship between sexual crimes and the penalty of stoning (instead of another form of execution) was that such crimes were deemed to have dishonoured the community's identity and thus required a shared response by community members. Unlike the punishments for other crimes, there was surely a particular dreadfulness on the part of the convict at being publicly stoned to death by family members and former friends and neighbours. It was hoped that the prospect of the sentence would mitigate the commission of future crimes that would call into question any parent–child relationship and threaten the integrity of tribal bloodlines.

The following are several accounts of Sharia justice over the past few decades. In Iran, usury is illegal under Sharia and anyone lending money for profit can expect 74 lashes and up to three years in jail. This mandate was strengthened to include the loss of four fingers from the right hand for a first offence, amputation of toes for a second offence, and life in prison for a third offence. One recent sentence demonstrates the lasting influence of talion. In 2011, an Iranian man was convicted of throwing a bucket of sulphuric acid in the face of a woman who rejected his marriage proposal and was sentenced to be blinded in similar fashion.[32] The victim was blinded and disfigured in the attack. She had the power to pardon the attacker by forgiving him for the crime, which took place in 2004, but refused to do so despite the pleadings of international human rights groups and the British government. Her defence was that it would be a warning to others planning such acts. In 2008 an Iranian court ordered that five drops of the same chemical be placed in each eye of the attacker, 'acceding to the victim's demand that he be punished according to a principle in Islamic jurisprudence that allows a victim to seek retribution for crime'. Only the victim may prevent a sentence by pardoning the condemned.[33]

Beheading is still used as a mode of execution in Saudi Arabia, and takes place at a location dubbed 'chop-chop square' by expatriates living in the capital of Riyadh. Here executioners use 4-foot-long curved swords during public executions, done just above a small metal grate over a drain to catch the blood.

It was a typical 100-degree day in September 1983, when thousands of Sudanese massed in a north Khartoum prison yard, anxiously waiting to watch Islamic justice in action. Two men sat in chairs, their faces covered by white cloths as they awaited the traditional punishment for theft. Before proceedings their charges were pronounced before the eager crowd, and the appropriate verse from the Quran was read out loud, with the crowd joining in to announce 'God is Great!' Then the executioner appeared with a knife and in a matter of minutes severed their right hands. Surprisingly, little blood was shed, with observers chalking it up to the probability of the use of tourniquets around their upper arms. For one of the men, it was still not over. An immigrant from Nigeria, he was set to have his leg cut off the following month.[34]

In 1996 an Islamic court in the United Arab Emirates sentenced a Filipino maid to 100 lashes for stabbing her employer to death. The canings were carried out twenty at a time on five separate days. Officials said this punishment was symbolic and that the person striking the maid placed a book under his arm to reduce the impact of the strikes. Although she claimed self defence, saying her boss had tried to rape her, she was sentenced nonetheless to the lashes, followed by a year in prison and deportation.

There are many supporters of Sharia law who would contrast the high rates of crime in non-Sharia regions to their low crime rates, which they claim Islamic law is responsible for. This is a matter strongly debated since crime data from these countries is rarely shared with the world at large. But one place where it can indeed be discerned to have worked was Somalia in 1996. At that time Mogadishu was deep into an epidemic of clan warfare, rape, robbery and what one *New York Times* reporter called 'almost post apocalyptic' random killings. Having expended all other methods, a Sharia court was convened and empowered, turning part of the capital from a 'state of anarchy into a relatively safe and civilized area'. If there was any doubt over the methods used to quell the crime wave, it was not hard to miss the severed hands and feet (amputated without anaesthetics in public) of local thieves and left out as a warning in front of a local stadium.[35]

The Taliban 'defined themselves' in the 1990s and during its revival in the 2010s through the adoption of a draconian version of Islamic law, as it rose to prominence in Afghanistan introducing its own brand of Islamic law. Contrary to popular perceptions, the stoning of adulterers in Afghanistan was not commonly practised prior to the ascent of the Taliban in the 1990s. Whenever it was used it was done under strict religious supervision, after a fair trial, and with limits on sanctions set by religious scholars. Stones were required to be small, and those who took part were prohibited from lifting their arms above the head to throw. The catch was that it must be done with a legitimate court. In one 2010 case in which a couple was stoned to death for eloping without permission, it was accomplished in a village not under government control. One religious elder criticized the stoning for its illegitimacy and noted 'it is not right to stone people unjustly with big, big stones'.[36]

In one case in 2010, hundreds of villagers took part in the stoning of an adulterous young couple in Kunduz Province. But more often it is the woman who bears the brunt of the penalty, especially if the male belongs to the Taliban or is well connected. In other cases, homosexuality is punished with individuals forced to stand against brick walls, which are toppled on to them. The Taliban follow the Sharia as literally as possible, even when it came to forgiveness. In 1999 a man was sentenced to death for homosexuality and was sentenced to be crushed by having a 15-foot-high wall knocked down on him. A tank was used to collapse the brick wall and the 60-year-old victim incurred serious head injuries and appeared dead. However, he lived; under Taliban law, a death sentence is commuted if the convicted person survives the execution. The victim complained of aches and pain and thanked God for having returned him from the jaws of death. He later told a journalist: 'I was wrongfully convicted for sodomy. And God has proven my innocence.'[37]

By 1996 the Taliban ruled nearly three-quarters of Afghanistan, where they imposed their brand of justice and before the end of the year had publicly executed the first person since capturing Kabul earlier that autumn. Prior to the execution, a mullah used a loudspeaker to announce the first execution made under Taliban rule, emphasizing, 'Let this be a lesson for others . . . In a short time, we will impose our Islamic law in all of Afghanistan.' He then repeated a list of Taliban punishments ranging from amputations and stonings to floggings. The condemned man's pleas for mercy were ignored by the solemn executioner, who with Kalashnikov in hand approached the man responsible for the murder of his wife and three small children just weeks earlier. There would be no forgiveness, as 'he walked the last few paces briskly, dropped to one knee, levelled the automatic' and fired from some 30 paces away. The execution was roundly cheered by the crowd of thousands, many of whom were hardened Taliban fighters.[38]

In another incident the Taliban treated a stadium crowd of 20,000 to the lashing of a woman for adultery. In most cases floggings are administered with a 3-foot whip, with the suffering often drowned out by the chants of Islamic slogans. Unmarried adulterers can be given 100 lashes and if married stoned to death. However, in the abovementioned case, the adulteress apparently walked away with no apparent pain or injury; in this case the goal was to humiliate her without inflicting pain. So the lashes were administered rather lightly in public without pain.

Forgiveness featured prominently in another Islamic legal case that came out of Nigeria, where currently the legal system is based on the common law by way of the English colonizers and draws from Islamic law brought by Arab traders and conquerors. An illiterate woman was sentenced to be stoned to death in 2002 for having sex outside wedlock. However, during an appeal before another court she was found innocent due to procedural errors. If she had been stoned she would have been the first in Nigeria since 1999, when twelve northern states adopted Sharia law. The ruling contained a novel defence, called the 'sleeping embryo theory', which under some interpretations of Islamic law asserts that some babies can remain in a mother's womb for over five years. If this was the case, this could have meant that her ex-husband had fathered the baby two years before their divorce. What's more it ruled that the policeman that arrested her for the crime violated Islamic law as well by not delivering the required four witnesses to the crime, since she was not caught in the act.[39]

Legal traditions are constantly evolving. This is often demonstrated by the softening of severe penalties for certain crimes. As late as the Ottoman Empire, when religious and secular authority was combined, stoning and other penalties were regarded as crude relics of the past. But almost 60 years after the break-up of the Ottoman Empire, the 1979 Iranian Revolution reinvigorated the criminal code to include stoning and established rituals for the procedure. Men were to be buried in a standing position up to their waists, women to above their breasts. Stones must not be large enough to kill with the first several strikes; nor as small as tiny pebbles. If adultery was proven by confession then the judge must cast the first stone. If proved by witnesses, then they must go first. Anyone fortunate enough to survive a stoning is set free without punishment, but this is unlikely, since victims are bound in cloth and have hands tied before being buried. In 2010 Iranian lawyers claimed only 100 stonings had taken place since the 1979 revolution and were on the decline. Between 2006 and 2008 at least six took place, while in Afghanistan stoning seems to be on the rise in morality cases.[40]

There is a penchant in the West for observers to regard Islamic legal traditions as harsh and unforgiving. But one recent Iranian case perhaps illustrates a growing debate among prominent clerics and judicial officials over support for the death penalty. In 2007 a seventeen-year-old lost his temper, as young men tend to do, and killed a romantic rival with his knife. He was tried and convicted and was sentenced to death. In most cases that would have been the end of the story in a country with one of the busiest execution machines (second only to China). However, seven years later the former teenager was still alive, languishing on death row, although at least 600 others had been executed the year before. Iranian society, like so many others, was experiencing a trend that saw declining support for the death penalty. Some observers have suggested this is perhaps due to a growing middle class and the expansion of social media. But, this case was more complicated than that, involving as it did conflicting interpretations of adulthood. According to Iranian Sharia law a girl is considered mature at the age of nine, a boy a man at fifteen. On the other hand, the legal age for a young man to receive his driver's licence or serve obligatory military service is eighteen. So, having committed the murder at seventeen, the boy presented the legal system with a conundrum of sorts (although it had not stopped other teenagers from being executed during the same time period). As a result, in 2012 the Guardian Council, whose purview is the constitutionality of laws, amended the penal code for juveniles, taking the death penalty off the table for 'discretionary' crimes, including drug-related offences.

Now 24, Safar Anghouti was scheduled to hang on 20 January 2014, and if not for the actions of the Imam Ali Popular Students Association, he would be dead. This group operates according to the principle of the country's interpretation of Islamic law, which allows victims and their families to seek retribution, in many cases pardoning with cash compensation. Under Iran's Islamic law convicted murderers and other criminals can pay the victim's family blood money. But since the young killer had grown up in poverty, when the victim's family demanded $50,000, it was a foregone conclusion that he would be unable to pay. Waging an extraordinary campaign on Facebook, the association raised $13,000 more than was needed. Although, the intervention of volunteers in the legal process is not looked upon favourably by the judiciary, claiming it undermines the Islamic right of victims to avenge, the student group proceeded to intercede with the deceased's family during 2013, trying to break down its opposition to accepting compensation. To the great credit of the victim's family and the student group, the victim's family was convinced that 'it would be merciful and compassionate' to allow his killer to live. Encapsulating the forgiving qualities implicit in traditional Sharia law, the killer's sister perhaps put it best, when she commented, 'Instead of applauding revenge, they paid money to spare my brother's life.'[41]

Unfortunately, the sporadic predilection for cutting off the hands of thieves and the stoning of adulterers in Iran, Pakistan, Sudan, Afghanistan and Nigeria in the twenty-first century has cast a negative light on what is in many respects a very just system. It needs to be understood that the typical Islamic judicial and evidentiary safeguards have been ignored in many cases, allowing fundamentalist regimes to embrace punishments and interpretations of criminality that run counter to the teachings and spirit of Islam.

Chinese and Mongolian Legal Traditions

China is rarely mentioned in the discussion of the world's great legal traditions. However, it boasts a legal system that lasted for close to 2,000 years. Chinese traditions influenced developments in Japan by way of Korea. Taken together, Confucian philosophy, Buddhism and the creation of Chinese script became an important model for Japan well into the eighth century, and in the process introduced many of the building blocks required for creating a centralized bureaucratic state. Chinese contacts with Japan are often considered the first sources of outside influence from the Asian continent; it would be another eight centuries before Japan had contacts with the West.

The key to understanding the vagaries of Chinese law is the fact that it developed in such isolation for so long. The Shang dynasty (c. 1700–1027 BC) was the first verifiable dynasty and also the first to introduce a penal code. But the first Chinese legal code, *Fa Jing*, or *Canon of Laws*, was built on the foundation of earlier legal codes. In it can be found laws dealing with theft and robbery, arrest and prison and even judicial rules. The Chinese used various corporal punishments in its earlier periods. Some of them were meant to operate as a system of identification. Malefactors could silently announce their presence when they appeared with tattooed faces, amputated noses and parts of their feet. Less obvious was castration. This earlier code was a major step forward for a society attempting to unify society with one of the few tools available – the law. Nonetheless, it would be almost eight more centuries before the next major turning point was reached under the Tang dynasty (AD 618–907).

Most evidence suggests that the majority of crimes committed in medieval China were committed by the young, unskilled and unattached – the core of the habitual criminal class then and today. From about the seventh to the eighteenth centuries no one could be sentenced without having confessed. The law allowed judges to question subjects under torture, but if a person died under questioning that turned out to be innocent the judge and his advisers would be executed. Various forms of torture were permitted including flogging with a light whip, beating on the backs of the thighs with a bamboo stick, applying screws to the hands and ankles and slapping the face with a leather strap. When the accused finally confessed the judges resorted to sentencing procedures that were used for 1,000 years dating back to the mid-seventh century AD.[42]

From their earliest era, the Chinese used the generic term *Wu Xing*, 'Five Punishments', in reference to the most severe legal penalties. However, the context of the term has changed over the centuries. In the pre-imperial era it referred exclusively to the corporal punishments of tattooing, amputation of the nose, amputation of one or both feet, castration and capital punishment. During the Han dynasty (206 BC–AD 220) punishments were less draconian, with amputation of the nose and feet and tattooing being abolished by imperial edict in 167 BC. Castration was probably ended in the third century AD. During the Han all corporal punishments other than death and beating were replaced by various forms of penal servitude.

According to the Sui Code of 581–3, the precursor to the Tang Code of 624, the aforementioned Five Punishments were more finely tuned and assumed the form that would last into the modern era. The five forms included: beating with a light stick (10–50 blows); beating with a heavy stick (60–100 blows); penal servitude (one to three years); lifelong exile (distances up to about 1,000 miles away); and death (by strangulation or decapitation).[43]

During the Tang, China was probably the largest, richest and most densely populated empire in the world. Its boundaries reached into Tibet, Manchuria, Iran and most of the Korean peninsula. We only have fragments of the earlier law codes, and so with the Tang as the earliest complete legal code of China to survive it is here we will begin. Like the Greeks, the laws were not of divine origin, but were manmade and created out of necessity. Similar to many other societies, punishment was meted out according to one's social standing and often depended on the relationship between the criminal and the victim.

The most serious crimes were considered those that threatened the emperor and the state, those committed by an inferior against a superior, and those that threatened the family. These three offences often required the execution of not just the perpetrator, but his whole family. In cases of treason both the father and son would be strangled, and anyone less than fifteen years old enslaved along with grandparents and great-grandsons. According to the Tang Code of 653 there were 233 offences punishable by either strangulation or decapitation. Three hundred years later the Song Code added 60 more capital offences; under the Yuan Code, we find slicing as a punishment for the first time. By the Ming Code of 1397, thirteen crimes were punishable by slicing, and 282 by the traditional methods. Lest one draws any assumptions about the draconian use of the death penalty, it should be remembered that China never exceeded 300 capital crimes, as Britain did during the halcyon days of its Bloody Code in the eighteenth century. (The term 'Bloody Code' has been used to refer to the English system of criminal law that roughly corresponded with the years 1688–1815, when literally hundreds of felonies carrying the death penalty were added to the criminal statutes.)

A major obstacle to reforming modern Chinese criminal law is the country's long history and deep-rooted traditions, in which criminal law was regarded as an extension of the emperor's power rather than an 'objective code' that applied to all inhabitants. Thus, 'Confession amounted to a submission to authority, while a plea of innocence was viewed as a form of rebellion.' In other words, according to Tang legal code, guilt could be accepted only through a confession (and cases could not be officially recorded without one). Ultimately, the judicial system was set up to protect the authority of government, not the rights of suspects.[44]

In order to understand the Chinese penal system one must grasp the significance of certain aspects of Confucianism, especially during the imperial era. Under the Confucian principle of *zhong* (respect for master, officials and emperor), public officials enjoyed a privileged status in ancient China, which sometimes allowed them to 'redeem their punishment with money and reduction of their ranks', even in lieu of certain capital offences. This protection was in keeping with the Confucian understanding that these upstanding members of society should lead by example through commendable behaviour. Conversely, when they did not live up to such expectations and committed crimes they would be subject to harsher punishment than commoners for the same crimes. This was especially true in the case of treason, which could include the execution of one's extended family up to the third degree, including parents, brothers, spouses and children. In the case of filial piety, or *xiao*, a son could be sentenced to death for beating this father, but in the reverse scenario this behaviour might go unpunished, since it is a parental duty to discipline one's children. On the other hand if an only son is sentenced to death, he might be spared since he would be the only heir available to care for his parents. The Confucian belief in *ren*, referring to benevolence, supports the notion that a society should protect its weaker members. This is probably best exemplified by penal codes that mandated that younger members of society under the age of fifteen, those older than 70, women (especially pregnant), and the mentally and physically infirm should get more compassionate sentences than their able-bodied counterparts.[45]

During his reign, Genghis Khan instituted what became known as the Great Law. His legal accomplishments are often overshadowed by his military campaigns, but deserve to be revisited here. This law code, as instituted by the leader of the Mongol Empire, is quite distinct from its counterparts. It was not based on divine revelations from God, nor was it derived from an ancient code of a sedentary society. Khan consolidated it from customs and traditions practised over the centuries by herding tribes. Groups were permitted to practise traditional law in their areas as long as it did not conflict with the Great Law, which was expected to be revered as the common law over everyone. According to one recent study of Genghis Khan the law did not represent a single codification of the law, but was more a work in progress, 'an ongoing body of legal work' that continued to develop during the last two decades of his life.[46]

Genghis Khan used the Great Law to regulate the most troubling aspects of daily life. Much of the Khan's law was rooted in his own story. His wife had been kidnapped and raped, and gave birth to her first child as a result (while not his own, Genghis raised the child as his own and considered him his eldest son). After this, he prohibited the tradition of kidnapping women on the steppes in an effort to end feuding. Furthermore, he declared all children legitimate, whether by wife or concubine, again drawing from his own recent past. He made great strides in removing whatever sources of conflict existed. He outlawed adultery. By definition, this did not include sexual relations between a woman and her husband's close relatives, nor between a man and female servants or other wives in the household, as it had in the past; now it applied only to relations between married people of separate households – not a crime unless it led to strife between families.

The Great Law of Genghis Khan lasted only 70 years, but during that period religious freedom was given to all, and unlike the Khan's Western counterparts, it asserted that no one was above the law, including the ruler. This law code would impact all corners of the Mongol Empire's justice system in the thirteenth century. Capital offences were reduced from 233 to 135, and were rarely used in any case. Records exist for all but four years of his 34-year reign and indicate that the highest number in any one year was 278, in 1283 (the lowest was seven, in 1263). What is most notable here is that while the Mongols were moving to limit capital punishments and torture, the more 'advanced' states of Europe and the Catholic Church were passing laws expanding the use of these punishments for an increasing array of crimes. While the Mongols limited torture to beatings conducted with a cane, western Europeans were ratcheting up the pain through more and more ingenious tools for inflicting it, such as the rack, impaling on spikes and burning at the stake.

Summary

From a criminological and historical perspective, the discussion of legal traditions has tended to be rather parochial, grounded mainly in those that have survived into the twenty-first century. However, in doing this we are missing references to customary and indigenous legal systems that did not often share a specific legal tradition, and were often confined to a particular locale while developing independently from outside influences.[47] The next chapter will examine the changing tapestry of crime and punishment as the feudal landscape eventually gives way to urbanization and state building. Feudalism was not just a Western phenomenon but was an important organizing factor for societies around the world well into the nineteenth century, in locales as far-flung as Asia, Africa, Europe and the New World.

3

Crime in a Changing Landscape: From Feudalism to the City and the State

Prior to the birth of the modern nation-state, a variety of similar social systems, often referred to as feudal (or feudalism), developed in scattered parts of the world.[1] In each region where it appeared it took on a provincial character reflecting specific features of the local culture. For some observers feudalism meant a set of legal and military customs that flourished in medieval Europe between the ninth and fifteenth centuries; others understood it more broadly as a system for structuring society around relationships derived from the doling out of land in return for service and labour.

The outlines of feudal society were drawn in early medieval Europe sometime between the fifth and eighth centuries, when societies were developing patterns of organization and cohesion in an epoch marked by the disruption of traditional kinship security groups. Much of the blame for the weakening of central power during this era has been laid at the feet of the disintegrating Roman Empire and the accompanying dislocation of bureaucratic state machinery in the Romanized West. This breakdown went a long way towards diminishing the importance of cities as centres of administration and of specialized economic activities, as public authority fell into the hands of the great landowners. Among the myriad other factors cited as contributing to the weakening of trad-itional units of government were the lack of competent administrators, an extremely low level of literacy and the restricted circulation of money. Nonetheless, between the tenth and twelfth centuries there was a clear lack of strong centralized states in Europe, meaning that there was no major authority invested with the power to collect taxes, promulgate laws, raise troops, keep the peace or dispense justice. Except for the sur-viving bastions of central authority – the papacy,[2] a handful of monarchies and the Holy Roman Empire – most governments were effective at exercising their power only over relatively small numbers of people in a local or on occasion a regional context. One of the hallmarks of feudal crimes and punishments was that government authority remained fragmented into small limited units of people under the purview of local feudal lords who exercised many of the functions normally associated with the state. Thus when it came to dispensing justice, your average malefactor would probably be most familiar with the lord's manorial courts, the only stewards of justice that a peasant or commoner would have contact with. Manorial courts were invested with the power to settle disputes and matters of law, and it was not uncommon for criminals to be handed over to the lord, imbued with the power to summarily hang thieves on the spot.

Observers from Geoffrey Chaucer to Monty Python and Quentin Tarantino have all contributed to a stereotypical view of feudal society. Yes, it was often a brutal and superstitious social order, but it was also a complicated and layered one, based on intricate hierarchical relationships that bound lords, knights, bishops, serfs, artisans and vassals in a vast web of mutual aid and dependence.[3] Few scholars agree on a precise meaning for the term 'feudalism'. It has been popular to use the term interchangeably with the word 'medievalism'; in most cases both terms have been used pejoratively, signifying something 'backward'. It is not my intention here to debate whether a society is feudal or semi-feudal, but to examine features of crime and punishment that have characterized societies where the basic features of feudalism prevailed. For those who have watched Tarantino's controversial film *Pulp Fiction*, the use of the phrase 'going medieval' on someone might have sounded like either a malapropism or an ahistorical slight; in reality this expression captured the violence that characterized and plagued life in various feudal eras around the world, both past and present. Medieval societies indeed were brutal, often 'violent societies'.[4]

According to the classic definition, feudalism was found in societies where 'a lord granted a fief to a vassal' and 'the vassal provided military service in return'.[5] Likewise, the French historian Marc Bloch expanded it to include the relationship of lords and peasants who performed labour in return for security and protection (manorialism).[6] Feudalism has appeared in a number of incarnations depending on time period and location, and has manifested itself in both Western and non-Western societies. On one extreme you have Marxist historians, who view feudalism as a universal stage in human history through which a society must pass sooner or later. Some historians have even identified feudal economies and social systems in such diverse regions as India, pre-colonial Africa and China, and in agricultural societies in central Asia and the Middle East, as well as medieval Europe. However, these examples run counter to traditional scholarship that restricts the use of the idiom 'feudalism' to a handful of societies in western Europe during the Middle Ages. For the purposes of this chapter, feudalism will be regarded as a social and economic system distinguished by inherited social ranks, where individuals possess inherent social and economic privileges. Perhaps feudalism is understood best as a 'method of government in which the essential relation is not that between ruler and subject, nor state and citizen, but between lord and vassal', a voluntary relationship between feudal lords and their supporting casts of free subordinates and heavily armed fighting men, who pledged their military service in exchange for a personal bond of loyalty.[7] As early as the Treaty of Verdun of 843, it was proclaimed 'Every man should have a lord,' with only the Pope and the Holy Roman Emperor in Constantinople exempt from its strictures, since they were regarded as vassals of the Lord.[8]

The best and most frequently cited examples of feudal crime and punishment come from western Europe and Japan. The Norman Conquest of England in 1066 saw northern French feudal institutions introduced to Britain, while in Japan, feudalism developed at the end of the twelfth century before becoming more dominant during the fourteenth century as the imperial central government lost control during a long period of internecine warfare. By the end of the fourteenth century, key figures called *shugo* had become regional powers and acquired both civil and military powers formerly held at the national level. The traditional Japanese feudal system would diminish somewhat by 1603 during the centralization of the Tokugawa regime, but continue nonetheless into the nineteenth century. Feudalism and its associated practices was an important organizing factor for societies well into the nineteenth century (and in some cases even into the twenty-first century). Indeed, Sicily did not abolish serfdom until 1812; Russia not until 1861. This chapter examines the variations of crime and punishment in feudal societies into the pre-modern era.

Medieval Crime and Punishment in Western Europe

Probably the best recognized of the early feudal eras was the period between 500 and 1500 in western Europe, an epoch overlapping the Middle Ages, or medieval period. While France and England are most often identified with feudalism and the period of medievalism, what could be said about England went for much of the rest of Continental Europe and elsewhere, albeit with some variations. By the turn of the tenth century, 'a military aristocracy of big landowners' controlled huge swathes of Europe's agricultural estates, leading to the control of a peasant population made up largely of serfs 'who were bound to the soil and whose lives were at the mercy of their lord'. Likewise, the developing criminal justice machinery was dominated not by judges, magistrates and police but by aristocrats, kings, ecclesiastical leaders, manorial lords and rich burghers (who gained control over town governments).[9]

By the eleventh century, growing medieval towns on the fringes of feudal estates had already begun to distinguish themselves from the longstanding feudal system that was defined by traditional obligations between lords and vassals. During the next two centuries these evolving urban entities developed their own new legal traditions. Ultimately, town law would become quite distinct from the feudal law that held sway in the countryside. Like feudal communities, the towns were challenged by their own particular brand of crime problems, which meant doling out punishments to thieves, bandits, highwaymen, pickpockets and assorted ne'er-do-wells. Towns relied on a particular exhibitory style of punishment, usually inflicted publicly, and included floggings and shaming penalties for minor offences, and executions for more serious crimes. Unlike the feudal realm, towns also employed hangmen and other executioners. Further distinguishing towns from feudal estates was the fact that all townspeople were liable for violating town law, while on feudal estates one was punished according to one's status since the punishment of crime hinged on one's position in the tightly controlled world of the peasant. In many cases those of equally high status might resolve conflicts on their own through fines or restitution. The poor on the other hand were burdened with increasingly cruel corporal and capital punishments (in lieu of an almost non-existent law enforcement apparatus). In any case, feudal penal sanctions, whether in England or Russia, were handled at the local level.

According to Pollock and Maitland, penalties became more cruel in England (and probably elsewhere) as the machinery of state began to emerge. Many crimes that in the past had been expiated with fines had become capital crimes by the twelfth and thirteenth centuries. Under the first Norman king, William I, better known as William the Conqueror, corporal punishments such as mutilations were introduced in lieu of capital punishment such as hangings. No criminal would be hanged for the next 40 years. However, this does not mean that no one perished from penal sanctions. Scores of the convicted must surely have succumbed to mutilations after having eyes gouged out and testicles cut off. William adhered to the Middle Ages' tradition of allowing conquered peoples to retain their legal systems and he went on to adopt most of the Anglo-Saxon criminal justice ideas while introducing other customs from Continental Europe. His successors ratcheted up sanctions; Henry I would institute the hanging of thieves caught in flagrante delicto, while Henry II hanged traitors and murderers if they were not lucky enough to lose a mere hand and foot. Beginning in 1166 (the centenary of the Norman Conquest), in the midst of a growing crime problem, criminal punishment was designed for its deterrence effect. For example, anyone who failed the ordeal was sentenced to be hanged or have a foot amputated and then banished from the realm for 40 days. Ten years later the Assize of Northampton introduced even more draconian sanctions. Mutilation, following conviction by ordeal, was extended to include the amputation of the right hand and foot. In the following century the death penalty replaced most mutilations for felons.

When it came to felonies, no crime offered such a contrast in punishments as theft, sanctions which would carry into the nineteenth century. The difference between petty and grand larceny was 1 shilling (12*d*). It was no accident that this limit was set: according to folklore twelve pence would allow a man to steal just enough food to keep him from starvation for eight days.[10] Grand larceny became a capital crime sometime in the thirteenth century. Sentence was often pronounced in local manor courts, with the sentence carried out by the 'sakebar', a pursuer who either cut the malefactor's head off or tossed him from a precipice to his death. As for petty larceny, the criminal might lose a thumb and then be forced to vacate the realm; or he could be shamed in the pillory or tumbrel, with an added loss of an ear. In some localities the thief would play the role of executioner, amputating his own ear, which was nailed to the pillory post from which only he could set himself free by using a knife. According to protocol the petty thief lost an ear for the first offence and the other for the next one. But, once the recidivist ran out of ears there was surely no sentence that would turn this malefactor around and he was usually hanged. In an interesting aside, in an era of knighthood and close combat with cutting instruments it was not uncommon for a knight to lose an ear in battle. This could stigmatize the warrior after his fighting days were over, since a missing ear usually marked an individual as a habitual offender. In such cases the warrior could obtain an explanatory charter from the king to carry on his person at all times in order to support his claims of respectability.[11]

Few sanctions were as widespread as the pillory. Its employment rose in popularity during the twelfth and thirteenth centuries and became known by an assortment of monikers. In northern parts of what is now Germany it was referred to as the *Katz*, while in the southern parts and Austria it was known as the *Prechel* or *Schreiat*. The French knew it as either the *pilori* or *carcan*, while the British called it the 'stretch neck' or simply the 'pillory'. No matter its name, this shaming device appeared in a number of incarnations, but all had the same goal: exhibitory punishment. Thus it was always located in a public place, often outside a town hall or other public building. A wide assortment of law violators saw time in this device (and the stocks, a sitting variation, with holes cut in a board for legs and irons for hands). Another similar type was known as the 'shame stool' or 'shame asses', a wooden structure in which the convict was forced to sit in a public place.

When it came to financial crimes in the Middle Ages, counterfeiting and forgery were the most prominent exemplars. Stocks and pillories were used to punish offenders who engaged in deceitful business practices, forgery, begging under false pretences, or masquerading as officials. One baker appeared in court so many times for giving false weights that he was nicknamed 'Pillory' for his habit of ending up in this shaming device. During the reign of the Anglo-Saxons, King Athelstan ordered coin forgers to be tortured and executed. Under King Canute they had both hands amputated and by the fourteenth century King Edward was sentencing some clerics to death by hanging for forgery violations.

In late medieval Europe the majority of crimes were along the lines of physical assaults and petty larcenies.[12] A number of records indicate that in the early fifteenth century more crimes were being committed in English towns and wooded areas than in villages and open fields. It was in the growing towns that cutpurses, petty thieves and their ilk tended to gravitate. Town taverns became meeting places for growing criminal fraternities and prostitution, which had become a well-organized profession in London as early as the fourteenth century. As connections were increasingly made between vice and criminality, new penalties were created, which sometimes included driving all the prostitutes out of any town where they were considered a problem.[13]

As families accumulated possessions, bands of skilled thieves concocted strategies to break into houses and pilfer concealed valuables. In order to get families to reveal where their most cherished possessions were hidden, thieves sometimes resorted to torture. In one case thieves covered their escape by gouging out a victim's eyes and cutting out his tongue in an attempt to prevent him from testifying against them once they left the scene of the crime.

When it comes to forms of financial crime, the modern criminal code is much more substantial today. By contrast, during the Middle Ages there were no such crimes as price fixing, monopolization, insider trading, securities fraud or false advertising. Prior to complex systems of banking and national treasuries, financial crime was committed on the local level and involved such shenanigans as using false weights and counterfeiting. Otherwise, looking back from a world of Bitcoins and hedge funds it is difficult to find many analogies between these two eras as far as financial crimes are concerned.

By most accounts the most common forms of punishments, and the least spectacular, were banishment and money fines. The offences most frequently prosecuted involved some form of physical violence; in return, assailants could usually expect one of various types of financial sanctions, determined in each case by the relative status of victim and perpetrator, the seriousness of the injuries and whether the assailant was a local inhabitant or not. The medieval crime historian Trevor Dean uses fourteenth-century Rome as an exemplar for how this so-called 'tariff justice' worked.[14] Fines were specific to the infraction: for chasing someone with a weapon, the fine was 4 lire, without a weapon it was only 40s. Those accused of grabbing a knife or sword with bad intentions paid 40s, deliberately making someone fall 100s, and brawling just 3 lire. The aforementioned penalties were doubled for knights, sons of knights and anyone who owned 2,000 lire in property. Some of the listed infractions give one the impression of a rude age. Those who knocked out or broke another's tooth, pushed someone into a fire or pulled another from a horse were fined 10 lire. However, if a miscreant had the gall to put dung, excrement or similar filth in anyone's mouth the penalty was more than doubled to 25 lire. All of these examples suggest a society plagued by social conflict.[15]

In all eras of early British history, no secular crime was considered more serious than treason, making it a virtually unatonable violation that no monetary compensation could remedy. By the Norman era, hanging was considered insufficient punishment for someone who killed his lord. It became an accepted notion that one who perpetrated such an act 'should perish in torments to which hell-fire will seem a relief'.[16] The punishment of hanging, drawing and quartering was developed in different stages to accomplish this. Initially, someone convicted of petty or high treason was placed on the ground on his back before being tied to the tail of a horse and dragged along to the gibbet. Apparently, some of the condemned would not make it alive to the executioner, after hitting their heads on sharp stones in the road as they were dragged behind the horse, so a hurdle was introduced to haul the offender there as a form of 'mercy'. In reality this was just as insurance that he would make it to the hangman alive. In time this was considered too benign for high treason and the protocol was lengthened to include drawing, hanging, disembowelling, penile amputation, burning, beheading and quartering. The established protocol stated that the person 'be drawn to the gallows' where he would be 'hanged by the neck, and let down alive'. At this point he would be stretched out on his back and have his bowels taken out, and if he was still alive, have them burned before his eyes (this was sometimes extended to include the genitals to signify he would no longer sire traitors). The *coup de grâce* was beheading and quartering of the body. Once this was accomplished, 'His head and quarters are to be placed where our lord the king shall direct.'[17] It has been suggested that this form of punishment actually represented punishment for *multiple* capital crimes. In one of its most notorious applications, in 1305 the legendary Scot William 'Braveheart' Wallace was punished for committing 'all crimes against God and man', requiring the suffering of four to five deaths. Thus, he was drawn for treason, hanged for robbery and homicide, disembowelled for sacrilege, beheaded as an outlaw and quartered for 'diverse depredations'. In any case the original drawing and hanging was used for lesser crimes such as petty treason and counterfeiting coins.[18] In 1352 an elaborate statute defined treason as the killing (or attempting to) of a queen, king or the eldest son; the defiling of the king's wife, eldest daughter or eldest son's wife; levying war against the king in his kingdom; giving aid or comfort to enemies; counterfeiting the king's seals or money; bringing false money into the realm; or slaying certain officers or justices at work.

A dual system of ecclesiastical and secular courts developed in England and on the Continent during the medieval period. By about AD 1000 the geography of what would become modern western Europe began to come into focus as common languages increasingly tied together societies within specific territories, as did a growing network of Catholic dioceses and parishes that bound 'a continent of believers through a detailed system of rules, regulations and church law'. Coincident with this transformation in patterns of power and authority was the replacement of older and more nuanced versions of crime and punishment with more violent and localized public structures of justice and its administration, based on the powers of strongmen and their fortresses.[19]

Ecclesiastical offences were in the main crimes not usually tried in lay courts and were typically related to sexuality and morality, such as fornication, adultery, bigamy or incest. While treason remained the highest secular offence, so heresy was in the world of the Church. Both demanded the ultimate sanction of death. For heresy the punishment in Continental Europe was death by fire. However, the first recorded case in England in 1166 was handled by secular authorities, who whipped, facially branded and exiled the defendant. Following the thirteenth-century Lateran Council (1215), English sanctions would be ratcheted up to include burning at the stake.

By the time of the Norman Conquest, the island had been Christianized for some four centuries. But William the Conqueror, the first Norman king, would also introduce Church courts in 1066, leading to the separation of the secular and the Church, or ecclesiastical law. The Catholic Church withdrew from the adjudication of secular disputes to concentrate on spiritual matters (and without secular interference). At first, Church law superseded English national law, with the Pope considered the supreme ruler. Ecclesiastical courts were immersed in matters regarding marriage, legitimation and status, as well as offences including adultery, perjury, blasphemy, usury and heresy. From the twelfth century on, the Church held its own courts and administered its own justice, controlling a jurisdiction that extended to clerics, Church property, sex offences and family law. Clergymen could be tried under these courts only and the worst punishment they could expect was excommunication. Some legal experts have suggested that excommunication of clergy was akin to ecclesiastical outlawry.[20] While excommunication might seem a rather benign punishment from a secular perspective, it was everything to a cleric: henceforth they were removed completely from the legal process and the clergy itself, whose members were prohibited from praying with him, talking with him or even eating in his company.

1215 and All That

There were few years in European history that impacted the future of European justice more than 1215. That year alone would have been momentous if just for the signing of the Magna Carta by King John at Runnymede on 15 June, establishing in writing the fundamental principles of human rights that would inspire the writing of the United States Constitution more than 500 years later. As one of the founding documents of modern democracy it introduced such judicial protections as no imprisonment without trial and justice to all men without fear or favour. But in an act even more far reaching than the Magna Carta in terms of crime and punishment, just five months later Pope Innocent convened the Fourth Lateran Council. Having already curtailed the use of compurgation (oath taking) in Church disciplinary actions in 1199, his reforms went even further during a three-week assembly of some 1,500 Church representatives, ranging from bishops and abbots to priors and proxies 'from every country in the Catholic world'.[21] Seventy reforms were introduced to the delegates, many of them designed to address clerical abuses. Henceforth priests were forbidden from throwing dice, watching clowns or wearing pointy-toed shoes. Princes were instructed to make Muslims and Jews wear unusual clothes, because too many Christians had been having sex with them and then claiming not to have noticed the difference. Every Catholic was required to make confession at least once a year, on pain of excommunication and burial in unhallowed ground.

More importantly, the Fourth Lateran Council prohibited priests from taking part in ordeals of water or fire, and in the process transformed European criminal justice. Over the course of several years these reforms would reach the far corners of Christendom. The prohibition of trial by ordeal left a legal vacuum. With the clergy forbidden from taking part in ordeals, alternative methods of retribution filled the void. Crude methods of justice aimed to fit the crime came into vogue. For example, hanging seemed a natural sanction for murder, as did burning for arson, castration for rape, and removing the tongue for slander and false accusation. Well into the thirteenth century anyone caught in the act of committing crime faced summary justice, often on orders of the local lords on their feudal holdings.

From a secular perspective, we can trace back incarceration in England to at least the tenth century, but it was not until 1250 that most towns used guild halls or castles as small prisons 'under a franchise arrangement'. In rare cases during this era purpose-built structures were erected.[22] After the Norman Conquest, Henry II introduced fixed periods of confinement for those waiting to go through the ordeal and ruled that gaols should be erected in every shire (county) to hold such malefactors. Demonstrating this early example of fixed sentences, perjurers could be held up to one year. Under Henry III, a breach of forest law could also result in up to one year in confinement while waiting the ordeal.

Pope Boniface VIII, in the late thirteenth century, is generally credited as the first sovereign authority in the Western tradition to designate the punishment of imprisonment as a 'legitimate instrument of a universal legal system'.[23] Outside the Church, medieval society lacked funds and facilities for long-term imprisonment and corporal punishment. Only the Church, prohibited by canon law from shedding blood since before the Fourth Lateran Council, used imprisonment for offenders under its jurisdiction. Life sentences operated by monastic orders were employed now and then, ostensibly for correction and penance. According to one leading authority, 'The Catholic Church was the first institution in the West to use imprisonment consistently for any avowed purpose other than detention as a practical way of handling disciplinary problems among all peoples within its jurisdiction.'[24] Prison historian Norman Johnston suggests there was a good reason for this, stemming from the Church practice of giving sanctuary to fugitives from justice; over time the special quarters that had been devised for this purpose made the transition to ecclesiastical prisons connected to religious venues.

Japanese and Norman Feudal Societies

Medieval Japan can be best viewed as an interregnum characterized by decentralized power sandwiched between two eras of stable central government. This feudal era was a turning point in Japanese history, with some historians finding it comparable to the beginning of the Middle Ages in the West. During this period Japanese society was creating new social forms as it distanced itself from Chinese models, becoming 'less Asiatic and more European'.[25] Mirroring events in medieval Europe, Japan was experiencing its own militarization of the upper classes in the provinces. The subsequent increase in vassal relationships connecting lords to their retainers, and the formation of feudal estates would soon dominate the land and those who worked it.

It has been de rigueur in historical scholarship to draw contrasts between feudal Japan and western Europe. Both shared military values that included loyalty to a lord, which in the case of Japan 'equalled or exceeded that of medieval Europe', leading at least one observer to assert that in some respects medieval Japan was more feudal than medieval Europe.[26] Around the same time that the Normans were organizing English feudal society and inaugurating a professional class of warriors, Japan was introducing its own version in the form of samurai (meaning guards or attendants) warriors. Before the centralization of the state and the formation of standing armies, some feudal societies encouraged the development of a martial class. On one hand, England had its knights and armed citizenry, while on the other Japan promoted the military arts, which became the preserve of a special feudal class, known as the *bushi*, or samurai class.[27] Security was considered a local issue and law and order was expected to be maintained by rich landowners. Under these large landholders a number of dependent small farmers and land-owners developed. Over time, master–servant relationships strengthened.

Both the Norman and Japanese military exemplars belonged to privileged classes that made fighting a vocation. By some accounts Japan's medieval period lasted from the twelfth to seventeenth centuries, an era considered an 'intermediary period between two stable societies'. During these years the government's power was decentralized, as Japan was ravaged by a series of factional conflicts and civil war. It was an 'Age of warriors with its shogun and vassals [that] launched Japan into the Middle Ages'.[28] In a society dominated by the presence of so many warriors it was necessary to create a strict penal system that would insure that order prevailed. In 1232 the customs of the warriors were codified in a collection of laws influenced by China's Tang dynasty, called the *Goseibai shikimoku* (a list of rules for distinguishing good from evil in a shogun household), and gradually imposed on Japanese society. Between the twelfth and nineteenth centuries, political power was in the hands of the shogun, the head of the military–vassal hierarchy. Between 1232 and 1432 it was up to the *shugo* to maintain law and order, acting as middleman between the military headquarters (*bakufu*) and the vassals in the hinterlands.

In a warrior society such as feudal Japan, severe penalties were invoked to pacify its members. In the past it was acceptable for a jealous husband to commit a crime in retaliation, but the government had stepped in to prevent potential vendettas and private wars from occur-ring. Many of the sanctions were directed at property, which was fiercely defended by warriors. Thus major infractions might lead to the confiscation of estates, sometimes coupled with exile. Incarcerative sentences were rare (and considered less severe than exile). Most commoners faced corporal punishments created with the goal of inflicting humiliation and shame. Common criminals often were marked by facial brands or tattoos. On the other hand, rape of an unaccompanied woman was not considered serious, and the perpetrator might be punished by merely having half of his hair shaved off, making him 'look ridiculous and disreputable until it grew back'.[29]

Much of Japanese feudal culture carried over into the subsequent Tokugawa era (1603–1867) and continues today in the great emphasis placed on duty, maintaining social harmony and placing the individual within the status-oriented relationships in groups. Whichever class you were born into, you stayed in for life. Indeed, the dominant characteristic of Tokugawa state law was its rule by status. Heavily influenced by Chinese Confucianism, which linked loyalty to superiors and expecting the government to act benevolently and responsibly, there was no conception of individual rights.

Prior to 1603 and the Tokugawa period (also referred to as the Edo period) Japan used such cruel sanctions as facial disfigurement through amputation of nose and ears, skull crushing with heavy mallets, flaying alive, tossing from cliffs, pulling apart by oxen, stoning, boiling, burying alive, or being tied upside-down on a cross set in a tidal flat to slowly drown the convict in the incoming tide. However, the inauguration of the Tokugawa bureaucracy in the early seventeenth century streamlined the death penalty by limiting it to decapitation, crucifixion, burning at the stake and sawing through the neck. According to one historian, 'Throughout the whole Tokugawa period criminal punishment was cruel, public and exemplary.'[30] The public was expected to respect state authority. This was done vicariously through the pain publicly inflicted on criminals. This could be manifested in numerous ways, ranging from decapitation, crucifixion and bodily mutilations to parading criminals through streets. In an age of limited mobility, exile or banishment from family and village was a more formidable sanction than it would be considered today, and conveyed the message that community forces could manage criminality at minimal cost to the government. Violators of village behavioural standards were punished with monetary fines, the surrender of rice or sake, or forced service as night watchmen. Serious crimes such as murder and arson were capital offences. During the Edo period an execution grounds was kept in several locations, where an estimated 100,000 to 200,000 criminals met their fates. Execution methods ranged from boiling, burning and crucifixion to decapitation, sawing and waist cutting (the cutting in half of an individual). Corporal punishment in the form of whipping and beating was the penalty for a number of common crimes, especially theft and fighting. In 1720, the judicial flogging penalty was introduced to replace the amputation of nose and ears, with 100 lashes the maximum.

Although Japan's criminal code was later influenced by French and Prussian elements, the modern Japanese criminal justice system is deeply rooted in the feudalism of the Tokugawa era, when class was determined by birth. This was best explained by one scholar who noted: 'the Western concept of natural law would have seemed like "unnatural law"', since 'natural law assumed that the rights of people were embedded in unchanging universal principles, which transcended the state and extended justice to all. It was in this way that the 'Tokugawa legal system was aimed at securing justice for the polity'.[31] Therefore there was little actual reliance on formal law; it was transcended by loyalty to the government and the family.

Feudal China

The Chinese Tang penal code and other laws influenced the Tokugawa model of justice. Japanese jurists studied the historical accounts of Chinese court cases. In fact, medieval Japanese pathologists had a basic grasp of forensic science, having adopted the text *Xi Yuan Ji Lu* (*Instructions to Coroners*), written by a Chinese official named Song Ci in 1247. It is considered one of the earliest treatises on forensic science. The law and the judiciary would be active supporters of the Chinese feudal system for almost 2,000 years. In a similar way to the European feudal system, one's experience with the criminal justice system was determined by the class status of victim and perpetrator. Chinese aristocrats, officials and big landlords were typically granted leniency and special consideration before the law when they committed crimes.

The Song dynasty, founded in 960, adopted the traditional system of Five Punishments (*Wu Xing*) introduced by the preceding Tang dynasty (618–907). These consisted of beatings with a light rod, or heavy rod, penal servitude, exile and death, and were typically listed in ascending order from lighter to heavier punishments. Similar sets of punishments existed in other East Asian states. The *Wu Xing* would remain almost unchanged until 1905. The least severe punishment was *chi*, 10–50 strokes from a light flogging stick. Following this in gravity was *zhang*, 60–100 strokes with a heavier flogging instrument. According to McKnight this traditionally was discounted up to 70 per cent in practice. Those condemned to either of these two punishments could pay compensation instead. (Beatings with flogging sticks have been common in numerous societies; the English preferred bamboo, while the French termed the sanction the *bastinado*.) In some cases deportation to a penal colony was used as a sanction. It usually required between one and three years of servitude far from one's village, or in worse cases exile from between 650 and 1,000 miles away, depending on the crime.

The most severe sentence was execution, either by strangulation or decapitation. Over the centuries the Tang code evolved, adding new gradations of penalties and offering judges finer sentencing distinctions. For example, over time beatings tended to become more punitive, with the introduction of longer flogging sticks, offering more leverage for the executioner to inflict pain. Exhibitory shaming in the form of wearing the cangue continued and for many was considered a 'humiliation worse than death' and produced 'shame that lasts a lifetime'.[32]

For the Chinese, death in the form of beheading or accompanied by any other bodily mutilation was considered the ultimate punishment since it was believed that the body of the deceased needed to be whole for the soul of the body to make a proper passage. This 'loss of somatic integrity' was the outcome most feared under the imperial system.[33] To dismember a body, especially the head, extended punishment beyond the grave. To add even more humiliation to the sanction in the earliest era the bodies and heads were often buried separately. Compared to beheading, the other main method of execution, strangling, was surely more painful, but was less feared since it left the body whole. Typically when someone was executed by strangulation, the condemned was attached to a post, allowing two soldiers to slowly twist a rope around the neck, not unlike a garrotte.[34] Traditionally, capital punishment was carried out on a seasonal basis, with late autumn considered the 'season of death'. Until it was abolished in the Song period, a pattern developed where convicted men were held in confinement until the proper season had arrived.[35]

The best-known irregular punishment from China has been referred to as 'death by slicing', 'slow-slicing' or *lingchi*. Its origins are still murky, but the earliest mention of it appears during the history of the state of Liao (907–1125). However, it was not used as a Chinese state penalty until sometime in the Later Zhou (951–960).[36] The punishment was deliberately conducted to produce the most suffering and degradation and was considered the most extreme death penalty since, like beheading, the prisoner would be left in several pieces after the sanction had been concluded. As a recent study of *lingchi* noted, 'The more the penalty reduced its victim to a form that could no longer be assumed to be human the more severe it was considered.'[37] It was originally used to punish such crimes as treason and the violation of temples, tombs or places representing the ruling house, as well as the murder of senior family members. Soon, bandits would face the painful wrath of the sharp knives, as would those who committed various types of robbery and sedition. Executions typically occurred between 1 p.m. and 5 p.m. in the vicinity of where the crime took place. It was not uncommon for those facing this painful and shameful execution to either hire a relative or someone else to kill them first. In order to protect the integrity of the legal process, anyone who assisted in the death of a convict prior to his formal execution would be subjected to the same penalty, albeit reduced by two degrees to penal servitude.[38]

It is rare to find any contemporary accounts of an actual execution during China's Middle Ages, but it is probable that if one was discovered it would read similarly to the following nineteenth-century account, in which the observer T. T. Meadows reported:

> [The criminal] simply kneels with his face parallel to the earth, thus leaving his neck exposed in a horizontal position. His hands crossed and bound behind his back, are grasped by the man behind, who by tilting them up, is enabled in some degree to keep the neck in the proper position . . . The executioner stands on the criminal's left. The sword ordinarily employed is only about 3 feet long . . . The executioners . . . are taken from the ranks of the army . . . The sabre is firmly held with both hands, the right hand in the front, with the thumb projecting over and grasping the hilt. The executioner, with his feet firmly planted some distance apart, holds the sabre for an instant at the right angle to the neck about a foot above it in order to take aim at a joint: then with a sharp order to the criminal of 'Don't move!' he raises it straight before him as high as his head, and brings it rapidly down with the full strength of both arms, giving additional force to the cut by dropping his body perpendicularly to a sitting posture at the moment the sword touches the neck. He never takes a second cut, and the head is seldom left attached and even by a portion of the skin, but is severed completely.[39]

The Feudal Roots of the Sicilian Mafia

Back in 1970 the travel writer Norman Thomas observed that 'the feudal system discarded elsewhere many centuries ago, has managed to survive'[40] in Sicily. This strategically located island at the crossroads of Mediterranean civilization has been conquered by a who's who of empires and countries including Roman, Greek, Arab, Norman, French, Greek, Austrian and Spanish invaders. The Romans introduced their version of feudalism during the third and second centuries BC, while the Normans brought their brand from the British Isles more than 1,000 years later. Foreign rulers consolidated their control of the island by cultivating the allegiance of local aristocrats, who obtained concessions in return. Thus, the law became whatever the rulers made it.

In 1812 feudalism was officially ended in Sicily by order of Ferdinand 1, King of the Two Sicilies (Naples and Sicily). With the abolition of the feudal estates much of Sicily was turned into a welter of large private estates owned by barons, the island's nobility. Finding urban centres more alluring, most of the landed aristocracy were drawn to the more compelling urban centres on and off the island, leaving their estates in the powerful hands of local middlemen, known as *gabelloti*, who in an earlier era were responsible for collecting taxes from peasants and managing estates, becoming de facto power brokers and patrons to the rural peasantry. Like feudal lords of yore, the *gabelloti* rented out small pieces of property to tenant farmers in return for a percentage of the harvest. They used a firm hand to control the peasants; as the old Italian adage goes: 'Those who controlled the lands controlled the people.' Some time during the nineteenth century, these 'men of respect' adapted their positions to exploiting those above and below them. They might have adopted the monikers 'men of honour' and 'men of respect', but when it came to the law they had no respect. Throughout the nineteenth century Sicilian justice was dispensed at the local level. With no faith in the government in Rome to protect them, peasants looked elsewhere for protection, forcing them into the orbit of the *gabelloti* and their henchmen. A leading modern authority on the Mafia has suggested that during this period 'the vestiges of feudal structures were still deeply visible and the spirit and legal forms of feudalism shaped most social relationships, especially in the countryside'.[41]

In their book *Made Men* (2013) the authors Antonio Nicaso and Marcel Danesi assert that 'crime in Sicily was primarily a product of its feudal system.'[42] Thus the modern-day Sicilian Mafia can trace its origins to the end of feudalism in the nineteenth century, a period of failed rebellions and reform efforts. The repeal of feudal laws in 1812 was followed by an increase in ownership of private property, the result of the break-up of the vast baronial and Church estates. The end of feudalism in Sicily resulted in an abundance of former *gabelloti* and their associates on the job market. Skilled in the use of violence and intimidation they were well prepared to take advantage of the opportunities provided by the post-feudal period.

Following Italian unification in 1861, some former *gabelloti* emerged as leaders of crime families, evolving into a shadow government capable of influencing most aspects of Sicilian life, while collecting taxes for their own coffers.[43] During the second half of the nineteenth century these former strong men made the transition from settling disputes and dispensing justice on feudal estates to controlling markets and communities through intimidation and bribery. Local peasants had long noted how the justice system short-changed the masses, as judges bought their posts and justice officials treated the powerful with leniency. It wasn't a great leap, then, for them to develop a deep distrust of most aspects of state institutions, creating a void in the power structure that allowed the Mafia to develop from the fallout from the end of feudalism.

Perhaps things might have turned out differently in Sicily if the nobility and the Church had been more inclined to invest in equitable policing, better schools and roads and better-paying jobs. But the clergy was as complicit as the landowners in keeping the status quo, since both benefitted from the hard work of peasants for deplorable wages.

The Russian Experience

The historian of Russia Jerome Blum suggested that in comparison with western Europe, where feudalism created a strong central power, it took a strong central power to develop feudalism in Russia. What's more, it took a much longer time for it to develop, and when it did it took on a harsher tinge than anywhere in Europe. Serfs had no rights whatsoever and it was said that they could be traded like livestock by their lords; even their families were not sacrosanct and like everything else they owned were considered to be property of the lord. According to Blum, 'Of all the millions of Europeans who in centuries past had been held in bondage, they [Russian peasants] were almost the last to be freed [in 1861].'[44] In eleventh-century Russia all free men enjoyed an equality that would be hard to fathom 600 years later as their lands were converted from communes to the private property of landowners. Ultimately, these once-free labourers found themselves renting fields that they themselves had previously owned, while others were pushed off their former holdings altogether and forced to become hired hands or contract labourers to survive. Between the fifteenth and seventeenth centuries Russian peasants were trapped in a social system of restrictions placed on them by the state and landholders. By the end of the fifteenth century the only time that a peasant renter could even legally leave his landlord was the two weeks surrounding St George's Day (26 November in the Julian calendar, a time of celebration after the year's harvest), and even then only after paying heavy fines.

The long process of Russian enserfment officially ended in 1649 thanks to a codification of laws and customs that regulated relationships between lords and peasants. However, it was deficient in many ways. Although it did not outlaw the rights of serfs to present petitions of complaint against lords, these were accorded little credence unless they involved treason. In fact, in 1767 Catherine II, while on a tour of Russian villages, was so overwhelmed with petitions that she decreed that it would henceforth be a criminal act to present masters with petitions and ordered violators to be beaten with a knout (a form of lashing instrument) and sentenced to labour in Siberia. Thus serfs lost the only mechanism they could use to call attention to injustices by their masters. And although the death penalty had been prohibited, masters had nothing to fear if their serfs died in the course of a beating. According to one Frenchman who lived in Russia for a number of years in the early 1800s, 'the serf owner's domination over his peasants was greater than of any sovereign in the world.'[45]

In time, the knout became the most visible instrument of punishment (and some might say of the state) and the most familiar penal sanction to Russians, particularly serfs, and to foreign observers. Introduced by Ivan III in the fifteenth century, the knout, sometimes referred to as *knoot* or *knut*, came in a variety of designs. There were a number of methods for applying it. It was described as being typically a 'wooden handle about a foot long, its thongs being plaited together to give a two-foot lash. At its end was fastened a further thong, eighteen inches in length, tapering to a point.' This extension could be detached when necessary and replaced by another length of lash. Although the lash was first soaked in milk and frozen, it was not uncommon for it to become softened by a victim's blood. When one was sentenced to be beaten with this type of knout, the malefactor was typically stretched over the back of an executioner's assistant. Extra punishment could be inflicted with the addition of a 'strappado'; in this case the victim had his hands tied behind him and was hoisted by his wrists so that the lashings compounded the pain of dislocated shoulder blades.

If a peasant killed a peasant from another lord's estate without premeditation he was sentenced to be beaten with the dreaded knout and then transferred with his family to the lord who lost his peasant. However, if the lord did not want the services of the malefactor who killed his peasant he could demand another peasant (and his family) from the murderer's lord. In the event the murder of a peasant was pre-meditated, the sentence was death for lord or peasant. According to one 1661 law, stewards who accepted runaway peasants were beaten with the knout as well.[46] Capital punishment was extremely rare in medieval Russia and was prohibited in numerous principalities. The eleventh-century Law of Yaroslav set restrictions on which types of crime should be regarded as capital offences. The law was eventually amended to ban capital punishment throughout most of the country. One of Russia's early penal codes enacted at the end of the fourteenth century mentioned only one capital crime: a third commission of a theft (which has been compared to the so-called 'three strikes' statutes used in some American states). However, as in most medieval societies moving closer to the modern era, more capital offences were added. The Sudebnik of 1497 extended it to include three specific thefts – those committed in church, horse theft, or two prior thefts – as well as arson and treason. In 1649 there were 63 capital crimes, which would be doubled under the reign of Peter the Great. The methods of executions were accomplished in public when possible and, though brutal, were not out of line with other budding modern states, including such sanctions as drowning, burying alive or forcing liquid metal down a person's throat.

Travelling through Muscovy and Tartary in the mid-1630s, a young German named Adam Ölschläger, who went by the name Adam Olearius, kept a record of his travels in Russia and gives some interesting insights into little-known instances of crime and punishment from this era. He asserted that 'False witness and deception are so prevalent among them they threaten not only strangers and neighbours but also brothers and spouses.' Theft was among the most seriously punished 'vices', and it was apparently not uncommon for neighbours to falsely accuse others who stoked their vitriol of this crime, and to let the justice system vicariously exact revenge.[47] Apparently swearing, slander and the verbal dishonouring of 'notables and commoners alike' became such an issue that special fines were concocted by the authorities to punish practitioners of this abuse. The fines were determined by the status of the abuser and the target of the invective. This so-called 'paying for dishonouring', or *zaplatit' beschest'e*, was often too steep for a commoner to pay. For example, an official of the Tsar might be awarded the amount of his yearly salary for some calumnious slight, and if the offender could not pay what was due after all the money or property he owned was forfeited, he could be 'sent to the house of the injured party, who may do with him as he pleases', which typically resulted in a public knouting.[48]

By the first half of the nineteenth century a number of restrictions were placed on the punishment of serfs by their owners. For example, beatings could not be administered with more than 40 blows from a rod or fifteen with a cudgel. Imprisonment in the seigniorial jail was limited to no more than two months. However, in case the serf owner felt this was insufficient, the malefactor could be sentenced to a maximum of three months in a government house of correction or to hard labour on a government works project.

In Russian villages there was a uniformity of punishment meted out to serfs, usually consisting of beatings, whippings, sitting in stocks, wearing spiked collars, stints in jail and fines. Certain acts were harshly punished such as idleness, vagrancy, theft and public drunkenness, which were punished with floggings with a cane, lashings with a cudgel or fines. Over time Russian whippings gained notoriety in western Europe, especially when prominent Russians nonchalantly recounted whipping their serfs and even bragging to have meted out triple the quota of strokes allowed.[49]

Although a number of gruesome accounts of punishment stand out, most serfs were probably treated in a civilized fashion. But the very fact of their social helplessness left them open to the sadistic caprices of their owners. For example, in 1756 the widow of a landowner inherited some 600 serfs and over a seven-year period reportedly tortured scores to death for petty or imagined crimes. This case was so notorious that authorities took the rare step of intervening. An investigation was launched into her activities which led to her being stripped of her noble rank and sentenced to be pilloried in Moscow for one hour, and from there sentenced to a lifetime's confinement in a convent. This left the brunt of the punishment to fall on those of her serfs who had assisted her reign of terror; they were beaten with a knout and sentenced to a life of hard labour in Siberia.[50]

By most accounts the most extreme punishment in the lord's arsenal was banishment to Siberia, which began in 1760, with the unstated goal of stimulating settlement there. But exile was limited to major offences with an age limit of 45 set for those deemed fit enough to work. Exiles were often accompanied by their spouses; under certain conditions children were sent along as well, and there is plenty of evidence to suggest that numerous rules were disregarded.[51] A policy was put in place that required seigniors to amply provide serfs with clothing and footwear and provide them with some financial aid before they left on their treks. Funding included 20 roubles for a bachelor and 30 if accompanied by a wife (with an additional 10 roubles for each child); most evidence suggests that up to 75 per cent perished as they made their way on foot to the Siberian wilderness camps.[52] Once they reached the camps they were either sentenced to hard labour or were given land and became state peasants.

Until Russian serfdom was abolished in 1861, large landowners depended entirely on serf labour. Some historians have even gone as far as comparing their lives to those of plantation slaves in the American South, in that both could be bought and sold at will.[53] Once purchased or given as gifts to other landholders they were expected to spend their lives toiling the soil or serving in the master's household. However, in most regions non-domestic serfs would work their master's land and in exchange were given land to farm for themselves. In this way they usually spent three days on the master's land and three days on their own. Beatings were common; serfs could be flogged for numerous infractions including theft, flight and even laziness. There is some conjecture that serfs did not necessarily oppose corporal punishment, especially for cases of theft or assault, since the alternatives would have been fines or prison, sanctions that could be ruinous for a serf's family.

During the late nineteenth century, brutal punishments still abounded in Russian villages, but what had changed was that it was now the villagers doling it out. It was not just backwater communities and rural villages that resorted to extra-judicial punishment. Although rare, it occasionally took place in some urban centres.[54] Russian peasants developed a practice in rural districts called *samosud*,[55] meaning 'judging by oneself', in which they took the law into their own hands, seemingly eliminating the middlemen of the criminal justice system altogether. However, prior to inflicting punishment it should be noted that the case was first brought before a village assembly. This was most common when the suspected guilty party was a member of the community.

Typically, the most severe physical punishments would be unleashed on outsiders. The determination of the punishment depended ultimately on the criminal act and, not surprisingly, on the individual's status in the community.[56]

Physical punishment featured prominently in a number of local press reports. The following is just a sample. In 1873 peasants punished a suspected criminal by completely crushing his head, chopping off his hands, and taking the plank used to beat him and forcing it into his anus, 'piercing the full length of his body' until it protruded from his mouth. Eight years later in 1881 peasants from the village of Mukhovitsie, in Kiev province, captured a thief and then sliced the tendons in his right leg and left hand. The same year in another village in Kiev province peasants brutalized a suspected thief. First they 'carved a toothed stake so that it resembled a series of arrowheads on one shaft'. It was then thrust up his rectum 'with the arrows positioned so that he could not remove it'.[57] However, incidents were often settled through shaming or some type of compensation. Some historians have even labelled *samosud* a 'predecessor of social control' that became the hallmark of the modern state, asserting that the 'growth of politically organized society can be measured precisely by the extent that the form of social control which we term law has superseded self-redress'.[58]

When it came to punishment, the harshest retribution was often reserved for horse thieves. Much like the American western frontier, horse stealing was not taken lightly, particularly in a time of negligible police protection and limited transportation choices. For Russian peasants a horse could mean the difference between survival and catastrophe. Without a horse a farmer lost the ability to raise crops, posing a severe economic threat. Captured horse thieves faced physical sanctions running the gamut from castration and having one's eyes put out to having stakes driven through the throat or chest, branding with hot irons and being beaten around the groin until death intervened. One common punishment for horse thieves began with the rigging up of a pulley system high on a gatepost, where the horse thief could be raised up into the air by a rope running through the pulley. Once the malefactor reached the requisite height the rope was released and he would fall to the ground, 'striking the lower part of his back in a terrible way. This is repeated many times in succession, and each time the snap of the poor devil's vertebrae can be heard.' Another clever method involved disrobing the horse thief and covering his upper body with a 'wet sack'. The peasants would then 'place a plank on his stomach and beat on it with whatever they could find – hammers, logs, or stones' until his bodily organs were destroyed. Like the modern art of torture, this method was used because no external signs of the punishment were left on the body once it was brought to the attention of investigators.[59]

Feudalism should be an anachronism in twenty-first-century Russia, yet it has survived in several regions still playing catch-up with the modern world. One recent crime captures the relative feudal nature of crime and punishment in some rural environs where big landowners continue to hold sway. This story could easily have been repeated in India, Mexico or Brazil, to name just a few countries still today coming to terms with their feudal pasts. But it took place in one of the developed world's leading economies. The evening of 4 November 2010 should have been a night to celebrate Russia's national Unity Day, as prosperous farmer Serever Ametov, his wife and a group of friends and family gathered for a traditional rural supper in the village of Kushchevskaya, located in the vast Krasnodar territory in southern Russia, an area that also included the host site for the 2014 Winter Olympics. Few could have imagined that daybreak would find Ametov, his wife and all ten dinner guests dead, including four young children – ten stabbed to death and two suffocated.

The economy in parts of southern Russia is still overwhelmingly agricultural, stemming from the Soviet era when many of the large landholdings were organized and directed by large state enterprises. But after the collapse of the Soviet Union most of these enterprises (*sovkhozes*) were privatized. This was followed by bloody battles pitting aspiring landowners against each other, much like the city gangs who fought over control of the new free-market enterprises in urban Russia. Following the massacre, suspicion almost immediately turned to Sergei Tsapok, a member of the local council, known for heading a group known as Tsapki that used violence and intimidation to control the region's fertile farmland. Like Tsapok, the most dominant and successful owners were those that retained their own private armies. The mother of Tsapok, the arrested ringleader, just so happened to be one of the territory's largest landholders. Her son, meanwhile, ran an organization called Centurion-Plus, a 'private security firm' – this being a model followed by many landowners, who establish armies to protect their property under the rubric of a private security firm. But most of their activities were extralegal, with 'the line between these private armies and organized crime' drawn fairly thin.[60]

Harking back to an earlier era, local Russian authorities far from the disapproving eye of Moscow preferred to let landowners sort things out on their own. But, staying out of the fray led to the very public deaths of this family after it refused to back down to the more powerful and politically connected Tsapok family during a power struggle over ruling the village. Some observers compared President Putin and his administration to a king and his court in the Middle Ages, as they proved exceedingly passive in supervising the bureaucracy. One journalist even likened the social system to a 'neo-feudal structure of power', noting that

> the source of the evident weakness of [Putin's] 'vertical' power is the same as it was for typical royal administrators during the Middle Ages. Putin, like feudal kings prefers to concentrate most of his limited resources on protecting his personal power; only interfering in life of provinces, or even the capital, during such high emergencies that the regime is in jeopardy.[61]

It probably should not be too surprising that this region was incorporated rather late into the Russian state in the nineteenth century. By most accounts this incident has been spoken about in terms usually reserved for feudalism; what one observer described as a medieval-sounding narrative in which the Tsapok 'family' gave villagers a place to work, allowed them to settle and establish farms and protected them from outsiders. However, in exchange Tsapok acquired 'vassal privileges' to steal, rape and maim, an agreement that 'would have been fine in the Middle Ages' but not the modern one.[62]

Summary

Numerous chroniclers have testified to the lawlessness that plagued the thirteenth and fourteenth centuries, much of it the result of a series of economic and social crises brought about by repeated epidemics and military conflict. Both war and disease generated new social problems, including urban unemployment, rural misery and predatory vagabondage. More importantly it also generated greater mobility among the labouring classes. The arrival of the bubonic plague, better known as the Black Death, in the fourteenth century came on the heels of famine and incessant war. Several historians have made a good case that it was climate warming between 1000 and 1250 that not only substantially increased the population but also facilitated growing population centres and increased trade contacts. As trade and population density increased, so too did the movement of flea-bearing rats, which passed on the plague to humans. Norman Cantor has noted that if the climate had not warmed, these rats would have stayed in their holes and died 'quietly' without passing on the disease. Others argue that the decimation of the European population in the wake of the plague accelerated the decline of serfdom and 'weakened the foundations of medieval kingship'.[63] The subsequent economic upheaval that allowed serfs to leave their feudal domains also generated a rise in crime in the growing cities such as London, as criminals, beggars, prostitutes and other ne'er-do-wells joined the movement from the countryside to the cities. This pattern continues to this day as witnessed by the growing urban populations of some sub-Saharan African cities and in Latin America, as agricultural workers flock to urban environs in search of economic opportunity of both the licit and the illicit varieties.[64]

If one thing is clear about crime and punishment as western Europe emerged from the late Middle Ages it is the fact that corporal and capital punishments had become increasingly punitive. Some countries added new and more venal corporal punishments limited only by what the imagination could conjure up. More and more punishments became capital crimes. As one observer put it, 'Reform was generally understood to mean the effect of punishment on those who witnessed it, not those who suffered it.'[65] Shaming, mutilations and branding gained wider support as the growing states sought not just to retaliate but to humiliate and stigmatize offenders, reaching its nadir in the seventeenth century as European justice became more and more elaborate and public, with spectacles that might have made the Roman emperors blanch at times. It is impossible to ascertain the number of malefactors that went to their deaths after being hanged, drawn and quartered, broken on the wheel, burned, boiled or disembowelled alive, stoned to death, torn by red-hot tongs, branded, blinded, their tongue torn out or clipped, having extremities amputated, being castrated or whipped.

If one looks hard enough, one can find various incarnations of feudal systems in almost all of the great civilizations of the past. Typically sandwiched between what some regard as 'Dark Ages' and the rise of modern states, feudal systems played a role in the evolution of centralized states. As societal transition occurred, so too did attitudes towards crime and punishment, as the growing transient population and the increased mobility of the poor required that what seemed to many authorities as a repudiation of the work ethic and the precepts of religion be addressed.

4

The Transformation of Punishment and the Rise of the Penitentiary

Their names now legendary – the Bastille,[1] the Tower of London, the Kremlin, Alcatraz – they conjure up images of fortress-like edifices, built to withstand siege, and in actuality that was originally what they were intended to do. What they have in common is that none originated as places of confinement, but they all served as prisons at one time or another. Like other prison holdovers into the eighteenth and nineteenth centuries they mostly started out as military fortresses with dungeons and cells that could be utilized to hold temporary prisoners before they were executed, transported or paid their debts. The development of the penitentiary was an uneven process, one of experimentation and failure, innovation and success. But it was a process in the making over many centuries.

Although the penitentiary is often regarded as a post-Enlightenment creation, there had already been a long history of utilizing whichever buildings were at hand for carceral purposes. For example, the Scottish employed redundant tollhouses as holding facilities in small villages as early as 1480, leading to the association by the middle of the seventeenth century of the term 'tollbooth' as shorthand for small jails. The tollbooth was originally a simple booth at a fair, where dues and tolls were collected and violators of fair propriety detained. Over time they were transformed into places of confinement and became more prominent buildings in Scottish towns.[2] In medieval Europe, hereditary royalty, bishops and city magistrates had established places of confinement. The main distinction between these earlier prototypes and what came later was the fact that they were not originally conceived of as places constructed for punishment per se, but rather served as provisional holding facilities for those awaiting trial, punishment, transportation or for debtors unwilling to meet obligations to their creditors.

A society's penal regime tells us much about a country and is a measure of how far a nation has progressed towards attaining higher standards of civilization. The development of the penitentiary in the late eighteenth century was a landmark in the evolution of punishment. Prior to this, medieval and early modern European penal measures reigned supreme, incorporating sanctions that later ages would regard as barbarous, ranging from physical mutilation and branding to breaking on the wheel. Public capital and corporal punishments were a part of everyday life not just in Europe but across the world. But beginning in the eighteenth century some societies began turning away from the spectacle of punishment in favour of radical new penal regimes that were heavily predicated on the use of incarceration. Along with parallel developments in policing, reformed judicial systems and legal codes, the emergence of the modern prison signalled the materialization of a new societal order that was much less enamoured with bloody displays of exhibitory punishments.

The eighteenth century, often referred to as the Age of Reason, or the Enlightenment, in western Europe, had a tremendous impact on the punishment of crime and criminals. The efforts of such penal reformers as Cesare Beccaria, Jeremy Bentham, John Howard, Montesquieu and others kick-started a transition from brutal, public corporal punishments to the development of incarcerative sentences, and in the process helped lay the groundwork for the modern penitentiary. In time their ideas would spread across the globe, carried near and far by modernizing nobles, intent on sharing Enlightenment concepts of law and government. Some of the most convincing reform notions came from the pen of the Italian nobleman Cesare Beccaria. Unburdened by the limited perspective of a lawyer or jurist, he was free to draw his own conclusions as an informed outsider. According to Beccaria, punishment should be certain and equal for all regardless of their place in society; furthermore, it should not necessarily punish people less, but better – in other words, punishment should be 'proportionate to the crimes'.[3] He was among the first modern writers not only to publicly oppose capital punishment in the mid-eighteenth century, but to indict the criminal justice system in the world at large. He forcefully condemned the use of torture in punishment and interrogation and of disproportionately severe penalties for minor crimes. Beccaria's lamentations found perhaps their greatest followers in America, which is somewhat ironic, considering the United States still locks up more people each year than any other country and is one of the few developed nations that continues to make use of the death penalty.

It was sometime in the eighteenth century, when western Europe witnessed a gradual reversal of what had been centuries of public execution and corporal punishment and the beginnings of modern European penal systems, leading no less an observer than the writer Victor Hugo to declare in 1874 that 'torture has ceased to exist'. He was not far off the mark when it came to the corporeal. Indeed, the transition away from torture and physical pain was already well under way by the mid-eighteenth century, as torture was declared illegal in Scotland and Prussia (1740), Denmark (1771), Spain (1790), France (1798) and Russia (1801). However, as European nations created foreign colonies, torture would reappear, albeit in a different guise. And although state-sponsored torture disappeared from Europe in the eighteenth century it would be revived in the modern era in Tsarist Russia, the post-Revolutionary Soviet Union, Nazi Germany, post-war Greece, Chile, Portugal, Spain and elsewhere.

One of the most oft-cited examples of public execution by torture is the death of the regicide Robert-François Damiens, famously recounted by Michel Foucault in his groundbreaking study of the advent of carceral society, *Discipline and Punish* (1975). In the first pages of the book Damiens' execution in March 1757 is recounted in excruciating detail. Until he was quartered by four horses Damiens endured an agonizing torture protocol that included having flesh torn from his breasts, arms, thighs and calves with red hot pincers, and being burned on various parts of his body with sulphur, boiling oil, burning resin and molten lead, before finally being quartered in a terrible process that required the severing of the sinews holding his joints, allowing the horses to complete the ghastly process.[4] However, this execution, for all intents and purposes, was already well out of sync with the new realities of crime and punishment in 1757; it was an anachronistic reminder of an earlier era. In fact, before the execution of Damiens in 1757, drawing and quartering was last used by the French after the attempt on King Henry IV in 1610, and except for the execution of Damiens, the French never used it again. Although this execution has been frequently cited as a transition point in punishment, other scholars have demonstrated that it 'should not mislead us into thinking many offenders were treated as harshly'.[5]

The persistence of judicial torture and exhibitory punishment into the early modern era was in part a reflection of the 'chronically insecure' central governments in their nascent stages of development.[6] Continuously besieged by natural disaster, epidemic disease and religious and civil conflict, developing states lacked the ability to enforce social order, prevent crime or deter civil unrest effectively beyond the threat of excruciating and humiliating criminal sanctions. Indeed, criminal behaviour was regarded as a challenge to the power of the sovereign. The sovereign responded in kind, by taking out his wrath on the body of the malefactor. In the wake of the eighteenth century a transformation of just punishment took root in the West. In time the reformative power of torture lost its lustre as corporal punishment became increasingly unacceptable in the West.[7] However, it was also true that the development of the prison was an inconsistent process across the globe, typically taking place at first only in countries that could afford to build and maintain them. Despite the decline in public executions and the parallel development of the penitentiary, corporal punishment and transportation to overseas penal colonies continued to be part of the penal regime into the twentieth century.

English Crime and Punishment

England is probably as good a place as there is to begin considering the relationship between the rise of the modern state and the transformation of crime and punishment. As the historian Alan Macfarlane put it, 'with the possible exception of Japan' England was 'generally acknowledged to have been the first "modern" centralized nation state . . . the first to establish the rule of law and to control violence'.[8] It didn't happen all at once, but in intermittent flourishes, stimulated by the rise of a market economy gradually between the fifteenth and eighteenth centuries. Writing at the end of the eighteenth century, the great economist Adam Smith even noted the links between the eradication of violence and the rise 'of what could be called capitalism'.[9]

As in other countries on the cusp of modern transformation, social disorder and violence lingered longest the further one travelled from major centres of urbanization. Commenting on this phenomenon, Thomas Babington Macaulay reported in the mid-nineteenth century that,

> No traveller ventured into that country [beyond Trent, Northumberland and the northern borders] without making his will . . . The irregular vigour with which criminal justice was administered shocked observers whose life had been passed in more tranquil districts. Juries, animated by hatred and by a sense of common danger, convicted housebreakers and cattle

stealers with the promptitude of a court martial in a mutiny; and the convicts were hurried by scores to the gallows.[10]

Indeed, the late sixteenth century and early seventeenth 'were for the English a great flogging age', when 'every village had its whipping post, which was in constant use as a means of preserving order'.[11]

Henry VIII (*reg.* 1509–47) was a firm believer, as were his Continental counterparts, in the use of brutal punishments. He was the first and only English king to allow state executions on Sundays and to permit boiling to death as a legal penalty, as he took an ever-increasing hard line towards civil disorder and criminality. In 1512 he made murders in church or on the highways 'non-clergyable' offences (capital cases). In 1536 he extended this to piracy, murder, rape, sacrilege, highway robbery, abduction, some burglaries and housebreaking. In 1530 Henry implemented the Whipping Act, directed against drifters and vagrants, who were ordered tied to the tail end of carts, stripped naked (later amended to only the waist) and beaten through town until their 'body be bloody by reason of such whipping'. This went for men, women or children. Those with a propensity for avoiding church services had their ears cut off.

Scottish penal code was considered more lenient than its English counterpart, but it was less punitive only by degrees. True, ordinary theft was not a capital offence (except on the third offence), but the Scottish employed a variety of disfiguring punishments. Thieves caught in flagrante delicto had their cheeks branded and their ears cropped, before being flogged and hanged. Executions included beheading, hanging, drowning, burning and wrenching off the head with cords; if these were too harsh than one could make do with tearing nails off with pincers, scourging with branding, cutting off tongues (or boring holes through them), and amputating hands and feet. Punishments of the fifteenth and sixteenth centuries fell hardest on political prisoners and accused witches. In 1437, one of the assassins of Scotland's King James had his right hand nailed to a gallows and was set up in a cart to be dragged to Edinburgh. On his arrival he had hot iron spikes run into his thighs and arms, and after being forced to watch the execution of his son, he was quartered.[12]

Scotland and England have had separate domestic legal systems for centuries. However, when crimes took place on the border between the two countries attempts were made to reach an international agreement on how to adjudicate the offence. Between 1249 and 1599 so-called

'Border Law' was revised and updated, but much about the application of these laws was still uncertain as late as the sixteenth century, in no small part due to the lack of written records. The way the system appears to have worked was if an English citizen was robbed by a Scot, the citizen would make a complaint to his (English) warden, who would pass it on to the Scottish warden.[13] The Scot would then investigate and if the charges were justified the offender would be summoned. Penalties varied considerably and less emphasis was placed on compensation and restitution than outside the border region. Those sentenced for robbery could pay basic restitution in 1367, but by 1384 it was a hanging offence. When it came to judicial executions, the most common method was hanging. The Scottish border frontier was dotted with such eponymous sites as 'Gallows Hill', 'Hangman's Hills', 'Hangman Hill' and other variations on a theme. Along with hanging, capital crimes were also punished by beheading and drowning. In one mass hanging 36 were strangled, and on another occasion 22 bandits were drowned en masse. By most accounts drowning was often favoured by the authorities because it was cheaper than the gallows. In 1563, border crime had become such a scourge that a law was passed that sounds eerily like the modern mandatory sentencing and 'three-strikes' laws that were popular in the United States until relatively recently. This 'three-time loser' penalty called for the death penalty after an individual committed 'three offences and attempts'. The caveat here was that the three offences had to have been committed consecutively and in separate incidents.[14]

During the rise of the English state no secular crime was considered as heinous as treason (or heresy under ecclesiastical offences). However, unlike in Continental Europe, except for punishment for treason, English criminal justice eschewed elaborate public executions and never broke prisoners on the wheel or tortured convicts for days on end as did its Continental counterparts. Petty treason, first defined by the Treason Act 1351, was used to criminalize certain activities that threatened the king. This could include the murder of a social superior by an inferior, which was included in the realm of treasonous acts, and typically included women who killed their husbands and servants who killed their masters; wives and female servants risked being burned at the stake for these crimes. But petty treason was rarely prosecuted. Punishment for most felonies was usually death by hanging. Precision was lacking, leading often to slow deaths by strangulation, accompanied by the so-called 'dance' of the victim as he or she struggled to breathe; until the nineteenth century this method could last anywhere between three and 45 minutes.

It was not uncommon for relatives and friends to charge the scaffold to help end the struggling by pulling down vigorously on the legs to speed up death.[15]

Early Financial Crime

The connection between national security and a secure state treasury was a growing concern during England's seventeenth century. Until then financial crimes had revolved around unpaid debts, fraudulent weights and measures, bribery, forgery and counterfeiting. Counterfeiting was about as sophisticated as it got. The trade in counterfeit coins had plagued England since at least the twelfth century when 'the penny was so bad that the man who had at market a pound could by no means buy therewith twelve pennyworths'. King Henry I took a strong stand against this crime by ordering castration and the loss of the right hand for debasing coinage.[16] During the seventeenth century two types of coins were produced in England – hand-struck coins (until 1662) and machine-made from the national mint (after 1662). The older coins were irregular and subject to wear, thus making it easy for 'clippers' to use shears to file and snip bits of silver from the edge of the coins. Since these coins had smooth rims, the clipper could then file the edges smooth again. In a short while he could amass a pile of silver at the expense of degraded currency. By the end of the seventeenth century clipping had become so rampant that Lord Macaulay commented: 'it was mere chance whether what was called a shilling was really ten pence, six pence, or a groat.' In his magisterial history of England, Macaulay reported, 'Three eminent goldsmiths were invited to send in a hundred pounds [sterling] each in current silver to be tried by the balance.' It should have 'weighed about twelve hundred ounces. The actual weight proved to be six hundred and twenty four ounces.'[17]

Coin clipping was certainly not a new crime and in England had been punished as high treason since the time of Elizabeth I. Traditionally, after conviction counterfeiters were sentenced to death by fire or rope, but it had little impact on the crime rate. For this crime, women were burned alive, but could appeal the sentences by 'pleading the belly', which allowed a pregnant woman to give birth first and hope for mercy. But, in many cases the only mercy they received was to be strangled before being burned alive. In fourteenth-century Venice a distinction was made between counterfeiters and clippers. Instead of being burned alive clippers could take solace in only losing the right hand and being subsequently banished. In similar fashion, women lost their noses instead of the right hand. In 1359, Venetian authorities added gouging out both eyes to the list of sanctions for this crime, joining right hand amputation and larger fines as an alternative sentence. Once again, women received some benevolence, suffering corporal punishment and life in prison.[18] Russian counterfeiters might have their false coins melted and then poured down their throats as molten metal.[19] The punitive measures taken against counterfeiters in England turned out to be counter-productive and often backfired, since it tended to make juries reluctant to subject the malefactors to death and disfigurement unless the evidence was more than obvious (possessing clipping tools and bad coins).

In one of the lesser-known chronicles of seventeenth-century crime and punishment, the English government selected Isaac Newton, 'the smartest man in England', as Warden of the Mint, to avert what was becoming by the late 1690s a national crisis, as it became increasingly difficult to find 'legal' silver in circulation. It grew into a major concern at the highest levels of government as the criminal underworld turned clipped silver into ingots to be sold on the Continent, leading to an inves-tigation by Parliament. Without sufficient funds England could not pay its soldiers on the battlefields of Europe. Newton's solution was, well, Newtonian, as he came up with the idea of calling back all coins, old or new, and having them remade into a consistent issue much more dif-ficult to clip. This task was completed against all odds in 1699. This, together with the production of Bank of England notes in 1695 led to 'the first bank issued paper money in the world', going a long way towards stemming England's financial crisis.[20]

During his term as Warden of the Mint, Newton found it difficult to prosecute counterfeiters, in no small part due to the 'very bloodiness of the bloody code'.[21] The last use of legal torture in England took place in 1641. Prior to its abolition, Queen Elizabeth 1 became the country's 'most prolific torturer monarch', authorizing it in 53 out of 83 warrants on record.[22] Parliament would eventually include coining as a form of high treason.

Following the Glorious Revolution in 1688 a plethora of new laws was passed targeting new forms of property crime, including fencing stolen goods, embezzlement, fraud and obtaining goods on false pretences.

Execution as Public Spectacle

A peripatetic English traveller named John Taylor arrived at the northern German seaport of Hamburg in August 1616. Soon after debarking, his attention was diverted to a rapidly forming crowd that, unknown to him, was gathering to witness a public execution set to take place the next day. The target of the crowd's wrath was a father who had been convicted of the axe murder of his young daughter. His interest piqued, Taylor decided to attend the execution due to take place the following day. Taylor found an excellent vantage point from which to memorably recount the gruesome scenario. According to his account published in 1617, the prisoner was

> mounted on a mount of earth, built high on purpose that the people without may see the execution a quarter of a mile round about; four of the hangman's men take each of them a small halter, and by the hands and the feet they hold the prisoners extended all abroad lying on his back: then the Arch-hangman, or the great Master of this mighty business took up a wheel, much about the bigness of one of the four wheels of a coach, and first, having put off his doublet, his hat, and being in his shirt, as if he meant to play at tennis, he took the wheel, and set it on the edge, and turned it with one hand like a top or a whirligig, then he took it by the spokes, and lifting it up with a mighty stroke he beat one of the poor wretch's legs in pieces (the bones I mean) at which he roared grievously; then after a little pause he breaks the other leg in the same manner, and consequently breaks his arms, and then he stroke four or five main blows on his breast . . . lastly he smote his neck, and missing, burst his chin and jaws to mammocks [small pieces]; then he took the broken mangled corpse, and spread it on the wheel, and thrust a great post or pile into the nave or hole of the wheel, and then fixed the post into the earth some six feet deep, being in height above the ground, some ten or twelve feet, and there the carcass must lie it will it be consumed by all-consuming time, or ravening fowls.[23]

Comparing this common German execution to the preferred method of capital punishment in his home country, Taylor noted that such savagery made 'me to imagine our English hanging to be but a flea-biting'.[24]

Taylor wasn't far off the mark, especially when it came to early modern Germany, where adultery was still punished with decapitation and arson by burning alive. However, even worse was reserved for the counterfeiter, who was boiled in oil, 'not thrown into the vessel all at once, but with a pulley or a rope to be hanged under the arm pit, and let down into the oil by degrees: first the feet, and next the legs, and so to boil his flesh from his bones alive'.[25]

On the European Continent perhaps no public punishment ex-emplified state power as much as breaking on the wheel, almost universally applied to male offenders convicted of aggravated murder of a family member or during a robbery. This method was applied from 'the bottom up' for more severe cases – which left the offender conscious throughout the punishment and caused greater suffering. Less extreme was from 'top down', in which an initial blow, usually to the neck, meant instant death. Although this was the most commonly used name for this pun-ishment, others have observed that it would be more accurate to describe it as 'breaking *with* the wheel'.[26] The more common derivation refers to the French technique, where the wheel was placed horizontally on the scaffold and the malefactor bound to it. This protocol called for the executioner to then break the individual's limbs with an iron bar.

Breaking on the wheel originated in medieval Europe and under-went a revival in France and Germany in the eighteenth century. Like hanging in Britain, death on the wheel remained very much a public torture. As previously noted in the description by Taylor, breaking with the wheel was more common in Germany. During early Germanic history it was customarily inflicted only on men for murder. The process varied, but usually involved a criminal being placed on his back on the ground with arms and legs stretched out to their limit and hands and feet tied to pegs and timbers laid out under each bodily limb so that hollow spaces were left beneath the arms and legs. The executioner would then break every limb (as well as the spine) with a heavy wheel. The number of blows inflicted was determined by law. Once the bones were shattered like broken glass in each appendage, the limbs were threaded alternately under and over the spokes of the wheel. Finally the wheel bearing the dead body was placed either on a post or gallows.[27] The wheel would see extensive use in the 1770s, as a ready supply of highwaymen, thieves, killers and other malefactors met their fates lashed to these killing contraptions. More criminals met death in this way than by hanging in France before it was abolished by Louis xvi in 1789.

In Europe countless forms of cruel execution were designed to hold the rapt attention of onlookers and deter potential criminals. For the upper classes the death penalty usually meant the sword and decapitation. The more stoic prisoners were allowed to kneel without the headsman's block. But any flinch at the final moment made the difference between a clean cut and a painful gash across the head or shoulders. A meeker sort, however, was encouraged to take a seat before being decapitated. Burning at the stake was reserved for blasphemers, heretics, coiners, poisoners and sodomites, with the intention to destroy the offender's body completely; even after reduced to ashes and bone fragments, these were then ground to dust and either buried under the gallows or dumped into a river.

In Germany, drowning was mostly used on women, particularly for perceived moral and religious offences such as heresy and adultery. Like fire, water was considered to also have a purifying effect. Women were in some cases lowered into a body of water from a bridge and kept under the surface by a hangman's assistant until dead. In more severe cases she might be stuffed into a sack with a cat, a hen and a snake and let down into the water (reminiscent of the Roman *poena cullei*, the 'punishment of the sack'). Since snakes were hard to come by in England, a picture of one had to suffice.[28] Those convicted of infanticide were buried alive and impaled. Sometimes they were drowned first; in other cases they might be tied up and laid in a shallow grave below the gallows, covered in thorns and then buried alive from the feet up. In the midst of the process or at the end, a stake might be driven through the heart.

By the mid-1750s the punishment of hanging, drawing and quartering was becoming increasingly rare. In fact, at its last use in Britain in 1803, during the execution of Colonel Edward Despard and his confederates, few were still alive who remembered its previous use, half a century earlier. Convicted of high treason for plotting to overthrow the state, Colonel Edward Despard along with six confederates were sentenced to this grisly reminder of the draconian past. The seven men were each duly drawn to their place of execution on the traditional hurdle, where they would one by one be hanged until not quite dead, taken down and have their entrails cut out and burned in front of them before they expired. Some 20,000 people massed to watch this historic occasion on 21 February, probably not realizing it was the end of an era in punishment. However, some monarchists might have been disappointed by the denouement of these executions when after the beheadings, their quartering and dismembering was waived.[29]

In time, many forms of public execution gave way to more 'compassionate' instruments such as the guillotine, although as recently as 1893 a German woman was beheaded with a sword for poisoning her husband. Likewise, two German women were beheaded with an axe in 1914. The introduction of the guillotine as the execution machine of the French state in 1792 was initially hailed as a humanitarian landmark, on a par with the use of the poison hemlock in ancient Athens and the introduction of lethal injection in the United States in the 1980s. The origins of the guillotine date back to ancient Rome, but it was with the Halifax Gibbet, inaugurated by the Scots in the thirteenth century, that the precursory design is most obvious. Utilized in England between 1286 and 1650, it rose to prominence in 1566 as the so-called 'Scottish Maiden' in Edinburgh. The original Halifax gibbet was little more than an axe fastened onto a piece of wood, drawn up by rope to the top of the frame, or as one early observer described it:

> The head blocke wheren the ax is fastened dooth fall downe with such violence that if the necke of the transgressor were so big as that of a bull it should be cut in sunder at a stroke and roll from the leadie by an huge distance.

Typically reserved for thieves, if the offender had stolen a beast, the rope attached to the pin retaining the axe aloft would be tied to the animal, which by moving executed its own abductor.[30] The Germans used a similar device known as the *Panke* or *Diele* in the early thirteenth century, which was actively used there until the sixteenth century. The guillotine, so firmly tied to French crime and punishment, was used in another incarnation in the fifteenth century, when it was known as the *doloire*, but passed out of use well before the late eighteenth century. Dr Joseph-Ignace Guillotin revived this 'old contrivance' as an alternative to the common use of the sword and axe by the executioners of France.[31]

Until the 1790s hanging was the preserve of the poor, beheading for the rich and the brutality of the wheel for religious offences. But in May 1791, Guillotin persuaded his fellow deputies in the French Constituent Assembly to accept decapitation as the punishment for all capital crimes. Among his most trusted advisers was Charles-Henri Sanson, representing a family that had served as state executioners for six generations (1688–1889). Sanson shared with Dr Guillotin the challenges of using the sword or axe for multiple executions, lamenting that the cutting instruments too often needed sharpening and that the task of cutting off all of those heads was often too physically demanding.

Perhaps no European country was more identified with public hangings in the early modern period than England. However, the British diverged from many European counterparts when it came to public punishment. For example, in the Dutch Republic courts did not distinguish between corporal and capital punishment during Amsterdam's so-called 'justice days', which presented the public with a cornucopia of punishment excess. In a single afternoon one could witness a parade of malefactors dragged up onto the scaffold. In the course of one ceremony the executioner meted out floggings, brandings and executions on the same stage (usually starting with the executions). England, on the other hand, drew a sharp distinction between the doling out of death and corporal punishments. Hangings rarely if ever were conducted at the same venue as other bodily punishments; while floggings were always good entertainment, these took place at a purpose-built venue, the whipping post. However, whippings never developed the same fan base and public interest as hangings.[32]

In England a standard defence when confronted with a hanging charge was to claim 'benefit of clergy'. This defence was initially used to ameliorate punishment for clergymen, but by the sixteenth century it was being used by lay men and women. Prior to 1706 it had been possible for members of the clergy and other literate citizens to escape execution for lesser crimes by pleading 'benefit of clergy', an ancient form of privilege enabling the clergyman to request he be tried in an ecclesiastical court rather than a secular one. The provision required a literacy test involving the recitation of a passage of Scripture, typically Psalm 51, the so-called 'hangman's verse'. By the eighteenth century this form of mitigation was permitted only for a first offence. During this period, punishment for cases of, for example, manslaughter included being branded on the hand with the letter M, for manslaughter, and/or transportation. As the modern historian Vanessa McMahon put it, manslaughter was a crime that was 'thoroughly developed by the sixteenth century', and 'unlike the pardonable acts of excusable and justifiable homicide, it remained a felony, technically subject to the death penalty', as were most felonies. The general application of benefit of clergy ensured that the vast majority of individuals sentenced to death were given alternative punishments instead.[33]

The Act of 1706 abolished the literacy test and in the process probably saved many illiterate malefactors from the gallows. On the other hand, 'what the elite gave with one hand it took back with the other', by ultimately expanding the scope of the death penalty. Authorities made sure that added new capital offences were 'non-clergyable', by abolishing the invocation of benefit of clergy protection, returning to the days of Tudor severity, with the gallows regarded as the only deterrent to serious crime. As one historian explained, this was the 'response of a society where capital enterprise was releasing new forms of wealth which could not be adequately protected without a regular police force'.[34]

It was in the treatment of property crime that the Bloody Code seemed so irrational, particularly its penchant for 'overkill', illustrated by the death penalty for stealing a horse or a sheep, pickpocketing more than a shilling's worth of goods, or stealing 50 shillings from a dwelling or 5 shillings from a place of business. Such acts as stealing linen from a bleaching ground or woollen cloth from a tenterground, cutting trees in a garden orchard or breaking the border of a fishpond to facilitate the escape of fish, were added to a rapidly growing list of capital offences.[35] In many respects the legal code became so much more punitive due to 'inflation' and the failure to repeal ancient statutes. At the onset of the eighteenth century, for example, theft of goods worth 5 shillings was a hanging offence. However, in the ensuing years everything rose in value while 'the life of a man had continually grown cheaper'.[36]

Fortunately, the verdicts handed down by judges during the years of the Bloody Code reflected their recognition that it was rather ludicrous to hang someone for such minor crimes, and except for pre-1688 offences traditionally treated with the death penalty, such as murder and highway robbery, sentences were more often than not converted to transportation to foreign penal colonies in America and then Australia (for the new capital offences added between 1688 and 1750). In effect, then, the Bloody Code was more bark than bite and did not actually lead to much higher levels of execution. It has been widely accepted that perhaps half of the people condemned to hang in eighteenth-century England were either pardoned or given some alternative punishment, all of this of course depending on the degree of violence used in the original crime. Also influencing the outcome of a capital trial was the prisoner's putative character.[37]

Among those attending an execution on 13 October 1660 was the noted diarist Samuel Pepys. He had come to witness the judicial execution of one of the regicides responsible for the execution of Charles I in 1649. Pepys, a 'fervent monarchist', had more than a passing acquaintance with this series of events, having as a young boy pushed his way through the assembled crowd to witness the execution of the late king. Now, eleven years later he watched death dealt out once more, recounting,

> I went out to the Charring [sic] Cross to see Major General Harrison hanged drawn and quartered – which was done here – he looking as cheerfully as any man could do in that condition. He was presently cut down and his head and heart shown to the people, at which there was great shouts of joy.[38]

Pepys attended several other executions in his lifetime, but the growing vindictiveness of English justice soon led him to weary of his fellow Englishmen's excessive thirst for revenge. However, the English predilection for public hangings continued and by 1724 the notorious Tyburn Triple Tree, first used in 1571, had become such a popular venue that grandstand scaffolding was erected in 1724 offering better seats to a paying public.

Precursors to the Penitentiary: Penal Colonies, Transportation and Servitude

As demonstrated here, well into the early modern era, European statute books were filled with capital offences. But alongside these creative punishments were a number of parallel penal developments that prefigured the rise of the penitentiary. Theoretically death was mandated for numerous offences, but capital punishment became more the exception than the rule as European states adopted alternative punishments that spared thousands of condemned inmates from death by sentencing them instead to lives of unremitting toil. Penal service had been a standard punishment in Spain and other Mediterranean countries since the days of the Roman Empire. In antiquity this might have included working on public works projects, cleaning sewers and the like. Harsher sentences could necessitate a life spent working in rock quarries and mines. Both sentences 'were regarded as sentences to slow and painful death and represented a kind of punitive imprisonment in the form of hard labor for the state'.[39] Most historians consider this form of penal servitude a primitive precursor to imprisonment. In contrast with antiquity, penal servitude was used infrequently in the Middle Ages. Except for the Church, most levels of medieval society lacked the funds and facilities for long-term imprisonment, thereby relying on the inexpensive standbys of corporal and capital punishments.

Like other Mediterranean countries, Spain had long utilized various forms of penal service. Some convicts were forced to labour on public works projects, while others were subjected to harsher sanctions such as working in mines and rock quarries. Bound in chains, it was not uncommon for prisoners to work until they died. However, both forms of state penal bondage were often nothing more than agonizingly slow death sentences. The recrudescence of penal labour in western Europe coincided with the emergence of the nation state and the coincident increase in wealth and power. Along with the extension of royal juris-diction and the greater degree of centralization that characterized state building in the early sixteenth century, the notion developed that states could use convict labour for the national interest.[40]

Galley service was another penal sanction that grew in use in the sixteenth and seventeenth centuries. In 1530 a new set of laws were promulgated extending galley service to all types of crimes. Male gypsies, unemployed and living out of the reach of any masters, faced six years of galley service. Vagabonds received four years for the first offence, eight for a second and life for a third. By the second half of the sixteenth century bigamists and blasphemers tried by the Inquisition or secular courts often found themselves sent to the galleys, where they frequently met commoners who had sold dice, committed perjury and resisted arrest. During these years it became a common sanction for most normal offences. But nobles and clergy, exempt from degrading punishments, only sat in the galleys after committing treason. Typically, those sent to the galleys averaged between four and six years (out of a possible two years to life) at the oars. Less than two years was rare, purportedly because it took at least one year to become serviceable at oar service. By the mid 1600s, sentences were limited to ten years. However odious the galley was, few would argue it was better to be 'hitting the waves' while still breathing than to be hanging from the noose on the gallows.[41] Male galley service increasingly stood in for the hangman and by the early seventeenth century houses of confinement, based on a number of the principles of galley service, were introduced for punishing men as well as women and delinquents. Recreating galley conditions behind four walls, the so-called *galera de mujeres* (women's galley), meant shaving heads with a razor, and diets of coarse, black bread or biscuits, and vegetables.[42]

With the popularity of the new sailing ships, Spain abolished galley service in 1748. Prisoners were then transferred onshore to work at hard labour in its North African *presidios*, which served as de facto penal colonies.[43] The Spanish also used service in the mines to refine Mexican silver, introducing this alternative in the 1560s. Convicts evidently preferred the living conditions of the mines to the galleys; here they could depend on daily portions of meat and wine, as well as sufficient clothing and access to doctors. On the other hand, mercury poisoning was rampant and many died insane and in agony in the course of the mining process. Ultimately, one could count on a longer life span in the galleys than the mines at Almaden. From a historical perspective the use of convict labour in the mines stimulated the evolution of a system of exploitation by private contractors that reached 'its fullest development in Spanish America'.[44]

Spanish punishments were transferred to its New World colonies in the sixteenth century, introducing severe European standards of justice to regions lacking a strong native legal tradition. Corporal punishments ranged from whipping and physical mutilation to hanging, regardless of one's gender. Like in Continental Europe, vagrancy was dealt with harshly. One Italian traveller recounted witnessing the public whipping of three women for vagrancy, who were then taken under the gallows and covered with syrup and feathers – exhibitory punishment at its most unpleasant.[45]

During the heyday of the Ottoman Empire, exile was reserved for arsonists (and for negligent guards who allowed it to occur), gypsies, lepers and immoral persons. During the sixteenth century a deficit of oarsmen in the navy led to typically eight years' penal servitude on galleys for numerous offences ranging from the more serious capital crimes of apostasy and homosexual sex to mundane infractions such as drunkenness, gambling and swearing at a muezzin. The reliance on this sanction decreased in the eighteenth century when oar-driven galleys were superseded by sailing galleons. Instead, prisoners were sent to work in forts and arsenals.

In the words of one historian, 'apart from Russia, with the vast spaces of Siberia at its disposal, no other civilized nation matched England in the scale and extent of transportation.'[46] Although transportation, or banishment, has been most often identified with England's colonial experience in America and Australia in the eighteenth and nineteenth centuries, the practice was actually introduced more than a century earlier by James 1. By the end of the seventeenth century several other European countries adopted it as well. However, until 1718 it was used only infrequently by the English. In the 1750s tsarist Russia replaced capital punishment with hard labour in its Siberian penal colonies.

France became more identified with transportation in the 1790s when legislation was passed requiring all men convicted of a second felony to be transported for life to Madagascar.

England's utilization of the transportation system paralleled the years of its 'Bloody Code' (1688–1815), when English criminal law was characterized by an enormous number of hanging offences. There were no more than 50 capital offences in 1688. But by 1765 these had expanded to 160, rising to 225 by the end of the Napoleonic Wars. English transportation policy had a dramatic impact on sentencing policy and possibly delayed the process of prison experimentation in England for a number of years. Prior to the 1718 Transportation Act, almost 60 per cent of those convicted of 'clergyable' offences were branded and dismissed. After the Act that same number were transported, with the death penalty largely reserved for murder, horse theft, gang crimes and other serious felonies. Between 1718 and 1775, the period of transportation to America, imprisonment declined in popularity. But the passage of the 1779 Penitentiary Act would soon stimulate a movement towards the modern penitentiary, fuelled in no small part by John Howard's investigation of prison conditions that resulted in his seminal work *The State of the Prisons in England and Wales*, published in 1777, in which he noted that between 1773 and 1775, more prisoners died in jails than by execution.

Penal colonies and regimes that featured hard labour in southern Europe were often designated as *bagnes*, where prisoners worked on various public works projects including harbours, fortresses and roads. Popularized in France during the nineteenth century, the idea also caught on in Spain and Italy, making use of former land detention cells that held galley slaves in earlier times. These cells then made the transition to holding offenders facing anywhere from ten years imprisonment to the death penalty. France would close its *bagnes* in favour of penal servitude in its colonies in Algeria, New Caledonia and Guinea. The regime required prisoners to be chained together in barracks-like prisons when not at hard labour. Of these penal colonies none was as infamous as Devil's Island, a rocky islet off the coast of French Guinea. The island had passed through the control of various European powers before it came under French domination in 1663. In 1791 the French penal system mandated that any man who was convicted of a second felony should be transported there for life, replacing France's original destination of Madagascar. However the onset of the Napoleonic Wars ended transportation until it was revived in 1851. Between 1852 and 1946 more than 80,000 convicts served sentences on the dreaded island. Less well known was the fact that the subject of transportation had been debated for years in France until Napoleon III came to power; it was his assertion that British transportation had led to the creation of their prosperous colonies in Australia that swung the debate in the favour of advocates. But as history would show, the French were never able to duplicate the success of the British and in 1946 shuttered Devil's Island for good.

During its colonial heyday, Australia became Britain's penal colony from 1787 until 1852. It has been estimated that 187,000 prisoners were transported there. The Australian penal transportation era had a significant impact on the post-1852 developments in British corrections by introducing innovations such as the ticket-of-leave system, the practice of parole, and parole supervision.[47] Another historian took it a step further, asserting the Australian transportation experience was 'the most successful form of penal rehabilitation that has ever been tried in English, American or European history'.[48] Despite the fact that Australia was created as a virtual prison populated by both free and convict settlers, it was necessary to establish other penal institutions to handle convicts who were uncontrollable under the existing regime. In response a home-grown transportation system was devised in which offenders were transported to remote communities such as Van Diemen's Land and Norfolk Island. Selected to run Van Diemen's Land was the British penal administrator Sir George Arthur, who would become, according to historian Robert Hughes, 'one of the most controversial figures in early Australian history'. Formerly superintendent of the British Honduras, where he presided over a 'slave state', his experience would influence the penal regime he established in the Australian penal colonies.[49] Arthur would make his mark at Van Diemen's Land (now Tasmania), where he supervised a penal regime that included seven levels of punishment. In increasing severity they included individuals holding a ticket-of-leave, those assigned to work for free settlers, forced labour on public works projects, labour on roads near established communities, forced labour on chain gangs, banishment to isolated prison communities, and penal settlement labour in chains. Individuals could improve their conditions through good work and behaviour. But it was at Port Arthur, where he came to prominence, where he created a penal settlement for additional punishment. Connected to the mainland only by a narrow strip of land, it was guarded by ferocious dogs and natural barriers consisting of precipitous cliffs, making the site 'a natural penitentiary'.

The Russian exile system was distinct from the Australian version. Founded as a penal colony, Australia's initial European population was almost exclusively composed of lawbreakers, while criminals were 'never the majority in Siberia, even though its criminal and exile population was much larger than Australia's'.[50] In addition, Australia only served as a penal destination for 80 years (1788–1868). Its total of 155,000 transported convicts paled in comparison to the tens of thousands deported to Siberia over its 300 years as a penal destination.

Exile was first mentioned in Russian legislation in 1648 under Tsar Alexis, but it was not yet regarded as punishment; rather it was a method of getting prisoners who had already been punished beyond the margins of civilized Russian society. Russian criminal code was rife with grievous bodily punishments – flogging, branding, amputations, removal of tongues and so forth. Perhaps none was so dreaded as being 'suspended in the air by hooks passed under two of their ribs until they died a lingering and miserable death'. At the end of the seventeenth century, banishment was introduced as an alternative to many of these punishments. It was even considered for such minor offences as fortune telling, prizefighting, driving with reins, and the accidental setting of property on fire; snuff takers, on the other hand, had the septum between their nostrils torn out before being exiled.[51]

Originally, exile in Russia was regarded as supplemental to corporal punishment. It eventually became accepted as a method of populating and developing a colony in subarctic Siberia, where it was hoped it would lead to agricultural growth. But few who were forced to make this trek had the skills or inclination to farm, and even if they were so disposed the conditions were unsuitable. With the spread of mining, forced labour replaced long prison terms, while the list of offences punishable by exile was steadily increased. In 1753, during the reign of Empress Elizabeth, the exile system saw its greatest expansion as she abolished the death penalty in favour of hard labour. In time the legions of common criminals headed to the mines were joined by tens of thousands of serfs who had been banished and sentenced to exile for additional new crimes including usury, fortune telling, debt, lasciviousness, drunkenness, wife beating, illegally felling trees, accidentally starting fires and begging under false pretences. By some accounts, perhaps one-third of the exiles were set free to settle, one-seventh at hard labour, and the remaining sentenced to prison terms or exile for varying periods of time. On top of this, almost one-fifth were not even charged with a particular crime, 'except they had rendered themselves obnoxious to the community' where they had formerly resided. In such cases, there was a presumption of guilt that trumped any chance of the appeals process, since these individuals had been handed over for exile by their own villages.[52]

At the turn of the nineteenth century new exiles averaged about 2,000 per year; by the end of the century this had increased to 19,000 per year. More than 10 per cent would perish on the almost 5,000-mile (8,000-km) slog from Russia's seat of imperial power to their final destinations. Once arriving at various penal settlements scattered over Siberia, they had to surmount their next challenges: brutal wardens, poor food, disease, unremitting stench and the ever-present threat of the knout. The historian Benson Bobrick has identified several classes of Russian exiles, including hard labour convicts, those merely deported and those who volunteered to follow them, usually family members. The hard labour convicts and the deported were banished for life. They were typically branded and tattooed for identification, and had their heads shaved in a peculiar manner, according to their status – the head was shaved lengthwise on the right side and the left was cut short. These two groups were loaded down with heavy, riveted leg irons. In the early years hot irons were used to brand the males with letters on their cheek or brow, indicating the crime committed. For example, 'K' stood for 'KAT', or *katorzhnik* (hard labour convict) and 'B' for *brodyaga* (vagrant). Ultimately this practice was modified, as many forms of corporal punishment, including facial disfigurement, were eliminated and replaced with knout lashings. By the 1860s, except for the knout, most gruesome corporal punishments were being consigned to the medieval past as Russia joined other European countries in taking a more 'enlightened' approach towards penal sanctions. Nonetheless, as late as 1873, prisoners were even chained to wheelbarrows for up to three years, and those trusted to dole out lashings were instructed to lay it on from several angles so as to form the 'shape of an asterisk or star'.[53]

Despite all of the reforms following the abolition of serfdom in 1861, the knout still stood supreme. No matter that a prison reform movement was underway, introducing prisons and preliminary detention centres, prisoners still faced the lash. Fyodor Dostoevsky recounted his experiences in a Siberian camp in his novel *The House of the Dead* (1862): 'Sentences of 500, 1,000, or even 1,500 strokes were normally taken in one go; but if the sentences called for two or three thousand, its execution would be divided into two or even three parts' as the executioner gave the prisoner's back time to heal.[54] Dostoevsky received his lashings for complaining about the quality of the food and remembered the pain as 'like a fire burning you; as if your back was being roasted in the very hottest of fires'. For prisoners who could afford it, it was worth trying to bribe the executioner to go lighter on his strokes. The Russian revolutionary Peter Kropotkin recounted how 100 lashes were ordered 'with the same easiness as one week's incarceration would be ordered in European prisons'.[55] Kropotkin's interest in prisons was piqued when he was selected to investigate the penal system as a young officer, and it would haunt him throughout his life as he made the transition to one of the leading theorists of the anarchist movement.

For the most part, transportation had receded into the penal past by the end of the nineteenth century. However it lingered in far-flung reaches of the British Empire until after the Second World War. First used as a transportation destination for prisoners following the aftermath of the 1857 Indian Rebellion, Port Blair in the Andaman Islands would also be used by British colonial authorities to hold Indian convicts and common criminals, though armed robbers and murderers made up a significant portion of the penal population there. Until captured by the Japanese in the 1940s, Port Blair held Indian nationalists as well. The institution was finally abolished at the war's conclusion.[56]

Workhouses, Houses of Correction and Bridewells

The demographic upheaval that followed the collapse of England's old feudal order left many agricultural workers chronically unemployed. Likewise, the Dissolution of the Monasteries in the 1530s by Henry VIII had a similar effect, casting former retainers of the monastic order on to the job market, leaving legions of bakers, gardeners and launderers without employment. These and others joined the waves of vagrants moving from town to town across the British landscape. Along with these actors was a developing cast of professional and petty criminals. The introduction of the house of correction and the workhouse were early steps taken to control this unruly lot before the modern prison. In 1553 King Edward VI donated Henry VIII's palace built at Bridewell in 1520 as a 'hospital for moral, not physical deformities', leading to its function as a house of correction. Over the ensuing years Roman Catholics, Nonconformists and petty offenders were forcibly housed here and by the 1630s it was common for vagrants and prostitutes to be administered lashings upon their first arrival. Adults were given twelve lashes, children half as many. In 1576 Parliament mandated the establishment of a 'Bridewell' in every county, eventually leading to the operation of 300 of them, many still functioning into the nineteenth century. It became a familiar sight to witness local officials called beadles making their rounds in their respective wards, collecting vagrants and idle ne'er-do-wells for delivery to a bridewell. Once there, officials decided who would or would not be incarcerated. Petty criminals, vagrants and the indigent often found themselves locked up at these facilities where they were required to work at a number of constructive (but mind-numbing tasks), mostly manufacturing items for sale, in order to make the institution self-supporting, a standard that would become a guiding force in future prison development elsewhere.

The bridewell played an important role in the development of the house of correction and the workhouse, which were similar early attempts to control the disenfranchised and the criminally inclined in the years before the modern prison. These institutions were more similar to each other than the modern prison, in that the workhouse movement was stimulated by attempts to control pauperism and fallout from the social problems related to rampant poverty. Due to the exigencies of old age, poor health and mental disabilities, many were not capable of supporting themselves. On the other hand were those who simply could not find work (who became associated with the idea of, and stigmatized as, being not willing to work). By the 1550s it was assumed that anyone physically fit that did not work had personally chosen not to do so. Various laws were established to punish them, including one British law in 1552 that proclaimed 'If any man or woman, able to work, should refuse to labour and live idly for three days', he or she would be branded with the letter 'V' for 'vagrant' with a 'red-hot iron on the breast'. On top of that, the individual would be 'judged the slave for two years of any person who should inform against the idler'. It was not until the 1650s that the workhouse was first used 'in its modern sense'.[57]

Prior to the prison reform movement of the late nineteenth century, prisoners condemned to years of idleness became accustomed to various 'make-work' strategies designed to keep them constructively occupied. These included the treadmill, the crank and oakum picking, perhaps the most tedious of all. It was abhorrent enough having to take part in work regimes making nails, beating hemp and cleaning sewers in the earlier renditions of the workhouse; by the nineteenth century, prisoners were required to unravel lengths of old tar-soaked rope and then dig out single fibre strands, or oakum, with their bare hands. These were then tarred and used for caulking in wooden ships. However, as the days of the wooden ships came to an end this practice became obsolete, although some reports has it lasting into the twentieth century well after the treadmill and crank had been abolished.[58]

Among the most infamous innovations added to the workhouse and jail regimen was the treadmill, sometimes called the treadwheel, a machine that has existed in less complicated formats since antiquity. By working the lower-body muscles, these were utilized to power pumps and mills. The first prison treadmill was designed by the engineer William Cubitt, who was inspired by a visit in 1818 to the Suffolk county jail at Bury St Edmunds, where he observed a crowd of prisoners loun- ging about near the prison gates. Noticing Cubitt's disdain at this spectacle, a local magistrate asked him to come up with something to occupy what Cubitt later described as 'repulsive groups' of prisoners. It was not long before Cubitt, no doubt much to the dismay of inmate populations everywhere, devised the human treadmill, which would become a com- mon sight to British prisoners into the late nineteenth century. In 1821 London's Surrey House of Correction, now Brixton Prison, introduced the city's first treadmill.

The treadmill was composed of a series of steps on a giant wheel and was propelled by the climbing motion of prisoners. On average 200 men and women could replicate the output of a water wheel. Some observers compared the motion to a very wide paddle wheel, in which workers held on to a bar and climbed the paddle blades. Others compared it to climbing stairs for hours at a time. Modern health club devotees would probably pay to take their places if given the chance. Its popularity among prison officials was its dual function as a method of punishment and a practical means of grinding corn and raising water. Initially pris- oners spent entire days repeating fifteen-minute shifts on and then being relieved for fifteen minutes. By 1824 more than 50 prisons had adopted it. In 1838 innovators added vertical separators between prisoners so that inmates would be forced to labour in isolation. Behind the decorative facade of Northern Ireland's Armagh Prison, until the 1850s prisoners were disciplined with the treadmill, expected to maintain a brisk pace of 48 steps per minute for ten minutes before getting a five-minute break.[59] Coldbath Fields Prison in central London opened its gates as a house of correction in 1794 and offered a penal regime that included carrying around cannonballs and spending three or four hours on a tread- mill that could hold 340 inmates at once. What's more, prisoners were limited to receiving only one letter per month and one visit every three months. The 1834 regime was conducted in total silence under threat of leg irons, solitary confinement and a bread-and-water diet. It closed in 1885. Various attempts were made to introduce this mind- and body-numbing regime to America but found few supporters. By the end of the nineteenth century the treadmill was regarded as labour-wasting and counterproductive. It was banned by Parliament in 1898.

As if the treadmill was not enough, prisoners also had to contend with the crank, common in many Victorian prisons. It was really not much more than a box filled with sand and operated with a handle. Prisoners were expected to repeatedly turn the handle, forcing it to scoop up sand inside a sandbox, and then dropping it, before repeating the process. Meant to wear out inmates, its use was monitored by an ingenious counting device that recorded the number of turns made by prisoners, who were expected to make almost 10,000 turns in one day. It too was outlawed, along with the treadmill, in 1898.

Similar to the house of correction, workhouses were meant to instil the rehabilitative value of hard work and inculcate an industrious work ethic. Britain was not alone in its ingenuity for keeping prisoners busy. During John Howard's tour of European prisons in the 1770s, he was rather taken with certain elements of the Dutch prison system. Among them was the aptly called *rasphuis*, or rasp house, where two inmates worked together to rasp at least 50 lb (23 kg) of sawdust per day. It was a strenuous process of pulverizing logs of dyewood in order to produce a powder for colouring goods. Depending on the workhouse, male prisoners convicted of serious crimes might spend between ten and twelve hours a day (comparable to the typical free-world workday of that period) preparing rough timber for carpenter's workshops. Howard reported how the inmates were constantly at work, no crowds lolling by the prison gates here. The *spinhuis* was its female counterpart, where women engaged in constructive routines of textile work, sewing and spinning. Most sentences to these facilities were open ended, or indeterminate, in length, with rehabilitation achieved only through work, a notion that seems at odds with the overwhelming idleness that characterizes most modern prison routines.

American Penal Progress in the New Republic

While England continued to add capital crimes to its Bloody Code, by 1790 America's new federal government only retained four capital offences: murder, treason, rape and arson. Although no American state abolished the death penalty in the eighteenth century, Pennsylvania came closest, when it eliminated the death penalty in 1794 for all crimes except first-degree murder. By the outbreak of the American Revolution in 1776, three major categories of confinement prevailed in England – debtor's prisons, jails and houses of correction. According to the customs of the day, debtors and their families were often confined together until their debts were absolved. But prison categories often overlapped to such an extent that it was not uncommon for jails to house together debtors, felons, children and the insane.

In colonial America, according to the author David J. Rothman, 'the threat of incarceration at hard labor was to discourage the needy stranger from entering the community and to punish him should he be apprehended.' Others suggest that when William Penn introduced his Great Law in 1682, the workhouse in effect became 'a true penal institution' in Pennsylvania, 'no longer limited to the treatment of the destitute and vagrant classes'. The law stipulated that 'all prisons shall be workhouses for felons, thiefs [sic], vagrants, and loose, abusive and idle persons'. Subsequently prisons were ordered to be constructed in each county.[60]

Penn established some of the groundwork for the prison reforms that followed in his Pennsylvania colony. Penn and other Quaker reformers led the way in prison improvement, abolishing the practices of charging inmates for fees and food and lodging, and their efforts would dominate American prison reform into the nineteenth century. In the early eighteenth century, American jail conditions mirrored counterparts in the Western world. Cell confinement was virtually non-existent; jails and prisons were little more than large rooms housing a range of malefactors, including debtors, felons, children, the mentally ill and the dissolute. The birth of Philadelphia's Walnut Street Jail in 1790 was a testament to the visions of such reformers as Benjamin Rush and John Howard. Its construction and other jails that followed led the way in the transformation of punishment, at least in America, from a punitive regime to one that emphasized reform, rehabilitation and, most importantly, penitence (hence the 'penitentiary').

A number of reformers advocated single-cell housing as a way of separating the most dangerous prisoners from others, eliminating the so-called element of 'convict contagion'. This refers to the phenomenon in which new prisoners are 'infected' by the criminogenic habits of career criminals. In the modern era, classification systems were developed to separate these types of inmates from each other, but in earlier times this notion was less developed. By the early 1820s two competing prison models had evolved out of the innovations of the Walnut Street Jail. The Pennsylvania or solitary system featured 24-hour isolation and some type of labour within the single cell. On the other hand, New York's Auburn system, predicated on rigid silence and congregate work, favoured cellular isolation only at night, allowing prisoners to silently work together in congregate settings during the day. Ultimately this scheme dominated prison design in the United States, due in no small part to the fact that this type of prison was more cost-effective, saving money and making more of a profit through prison industries – the bottom line for any prison administrator.

Of all the prisons built in America during the early nineteenth century none received more attention and publicity than Eastern State Penitentiary. Built between 1822 and 1829 near a cherry orchard in Philadelphia, it cost more than $750,000, America's most expensive building at the time. One architectural historian was so bold to assert it was the country's 'first building to have real influence abroad'.[61] With 12-foot-thick (3.5 metres) granite walls extending 30 feet (9 metres) high, the prison was probably the nation's first building with indoor plumbing. It covered 11 acres and every cell was built for one prisoner to be kept in solitary confinement for the entire sentence, its system influenced by Quaker impulses of reform and penitence. Charles Dickens became one of its most vocal critics after visiting it in 1842. Arriving in the United States, Dickens had been asked what he would like to visit, and he responded: 'Niagara Falls and Eastern State Penitentiary.' In his book *American Notes for General Circulation* (1842), about his travels there, he would describe the so-called Pennsylvania system as 'rigid, strict, and hopeless solitary confinement', adding he believed it was 'cruel and wrong' and that the 'slow and daily tampering with the mysteries of the brain' was 'immeasurably worse than any torture to the body'.[62] Most of the 300 prisons that adopted this model were located outside the United States and included China's Beijing Prison (1912), Belgium's Louvain Prison (1860), Japan's Hakodate Prison (1931), London's Pentonville Prison (1842) and Russia's Kresty Prison in St Petersburg (1890).

The Russian Enigma

In 1781 the great British penal reformer John Howard visited Russia for the first time.[63] He had become especially interested in its penal system after hearing that capital punishment was no longer used there.

However, the more he was apprised of this the more he searched for other punitive measures that surely must exist. He found this in the ghoulish person of the knout, which in many respects was more vicious than any hanging or decapitation England had to offer. Russia had relished the fact that it had risen above the uncivilized nations of Europe by abolishing capital punishment, making it a source of national pride. But Howard found that the use of the knout had led to numerous accidental killings. He queried an executioner as to how this punishment could be fatal. He responded, 'By one or two strokes to his sides, which carry off large pieces of the flesh.' Howard asked if he had ever been ordered to inflict mortal damage, and he replied, 'Sometimes.'[64] The always inquisitive Quaker decided he had to personally witness its infliction, which he did on 10 August:

> I saw two criminals; a man and a woman suffer the knout. The woman was taken first and stripped to the waist, hands and feet bound by cords to the whipping post. A servant attended the executioner, both powerful men. The servant marked his ground and struck the woman with five lashes, every stroke penetrated the flesh; but his master thought him too gentle and pushed him aside and gave the remaining twenty strokes himself.[65]

Before leaving Russia, Howard, who would perish there from typhus in 1790, was given a tutorial on the grim instruments used for inflicting pain by the chief of the St Petersburg police. Among the items Howard noted were a machine for breaking arms and legs, an instrument for splitting nostrils and one for branding by puncturing the skin and rubbing a black powder on wounds.

As noted in the previous chapter, Russia had a long tradition of using corporal punishment, as other countries did before (and in some cases after) the advent of the penitentiary. In the time of Peter the Great (1672–1725) torture was used for three purposes – forcing someone to speak, punishment, and as a 'prelude to or refinement of execution'.[66] Among the grisly instruments used for this purpose was a small rod about as thick as a finger called the batog, used for common crimes. The procedure required a victim to lie flat on the ground or floor with legs extended and back bared. Two men simultaneously applied the strokes, with one sitting or kneeling on the victim's head and arms and the other on his legs and feet. As they faced each other each wielded his batog 'rhythmically in turn, keeping time as smiths do at an anvil until their rods were broken in pieces and then they took fresh ones until they were ordered to stop'.[67] It was not uncommon for the weakened victim to die from these prolonged beatings.

But no instrument was as notorious as the knout, used for serious criminal cases. More than a century before Howard witnessed its use a visitor described a beating in which 'blows tore skin from a bare back, in some place could reach through to bones'. The standard number of strokes was between fifteen and 205, depending on the crime. Punishment with the knout used a curious procedure that began with the victim 'lifted and spread across the back of another man selected by knoutmaster from group of spectators'. His arms are then tied over the shoulders of a stationary porter and his legs around the porter's knees, 'then one of the knoutmaster's assistants grabs the victim by the hair and pulls his head out of the way of the rhythmic lashing on his back'. In other cases a more horrid posture was assumed by the victim, in which his 'hands were tied behind his back and a long rope tied to his wrists and then passed over a tree branch or beam': when one pulled down on the rope it would lift the victim into the air with his arms twisting backwards the wrong way in the shoulder sockets. Other procedures were added to this that facilitated pulling the shoulders out of their sockets. One observer in 1716 recounted:

> so many strokes on the bare back as are appointed by the judges, first making a step back and giving a spring forward at every stroke, which is laid on with such force that the blood flies at every stroke and leaves a weal behind as thick as a man's finger. And these knoutmasters, as the Russians call them are so exact in their work they very rarely strike two strokes in the same place, but lay them the whole length and breadth of a man's back, by the side of each other with great dexterity from the top of a man's shoulders down to the waistband of his britches.[68]

The knout might be used on a weekly basis to garner a confession. In other cases fire might be used to loosen tongues, as the victim's bound hands and feet attached him to a pole like being roasted on a spit and his raw back roasted over fire until he confessed; in some instances this was done to the raw back of someone just knouted.[69]

Ottoman Crime and Punishment

The Ottoman Empire (1299–1922) was one of the most expansive and enduring empires in history, reaching its apogee in the sixteenth and seventeenth centuries during the reign of Suleiman the Magnificent. At that point it was among the most powerful states in the world, a multinational empire stretching from its southern borders to the gates of Vienna and the Holy Roman Empire. Its success was predicated on a number of factors that are commonly associated with successful states. It was highly centralized with power in the hands of a central ruler. Its judicial system was run by the state as well. And as an empire united by the Islamic faith, its leaders were highly pragmatic, borrowing the best ideas from cultures it subsumed in its expansion.

When it came to the Sharia, which the Ottomans saw as their duty to protect and uphold, they also recognized it was 'not always practical for handling the day to day issues that arose in the empire'.[70] In response imperial laws were promulgated that often borrowed a sharply different interpretation of Sharia penal law. What becomes apparent is that Ottoman penal practices varied widely, both from a temporal and regional context. The use of fines became a prominent sanction, and served as an alternative to more brutal methods such as stoning and flogging. This shift from physical to fine-based sanctions has been a source of debate. However, once one understands the extent of the vast empire that in the sixteenth century ranged from present-day Iraq across North Africa and north to the Balkans, it should not be unexpected that it was often necessary to modify existing legal practices to meet the needs of an incredibly diverse population that included Christians and Jews, tribesmen and villagers. Whereas some European observers praised the Ottoman justice system for 'its swift justice [which] compared favourably with European legal practices, characterized by long drawn out and costly procedures', others criticized it for its 'hasty capital sentences and sometimes cruel punishments'.[71]

Ottoman crime and punishment contrasted sharply with many of the traditions established by Islamic legal code. In fact, in places such as Aleppo, Syria, under the Ottomans sexual indiscretions, or *zina* crimes,[72] were often treated with non-violent sentences such as banishment from the community, rather than stoning. One authority asserts there was not one case of stoning listed in the Sharia court records of Aleppo in a 300-year period.[73] But there were distinctions from city to city. While Aleppo preferred banishment as a sanction for prostitution in the eighteenth century, Anatolia favoured fines accompanied by the bastinado, a form of flogging. The following account captures this method in action:

> The culprit was laid on the ground and his feet were immobilized between a stout pole of board and a rope passed through two holes at its ends. Two men lofted the pole so that the offender's shoulders touched the ground. Two others then inflicted strokes on the bare soles (and other parts of the body) with long pliant sticks about one finger thick.[74]

What these variations suggest is that rather than consider Islamic law as a singular law code it would be much more accurate to view it as 'a series of legal codes that differ according to time, place and context'.[75]

The inventiveness of Ottoman punishments gives insight into the pragmatic possibilities of Islamic law. By most accounts fining was the most often used sanction. Whenever some type of flogging was required, as in *tazir* offences (non-mandatory), a corresponding fine was determined by the number of strokes in the sentence. Those sentenced to death also faced matching sanctions, especially the confiscation of personal property. In some cases torture was utilized before death if there was reason to believe there were still treasures hidden elsewhere. Complementary sanctions such as forms of shaming were sometimes imposed with other penalties, as in the case of an individual forced to navigate city streets with the carcass of a chicken hanging around his neck after he was caught stealing it.[76] Other documented shaming punishments include an individual who had wounded someone being led through town with an arrow or knife stuck through his arm. Those who violated business regulations could be seen from time to time being led through the streets with his defective merchandise hanging from his pierced nose. Like the Chinese cangue, used for shaming, the Ottomans introduced a heavy wooden board which the perpetrator was forced to wear around his neck, with a sign adhered to it and the faulty goods arranged on the board. In other cases the merchant might have his ears nailed to the doorposts of their place of business with their feet barely touching the ground and left there for the amusement of his dissatisfied customers.[77]

But of all the Ottoman penal sanctions, the most popular remained flogging and caning. Typically, lashes were applied to either the back or the bottom of the feet, with the number of strokes decided by the seriousness of the transgression. Lashes were limited to prevent the death of the malefactor; if he perished under the whip the state was liable for half his blood price (after 100 strokes). Recidivist criminals were always a problem and amputation of the right hand was adopted to remind habitual purse snatchers, forgers and others of the rule of law, although from the mid-sixteenth century on they were probably sent to the galleys. Amputation was not limited to the hand, with recorded cases of penis amputation for abduction (and branding of vulva of women complicit in this offence). Other physical punishments entailed branding the forehead for forgery and procuring women, and slitting the nose and removing ears of those who deserted the army. But here again, like capital crimes, beginning in the sixteenth century these sentences might be commuted to galley slavery.[78]

When it came to crime and punishment no sentence represented the power of the state more than the death penalty which was often rife with symbolism. Enforcing the connection between the authority of the sultan and other high-ranking leaders such as governors, after decapitation the heads of offenders were often placed in front of the Istanbul palace gates with signs explaining the reasons for executions. It was not unheard of to see sometimes hundreds of heads exhibited there, including those of bandits killed in far-off locales. In order to transport the heads it was necessary to fill them with straw and preserve them in brine; in other cases they were placed in sacks and preserved in honey until they reached Istanbul. Common methods for decapitation included the axe or scimitar. Strangling with a bow string was reserved for high-ranking officials, a tradition dating back to the Mongol-Turkish taboo against shedding blood of senior servants of the state. Like hanging, drawing and quartering, grisly remedies with maximum suffering were concocted for deterrence value and to emphasize the power of the state. Insurgents and others convicted of political offences were treated to impalement, which was conducted by throwing them onto sharp hooks that extended from a wall or on pointed stakes. Others were pounded to death in an oversize mortar, and still others either sawed in half or had their skin removed while still alive.

The Mamluk military system that evolved in Egypt during the Ottoman period demonstrated its commitment to preserving public order through the use of intimidating punishments meant to curb crime. One inspector of Upper Egypt, appointed in 1433, 'devised diverse torments of criminal elements and highwaymen'. On one occasion he had a criminal arrested, then ordered him to be inflated 'through his buttocks with a bellows so that his eyes popped out and his brain burst'.[79] The inspector sought to contradict his cruel reputation, at one point releasing Cairo's prisoners from imprisonment, but with the warning that anyone who was arrested for theft in the future would be bisected, with no chance of incarceration. His brutal methods seemed to bring theft in Cairo to 'a virtual standstill' during his regime.[80] In one mass execution of repeat offenders in 1402, together they 'were suspended from hooks driven through their orifices' and left to perish slowly. The inspector was apparently well aware of its shock value, but condoned it nonetheless, since this band of criminals had been murdering and plundering at will. In another case almost 100 years later, a thief who stole from a tomb had his face flayed while he was still alive, with the skin hanging down to his chest and his facial bones exposed, and was then hanged (as if being strangled to death is not bad enough). The obvious question is whether this deterred crime. By most accounts the results of extreme punishment were 'ambiguous' at best.[81]

The Qing Dynasty

Modern China came of age during its last dynasty. From 1644 to 1911, the Qing dynasty made great strides in modernizing its legal system. Signs of a movement towards less extreme forms of corporal punishment were on the horizon. During this era the *Manual for Local Magistrates*, first published in 1699, served as the handbook for the local administration of punishment. Its author, Huang Liu-Hung, a local magistrate (one of 100 in seventeenth-century China), noted that the 'Instruments of torture used today are lighter than those of olden days . . . For the purpose of chastisement, bamboo paddles are used.'[82] According to the manual, bamboo paddles came in various models. Heavier ones were used to lash robbers, hoodlums and '*yamen* runners who take bribes', while medium ones were preferred for 'ordinary cases'. The lightest were reserved for cases involving 'ignorant villagers who are tax delinquents or minor litigants'.[83]

For individuals who refused to confess during hearings, finger and ankle squeezers were utilized, as was humiliating public exposure in the cangue. Manacles and shackles were employed to prevent escape. Although permitted by law, the usage of these devices varied according to the circumstances. Ankle squeezers were used only on homicide and robbery suspects who refused to confess. By most accounts the administration of this type of punishment was best accomplished by an experienced executioner, who would be aware of the necessity of adjusting the feet properly to avoid causing death. Properly done, the feet would be placed through holes in three boards and tightened with ropes from both sides gradually, producing severe agony but preventing the 'sudden rush of blood that attacks the heart'. If done incorrectly it could break the ankles. Well aware of what awaited them, some prisoners were savvy enough to take bone-softening pills ahead of time, which purportedly prevented damage to bones no matter how tightly pressed. In the long run, except for ankle and finger squeezers, no other torture was permitted.[84]

The shaming punishment of the cangue was preferred for offences involving moral turpitude and typically took place in public. The miscreant was humiliated by having his head shaved on top so he could not hide his eyes from the public (hoping to prevent future recidivism). The cangue was a rather flimsy device carried on the shoulders to limit movement and was only used on local vagrants and layabouts. It was not used on those of high social status since such humiliation would be a fate worse than death for them.

The Qing demonstrated one of the important hallmarks of the modern state by singling out treason (and rebellion) as deserving of the most severe punishments. High treason, in which an act was committed to subvert the established government or purposely destroy the imperial temple, mausoleums or palaces (whether a principle or indirect actor) was met with the 'penalty of lingering death'. In such cases all the male relatives of the perpetrator – grandfather, father, sons, grandsons, brothers and others living under the same roof and 'irrespective of surnames' and over the age of sixteen were decapitated.[85]

One of the more interesting principles of Chinese law, *fan-tso*, or 'retribution of punishment', required anyone who made a false accusation to be sentenced to be punished for the same crime which the accused would have merited. This could include strangling, beheading and other sanctions. If the false accusation was discovered before the sanction was used, the false accuser would suffer 100 blows and perpetual banishment to at least 3,000 *li* from residence.[86]

Chinese law recognized seven categories of homicide, each with its own punishment. Premeditated murder was punished with decapitation and any accessories were strangled. No crime was considered more serious than murder committed in the course of a robbery, which required beheading for all accomplices. Judges had discretion when death was caused by accident. Those who killed in the course of 'playing with the fist, with a stick, or any weapon or any other means whatsoever', accidentally or not, 'shall suffer the punishment provided by the law in any ordinary case of killing or wounding in an affray'.[87] In such cases death might be the punishment, but judges had some discretion in applying the sentence. Indeed, the perpetrator could redeem himself from punishment by paying compensation in the form of a fine to the family of the person injured or killed.

During a British expedition in 1793 attempting to open China up to Western trade, the twelve-year-old son of one of its officials, Thomas Staunton, kept a diary, remarkable for its maturity and candour. The young Staunton suggested that the death penalty was 'seldom . . . inflicted without the confirmation of the Emperor; but it takes place sometimes by order of the viceroy of the province in cases of emergency, such as rebellion or sedition'. However, like other first-person accounts, Staunton's findings often fail to pass the scrutiny test. He asserted that the general rule was that criminals due to be executed were to be delivered to Peking, where it was common for sentences to be downgraded by a special tribunal. He also explained that the executions took place just once a year, during the autumn season. If his observation that only 200 executions took place each year was correct, this is in great contrast to the modern Chinese proclivity for judicial executions. By most accounts these figures sound quite low. But if it was true, consider that by the 1830s, France, with one-twelfth of the population of China, was doling out hundreds of death sentences each year.[88] According to another China observer, Father Lamiot, the criminals that were executed in autumn were executed not just in Peking but 'in all the capitals of the provinces', unless granted clemency by the Emperor, with some provinces witnessing hundreds of executions annually. However, no matter how one accepts the findings of the younger Staunton, his argument that Chinese punishments seemed more moderate 'than the rope which English thieves were hanged at the time' would be difficult to argue with.[89]

The earliest references to incarceration as a criminal sanction in China come from Confucius, who recorded in the *Shujing* (Book of Documents), a collection of writings said to have been edited by him, that as far back as 2300 BC the emperor Yao had exiled three political malefactors and punished another with 'strict imprisonment'.[90] Other testimony to its early use was found on an excavated stone tablet dating to around AD 723, noting that Buddhist temples were expected to be constructed near prisons, probably to contribute towards the rehabilitation process.[91] Despite this rather sketchy evidence, these prisons were probably not much more than dungeon cages in local castles and fortresses.

By the late Qing period the majority of criminals sentenced by county magistrates were sanctioned with fines, beatings, penal servitude, exile and death. Imprisonment was not yet a legal penalty at this juncture, but mostly a short period of confinement while prisoners awaited trial, convicts awaiting exile logistics or execution. Mention is made of a 'dark gaol' where bandits and murderers were sent prior to execution. During the late eighteenth century China was undergoing a period of incredible demographic growth that led to a breakdown of social and economic conditions. In response the government began expanding its exile system. Penal historian Frank Dikötter has made a case that this banishment system was in many ways similar to the French and British disposition towards the transportation of convicts, especially since it was perceived as being more benevolent than the death penalty as an alternative punishment.[92]

During its move towards modernization China sent envoys abroad in the 1860s seeking other alternatives as the current penal system fell out of favour. Their first visit took them to London's Pentonville Prison, just completed in 1842. Modelled on the separate and silent system of confinement, it was initially reserved for those awaiting transportation to Australia. The visitors quickly formed the opinion that this might be a desirable alternative to banishment since prisons were more associated with the notions of 'repentance and self-renewal', concepts that seemed in keeping with Chinese cultural tradition and conformed with their perceptions of the modern prison.

Chinese penology languished behind the West until the beginning of the twentieth century, when construction of its first modern prison was influenced by the Japanese interpretation of Western prison reforms. One leading expert on the Chinese penitentiary has suggested that, 'prison reform only became a government priority with the advent of a radically new vision of political order', and this was provided by the collapse of the imperial system beginning in 1895. But until then the mainstay of the penal regime was predicated on hard labour, including brick making, making blankets and straw hats, weaving, manufacturing hairnets and printing. As was the case elsewhere women prisoners were placed in gender-prescribed occupations such as sewing, weaving and braiding. The first model prison opened in Beijing in 1909. Based on the Pentonville model, other prisons were constructed in various provinces, but the onset of the Communist Revolution would stall this stage of prison reform in the coming decades.

The rise of the penitentiary was central to the transformation of Europe's penal regimes beginning in the eighteenth century, as the scaffold and other holdovers from previous centuries 'yielded primacy to imprisonment and transportation'.[93] Some scholars and writers have focused on the transition from the body to the soul as the target of punishment. Dickens's previously mentioned account of his 1842 visit to Eastern State Penitentiary, in which he asserted that the 'slow and daily tampering with the mysteries of the brain' was 'immeasurably worse than any torture to the body', prefigured the stance of Michel Foucault and others, who suggest that this transformation in punishment was perhaps less convincing when continuing corporal punishment and penal servitude are thrown into the mix. In any case, the addition of the penitentiary to the punishment arsenal gave officials a much larger selection of penal (and less lethal) alternatives to choose from. Transportation, galleys and various forms of purpose-built prisons gained wide support on many fronts and ultimately the decline of public executions and the rise of the penitentiary demonstrated that there was indeed a transformation of punishment occurring in the Western world, as centralized states became the rule rather than the exception.

5

Highwaymen, Bandits, Brigands and Bushrangers: Bands of Thieves and Early Organized Criminality

One of the unintended results of state centralization was the opportunities that gave rise to the advent of organized gangs of local criminals who took advantage of the roads that linked communities together and were so essential for commerce. They were known as highwaymen, bandits and bushrangers; others were branded brigands, thugs, dacoits and worse. They shared a propensity to appear wherever governments were weak, policing ineffective and the population stratified. Some observers have linked banditry to agrarian class societies, while others have detected them in industrialized ones as well. Bandits flourished when jobs were scarce, or as a result of lack of opportunity after the mustering out of temporary soldiers after wars. In some cases we can detect precursors to modern organized criminal groups, but more often they were regional menaces of a more ephemeral nature.

The term 'outlaw' dates back to at least ninth-century England, when the concept of outlawry referred to individuals placed outside the protection of the law, hence 'outlawed'.[1] In Anglo-Saxon society anyone who refused to appear in court, failed to pay the *wergild*, or sought to evade the machinery of justice by fleeing the realm, was outlawed, and thus forfeited all property and civil rights. According to the procedures of the day, once outlawed, an individual who, say, failed to appear in court four consecutive times, would be essentially branded an animal to be hunted down and vanquished. If not killed outright while resisting capture, he would surely face the executioner once proof of his sentence of outlawry was established.

It has been oft-chronicled that warfare stimulates violence and has been a frequent precursor to the development of outlaw bands over the centuries in the aftermath of wars. Banditry became a major problem at the end of the War of the Spanish Succession (1701–14) as men skilled in battle added their skills to existing criminal bands, and in the following century, as Napoleon invaded Italy and Spain, local peasants and others flocked to join the bandit gangs. Many remained in this line of crime even after the French withdrew. In the United States, the end of the American Civil War in 1865 inaugurated an era of banditry unequalled until the 1920s and '30s.

It should not be very surprising that war was often a precursor to bandit activity, since it was common to recruit convicted criminals into armies in return for pardons in countries such as England. For example, the Hundred Years War between 1337 and 1453 was a series of wars between England and France for control of the French throne. It was not uncommon for demobilized soldiers to return home with a taste for looting and to form small bands that subsisted on robbery. In a similar vein, free peasants in the aftermath of the depopulation wrought by the recent Black Death sometimes turned to outlawry after having their demands for higher wages ignored by potential employers. The Hundred Years War generated organized rural crime as gangs of demobilized soldiers, heavily armed and skilled at violence, attacked villages and civilians at will – when they weren't sacking French towns and villages, that is. English veterans who accumulated a record of good behaviour were most likely to receive pardons later on. Few could argue with the fact that armies taught men skills that came in handy in both war and peace, as many refused to return to the dull routine of previous lives and had trouble reintegrating into society.

Between the fifteenth and seventeenth centuries many regions of Europe, including parts of France, Italy, Spain and Germany, had been economically devastated by wars, which left in their wake bands of army deserters, discharged soldiers and smugglers, robbers, and un-employed soldiers and mercenaries. Following the Hundred Years War France suffered from gangs called 'skinners' or 'flayers' (*écorcheurs*), so-called for stripping people of their money in the mountainous regions of central France and elsewhere.

Some historians have traced the origins of the British highwayman tradition to activities of ex-Royalist soldiers in the aftermath of the English Civil War (1642–51). It was no coincidence that the apex of the era of the English highwayman followed the war between the forces of Charles I and Parliamentarians. Following the king's execution in 1649, many former Royalist officers were dispossessed of their holdings and took to the roads to sustain themselves. Typically mounted on well-bred horses and dressed in cavalier costume these 'gentlemen of the road' would set the standard for the 'knights of the road' that would follow in their hoof prints over the ensuing decades.

While English highwaymen preferred the roads of commerce, in other regions topography was often a determinant as to whether a bandit gang would flourish or not. Chronicling the roots of banditry, one mid-nineteenth-century observer noted:

> In looking over the different countries infested by banditti, it will strike us that their existence may also be reduced to a branch of statistics and geography. Certain districts, as formed by nature, seem of themselves to suggest the trades of robbery and piracy; and where the progress of good government, civilization, prosperity, and population have not corrected the dangerous facility, it will be found that robbers and pirates pursue their calling now, as they have done in all ages, in certain spots which offer favorable points of attack and retreat.

As exemplars, the author pointed to mountainous areas, regions with long coastlines, or divided into many little countries, with many borders, such as in the case of Italy at the time of his writing.[2]

The reivers were among the lesser-known archetypes of the bandit tradition. The Scottish border reiver has been described as 'a unique figure' that transcended class boundaries. While some of them lived with their outlaw gangs, others worked as agricultural workers, often tending their own plots of land near the border line between Scotland and England. Reivers were distinct for their abilities as cattle rustlers and their skills at guerrilla warfare and handling weapons. According to their chronicler George Macdonald Fraser, the reiver 'was also often a gangster organised on highly professional lines, who had perfected the protection racket three centuries before Chicago was built'.[3] What's more, the activities of these rogues introduced the term 'blackmail' into the English lexicon, a tradition that began sometime in the 1550s when Scottish blackmailers offered protection against English invasion to towns in the English East March. Those that refused to pay this extortion saw their communities burned to the ground.

Perhaps no one has contributed more to the discussion of banditry than the British historian Eric Hobsbawm, who coined the term 'social bandit' in 1959.[4] Over the next half-century his concept was increasingly debated. According to his basic category of bandit, the 'noble robber' best exemplifies 'peasant outlaws' such as the American Jesse James. However, his thesis becomes less persuasive in the eyes of some scholars when it is argued that there never were 'American peasants to champion'.[5] Hobsbawm portrays his social bandits as a special type of criminal, 'Peasant outlaws whom the lord and the state regard as criminals, but who remain within peasant society' where they are seen as 'heroes', 'fighters for justice' and 'men to be admired, helped and supported'.[6] The noble robber finds its best expression in the Robin Hood myth. While the nomenclature of outlawry has evolved over time to include a wide variety of actors and criminal bands it has remained both historically and geographically a remarkably consistent and uniform phenomenon.[7] Hobsbawm demonstrated that similar situations within peasant societies around the world have created social bandits. However, as initially conceptualized, his social bandit is basically a European-American construct and does not fit every historical experience, and could also be found in non-agrarian societies such as America, Australia and England in the nineteenth century.

Outlawry Outside the Common-law Experience

Some of the earliest accounts of banditry come to us from Asian history. During China's twelfth-century Song dynasty, the conquest of banditry, or *tao-tsei*, was considered 'central to the problem of law and order' due in no small part to the fact that this form of criminality combined violent activities with 'some degree of organization and cooperation'.[8] Traditionally, criminal activity that required cooperation between multiple actors represented significant threats to the power of the state, what modern criminologists might label 'security threat groups'. Perhaps one twelfth-century official put it best when he acknowledged that 'the world's having bandits is like a house having rats . . . Houses will always have rats.'[9] This analogy between bandits and rats was apparently common in the Song era. Distinctions, however, were made between bandits and foreign enemies, who were viewed as 'tigers', to be vanquished with weapons and traps, as opposed to bandits who could be 'surrounded and smoked out'.

In seventeenth-century China no crime was treated more seriously than robbery. Punishment reflected this by usually demanding the beheading of all accomplices (and even of those who fenced stolen merchandise). Robbery committed by a small group of unarmed actors was considered 'plundering', and when it took place in broad daylight it was considered less clandestine, and the penalty was thus less severe, mostly limited to flogging and penal servitude. However, in the event a victim was wounded, the gang's ringleader would be executed. When large armed gangs of brigands committed their crimes in daylight, all faced beheading and having their heads displayed in public, no matter whether anyone was wounded or the size of the gang.[10]

Officials during Japan's thirteenth-century shogunate paid particular attention to the problem of 'evil bands', or *akuto*. The threat was mentioned for the first time by an administrator in 1258: 'The evil bands of various provinces have arisen, and we have heard to the effect that they plan to commit night attacks, robbery, banditry, and piracy.'[11] The threat became even more acute in the next century as *akuto* robbed taxmen, mounted night attacks, cut down and stole crops, and illegally harvested mountain timbers to build protective fortifications. Despite more modern claims linking this brigandage to the samurai tradition, as early as 1348 one anonymous monk disputed this, insisting there was no resemblance at all.[12] Compared to immaculate and martial samurai, these bandits were described as 'unkempt', bearing bamboo spears and long, rusted swords. They wore eccentric six-sided caps and sleeveless, elaborately decorated war kimonos and covered their faces with yellow scarves rather than the traditional *eboshi* (tall headdress now worn by Shinto priests) that were worn by most men. 'This unconventional appearance was chosen by the *akuto* as a badge of non-conformity, as the bandits sought to distinguish themselves from the rest of the population by presenting their marginality in the form of a challenge.'[13] The etymology of the generic term yakuza refers to a losing hand of cards in the Japanese game *oicho-kabu* – 8, 9, 3 or *ya*, *ku*, *za* – hence its affiliation with the gambling tradition. In this variation of the game Blackjack, numbers adding up to twenty is a losing hand. Over time, the term *yakuza* came to be used to describe a worthless person, loser or misfit. The most significant modern form of Japanese organized crime, the yakuza revels in its marginality as well, with members portraying themselves as worthless, losers and misfits to burnish their image as underdogs and societal rejects.[14]

There was no uniformity to early Japanese criminal bands, with some occasionally hired out as mercenaries while others cheated at games of chance or committed acts of petty larceny. Often, shielded by local peasants, *akuto* might even offer to help harvest crops and cut hay, and yet they might repay the locals by setting houses on fire and pillaging when their supplies needed replenishing. Initially, *akuto* were rejects from various social classes, and not simply marginalized inhabitants who turned to outlawry. In fact, the leaders of these gangs often proved to be leaders of the local ruling classes – warriors and estate managers fighting over control of the land who were later denounced as bandits to the authorities by landowners. By the 1330s criminal bands became much better organized and had adopted battle techniques that made them capable of conventional warfare against shogunate forces.

In Africa, most examples of classic banditry are 'confined to South Africa'.[15] Organized criminal gangs have been operating there since the nineteenth century, stimulated by the discovery of diamonds and gold. Australian immigrant Scotty Smith rose to prominence as one of South Africa's first major highwaymen and gang leaders, conducting most of his operations in the North Cape and Orange Free State. One expert suggested that by smuggling a large herd of horses across the South African frontier to German cavalry troops in German southwest Africa, the Smith Gang should be considered 'one of the first transnational criminal operations in South Africa'.[16] During the early twentieth century, the Foster Gang achieved prominence for a spectacular run of violent bank and post office robberies. But the gang played out its string after being cornered in a Johannesburg mine dump in 1914 when the gang took their lives rather than surrender.[17] By mid-century the region's gangs were more likely to come from the indigenous population, such as the Msomi Gang, one of the country's more formidable gangs in the 1950s and significant for its adoption of American gang strategies.[18] Its leader, Shadrack Matthews, better known by his moniker 'Prime Minister', earned a reputation for cunning and brutality before mounting the gallows' steps.

The English Highwayman

The biggest challenge to maintaining public order in England in the early modern period was the proliferation of organized bandit gangs. Many types of crime committed by commoners – land seizure, mayhem, abduction, highway robbery and feuding – required the coordination of numerous malefactors. In an era when most men carried weapons and kinship welded extended families together, these bands often contained men closely related by blood. When one failed to appear in court and was outlawed it was common to join in with other like-minded individuals for mutual protection and potential lucre. For example, the fourteenth-century Coterel gang was made up of James and his two brothers along with a handful of locals, reaching its apogee at perhaps twenty men. According to one study of criminality during this period, most gangs had a nucleus of six, often related men, who combined with other groups for mutual protection. In an era before organized policing, the best that the English crown could hope for in many cases was to allow gangs and their leaders to purchase pardons through cash or some type of service.[19]

When it comes to the stereotypical outlaw, English common law has given birth to its fair share of exemplars, from Robin Hood to Dick Turpin. For many chroniclers, highway robbery was 'perhaps the most colorful crime in the later Middle Ages', summoning up images of 'noble robbers' and 'Merry Men'. In reality the actual practitioners of this form of criminality were rarely 'merry men', and were probably more likely to be loathsome killers. Highwaymen usually operated in a selected locality, a comfort zone if you will, typically favouring stretches of roads notable for providing cover for ambush and retreat.[20] English highway-men typically operated on horseback and wore masks during their robberies. Sources claim they killed less than their horseless counterparts because they could quickly escape. Among the best known was Dick Turpin (bap. 1705–1739). Mounting the gallows steps just outside the town of York he bowed to the vast crowd of witnesses 'with the most astonishing indifference and intrepidity'. After a brief talk with his exe-cutioner, Turpin presented him with a small ivory whistle to remember him by. Without waiting for the cart to be drawn from under him as he stood resolute with his neck in a noose, Turpin flung himself from the ladder and died instantly, preferable to a slow strangulation as the rope took his weight.[21]

Highwaymen were comfortable plying the roads leading to and from large cities where victims were numerous and more prosperous than the village- and farm-bound peasants. Highway robbery flourished in England as in no other country in the seventeenth and eighteenth centuries. During this era England was still without anything resembling a professional police force; while Continental countries embraced military patrols or national gendarmerie to keep the peace on rural roads, the English traditionally saw this as a threat to liberty. Furthermore, the high cost of maintaining it in a way similar to a standing army was not regarded as cost effective. So for protection England relied on time-tested amateur local bodies such as ineffective constables, beadles and nightwatchmen, much as it had in previous centuries. By the end of the seventeenth century, lone highwaymen as well as gangs infested the roads, holding up middle-class merchants and wealthy aristocrats, farmers going to market and even solitary pedlars, prefacing their actions with the fabled 'stand and deliver', or the less fabled 'your money or your life'. The opiate-addled writer Thomas De Quincey (1785–1859) would later comment that the profession of highwayman 'required more accomplishments than either the bar or the pulpit, since it presumed a bountiful endowment of qualifications'.[22]

Beginning in 1658, when the first public stagecoaches began delivering mail and valuables on the highways leading in and out of London, bandits found financial opportunities bountiful. It was not uncommon for local innkeepers to conspire with outlaws for a share of the loot. The era of the English highwayman peaked between the second half of the seventeenth century and the early eighteenth, a time of abject poverty and subsistence living for many British families and shortly before the birth of more effective policing in the guise of the Bow Street Horse Patrol (1805) and Sir Robert Peel's Metropolitan Police (1829). By the end of the 1700s, roads were becoming much improved, faster and safer. In addition, the government stopped authorizing inns that were known to harbour outlaws along the toll roads outside London.

The eighteenth century might have been an 'age of highwaymen' but it was also an age of hanging. Lest anyone forget the ultimate penalty for highway robbery, there were constant grim reminders such as the one described by the noted diarist Samuel Pepys, who recounted his run-in with a hanging corpse while riding along the Diver Road on 11 April 1661, describing his ride 'under the man that hangs upon Shooter's Hill, and a filthy sight it is to see his flesh is shrunk to his bones'.[23] But this was just part of an age-old tradition, in which the more nefarious would be gibbeted post-execution, their body coated in tar for preservation and then hung in chains near the site of their crimes as a warning to others.

London's most prominent criminal of the first half of the eighteenth century was Jonathan Wild (c. 1682–1725). During the last decade of his life he dominated the underworld like no other of his time as a fence extraordinaire who would restore stolen property to its original owners for rewards. During a previous four-year stint in a debtor's jail, he learned the vagaries of the criminal underworld. Released in 1712, he subsequently ran a brothel and furthered his criminal education as he became well acquainted with the methods of robber gangs, whose members indulged at his establishment. Wild soon found that the major problem with stealing valuables was disposing of them and making a profit, and so began his career as a fence. He soon advertised his new business and victims of recent robberies lined up for his services. Taking stock of stolen valuables, Wild used his vast underworld connections to locate the thieves, so that he could return cherished items to their proper owners and collect promised rewards, an enterprise that would take him to the top of the London underworld for almost a decade. His near-universal knowledge of criminal activity gave him enormous power, which he manipulated for his own good. Parliament reacted in 1717 by passing legislation making it a capital offence to take a reward under the pretence of helping an owner retrieve stolen goods; the original thief was not prosecuted under the law. Entitled the Receiving Act of 1717,[24] it was conceived with Wild in mind, so it was only natural that it was commonly referred to as the 'Jonathan Wild Act'.

During the London crime wave of the 1720s, most powerful criminals were able to bribe their way out of prosecution. In response, the government began paying rewards for the capture of robbers. Well versed in the trade of receiving stolen goods, Wild set up an office near the Old Bailey where he represented himself as an agent between thieves and their victims. He exploited the law to the fullest and created a posse of thief catchers. Some historians have had the temerity to suggest Wild's business was a precursor to modern policing. As the self-proclaimed 'Thief-Taker General' he became the most efficient gangbuster in England. The writer Sir Henry Fielding even suggested: 'Nature intended Jonathan Wild for a sleuth, and had he been born two centuries later it is probable that he would have won a responsible position at Scotland Yard.'[25] Perhaps he was a man before his time, but in reality Wild had merely refined a system conjured up in the previous century by Moll Cutpurse (Mary Frith[26]) that involved selling stolen goods back to their original owners, who usually paid an inflated price for the return of their personal property. But Wild went a step further, by posing as a private thief-taker who went after offenders to later collect a reward once the objects were returned. He then organized a band of thieves whom he directed in his various schemes. Any thief who had the audacity to compete with him quickly found himself arrested and soon executed, since anti-thief-taker legislation in 1717 made theft a capital crime. Apparently highwaymen gave London a wide berth between 1723 and 1725, since none were hanged at the Tyburn Tree during this time. Despite supporters who claimed he helped control the gang problem, Wild joined his competitors on the gallows in 1725 after one of his accomplices turned on him.

European Outlaws

The European continent has endured centuries of conditions conducive to outlaw activity, often accompanied by political upheaval. During the late fourteenth century it was visited by pandemic disease, famine, wars and peasant uprisings, which often crippled local governments and feudal regimes. Lawlessness, together with extreme poverty and hardship, demoralized entire communities. This, combined with agrarian distress, unfair taxation and class resentment, provoked social unrest. However, no matter the posture assumed by outlaw bands – social bandit, gentleman of the road or common criminal – the vast majority here and elsewhere remained part and parcel of a common criminal milieu that banded together for selfish goals and for protection from the gallows that surely awaited them when caught. For most of Europe, this scourge would finally be resolved by the development of strong administrative governments, the tightening of borders between states, harsher penalties and improved rural policing supported by local communities. But most countries would have to wait until the nineteenth century for this.

Compared to their common-law counterparts in North America, Britain and Australia, Continental European gangs were typically larger, more isolated from organized society and at times even potent enough to challenge weak and unstable governments. In parts of Italy and Spain during the sixteenth century they sometimes held greater power than regional governments, in large part due to the fact that the nobility were often in cahoots with them as a strategy to protect their parochial feudal interests from the machinations of a developing state apparatus.

Initially the term *bandito* referred to Italian outlaws and was later extended to include large criminal gangs in war-stricken areas. Similarly, the word *brigante* meant a partisan or irregular soldier, but was also identified with sixteenth-century Italian bandits, who were among the most accomplished in Europe. In fact, by 1860 two-thirds of the Italian military was tasked with controlling banditry in the south, mostly in Calabria and Apulia, as well as the islands of Sicily and Corsica. All offered the requisite mountainous and rugged terrain that allowed them to become the most prominent and successful examples of long-term European banditry, especially in the eighteenth century when taxation was prohibitive and land tenure almost impossible for poor farmers. This was also magnified by the fact that common people in Sicily and elsewhere felt little allegiance to central governments that were remote and unsympathetic.

AN EYE FOR AN EYE

Italy was divided into a number of separate small papal states, which made it easier for bandits to slip across borders for jurisdictional protection until the mid-nineteenth century. What made the Italian outlaws so formidable in the years before national unity was the support and shelter supplied by feudal nobles, who acted as bandit lords. Numerous attempts were made by the government to suppress this scourge. Near sixteenth-century Naples, authorities burned large areas of bushes and trees to remove natural cover. At other times weapons bans were implemented. However, as the forces of law and order began to get the upper hand, bandits made the mistake of attacking peasants, thereby losing their vaunted support and protection. Nonetheless, it was impossible to totally eradicate this problem, since poor farmers and others made a living selling them food and supplies, while other corrupt individuals continued to protect them.

Banditry in Spain was mostly confined to the mountainous regions of Catalonia in the northeast and to the south below the Sierra Morena mountains. In both areas the rural nobility played a role. Late sixteenth-century Catalonia was the scene of brutal peasant repression as bandit gangs raided the estates of wealthy landowners. Among those who achieved hero status was Perot Rocaguinarda, thanks in part to Miguel de Cervantes who modelled his Roque Guinart after him in the second part of *Don Quixote*. Unlike many of his counterparts, Rocaguinarda lived to receive a pardon on the condition he fought in the army in Italy.[27]

During the mid-eighteenth century, Corsican bandits proliferated in part due to the struggle against the Genoese, and featured prominently in the resistance against French rule during the Revolutionary and Napoleonic eras. These gangs shared with others the propensity to develop in times of political crisis and government weakness. In response, the government turned to a variety of measures such as setting up the Voltigeurs Corses to track them down in 1822, and weapons' bans.[28] This police group reached 1,000 members before it was disbanded as government officials turned to more localized bandit hunting groups and later more military-oriented strategies using gendarmes and soldiers.[29]

Among the many avenues leading to banditry was resisting conscription and deserting from the army. Teodoro Poli, 'the Robin Hood of Corsica', notably took this route in 1821 after killing a local officer who tried to apprehend him for evading the draft. Still others were attracted by the lifestyle, fame, power or in the defence of family honour. In the case of Poli, he came from one of the richest families in the region, but his followers were overwhelmingly poor herdsmen, artisans, labourers, muleteers and from other less elevated occupations. This further demonstrates how local banditry was often used as a weapon in local power struggles by both the poor and the wealthy. Except during times of national crisis, such as French invasion, gangs typically averaged about six men, and rarely more than twelve. By the early twentieth century the noble bandit was a thing of the past. As one Corsican subprefect lamented in 1896, 'Today the situation is quite different. The bandit has become an ordinary malefactor, a brigand who holds up mail coaches, robs travellers and lives from theft and rapine.'[30]

In France the highwayman Louis Dominique Bourguignon (1693–1721), better known by his moniker 'Cartouche', or 'the Cartridge', plagued commerce to such an extent that his nickname would become shorthand for 'highwayman', but not until after he was sentenced to be skinned alive and broken on the wheel in 1721. Conforming more to the 'social bandit' motif was the brigand Louis Mandrin (1725–1755), who left the army for a life of extortion, murder and smuggling. He was well versed in the highway life, having served as a tax collector; he knew which strategies to employ when robbing tax collectors or smuggling large caches of untaxed tobacco and cheap textiles across the French border. He was said to command 500 men at one time, and enjoyed success only with the support of local peasants. In response, a *maréchaussée* (mounted constabulary or gendarmerie) was formed. But with only 3,000 constables to cover all of France it was of limited assistance to local officials. However, when they did catch a bandit leader, the sentence was usually to be broken on the wheel, but not before the convict carried a banner to his place of execution, proclaiming in large letters his role as 'Leader of Smugglers, Treasonous Persons, Assassins, Thieves and Disturbers of the Peace'. Towards the end of the eighteenth century, while the French government was in the throes of the Reign of Terror, there was still a paucity of police to deal with the growing number of outlaw gangs, and those who were not executed were sentenced to the galleys.

Germany was plagued by inadequate policing to meet the outlaw problem through much of the late sixteenth century and early seventeenth. In succeeding years Johannes Bückler, alias 'Schinderhannes', or 'Hans the Skinner', earned a nefarious reputation for robbing Jews. In the early nineteenth century a criminal judge in the province of Upper Hesse identified some of the same criteria used to measure modern organized crime gangs, noting that crooks 'are people who make a trade of robbery and theft and, by using this trade to their advantage, develop their own rituals and language. All those who adopt the same philosophy of life and rituals are their allies and the cant is the tool that helps them to recognize each other.'[31] Contrary to popular conceptions, Jewish and Gypsy bandits were sometimes on the receiving end when it came to highway robbery, especially in Germany and the Netherlands from the late seventeenth century until the end of the eighteenth.[32] Their involvement fits the Hobsbawmian paradigm which asserts that criminal robbers can be distinguished from social bandits 'by their composition and their mode of operation' and 'are likely to consist of members of criminal tribes and castes, or individuals from outcast groups'.[33] One of the better-known gangs was the Grosse Niederländer (Great Dutch), composed mostly of Jews. According to one authority on German outlaws, this phenomenon can be explained by the fact that in previous eras the Jewish social system had been able to take care of its own destitute, but the system collapsed when overwhelmed by an avalanche of refugees expelled from Eastern Europe after the 1648 Cossack rebellion in Poland. As a result of this onslaught, Jewish paupers and vagrants began travelling in groups from one community to another.

Likewise, Roma people, who were even more ostracized than the Jews, formed gangs as well. Prohibited from living in or passing through most communities on threat of death, the Roma sometimes formed gangs for self-protection. One of the best known was the Grosse Galantho gang in the 1720s. In 1728 it was brought to bay and the members, including women, were either broken on the wheel, hanged or beheaded.[34] Ultimately, these gangs more often resembled forms of 'temporary companionship' rather than organized criminality. Lacking elaborate rules, formal organization and a permanent leader these groups were often flexible and operated on an irregular basis.[35] Some of these gangs operated in particular vicinities where they could depend on some local support, while by contrast it was not unheard of for Jewish gangs to strike hundreds of miles away. If one thing is clear about these 'non-traditional' bandit groups, it is that their activities and modes of behaviour varied widely. Like criminal gangs and subcultures, they often had secret modes of communication (gestures, sounds, hand movements) that gave them safe passage in certain communities.

Eastern Europe had its share of outlaw gangs, especially in the mountainous Balkan region. Before his execution in 1925, the Serbian outlaw Jovo Stanisavljević, known as Čaruga, earned the reputation as the 'Robin Hood of Yugoslavia'. He escaped prison and joined a gang of military deserters turned outlaws known as the *kolo gorskih tića*, or 'mountain birds', as they robbed and killed without mercy, until Čaruga was hunted down and hanged by the Austro-Hungarian Army in 1925. Perhaps one of the best-known criminals from the region was Juraj Jánošík (1688–1713), who was born in Slovakia when it was still in the grips of medievalism, ruled by a feudal aristocracy and corrupt justice system. The region had long been a breeding ground for outlaws. Jánošík quit the army to join a band of bandits roaming the Carpathians, robbing and murdering, until he was captured and hanged in 1713. This only further contributed to his continued stature in Slovakian folk history.

American Bandit Traditions

Hobsbawm asserted early on that episodes in banditry seem most likely to occur when a traditional social equilibrium is upset 'during and after periods of abnormal hardship such as famine or wars, or at the moments when the jaws of the dynamic modern world seize the static communities in order to destroy and transform them'.[36] This was especially true in America in the aftermath of both the Civil War and the First World War. For a relatively young country, America has had more than its share of outlaw gangs. The best known appeared in the aftermath of the Civil War, when the country still remained highly politicized over the recent sectional conflict. One important study has linked the various outlaw gangs and famous gunfighters to their political allegiances as either loyal Republicans (who had supported the North), or Democrats (who favoured the Confederacy). When it came to post-war conflict, the Republican affiliated factions were less likely to be branded as outlaws or bandits, and were more associated with what one historian has labelled 'the conservative forces consolidating the authority interest of property, order and law',[37] a trend general in late nineteenth-century America. This faction was best represented by vigilantes and lawmen such as Wyatt Earp, Pat Garrett and James Butler Hickok, better known as 'Wild Bill'. On the other hand were the 'dissident resisters' of western incorporation and supporters of the Lost Cause of the Confederacy, who were best exemplified by Hobsbawmian 'social bandits' such as Jesse James and Billy 'the Kid' Bonney. American historian Richard Maxwell Brown has called this the 'Western Civil War of Incorporation', according to which members of outlaw gangs were more often than not resisting 'civilization'. They opposed the dominant trend in society towards an emerging class structure that favoured a growing elite and rapidly rising middle class represented by professional men, ranchers, farmers and others who threatened the 'traditional values' of a rural pastoral culture. The James brothers, Younger brothers and other former Confederate guerrillas became heroes to many Democratic- and Confederate-minded people that were alienated by the 'incorporation process stressing the aggregation of wealth, consolidation of capital and centralizing of authority at all levels of authority'.[38]

Bandit gangs appeared in a variety of incarnations during the middle decades of the nineteenth century, ranging from rebel guerrilla gangs in Missouri and Kansas to cowboys and farmhands-turned-badmen in rural Texas and Oklahoma. In 1866, the year after the war ended, America experienced its first organized bank robbery, when ex-Confederates led by brothers Jesse and Frank James robbed a bank in Liberty, Missouri. By most accounts, bank robbery was the ultimate form of protest. It was easy to link the bank owners who cheated customers with the railroad magnates who had a hand in fencing off grazing lands to construct train lines across cattle country. Both economic symbols were targeted by robber bands during the post-Civil War era. Over the next fifteen years the 'glamorous' James Gang inspired other former guerrilla fighters, including the Daltons, the Doolins, the Hole-in-the-Wall Gang and many others. However, the Hobsbawm thesis begins to unravel when applied to the James Gang. After studying the legends and heroes in mostly peasant or agricultural economies, Hobsbawm suggested that his so-called 'social bandits' should not be considered criminals, because they were engaged in a legitimate struggle against injustice and oppression on behalf of peasants against the wealthy and powerful interests that bound them to the land – but, as for the James Gang, the social bandit thesis 'tends to break down when measured by specific examples'. Nowhere was this truer than in the nineteenth-century United States where 'there were no American peasants to champion'. Furthermore, both the outlaws and their supporters 'came from modern, market-oriented groups and not from poor traditional groups.'[39]

The admiration for these nineteenth-century bandits would carry well into the twentieth century in a number of southern and border states as these regions went through economic downturns and social upheaval. As the frontier continued to shrink in the new century the number of bank and armed robberies plummeted until the 1920s and '30s, when bad economic times left a generation of desperate, unemployed young men. However, a series of particularly brutal killings caused a public backlash against these malefactors, even among their agrarian supporters.

Until the 1930s American bandit gangs took advantage of the lack of federal policing, due to the fact that few crimes were federal ones. With the added benefits of the automobile and the Thompson sub-machine gun, gangsters took advantage of the lack of state police forces and coordination between police jurisdictions. However, this would unwittingly lead to the expansion of federal law enforcement, as the majority of Americans supported new federal crime statutes and the elimination of what in the previous century would have been considered agrarian social bandits. In quick succession a variety of law enforcement efforts led to the killings of John Dillinger, Pretty Boy Floyd, Bonnie and Clyde, Baby Face Nelson and others.[40]

Gold Strikes and Boomtowns

The search for precious metals and subsequent gold strikes and diamond finds often stimulated bandit activity in regions with ineffective law enforcement, whether in the South African Transvaal, the American West or Australia. In South Africa, Scotty Smith led a local gang that took advantage of gold and diamond booms, periods when there was a rare chance for substantial lucre. Smith was born in 1845, he claimed in Perth, Australia, and ended up fighting in the 1877 Kaffir War before cashiering out to steal horses and rob banks. It wasn't much of a stretch to reach into gold and diamond theft.

Joaquin Murrieta became America's most famous Hispanic outlaw and one of its most notorious during California's mid-nineteenth-century Gold Rush. Murrieta's star rose at a time when much of the California coastal region was beset by lawlessness as 'hordes of Hispanic outlaws ravaged the countryside'. Murrieta's story, like those of many of his ilk, was mostly speculative, thanks to a healthy dose of mythmaking and popular lore. Born in Sonora, Mexico, in 1830, he apparently reached North America after the 1848 discovery of gold in California. Popular legend has it that he developed a hatred for Anglo miners after being mistreated. However, recent research asserts that Murrieta never led a regular organized gang, and 'like most outlaw gangs', he and his followers usually 'acted on impulse and opportunity'.[41] No social bandit here. In any case, the backdrop for such activity was ripe, since the 'Gold Rush had uprooted many Hispanics from their traditional rural families, away from the stabilizing influence of home and family, and landed them on a rough frontier where riches were everywhere and Hispanics systematically excluded'.[42] Some of the stories of Murrieta's activities have been called into question by researchers, including one who noted that of Murrieta's 24 victims, nineteen were from the Chinese minority, and that rather than leading a band of hundreds, he never commanded more than eleven men. Writing in the late nineteenth century, one California peace officer described Murrieta's gang as composed of Mexican outlaws, cut-throats and thieves, who had the run of the country from San Diego north to the Gold country. However, the writer turns to hyperbole, suggesting that 'in any other country other than America' the operations of Murrieta's gang 'would have been dignified by the title of revolution, and the leader with that of rebel chief'.[43] However, close reading of his exploits in the era leading up to his death in 1853 points to him being a run-of-the-mill opportunistic horse thief, who when he wasn't targeting docile Chinese miners, whom he probably viewed as easy prey, or lone Anglo travellers, was robbing Mexican ranches.[44]

The bandits or 'bushrangers' of Australia's gold rush era were known as the 'wild colonial boys'. They were distinct from earlier incarnations of the Australian outlaw for their sartorial improvements and healthier countenance. Prior exemplars of the tradition had begun their criminal careers after having endured years on prison hulks and English jails before fleeing into the bush. Unafraid of the police, this new breed of freemen became bushrangers by choice. The 1851 gold strikes in New South Wales simply offered new sources of plunder. Better armed and mounted than the earlier 'bolter' prototypes, who were escaped convicts and military deserters in the 1830s, the bushrangers were also better rewarded in terms of plunder.

Mexico and Latin America

Prior to independence in 1821, there were few problems with banditry in colonial Mexico. As long as property was well distributed among the peasants, banditry remained relatively absent in certain communities. But, beginning in the 1850s, Mexico was beset by a variety of bandit gangs due in no small part to the economic upheavals of the era, which ranged from traditional village feuds to the seasonal nature of parts of the Mexican economy. With no effective federal police force it was often up to the majordomos of haciendas to furnish weapons and effective protection to local peasants. Best known and most feared during the period 1857–67 were the Plateados of Morelos, recognizable for their ornate outfits incorporating a gaudy display of silver – silver spurs, guns, machetes, saddles and buttons – hence their reputation as the 'Silver Ones', literally *plateados*. While they did not consider themselves bandits, these 'dandified' outlaws certainly acted the part. Pity the poor penniless victim waylaid by bandits; one bandit gang from this era posted a message in Mexico City warning that any traveller who did not have at least twelve pesos should expect to be severely beaten. As previously noted, outlaws often came from the ranks of cashiered troops. Some of the Mexican bandits had formerly served in the volunteer army, only turning to brigandage during an 1860 campaign when they felt slighted by their miserly remuneration, plundering unprotected haciendas and villages.[45]

Brazil made one of the best-known contributions to the Latin American outlaw tradition through the activities of the Cangaceiros. Like the Mexican Plateados they were not above entering contracts with politicians and landlords to provide mutually beneficial services. Their field of activity embraced the northeast region where 'agrarian decay weakened the old power blocks and stimulated social competition', instead of the south, which was dominated by a strong centralist government.[46] Cangaceiro recruits were often a sordid lot, comprising army deserters and escaped convicts, those looking for adventure, opportunists, those ostracized by their family and disgruntled peons. None matched the prominence of Lampião, 'the Lantern', who won his moniker for shooting off his firearms in such quick succession that the flashing powder lit up his silhouette. Born Virgulino Ferreira da Silva (1898–1938), his was a classic tale: living a law-abiding life, he pulled himself out of peasant poverty to become a leather artisan by 1919; he turned to violence only after his father was killed in a local feud. According to his biographer, Lampião was not so much against the reigning social order as seeking a place in it as either a businessman or rancher.[47] He avenged the murder and took exile as an outlaw for the last twenty years of his life. He led a Cangaço gang over seven states, torching towns and farms, while engaging in cattle theft, rape and murder. Silva was hunted down and killed along with ten others; all were beheaded to serve as identification. His rise and fall had much in common with similar gangs such as those led by bandit chieftains Antônio Silvino 'Sinhô' Pereira, especially when it came to administering justice. It was rare in an agrarian setting for a bandit leader to get a trial or access to the protections of the criminal justice system.

Thuggee and Dacoity

Over the centuries, India has been home to some of the world's most storied forms of banditry, including the Pindaris, Thugs and Kanjars.[48] From early Sanskrit hymns compiled in the Vedas around 1000 BC, highwaymen and thieves have been a feature of daily life in the Indian subcontinent. In ancient India, the Rigveda mentions the Dasyus, who robbed the rich with a heavy dose of violence. The British had been in India since 1615 setting up a network of trading privileges. As far back as the 1660s one British merchant was forced to employ 50 soldiers to protect his caravan since 'the country is so full of outlaws and thieves that a man cannot stir out of doors without great forces.'[49] By the mid-eighteenth century, banditry was common throughout the entire Indian subcontinent. Of the thousands that survived in this manner most were dacoits, that is, 'members of well-disciplined gangs of thieves, who robbed merchants and operated out of towns and villages'.[50] The much-feared bandits of the Bundelkhand and the Chambal Valley of central India carried on well into the twentieth century. In addition to looting, arson and murder, these home-grown bands have been connected to a variety of repugnant crimes. Harjan Singh, killed in 1939, was known to castrate men, while Batri, who was eliminated in 1930, and Gabbar in 1959, would chop off the noses of victims. Hazuri, who met his demise in 1958, raped women, while Lal Singh, killed the following year, preferred beheading victims.[51]

At the end of the Mughal dynasty (1526–1707) ferocious bands of Pindaris, literally referring to 'plunder by a mounted horde of freebooters', ravaged parts of central India, undertaking looting expeditions that ranged up to 500 miles from their home bases. Bearing bamboo spears and sometimes guns, the very mention of their arrival foreshadowed devastation of villages, rapine and murder. One 1907 observer recounted,

> The horrors perpetrated by these demons at other places made the poor villagers, totally unarmed and incapable of resistance, fly to the desperate resolution of burning themselves with their wives and children. All the young girls are carried off by the Pindaris, tied three or four like calves on a horse, to be sold.[52]

Indian banditry grabbed the world's attention beginning in the early years of the nineteenth century as Britain expanded its control over the subcontinent. As early as the late eighteenth century,[53] soldiers and officials of the Crown became privy to the existence of gangs of stranglers that seemed to operate unimpeded in numerous locales. It was not until the British surgeon Dr Richard C. Sherwood gathered insight from Thug informers and published an article about the secret brotherhood of murderers in 1816, that British officials put together a game plan to suppress what they called the Phansigars, or 'Stranglers' (*phansi* is Hindustani for noose; in northern India they were called Thugs, or 'Deceivers'). What made this phenomenon so successful was the protection they could count on from local rulers in exchange for a percentage of their stolen loot. Early on they recognized that as long as they refrained from killing Europeans they would evade retribution, but their distinct methods of killing would not hide them for ever.

If one was to believe the traditional interpretations of Thug history, it was one of the world's longest-lasting criminal gangs. The earliest mention of this phenomenon dates back to the thirteenth-century writings of a Delhi sultan; Thuggee was probably well established by then. Members were both Hindu and Muslim. They travelled in bands and preyed on other travellers, whom they strangled. This menace represents the darker side of earlier criminal organizations. There are no ballads or folk tales to herald their deeds. Thugs came to prominence for their distinct methods of operation. According to the traditional view, 'the *phasidars*, or "noose holders", were unusual' for their invariable method of killing by strangling with a yellow scarf (or *roomal*) and always murdering before robbing victims.[54] Typically, for each victim it took two to three Phasidars to complete the killing, two to hold each end of the scarf around the target's neck and a third to pull the legs out from under him. As groups of Thugs insinuated themselves into travelling caravans each member of the group played a role. For example there was the conman or inveigler (*sotha*), strangler (*bhuttote*) and grave digger (*lugha*).[55]

There is still a lack of consensus about the Thugs and their activities.[56] By most accounts, the earliest European perceptions were influenced by the 1839 publication of *Confessions of a Thug*, by the British author Philip Meadows Taylor. Purportedly based on documentary evidence and his first-hand experience investigating these gangs as Superintendent of Police in India in the 1820s, this novel offers penetrating insight into the Thug phenomenon. Along with Rudyard Kipling's *Kim* (1901), it was one of the most influential novels about India, and one of the best-selling crime novels of the nineteenth century.[57] During the latter half of the nineteenth century it was readily accepted that Thugs comprised a hereditary fraternity dedicated to killing by strangulation without shedding blood. Over ensuing decades the perception was held that for over 700 years they were responsible for up to 50,000 murders a year. Late-twentieth-century revisionists have suggested that the existence of the traditional view of the Thugs was highly exaggerated and that they were no more than gangs of ordinary bandits, thieves and rebels challenging British hegemony on the subcontinent. The revisionists score some points insisting that since it had no central organization, hierarchy or boss, that Thuggee was not organized crime, nor, say some, was it a religious cult since the gangs did not utilize specific religious texts or agreed forms of worship. Some historians suggest early investigators misinterpreted conversations with captured Thugs and that this, combined with prejudice against Hinduism, textured many of the accounts.[58]

William Sleeman, a British Army official and the eventual nemesis of this scourge, had read Sherwood's findings and, with no police presence outside British possessions, had to create his own police network while obtaining permission from local courts to try criminals from other districts. Writing in 1843, Sleeman stated that Thugs lived and behaved in homes like other docile villagers until it was time to go out on a mission, when together they morphed into a secret fraternity. Over the years a whole subculture evolved with distinctive belief patterns, macabre rituals, argot and modes of behaviour. Thug groups operated on roads and pathways, befriending unwary travellers on the road or at roadside inns. At the appointed place they would pounce on victims, garrotting them in a flash of 'swift and well-practised motions'. Graves were often dug in advance and the dead were buried dozens at a time, as the attackers collected their booty and vanished, leaving behind few traces.

More recently, Thug chronicler Kevin Rushby noted that the British played an unwitting role in the lucrative activities of Thugs and other bandits through their support of the opium trade between the poppy fields of Bengal and the Chinese market. Production multiplied in the first decade of the nineteenth century as farmers made up for their other crop failures by planting the always profitable poppy. Meanwhile, Bombay merchants sent vast sums of money, gold and jewels ahead to buy the product in advance through traditional treasure carriers during the same time of year, making mid-October the Thug's hunting season. However, Rushby argues that the Thugs were little more than bands of 'freebooters' created by British conquests and the concomitant development of the opium trade.[59]

In 1933, William Sleeman's grandson James L. Sleeman estimated that a typical Thug strangled eight men per month and usually was active for twenty years. He calculated that if one was to consider all the Thugs active in India from their emergence until their demise in the 1840s, they would be conservatively estimated to have been responsible for 1 million murders, most committed using a pocket handkerchief. According to the *Guinness World Records* one Thug murdered 931 people, by his own testimony.[60] Beginning in the 1950s, the authenticity of these accounts came under scrutiny by revisionist scholars. Some saw the thugs as simple bandits with 'no fixed modus operandi, who had been given the label "Thug" by their British captors', while others were inclined to regard them as ordinary criminals, often 'the product of British dominion in India', and that rather than murderers they were more likely to be 'soldiers thrown out of work by the imposition of *Pax Britannica* on the Subcontinent'.[61] Most of the evidence used against the accused Thugs at court was derived from the testimony of cooperating witnesses, or 'approvers', and the use of what were virtually kangaroo courts. Ultimately, approvers were pardoned for their cooperation, while those convicted were either executed or imprisoned. Of the 3,689 tried before 1840, 466 were hanged, 56 pardoned and most of the others transported to the Andaman Islands or imprisoned for life.[62] Some Thugs became informers to avoid execution or transportation, where they were tattooed below their eyes with the word 'Thug'.

Indian banditry did not disappear with the British dissolution of the Thugs. After the Pindari and Thug gangs had been eradicated, official focus turned to various major dacoit gangs. Bands of armed bandits, dacoits followed in the footsteps of the Thugs. In 1889, one observer described the dacoit as

> a member of an organised gang, armed with sword or blunderbuss and working generally by torchlight but occasionally also in the day-time. The gang is headed by a known leader of approved merit in his profession. Occasional members may be admitted, or even pressed into service, for an expedition or two, but the regular members look upon dacoity as their permanent calling, which they ply as occasion offers from the time the rains cease until the rainy season recommences.[63]

As the nineteenth century gathered steam these gangs revved up their firepower, adding percussion muskets and French rifles (*fusils*) to their arsenals of *lathi* batons, swords, spears and *pharsas* (a sharp-edged baton, sometimes a battle-axe). But, unlike the American and Australian outlaw gangs of this era, they rarely engaged the police in battle, preferring to loot, kill and burn villages. Until the 1970s the Bundelkhand and Chambal Valley in central India had been identified with the dacoity problem, which persisted until 1972, when hundreds surrendered en masse. According to one expert, dacoity was merely 'a historical continuation of group behavior' dating back centuries to the princes uprooted by feudal struggles or foreign invasions.[64] Others point to India's topography being highly favourable to bandits on the run, with winding hills, rivers and tropical vegetation. Still others insist dacoity resulted from the social tension created by caste cleavages and political strife, and other sources of frustration caused by economic travails.

Over the past 200 years a host of Indian bandits captured the attention of authorities and the public, usually on the regional level, but sometimes internationally. Koose Muniswamy Veerappan (1952–2004), linked to at least 100 killings, was the country's most wanted bandit of the twentieth century. He had started out smuggling sandalwood and killing elephants for their ivory before branching out into murder, extortion and kidnapping. Crafting a Robin Hood-type image, Veerappan enjoyed the support of poor villagers, who resented official interference in local smuggling and poaching operations. Joining a neighbouring gang of poachers while still in his teens, he was arrested in 1986 but paid a $2,000 bribe to be freed, and swore that from that day on he would not be taken alive again. He pursued a special vendetta against forest rangers, whom he felt oppressed villagers and hindered the poaching of elephants and the illicit logging of sandalwood. At his apogee in the early 1990s he had vanquished his rivals and controlled 3,600 square miles in southeast Mysore. He found the kidnapping of prominent people to be a most lucrative endeavour, particularly when he kidnapped Bollywood's reigning star, Rajkumar, for 109 days beginning in July 2010. In return he demanded a pardon, in hope of entering politics, like the notorious female bandit leader Phoolan Devi (1963–2001), the renowned 'Bandit Queen'.

Devi had been born into a poor low-caste (Mallah, boatmen) family in the northern Indian state of Uttar Pradesh. Married off at eleven, beaten and molested, she returned to her family but was sent back to live with her husband and his new wife and subjected to worse treatment. Her family became involved in a conflict with richer relatives over family land, but was able to escape by joining a bandit gang led by Babu

Singh, a low-caste member like Devi. They married and together formed a low-caste gang in the Chambal River valley. One of their ruses was to dress as members of the police to stop trucks and hijack them, and rob landowners. Unlike so many of her counterparts over the ages, Devi made sure to share her loot with villagers. She came close to meeting her demise when her gang was tricked into joining a higher-caste gang. Most of her fellow bandits were shot and killed and she was held hostage in the village of Behmai, where she was repeatedly raped. Devi escaped and joined a dacoit gang; she quickly became its leader and led it on numerous raids, looting bazaars and sharing the lucre with the poor, leading her, as a woman, to achieve Robin Hood-like status. In 1981 she led an attack on Behmai, the village where she had been raped, and took part in the killing of 22 upper-caste villagers. Devi managed to elude capture, despite the government's mobilization of thousands of police. In 1983 she laid down her arms and surrendered with her gang members, on the understanding that she would spend no longer than eight years in jail. Never tried in court, Devi was given an eleven-year sentence, and converted to Buddhism. In 1996 she parlayed her popularity to a seat in parliament, where she looked out for the interests of low-caste members of society. But in 2001 she was assassinated, some say by a higher-caste man from Behmai in revenge for the 1981 attack.[65]

Australian Bushrangers

Along with legions of convicts, Britain would also export its criminal traditions to Australia, as it did over the centuries to other far corners of the Empire, from the Americas to Australia and the African veld. None was more distinct than the tradition of the highway footpads and horsemen. The British transportation of convicts to Australia in the late eighteenth century created a carceral system in a wilderness that was easy to escape to – 'the hard thing was to survive.'[66] The Australian bushrangers often proved more violent and ruthless than their British highwaymen counterparts, due in no so small part to the fact that most were direct products of the convict colony.

The first stage of Australian bandit activity began at the end of 1790s, and included escaped convicts and military deserters. Those who could not escape by sea as stowaways or on rafts and hijacked vessels turned to banditry, better known in the parlance of the day as 'bolters'. These early purveyors of the bushranger tradition, regarded as outsiders, were feared as a violent menace by free settlers of the colony and thus never elicited the sympathy that the Australian-born convicts who followed would enjoy. Within a few years convicts tired of the lash and harsh regimen began escaping to the bush and other wide-open spaces that, despite the numerous natural obstacles, were preferable to the appalling conditions in the convict settlements. The early prison settlements were punitive experiments that brooked no resistance. Some who escaped attempted to live off the barren land and robbed free settlers for food and clothing. Most of the early convicts were Irish. The experience of the bolter James Barry is emblematic of the regime that led many to choose life in the bush over the penal system. Barry had been sentenced to 1,000 lashes after burgling a settler's home. He collapsed, near death, after the first 270 strokes. The remaining 730 were doled out in four instalments of 150, and one of 130. After the flogging, prisoners were either returned to their chores or were imprisoned on starvation rations.

Since prisoners substantially outnumbered troops and correctional officers, governors were often reduced to offering inducements for good behaviour such as free pardons and sometimes passage home; when that didn't work, clothes and barrels of rum were thrown in to sweeten the deal. When this didn't work a campaign by mounted police was initiated that sent many to the gallows. However, compared to the gallows fate of most highwaymen in England, the majority of captured bushrangers were spared execution and imprisoned instead.

By the early 1820s bushrangers were active throughout New South Wales, necessitating the establishment of a mounted police to counter the scourge. Paramilitary in spirit, this mounted police apparatus was regarded as 'only tolerably average' by one commanding officer. Similar to early police departments in London, New York City and elsewhere in the early nineteenth century, the police would often refuse to pursue criminals into the bush until they were 'worth catching'.[67] In response to the continuing lawlessness, smaller and better-policed penal settlements were established on Norfolk Island and Tasmania. In 1834 a Bushranging Act was passed requiring execution for crimes such as robbery or plundering houses with violence within 24 hours of conviction. This was repealed four years later, and the last hanging for robbery took place in 1839. The vast majority of convicts in 1841 had ten years of transportation added to their sentence. After ten years they could expect at least four years of hard labour on public works projects.

No other bushranger attained the prominence of the legendary Edward 'Ned' Kelly, often referred to as the 'Iron Bushranger' for the imaginative homemade body armour he wore. Unfortunately for Ned, his Achilles heel was his unprotected legs. In his final confrontation he was brought down by shotgun slugs to his legs. He recovered from his wounds, to be hanged on 11 November 1880 after being found guilty of wilful murder. His last words before the gallows trap was sprung were 'Such is life'. Kelly was the son of an Irish convict who served years in Van Diemen's Land (Tasmania) for stealing two pigs in Tipperary. His family lived on a remote property, where the Kellys apparently became involved in a conflict with powerful cattlemen; again we see the emergence of outlawry in response to the inequitable distribution of land. Kelly's almost pathological hatred for police was fed by the class antipathy between Catholics and Protestants: weaned on stories of Protestant abuse of Catholics back home in Ireland, he was one of many who believed that Irishmen could not expect justice, especially as long as the police were in the employ of powerful landowners.

However, Ned failed where so many other charismatic gang leaders did – by actually believing his media coverage and lapsing into delusions of grandeur. Despite all his press clippings and his many heroic or daring exploits, he was hanged as a common criminal at the age of 26. Like other regions undergoing the transition from frontier to civilization, the bushranging period would play out by the end of the nineteenth century as roads, railways, telegraph and telephone services reached the bush.

By the end of the nineteenth century a number of bushrangers had formed gangs adhering to the outlaw traditions. For almost a century the Australian bush would shelter a variety of criminal gangs who pillaged homesteads, stole cattle and horses while 'bailing up' travellers when holding up stagecoaches (bushrangers would demand: 'Bail Up!', an expression similar to 'Stand and Deliver!') and ambushing escorts delivering gold and other precious metals from the mines to the banks.

Summary

Organized criminal bands have emerged in various guises throughout much of the historical record, chiefly flourishing in pre-industrial societies and maintaining some form of support in rural districts rather than in the urban centres, which would become strongholds much later. Gangs of highway robbers, thief-taking networks and myriad examples of banditry were precursors to the more sophisticated, organized and international gangs that would follow. Criminal gangs and occasional solo operators established their operations as populations became more mobile and prosperous. Criminal bands were especially prevalent where the topography could be used for protection, especially in the aftermath of major civil and international conflicts. Their persistence was aided by the paucity of law enforcement, a characteristic of the pre-modern era. When this form of criminality emerged in England in the fourteenth century the criminal justice apparatus had begun to collapse because of the rivalry between the courts and local lords of the declining feudal system. Similar ecosystems developed in Slovakia in the 1700s, Greece in the 1890s, and Sicily in the 1950s, to name just a few. Likewise, when these gangs did exist, usually at times of dramatic modernization and social change, the individuals involved, once captured, were punished in what was often a very public display of brutality such as hanging or breaking on the wheel, thus assuring citizens that the forces of the nascent state would not allow lawbreaking. One of the most effective strategies of gang suppression that developed in response to horse-mounted bandits were the various incarnations of the mounted policing tradition, including the Bow Street Mounted Police, the Texas Rangers, New Mexico Mounted Police, the Mounted forces in Australia, and so forth.

The following chapter will chronicle the next stage in the development of organized criminality, contrasting sharply with the mostly local and regional activities of the gangs that dominate this chapter, with the transnational nature of pirates plying the high seas in the seventeenth century and continuing through the nineteenth and twentieth, as opportunities created by various prohibitions in the Western world gave rise to global drug traffickers, slave traders and other organized forms of crime.

6

Prohibitions, Pirates, Slave Traders, Drug Smugglers and the Internationalization of Criminality

The roots of international criminal networking can be traced to the activities of a variety of pre-modern smuggling groups that existed long before most present-day national boundaries were established. The classical overland trade route connecting ancient Byzantium to Rome through Greece and the Balkans into western Europe, for example, is still utilized by contemporary weapons and drug smugglers; likewise the 'amber route' connecting the Black Sea to the Baltic plays an integral role in smuggling and human traffic operations from China and other parts of Asia. In fact, as one American journalist noted in 1931,

> There is really nothing new about [organized crime]. Organized robber bands preyed on merchants in the past and exacted tribute from them. Pirates took their toll from commerce on the high seas. It is almost beyond belief, however, that in the present day the methods of the robber gangs can still be applied so successfully.[1]

The trailblazing Magellan circumnavigation of the world from 1619–22 would be followed by more and more innovations that cut sailing times even further. The rise of steam power at the end of the eighteenth century provided the next big technological leap in oceangoing technology. With steamships came a noticeable reduction in travel time. Shortening sailing time increased turnaround times, in the process intensifying global contacts between nation-states. Moreover, vessels were also increasing in size, leading to higher trade volume; it was only a matter of time before legitimate and illicit entrepreneurs were seeking and making fortunes at each step of the globalization process, making sea pirates, slave traders and contraband smugglers among the first international criminal entrepreneurs. Increasing contact between nations and territories on a global scale also meant that financial crime could be that much more rewarding, sparking the development of more sophisticated criminal entities, as illustrated by the successful pirate entrepreneurs on America's colonial eastern seaboard. What's more, advances in transportation meant that these criminal groups could react more quickly to changes in the marketplace whenever a new prohibition against a popular commodity offered new 'business' opportunities. Consorting with countless corrupt officials, underground economies and black markets became commonplace within and along national borders.

As nation-states increasingly turned to tariffs and taxation to fill the national treasuries and pay for armies abroad, smuggling operations became more and more lucrative. Attempting to avoid usurious taxes, and prior to offshore banking systems and money laundering, British colonists smuggled perhaps five-sixths of its tea into port along with other must-have products. Colonists were willing to follow British law up to a point, but when it came to free trade they essentially all but nullified existing laws and turned to smuggling ventures. By the mid-1700s the American colonies were home to a number of clandestine economies. Some made considerable fortunes smuggling Dutch linens and French brandies. By one estimate, colonial businessmen smuggled 2 million gallons of illegal molasses into ports between 1738 and the 1750s.

The illicit trade in humans, maritime piracy and the smuggling of mind- and mood-altering substances are some of the earliest exemplars of what criminologists now describe as 'transnational crime', better understood as crimes that involve 'two or more sovereign jurisdictions',[2] in that the activity takes place across or between national borders. For most of the historical record, crime was a local or regional concern, rather limited geographically and mostly a threat to communities from local malefactors, such as the horseback bandits and highwaymen of the previous chapter.

The commencement of the Industrial Revolution, first in England and then in other parts of the Western world saw rural peasants flock to newly urbanized settings in search of better opportunities and sustenance. This, together with developments in faster forms of transportation, hastened the development of longer-lasting and more efficient crime syndicates that allowed them 'to adapt to rapidly changing markets, consolidate their power, accumulate capital, expand from their orginal bases, and continue to operate in the modern world'.[3]

The First Drug Wars

Global crime networks owe a debt of gratitude to the attempts by the international community to foist prohibitions on certain commodities and behaviours. This is not a new phenomenon. The ubiquitous modern war on drugs, for example, is just the latest chapter in a crusade that has persisted for more than 600 years. Prior to the drug prohibition movements of the modern era, many countries were coming to terms with newly discovered psychoactive substances. In fact, over the centuries various cultures have had what one medical anthropologist labelled an 'inexplicable difficulty' in dealing with the introduction of 'peculiar substances'.[4] Overwhelmingly agrarian European societies were firmly entrenched in their 'patterns of consumption' of foreign products, comfortable with the familiar.[5] The age of exploration beginning in the late fifteenth century with the so-called 'Columbian Exchange' of foods, medicines and other products between the New and Old worlds dramatically challenged societies with routines and products that many saw as alien, therefore threatening to their longstanding cultural practices. Long before amphetamines, crack cocaine, heroin and other narcotics and purpose-made drugs were available, familiar modern culinary items such as coffee (from Ethiopia), chocolate (from Mexico) and tea (from China), along with tobacco and opiate products, were targeted with suspicion and in some cases criminalized by autocratic rulers. Everything from tobacco and snuff to chocolate and the coca leaf came under the inscrutable eyes of colonial authorities in Spain, France, England, the Dutch Republic and elsewhere. As early as 1569, King Phillip ii of Spain received a report from the Second Council of Lima stating, among other things, 'Coca is a thing without benefit and . . . takes the lives of many.'[6] While Spanish colonizers became well acquainted with coca in the sixteenth century, until their arrival it was actually used rather sparingly by the indigenous Incas, and mostly for medicinal and religious purposes. It was used to prevent altitude sickness and to avert hunger and fatigue among workers.

The story of tobacco and its road to societal acceptance, and its evolution from satanic to euphoric, is an instructive lesson for attempts to regulate popular substances through prohibition and criminalization. Among the most widely used drugs in the world today, tobacco and its related products have been targeted by numerous prohibitions over the centuries, with smokers sometimes facing severe penalties for indulging, as exemplified by a Chinese law of 1638, which ruled that decapitation was the penalty for using or distributing tobacco. But, with the arrival of the Manchu from northeastern China, and the subsequent founding of the Qing dynasty in 1644, their affinity for tobacco having already been well established in their native Manchuria, they not surprisingly supplanted prohibition with legalization; thus their familiarity with the product determined its acceptance. This contrasts sharply with the Russians in the first half of the seventeenth century, a time when smokers were persecuted with draconian sanctions, ranging from splitting the lips of smokers to flogging with a knout, and even castration; wealthier smokers got off slightly easier, exiled to the Siberian tundra and their property confiscated.[7] In the United States between 1895 and 1921, fourteen states prohibited tobacco sales due to health concerns related to smoking by women and children. But during the First World War the anti-smoking movement collapsed, probably due in large part to the popularity of smoking among soldiers and thus its temporary association with patriotism.

Botanically, although there are 64 species of *Nicotiana*, only two are smoked, and both *Nicotiana rustica* and *Nicotiana tabacum* originated in the Americas long before the North American continent was populated. It has been estimated it was first cultivated somewhere between 5000 and 3000 BC.[8] By the time Christopher Columbus reached the New World in 1492 it was being smoked throughout the richly populated Americas. The eventual spread of the tobacco habit to Spain resulted in the world's first recorded tobacco prohibition, when in 1588 a Church decree was issued in Lima that prohibited 'under penalty of eternal damnation for priests, about to administer the sacraments, either to take the smoke of . . . tobacco into the mouth, or the powder into the nose [snuff], even under the guise of medicine, before the service of the mass'.[9]

Tobacco use came in various forms, including the snorting of ground-up tobacco, which became known as snuff. It is believed that the indigenous people of Brazil were among the first to use it in this way. But, thanks in part to French court physicians impressed by its medicinal powers, the so-called 'powder habit' found a growing market among upmarket consumers. Small amounts of tobacco were initially imported from Cuba, until the appetite for it by Spanish and Portuguese seamen saw tobacco transported to a wider market. For a time, the retail price became so prohibitive that only the wealthy could afford to indulge. Nonetheless, the demand continued to rise, leading to its New World cultivation and transportation becoming an international business. Tobacco use found its adherents in Europe's Northern Lowlands and in the budding Italian and German states, with each country developing a characteristic use for the plant. The French, for example, adopted it to 'ward off illness and preserve beauty'.

When English mariners and heroic sea dogs popularized smoking, following ventures to America, this seemed to justify its consumption from the 'pleasure of the aromatic smoke'.[10] The English did not associate smoke with Satan as did the Catholic Spanish. The Elizabethan sea captain, privateer and slave trader Sir Francis Drake encountered tobacco during the second circumnavigation of the world in the late 1570s. The English had been at war with Spain since 1558, with much of the conflict taking place on the high seas from the coast of Europe to the New World. Without a colony in the Americas the English found it more convenient to rob galleons of tobacco than to grow it at first. Making use of their speedier ships, the British succeeded in carrying many a ship, looting tobacco along with gold ingots. From there the popularity of tobacco spread rapidly. By most accounts the English preference for the pipe over the cigar (which was the custom of the Spanish), mirrored the smoking practices of the indigenous tribes they made contact with in North America. Like many other new drugs and stimulants, its initial use made the transition from curiosity to craze. By the end of the sixteenth century, foreign visitors were commenting about the ubiquity of pipe smoking in social situations.

But not everyone favoured what would become known as the 'stinking weed' during the reign of King James I. Objections ranged from its smell and the expectoration of smokers to its association with fire and soot. Among the first to comment on its habit-forming properties (addiction was not yet understood) was Francis Bacon, who noted the ability of tobacco 'to control its users', commenting that 'in our time the use of tobacco is growing greatly and conquers men with a certain secret pleasure, so that those who have once become accustomed thereto can later hardly be restrained there from.'[11] In Russia in 1643 Tsar Michael prohibited the sale of tobacco, ordering nose amputation for snuff takers and execution for persistent tobacco use.

Initially the Catholic Church took an ambiguous stand on tobacco use by limiting prohibition of it to houses of worship, and in the seventeenth century Pope Urban VIII banned its use in churches and threatened to excommunicate snuff takers. Upon James I's succession to the English throne in 1603 any doubts as to the place of tobacco in English society were made clear. In a pamphlet entitled *A Counterblaste to Tobacco*, the king compared tobacco users to alcoholics. Despite his ardour he failed to gather much support and thus decided to increase taxes on tobacco by almost 4,000 per cent, not unlike the crusade by America's modern-day anti-tobacco lobby which continues to push for higher taxes on cigarettes as a way of limiting their consumption.

Tobacco became 'a natural adversary for James', as an association was made between the 'deceivable weed' and witchcraft. Tobacco was soon linked with witchcraft as an elixir for flying (once mixed with the traditional belladonna and henbane). The leaves of the plants were thus mashed into a sticky paste, according to popular legend, and smeared on broomsticks, allowing witches to trip the light fantastic. James had been in the forefront in the battle against the 'Antichrist', a battle that he had waged in print and later through persecution, buttressing his claims with his 1597 treatise on demonology. In it he advocated the harshest sanctions for Satanists, whom he believed – to the point of paranoia – were bent on his ruination. Thus James would take a personal interest in the discovery of witches and even direct tortures and edit their confessions. Among his victims was a Dr Cunningham, who had been implicated in a plan to drown the king while on a sea voyage. The doctor subsequently had his fingernails pulled out, eyeballs stuck with red-hot needles, and suffered torture of the 'boots', by which his legs were encased and beaten to the point that 'blood and marrow spouted forth', making his legs useless.[12]

Around the same time that James I was crusading against the 'stinking weed', the Japanese were doing likewise, initiating bans on it in 1609, 1612, 1615 and 1616, and with each new law came increasingly more punitive penalties, so that by 1616 it was common for smokers to face fines, imprisonment and the confiscation of property. The Japanese stance was due in no small part to tobacco's foreign origin, which was seen, like many other Western commodities and rituals, as a negative symbol of foreign influence.

Islam was apparently less reticent in its acceptance of tobacco. On the one hand, it is not mentioned in the Quran, but on the other, the proximity of Muslim settlements in East Africa to the Saudi Arabian peninsula surely contributed to early Arabian exposure to smoking and thus probably facilitated its acceptance in Islamic society.[13] However, this did not hold true throughout the Islamic world. Due to its absence in the Quran, for some despots smoking bespoke of 'otherworldliness' and thus deserved harsher penalties. The most extreme examples can be found in the Ottoman Empire under Murad IV, earning him the moniker 'the Cruel'. He had supposedly loathed smoking ever since a fireworks display celebrating the birth of his first son burned down half of Constantinople. By some accounts he would go to great lengths to stamp out its use, even donning a disguise and walking backstreets and alleyways pretending he needed a nicotine fix. Once he found someone who would comply, it was common for him to have the Good Samaritan beheaded for his troubles. Murad the Cruel was estimated to have put to death more than 25,000 suspected smokers during his fourteen-year reign. Persian officials were no less cruel, following Murad's lead: any merchants caught selling tobacco were executed by having molten lead poured down their throats.[14]

The Origins of the Illicit International Narcotics Trade

From a criminological point of view, no drug has impacted the historical record and had such a controversial history as much as opium. Introduced to the West in the 1850s, European sailors, travellers, drifters and prostitutes – individuals already associated with nothing but bad habits – brought the habit back to their countries of origin. For the most part, the use of opiates was relegated to the fringes of society. Opium was introduced to China as a medicinal item by Arab traders in the late sixth or early seventh centuries, during the early Tang dynasty (608–907). By the first decades of the eighteenth century, opium smoking had spread to such an extent that the Chinese emperor Yongzheng issued a prohibition against opium smoking houses and the sale of the substance, declaring it 'odious and deplorable'.[15] Shortly after, a decree was implemented making the sale and use of opium a capital offence. In the process this ban created what many scholars regard as the first drug smugglers, in the guise of the stereotypical pipe-smoking English-gentleman-cum-drug-dealer, representing the British Empire. Several decades later another edict targeted anyone involved in the opium trade – from the brokers and den operators to the farmers and the corrupt law enforcers – with severe sanctions. However, those that wilfully gave up their opium were pardoned, and addicts were given a year and a half to seek a cure. Nonetheless, for the first time foreign opium dealers were beheaded and Chinese accomplices strangled, while others were subject to the Manchu penal code, which included beatings, transportation and banishment.

The story of British involvement in the opium trade in China is an oft-chronicled tale. Since the early eighteenth century the Chinese opposed not only the importation of opium but also tried to limit all trade with the outside world. But this had little effect on traders who evaded these prohibitions through cunning, bribery and smuggling. Britain gained control of India's Bengal opium fields in 1773 and over the ensuing century created legions of addicts among users unfamiliar with its addictive propensities. According to one 1838 report, opium smokers and dealers were sentenced to have a portion of the upper lip cut out to prevent the smoking of the substance.[16] However, the onus of punishment fell heaviest on those members of the local population who collaborated with foreigners (who were rarely punished for breaking Chinese laws). Laws were haphazardly applied at best, while penalties remained severe. Opium sellers could be banished, forced to wear a cangue (heavy wooden collar), while den keepers could be strangled.

After the Manchu imperial court banned the opium trade, the British paid little heed. The Chinese responded by destroying an estimated $11 million (at least $240 million today) worth of opium, kick-starting the First Opium War in 1839 (a second followed in 1856). A British victory required China to reimburse it for its losses and lift the opium prohibition. Until the twentieth century, most international criminal activities were carryovers from previous centuries. Indeed, there were few significant innovations in global communication and transportation before the twentieth century outside simple cross-border smuggling operations.

By most accounts the convening of the 1909 Shanghai Opium Commission stimulated the crusade against international drug trafficking, a crime that best illustrates the complex web of associations required by the global drug trade. Among the first individuals to grasp the opportunities offered by the drug trade were Jewish-American gangsters who organized a smuggling network with China,[17] the leading supplier of the day. Subsequently laboratories were built to dilute and package drugs for the market, and distribution networks established to market opiates to addicts.

During Japan's expansion into China in the 1930s, one of its strategies was to flood China with opiates. It seemed sensible to pursue this market given the fact that at that time there were an estimated 100,000 addicts in the u.s., compared to perhaps 8 million in China.[18] But what set the stage for global innovation was the passage of new legislation in the United States in the first decades of the new century. The Harrison Narcotic Act of 1914 criminalized nonmedical use of opium, morphine and coca derivatives in the usa. Other international treaties would build on this prohibition after years of crusading against opiates by mostly

Western powers. The internationalization of drug prohibitions stimulated the formation of drug trafficking syndicates to supply whichever
drug was in demand at the moment. From a contemporary perspective,
after more than a century of drug prohibition, few alternatives have
been considered by the world's criminal justice systems, making the
international smuggling of illicit drugs the most lucrative form of
organized crime in the twenty-first century.

Piracy

When the pirates of legend are put under the historical microscope
researchers have revealed that much of what we think we know about
them is bogus. They rarely if ever buried treasure (try finding it in the
shifting sands later), nor did they walk the plank. Most pirate organizations were rather transitory, lasting about as long as their charismatic
leaders, who by the eighteenth century were being hunted into extinction.
But while they did roam the high seas they shared a number of attributes
with international crime syndicates, in that they bribed officials, operated
on occasion with state support, sold stolen and prohibited goods to
legitimate businessmen, and used violence and the threat of violence to
get their way. Piracy existed in a variety of incarnations, depending on
region and time period, and thus often varied widely in character. Most
pirates were aged in their twenties, rarely did one come across an old
pirate (that is, over 40 years old). Piracy was a young man's (and on
occasion a woman's) game. Like modern-day gang members, if they
weren't caught, killed in action or died from exposure to the elements,
they aged out of the life.

More than 2,000 years have passed since the Roman historian Dio
Cassius asserted that 'There was never a time when piracy was not prac-
ticed. Nor may it cease so long as the nature of mankind remains the
same.' By most accounts, there is perhaps no form of transnational crime
that better illustrates the continuum of international criminality than
the ancient practice of piracy. In contrast to their precursors, modern
pirates have taken advantage of high technology, bases in failed nation-
states, potential alliances with transnational terrorists, and a global
economy dependent on secure shipping lanes. Nonetheless, modern
powers have proved no more able to fend off pirates, as demonstrated
by the April 2009 stand-off between an $800 million u.s. Navy destroyer
and a handful of pirates in a lifeboat; the first incident in two centuries
in which foreign pirates had captured a u.s. vessel for ransom.[19] In fact,

the last time such a stand-off occurred between America and a foreign power over piracy was when the Barbary pirates of North Africa took sailors hostage in the early days of the American republic. It might have been new for America, but it was an old story in the Mediterranean world, where piracy had been endemic as long as valuable commodities have been shipped between ancient territories.

Early historians of antiquity such as Herodotus and Thucydides were among the first to record the exploits of pirates. Piracy became increasingly problematic in the last century of the Roman Republic as a result of a miscalculation in foreign policy by the Roman senate in the second century BC. Formerly, the sea power of Rhodes had been responsible for policing the eastern Mediterranean, that is, until it was destroyed by the Romans. Rome, with no standing navy of her own to replace what it had destroyed, left the Mediterranean open to organized piracy. Pirates were headquartered in Cilicia, on the southern coast of Asia Minor, dominating the Mediterranean with great fleets. No direct action was taken against them until 102 BC. According to one observer, the reason that the Romans had not vigorously suppressed piracy was that pirates had also become the main source of slaves for the ruling classes. By 69 BC the seas were almost closed to travel and trade and pirates were able to strike at will along the Italian coast and even make forays into the harbour of Rome at Ostia. Famine and financial disaster beckoned if the pirates were not vanquished. In 67 BC the Gabinian Law was passed granting Pompey some of the most extraordinary powers ever granted to a Roman leader – almost unlimited powers over the entire Mediterranean – to deal with the pirate threat. Within three months the pirate menace and freebooting ceased to plague the Empire.[20]

By the Middle Ages, then, piracy was already an established criminal vocation. As trade increased over the centuries, so did the volume of piracy. With the expansion of oceanic trade routes during the commercial expansion of the sixteenth and seventeenth centuries, pirates likewise expanded their routes, following the money trail from the Old World to the Americas. As the French, English, Dutch and Spanish each carved out colonies in the New World, competition between these powers to establish trade monopolies often led to war on the high seas.[21]

In 1696 a British court defined the crime of piracy as 'only the sea-term for robbery within the jurisdiction of the Admiralty . . . If the mariner of any ship shall violently dispossess the master and afterwards carry away the ship itself or any of the goods with a felonious intention in any place where the lord Admiral hath jurisdiction, this is robbery and piracy.'[22] More modern researchers refer to it as a form of 'maritime macro-parasitism', or simply the 'indiscriminate taking of property with violence, on or by descent from the sea'.[23]

According to early English common law, piracy committed by English subjects was likened to treason, the highest felony of this period. Statutes were introduced that added trading with known pirates or furnishing them weapons as forms of treason. According to the jurist William Blackstone, the crime of piracy, or trading with known pirates, was equivalent to 'robbery and depredation upon the high seas'.[24] Sir Edward Coke regarded these actors as *hostis humani generis*, enemies of mankind, who 'renounced all the benefits of society and government' when it came to justice.

The years of the 'Golden Age of Piracy' are traditionally given as between 1650 and 1730, an era one historian described as 'a period of unrestrained murder, robbery and kidnapping on the high seas'.[25] An evaluation of this era offers a number of striking parallels to modern transnational criminal activities. Illegal pirates as well as state-sponsored ones, called privateers, had vast economic incentives to participate in the looting of cargoes of gold, grain, jewels, wine and even drugs. The import and export of these commodities was heavily controlled and for a successful smuggling network to flourish it required the willing participation of corrupt officials and merchants, particularly when it came to laundering their ill-gotten treasures.

They were called pirates, buccaneers, privateers and corsairs, but not all were bona fide desperadoes. Like their land-bound counterparts covered in the previous chapter, there were variations and permutations within the pirate universe. Unlike privateers, the 'pure pirate' always acted outside the law, preying on merchant ships for their own lucre. On the other hand, privateers were sanctioned by various nations and commissioned to attack and seize enemy merchant ships during war, and really should not be considered pirates at all, since they had government support. In a similar vein, corsairs also plundered on behalf of governments, with the main difference being that they targeted victims according to religion. For example, Barbary corsairs of the North African coast attacked vessels from Christian nations; Christian corsairs such as the Knights of Malta performed a similar service (privateers and corsairs were typically not considered outlaws).

The attitudes of authorities towards piracy have always been un-sympathetic to say the least, leading one expert to ponder why, 'in view of almost universal condemnation of it and the treatment when caught', piracy 'flourished in much of the world from earliest times and continues today'.[26] From the medieval period, England hanged pirates and other lawbreakers from gallows located at Wapping on the banks of the Thames; there a simple wooden scaffold was erected between the low- and high-tide marks alongside the wharf, earning it the moniker 'Execution Dock'. The reason for hanging malefactors between the flood-marks was to demonstrate that their crimes had been committed within the jurisdiction of the Lord High Admiral, who was responsible for all crimes committed on the high seas and waterways up to the low-tide mark. Thus, if the crimes had occurred above the tide line it would have been a matter for the civil courts instead.[27]

The gallows rarely consisted of little more than two wooden uprights connected at the top by a crossbeam. When in use, a ladder was placed against it and the hangman's rope suspended from the top beam. The pirate then ascended the ladder, assisted by the executioner, who was responsible for placing the noose around his neck and, after receiving the signal from the marshal, for pushing the convict off the ladder to his death. It was not uncommon for the prisoner to slowly strangle and to struggle for some time – that is, unless he could count on friends or family to pull down on his legs and complete the strangulation in a timely manner. In rare cases, if the rope broke, the prisoner was given a second hanging. Such was the case for Captain Kidd, whose noose broke, sending him to the ground. Some onlookers remembered his pee-stained crotch as the executioner repeated the execution routine just ten minutes later. This time the noose held.

The legendary Captain William Kidd met his maker at Execution Dock on 23 May 1701. Kidd was taken from Newgate Prison in a procession led by a deputy marshal who carried on his shoulder the silver oar, symbol of the Admiralty Court. As per custom a noose was placed around Kidd's neck and he was positioned in an open cart draped in black. Kidd was apparently well fortified with rum on his way to the gallows, reportedly thanks to a sympathetic warden, so that by the time he approached the muddy shores of Wapping he was almost falling down drunk and scarcely aware of his ghastly march through the fetid slums to the shore of the Thames. After his hanging, as dictated by Admiralty law, Kidd's corpse was chained to a post at the water's edge until three tides had washed over it. As was the tradition with the corpses of more notorious criminals, the now bloated body would be preserved in tar and placed in a human shaped cage of iron bands designed to hold the body in place as it rotted away.[28] It was then suspended from a gibbet along the Thames Estuary for as long as several years, as a warning to every passing vessel – unless birds stripped it to the bone first. Those who were not consigned to this aftermath were either buried in an unmarked grave or transported to the Surgeon's Hall for dissection. The latter stage was introduced by Henry VIII in the sixteenth century and by the eighteenth century the dissection of executed criminals had become de rigueur in the medical field. In one of the more remarkable post-hanging sagas, the 'corpse' of the recently executed William Duell was delivered to the Surgeon's Hall in 1740. His body was cleaned prior to dissection, but Duell was soon observed breathing. He was then bled by a surgeon and after two hours recovered, and was left sitting in a chair, no doubt trying to make sense of the recent turn of events. Duell was sent back to prison and the courts magnanimously decided that another hanging was not warranted: he was transported to the American colonies instead.[29]

In the seventeenth century, pirates often joined crews under the false impression that if their ship was captured by pirate hunters only the leaders of the pirate company would be executed. This might have been true at one time but by the next century they were more likely to share the same fate as their captain, as in the case of the 30 of 34 crew members hanged with Major Stede Bonnet in 1718. It was not uncommon for authorities to make a statement by putting pirates to death in mass executions. During the first decades of the eighteenth century, groups of pirates were dispatched at London's Execution Dock; along Boston, Massachusetts's Charles River; at Leith Sands, Edinburgh; at Gallows Point, Jamaica; and Nassau's, near Charleston Harbor in South Carolina.

The hanging of 52 members of Bartholomew Roberts's pirate band at the Cape Coast Castle waterfront on the west coast of Africa in 1722 was probably the largest hanging of the era. This region had long been a hotbed of pirate activity. Trials were usually held at the ivory and slave trading centre at Cape Coast Castle, including the Roberts trial, reportedly the largest pirate trial ever held. More than 260 surviving pirates from Roberts's crew were put on trial here and 52 sentenced to hang; the others were either imprisoned or sentenced to hard labour in the Gold Coast mines of the Royal Africa Company (headquartered at the castle). Twenty would be worked to death. The pirates were hanged in batches during a two-week period in April 1722. Following British tradition, the bodies of eighteen of them were tarred and wrapped in metal bands to be strung up from gibbets on the hills overlooking the harbour. As one historian put it, the spectacle of rotting cadavers 'gave notice that there was no longer any place for pirates in a world dominated by global European imperialism – a world that ironically, piracy had helped make possible'.[30]

In another case authorities made a statement with the hanging of thirteen followers of Edward Teach, better known as Blackbeard, along the 'Gallows Road' running between Williamsburg, Virginia, and the James River. One historian suggested it closely paralleled 'the fate of Spartacus and his fellow slaves' when in 71 BC they were crucified along a length of road following their failed rebellion. In the case of Blackbeard's crew, every half-mile the entourage of prisoners, officials and onlookers stopped at an accessible tree or a purpose-built gibbet. The prisoner was instructed to stand in the back of the cart with hands tied behind his back. Already wearing the noose around his neck, he was allowed to make a short speech before the cleric followed with probably an even shorter prayer; the cart and horse was then led away leaving the prisoner kicking in mid-air.[31]

England was not alone in its low regard for piracy, as witnessed by the harsh stance taken by other European countries. In 1573 a German pirate named Klein Heszlein along with 33 crew members was beheaded in a Hamburg marketplace, ending their long run of plundering ships on the North Sea. The French and Spanish were not ill-disposed to execution, but there were also numerous pirates who were condemned to galley service for life. Pirates captured by China and other countries on the Pacific Rim, on the other hand, were likely to be beheaded.

At the same time that English privateers and pirates were plundering Spain's enticing New World Empire, almost a world away and often transporting even more lucrative cargoes, various pirate bands were attempting to capture Mughal and Arab treasure ships plying ancient trade routes in the Indian Ocean. Besides gold, silver, precious gems, spices and silk, these ships were often ferrying the pilgrim faithful and Arab merchants from India to the Red Sea ports and thence on to Mecca. By the late seventeenth century, pirates were facing more resistance and less opportunity in their traditional Caribbean plundering grounds. The more pragmatic pirate captains found new opportunities along the routes between India and Red Sea and turned to Indian Ocean trade routes to the east. These were among the oldest pirate preying grounds, the Arabian Gulf having been menaced since around 1600 BC. No less an observer than the Greek geographer Ptolemy dubbed the trade routes on the west coast of India the 'Pirate Coast'.

Some pirate captains were among the most sadistic criminals of their era. Captain Edward Low, for example, was so incensed that a Portuguese merchant threw a sack of gold coins overboard that he cut the man's lips off and broiled them in front of his very eyes. Then the terror ensued: after forcing one of the Portuguese sailors to eat the broiled lips, the entire crew was massacred. Low reportedly cut the ears off a New England whaling captain and made him eat them seasoned with salt and pepper. In another instance, Low removed everyone from a French ship except the cook, whom he strapped to the vessel's mast before setting the ship on fire; Low noted that 'being a greasy fellow', the man would fry well.[32] The infamous Blackbeard himself, once the terror of the high seas, was brought to justice in 1718 during a battle in which he suffered five gunshot wounds and twenty sword wounds before succumbing to his injuries. As proof of Blackbeard's death, the pirate hunters returned his head to the Virginia colony where it was stripped of its flesh and hung from a pole on the Hampton River.

Until the end of the seventeenth century, Massachusetts colonial officials lobbied to adopt England's punitive anti-piracy laws. Until 1699, pirates were punished as if they had committed larceny, and were required to pay triple the damages of stolen property.[33] This soon changed as piracy flourished. In the American colonies dozens of pirates strode the gallows after waging an unremitting crime wave along the Eastern seaboard. In one month alone almost four dozen were hanged in Virginia and South Carolina. Barbaric treatment went both ways. As the Golden Age of Piracy was winding down in 1725, captured pirate captain John Gow refused to plead at his trial and was pressed to death – the only torture at that time allowable by law. If he had simply taken a guilty plea, hanging would have sufficed.

There are numerous accounts of pirate executions in the American colonies during the eighteenth century. The prisoner often suffered a similar ordeal as his counterparts in England. Led through streets crowded with onlookers, in a time with little in the way of public enter-tainments, he could expect to be bombarded with crude salutations such as 'Ye be doing the sheriff's dance!' or 'You'll piss when you can't whistle!' But it is probably doubtful that doomed prisoners would notice the razzing as they ducked dead cats, excrement and eggs tossed by the crowd at them on the way to the gallows. Meanwhile, it was not uncommon for pleasure boats filled with onlookers to watch the festivities from just off-shore. In most cases the convict had his elbows lashed together behind his back, rather than his hands. Experience had demonstrated that dying men tied at the wrist were capable, in their desperate struggle to live, of rolling their hands free of the restraints. The feet were virtually never tied either, since this would rob spectators of the eagerly awaited 'dance upon the air'. It was not uncommon for executioners to purposely leave hanging ropes short to avoid breaking the neck, so as not to deprive the onlookers of this spectacle. Not unlike crime memorabilia collectors of the present day, there was always a chance that drunken souvenir hunters might cut off a body part or button as a keepsake or, more likely, trade it for a pint of beer at a local tavern. Sheriffs were sometimes paid to protect the body at the water's edge until the corpse was carried off to its final resting place.[34]

Spain regarded foreign traders as pirates and heretics in the late sixteenth century. In 1593, ten Dutch merchant ships were captured by the Spanish Navy. The ship's masters were summarily hanged and the rest sent to toil in the galleys. Among the most notorious buccaneers operating in the Caribbean was the Frenchman Jean-David Nau, better known as François l'Olonnais, or as one observer described him, a 'psychopath by any century's measurement'. Among his strategies was to torture anyone that did not answer his questions by cutting them into pieces with his cutlass and pulling out their tongues. Others reported his habit of burning prisoners with matches, or cutting a man to pieces, 'first some flesh, then a hand, an arm, a leg, sometimes tying a cod about his head' and 'twisting it till his eyes shoot out' (better known as 'woolding').[35] L'Olonnais evaded Spanish justice, only to be captured by Native Americans and tortured to death himself, his body incinerated and its ashes scattered in the wind.

The seas around Japan were infested with pirates from antiquity to the Edo Period. During the fourteenth century, with Japan in the midst of civil war, made worse by an absence of central authority, piracy grew to unprecedented levels throughout East Asia, ranging as far as the Korean and Chinese coasts. Like other criminals and criminal bands, these pirate groups were sometimes driven to this lifestyle for economic survival. One historian described this strategy as 'petty piracy' by individuals unable to make it any other way.[36] Chinese and most other East Asian authorities sentenced captured pirates to beheading.

Smuggling and piracy are two variations of crime that requires some form of organization. Piracy is distinguished from smuggling by its very nature, requiring direct confrontation with victims and the threat or use of violence, whereas smuggling is accomplished in a more clandestine fashion, with violence only a last resort. Pirates were for the most part drawn from the labouring classes in the Atlantic World. By contrast, they seemed to represent a 'broader social base' in the South China Sea in the eighteenth and nineteenth centuries.[37] Smuggling, of course, has always been more common than piracy, but has not received the depth and breadth of research as piracy, due in no small part to its relative lack of dramatic panache on the part of its practitioners. One authority has suggested that 'Smugglers in the Caribbean' lacks the flair of a *Pirates of the Caribbean* and would probably not come close at the box office.[38]

The Slave Trade as Crime and Punishment

Slavery, or enslavement, has been a licit business as well as a penal sanction for millennia; or, as the psychologist Steven Pinker put it, for most of history it was the 'rule rather than the exception'.[39] References to slavery as a formal punishment can be found in both the Christian and Hebrew bibles, and was even defended by such eminent voices of the ancient world as Plato and Aristotle. The Greek philosopher Aristotle famously defended the practice, commenting, 'humanity is divided into two: the masters and the slaves.'[40] Ultimately, the ancient Greeks were among the societies that considered slavery an inherently natural condition essential to highly developed societies. But unlike Rome, enslavement was used only sporadically in Greece, mainly applied to *metics* (resident aliens), foreigners and freemen. Slave markets flourished in both ancient Rome and Athens and by the fifteenth century was still a legal enterprise in various regions of the world. Slavery became an established institution in Rome, but mainly for those condemned to death, who served as penal slaves between conviction and execution. Slavery vanished from the European landscape for almost a millennium before re-emerging in the sixteenth century as European powers, including Portugal, the Netherlands, France, England and Spain, increasingly required slaves for their New World colonies.

Penal slavery was prohibited by Islam. Thus, whenever the religion was introduced to a new region, there was a good chance that it would also diminish the role of slavery as a local criminal sanction. This was not always true, though. African societies as well as Islamic states in North Africa and other Arab regions were enslaving Africans long before the Europeans. Some did not abolish the practice until the twentieth century, as in the cases of Qatar (1952), Saudi Arabia and Yemen (1962) and Mauritania (1980).[41]

Beginning in Chinese antiquity a pattern was established of enslaving not just individuals but the entire families of recently condemned individuals. For centuries this remained the 'only recognized source of slaves in Chinese law'. Extra-legally, of course, there were always other methods for securing slaves, but unlike in Rome, the strong emphasis on familial responsibility in China meant that a person's wife and kinsmen were fully liable for his criminal actions. However, the seriousness of the offence often determined the number of family members subject to this sanction. By most accounts, prior to the Han period (206 BC–AD 220) convicted persons were almost always executed and their family enslaved; after the Han, there was a mounting tendency to, in lesser capital cases, enslave (rather than execute) both the offender and his family. One of the earliest laws related to slavery dates back to a mid-seventh-century Chinese law which stated,

> Those plotting rebellion or major crimes shall all be beheaded. Fathers and sons over sixteen years old shall be strangled. [Sons] fifteen years or younger, mothers, daughters, wives, concubines, sons' wives and concubines, grandfathers, grandsons, older and younger brothers, older and younger sisters, and such others shall be enslaved, and property confiscated by government.

However, the lives of men over 80 years of age or who were incurably ill, and women over 60, were spared.[42]

In an era before complex identification systems, third-century China used branding or facial mutilations to identify the status of various classes of malefactors. Prisoners and slaves often laboured side by side and since both wore shackles and similar clothes and bore identity marks, slaves were distinguished by specific facial markings. It is not clear exactly what these marks consisted of, but one account from an official order noted that runaway male or female slaves were tattooed near their eyes with a copper-green ink-like substance. On a second attempt marks were added to both cheeks. On the third escape, an inch-and-a-half-long horizontal mark was added under each eye. The sale of innocent individuals into slavery was considered abhorrent in Chinese society, leading kidnappers of free persons to use the subterfuge of immediately branding them – making it easier to sell them due to their concocted criminal pedigree (guaranteed by the brand), much the way someone would brand domestic livestock to insure ownership. Of course, this did not keep cattle and horse rustlers from simply altering the brand.

If being enslaved was not harsh enough punishment, slaves were also subject to a punitive dual justice system administered by their masters, rather than an official judiciary process. Compared to freemen and citizens, slaves could expect the harshest sanctions available. It seems that in some cases punishment was only limited by the imagination of the executioners. During one eighteenth-century Haiti slave rebellion, French overseers reportedly smeared runaways with sweet substances such as molasses and then tied them down to the ground so that starving ants would strip the flesh from the body. The French were also known to put gunpowder 'up the backsides of errant slaves and set [it] alight'. Following the 1802 slave revolt at St Domingue, led by Toussaint L'Ouverture against the French, several witnesses reported accounts of rebel leaders having their makeshift epaulettes nailed down into their shoulder blades, in full view of kith and kin. Even more grisly were the fates of slaves staked to the ground and fed to starving dogs. One chronicler has suggested that the punishment of forcing black prisoners into a ship's hold and then burning sulphur throughout the evening created 'what may have been history's first gas chamber'.[43]

When slave populations needed replenishing it was not unheard of for some unscrupulous tyrants to increase the number of crimes for which either capital punishment or enslavement were the sanctions, as in the case of West Africa during the expansion of the Atlantic slave trade. Among the Ibo tribe, slavery became the punishment for such capital crimes as witchcraft and sorcery, disobedient children and people who leased or sold communal property.

During the seventeenth and eighteenth centuries American plantation overseers rarely spared the rod on their slaves, who were much more vulnerable to this type of non-capital punishment; they were too valuable to destroy, and imprisonment (if it was available) would probably have been considered a vacation for the slaves of that era. Slave-holding Southern u.s. lawmakers often found the traditional criminal law to be inadequate for the rapidly growing slave populations and adopted harsher punishments for slaves and freemen, particularly if they were rebellious. These sanctions multiplied after Nat Turner's bloody slave rebellion in 1831, and provided the cornerstone for the South's 'black codes'. As early as 1705 runaway slaves were outlawed and could be killed with impunity. If caught alive, slave catchers were given free rein to castrate them or amputate limbs; these horrific sanctions and ministrations of the special slave courts were designed to set an example for like-minded slaves. By some accounts, if slave owners wanted others to do their dirty work, they could pay the local executioner a fee to lash their property at the local jail, which in some cases could be as many as 25 strokes for misdemeanours.

Ever since slavery was introduced to America in the 1600s, slaves had tried to escape bondage, leading to the passage of various laws prohibiting this practice; sanctions were specified for recaptured slaves, most requiring some form of bodily mutilation that was not serious enough to prevent subsequent plantation labour. Southern colonies introduced their first slave codes beginning with South Carolina in 1712, establishing brutal slave patrols to hunt down and punish runaways.[44]

In was not uncommon for some societies to substitute enslavement for execution in the course of capital cases, with several European states using this strategy into the nineteenth century. Slavery as criminal sanction has been an important source of slaves for the Ibos of West Africa and the Guajiros of northern Colombia and Venezuela. Likewise, several Asian societies adopted penal slavery, particularly the enslavement of criminals and families of men executed for treason and rebellion during the ancient Han period. From the Han to the late Qing period, it was not uncommon for families of individuals guilty of such crimes as treason and rebellion to be enslaved in this manner. What's more, the earliest records of China's Shang dynasty (around the mid-eighteenth century BC) indicate the extensive use of slave labour. One historian has even suggested that, 'At the time of Christ, an estimated five per cent of the Chinese population was enslaved', many of them for debt, captured in war, or simply family members of executed prisoners.[45]

From the late Middle Ages into the nineteenth century, penal slavery became the main means of recruiting labour for the mines, galleys and public works projects, particularly in Spain, France, Italy and Russia. In 'quantitative' terms, except for Russia, where criminals were enslaved to work the mines and settle the Siberian wilderness beginning in the seventeenth century, the number of slaves was actually never immense among western Europeans. Nonetheless, at the turn of the nineteenth century, according to Adam Hochschild, 'well over three quarters of all people alive were in bondage', either in correctional systems or conditions of slavery or serfdom.[46] In some regions of South America and Africa, 'slaves far outnumbered free persons.'[47] Elsewhere, the majority of Russians found serfdom the norm, as did multitudes in the Ottoman Empire, parts of India and Asia, who toiled in varying states of debt peonage and absolute enslavement. By the end of the 1700s, 'freedom, not slavery, was the peculiar institution.'[48]

Well-documented mass killings of slaves, once disseminated to a wider public, were used by abolitionists to gather support for their campaigns, but with varying degrees of success. The worst tragedy of the Atlantic slave trade in terms of lives lost was the deaths on 1 January 1738 of close to 700 African men, women and children aboard the Dutch slave ship the *Leusden*. Caught in a dreadful tempest off what is current-day Suriname, the outnumbered crew was ordered to lock the hold of the ship, essentially leaving the Africans to drown below decks, fearing they might rush for the ship's too few lifeboats. About a half-century later, 132 slaves (about one-third of the slave cargo) aboard the British-owned *Zong*, on a journey from Africa to Jamaica, were unceremoniously ejected from the ship to their deaths. Some sources suggest this was done for insurance money, while others suggest that its captain believed the ship to be off course and running short of water, and feared an uprising over the shortage. The case was later brought to court, not for mass murder but because the insurers refused to believe the owner's claim that their cargo 'had been necessarily jettisoned'.[49]

By the mid-nineteenth century, no branch of the international contraband trade was as widespread as the international trafficking of African slaves. Although the trade had been abolished by Britain in 1807, there continued an enormous demand for them in not just the United States but also Brazil, Cuba, India and the Arab world. So, the trade continued, but in a much more clandestine format. The British Slave Trade Act of 1807 was considered a landmark event in the crusade against international slavery, although it was bogged down with too many limitations to be effective. Slavery continued to flourish despite efforts by the British and Americans; there was no shortage of other European nationals ready to take the lucrative risks. Midway through the era of Napoleonic Wars, slavers were unlikely to encounter abolitionist patrols on the vast seas, and if they did there was a good chance they could either outrun the few ships available to chase them, since many were sluggish relics from recent maritime campaigns, and then even if the chase was close, the traders could still just throw their precious cargo (and evidence) overboard.

In cases where a vessel was brought to justice, it was rare for any slave trader to be punished beyond forfeiting their cargo and equipment. During the nineteenth century a number of European maritime powers created bilateral courts to adjudicate ships suspected of slave trading. These Courts of Mixed Commission convened in Sierra Leone, Angola, South Africa, Jamaica and New York. The courts were empowered to seize vessels, equipment and merchandise, and release captive Africans. Similar to the toothless international courts of the modern era, these courts were not empowered to punish ship owners or their crews.[50]

By the early nineteenth century, Britain and the United States had a long tradition of equating piracy with slave trading. This link was foisted by abolitionists who thought that drawing the connection would empower the British Navy to arrest slave ships from other countries. Unfortunately, other European powers were less convinced, regarding it as a specious argument. Both countries, at one time or another, categorically declared slave trading to be piracy, a maritime offence which theoretically any country was authorized to suppress. This characterization is linked to nineteenth-century international law that viewed pirates as 'common enemies of [all] mankind', thus subject to universal jurisdiction and open to legal arrest, trial and punishment by any country. One historian has even gone as far as likening this perception to modern concepts of crime against humanity.[51] Ultimately neither was ever successful at prosecuting slavers for piracy. After the u.s. (1820) and Britain (1824) declared the slave trade a capital offence, only one person was ever executed for the offence. The unlucky Nathaniel Gordon was executed in 1862, despite pleas passed on to President Lincoln to commute his sentence into something more temporary than death.

From the Slave Trade to Modern Human Trafficking

A number of scholars have responded to the predilection of some human rights activists as well as experts in the field to equate the modern scourge of human trafficking with traditional slavery. Steven Pinker is among those that take umbrage with this tenuous connection, noting that 'Modern human trafficking, as heinous as it is, cannot be equated with the horrors of the African slave trade.'[52] The fact that between 17 million and 65 million Africans were forcibly relocated to the Americas, and that at least 1.5 million of them perished between the sixteenth and nineteenth centuries makes this link with the modern horrors of human trafficking unsustainable.

As noted previously, human trafficking is probably older than the written word, yet it has been criminalized only since the mid-nineteenth century. International cooperation against the venal trade received its greatest stimulus in the early twentieth century during the campaign against 'white slavery'. First recognized in the mid-nineteenth century, the phrase 'white slavery' originally referred to 'the entire system of licensed prostitution'. But over the last decades of the nineteenth century, it became analogous to all prostitution for many observers. Implicit in its definition was the 'recruitment to prostitution by force or fraud'.[53] In 1904, representatives from thirteen nations agreed to coordinate their actions by signing the International Conference for the Suppression of the White Slave Traffic, agreeing to punish any individual who facilitated the entry of females under the age of twenty into the sex trade, or procured an adult by force or fraud.[54]

Some observers compare the trafficking of victims to 'migration gone wrong', since the vast majority caught up in human trafficking originally set off for other shores for better opportunities or were victims of coercion. Human trafficking is indeed distinct from the slavery or enslavement, particularly since slavery was often a condition that lasted a lifetime.[55] Moreover, the children of slaves became part of a permanent and hereditary class of unfree people; most trafficking victims are often only temporarily 'enslaved'. Indeed, the difference between human smuggling and trafficking is often blurred. The main distinction is based on coercion and consent. Human smuggling often begins as a simple smuggling operation, but towards the end of the transaction might take an unexpected turn, with the customer being victimized by the trafficker, who insists s/he is still owed money by the trafficked individual. In these cases the victim is forced to pay for what are often described as 'hidden costs' or 'unforeseen debts' by working it off through forced labour, such as prostitution.

There is no debating that modern-day human trafficking is horrific. What often hampers any intelligent discourse is what one scholar refers to as the numbers of victims 'usually pulled out of thin air' by well-meaning activists, journalists and other observers. As a result of recent publicity about this phenomenon, Steven Pinker perhaps puts it best when, in his book *The Better Angels of Our Nature*, he challenges what he calls 'the statistically illiterate and morally obtuse' who 'claim that nothing has changed since the 18th century.'[56]

Summary

If there is one given about organized criminal gangs, it is that they are always on the prowl for the next big financial opportunity. Many gangs are branching out into modern-day types of fraud. In early 2014, Interpol and Europol led an investigation into the attempt to fraudulently sell 22 tonnes of long-grain rice as the more expensive Basmati rice. In another case, authorities seized 2,500 jars of honey that were found to be nothing but sugar syrup. Cheap species of fish may be substituted for pricier ones, soybean oil for olive oil, horse meat for beef and so forth. The bootlegging of alcohol has even seen a revival: one Italian organized crime group has been linked to the manufacture and sale of fake Champagne, while a gang in Bangkok, Thailand, sold 270 bottles of fake whisky. In one headline-grabbing incident a 40-foot-long lorry stocked with counterfeit vodka, estimated to be valued at £1 million, was seized by authorities in the UK in 2014.[57] But what is most concerning is that gangs that once trafficked in drugs are now switching to foods, an economic decision predicated on the declining profitability of the drug trade. What's more, penalties for smuggling foods pale in comparison with drug charges.[58]

As trade and travel restrictions between countries disappear and world economies become increasingly interdependent, so do international criminal syndicates. Organized criminal activity can be found in various incarnations throughout the historical record. Pre-industrial societies in China, Italy and Japan gave rise to such groups as the Triads, Sicilian Mafia and the yakuza. As demonstrated in this chapter, sea piracy and the illegal trade in humans are the earliest examples of multinational crime on a global scale. Criminal entrepreneurs continue to exploit global prohibitions on a variety of popular products ranging from cocaine and heroin to new, synthetic concoctions. No crime-fighting regime has stimulated the development of international crime more than the various prohibitions that have barred certain in-demand products from being traded freely across and within national borders. Similar to America's Eighteenth Amendment, which initiated alcohol prohibition in 1920, England created a black market for commodities when Parliament passed the Navigation Acts in the late seventeenth century. These Acts, passed between 1651 and 1696, did for seventeenth-century pirates and smugglers what alcohol and drug prohibition did for the development of twentieth-century transnational crime syndicates. Indeed, the Navigation Act of 1651 was formulated to suppress smuggling activities, particularly in relation to tobacco.

Smuggling activity as a form of criminality dates to antiquity, when the collection of tribute was an established practice. The introduction of coins and other forms of money facilitated commercial ventures and the exchange of goods, and at the same time made it easier for monarchs to collect tariffs[59] and other taxes to expand their coffers and empires. These advances stimulated global financial crimes ranging from monopolization to price fixing. The latter was exemplified by the English laws that forced their American colonists to trade with the mother country at exorbitant fixed rates. Thus the Navigation Acts proved a barrier to American merchants trying to earn a profit and, like alcohol prohibition in 1920, led to organized tax evasion and smuggling syndicates. Tobacco smuggling became a global criminal enterprise once England ordained that it could only be taken directly from the country where it was produced to England, and only by its own ships or ships from the country of origin. The subsequent 1660 Navigation Act went even further, prohibiting the American colonists from selling tobacco to any country other than England. Thus the colonists embarked on creating their own markets through various smuggling strategies. What's more, by prohibiting numerous luxury items from competing nations from being sold in the American colonies, the Navigation Acts spurred the creation of an underground economy operated by diverse pirates, smugglers and black marketeers eager to fill the void in certain prohibited market goods. Some items were smuggled to avoid onerous taxes, as in the case of tea, which by some estimates perhaps five-sixths of the tea consumed in the colonies was illegally smuggled into eastern ports.[60]

Recent scholarship suggests that as 'the first global prohibition regime', the campaign against the slave trade 'added new dimensions that have been replicated in more recent global prohibition regimes'.[61] Not unlike attempts to uphold the current drug prohibition regime, a concerted effort against the slave trade was implemented in the nineteenth century, but it did not end the trafficking of slaves from Africa, as smuggling operations came up with new strategies to beat the system. The prohibition against the slave trade included a number of firsts in the crusade to suppress international criminal enterprises. It was the first time that a prohibition regime was institutionalized in a series of international conventions and signed by a majority of nations; likewise it was the first to criminalize international commerce in a particular commodity, and was the first to develop into a far more ambitious regime aimed at the criminalization of all activity involving the production, sale and consumption of that commodity in every country.[62]

But one theme becomes clear, following a pattern that is a discernible one throughout this book. It goes something like this: no matter what punishments a society conjures up to stymie particular behaviours, it usually takes a sea change in regional, local and global human values to eliminate behaviours that were formerly widely acceptable, as in the case of exhibitory punishments and public torture. For most of human history slavery was an accepted part of the social contract – that is, until a shift in human values and attitudes towards slavery led the world's sovereign states to arrive at a time where no state currently (publicly) supports it.

7
The Face of Modern Murder

I n 1991 German hikers in the Italian Alps stumbled upon what some
have suggested might be the world's oldest 'preserved' crime scene.
The frozen corpse, known as 'Ötzi the Iceman', had been lying there
undisturbed for 5,300 years and was so well preserved that further investigation revealed that his intestines contained remnants of his final meal
of bread and meat. Ötzi was well armed at the time of his death: found
alongside him were an archer's bow and a quiver containing fourteen
arrows. Several theories for his death were initially proposed, including
freezing to death, falling and perhaps becoming incapacitated, or being
buried in an avalanche. But, with the assistance of CT scanning, it became
apparent that Ötzi died after an arrow ripped into his back, causing
internal bleeding. In his hand he still clutched a dagger; what's more,
he had defensive wounds on his forearms and hands. DNA testing revealed
the blood of two other individuals on his body as well.[1]

The exact circumstances of the Iceman's death will probably never
be known for certain, but there is no doubt that it was a violent one.
Like many homicides that have taken place since it will go unsolved
– become a cold case – if not the coldest of cold cases. So, why a chapter
on murder, when there are so many more common crimes a chapter
could have been devoted to. Murder, as the rarest form of crime, is
more extensively covered than any other type of crime. There are substantially more people studying serial killers and mass murderers than
there are perpetrators of this crime. Perhaps this fascination stems
from the fact that it is the crime that humans are least likely to contend
with on a daily basis. The human species has graced the earth with
remarkable accomplishments over the millennia: from the pyramids
of Egypt to the great cathedrals of Europe, from curing epidemic

diseases to reaching the moon, humans are capable of such wonderfully constructive behaviour. Yet there is one less attractive propensity that humans have demonstrated over and over again – the ability to murder each other at alarming rates and with a variety of methods throughout history.

No crime is more chronicled than that of taking a life, the act of homicide. Distinctions between different forms of this crime have become more pronounced over the centuries. Some cultures treated accidental homicide as seriously as premeditated murder, while others have made distinctions between various degrees of homicide. The terms homicide, murder and manslaughter have been used interchangeably over the years. In fact, one of the longest-lasting debates has been over the differences (if any) between 'murder' and 'killing'. In the Bible, for example, killing is permissible in self-defence, capital punishment and warfare. However, in the Torah the commandment is generally understood as 'you shall not murder', while the King James version says 'Thou shalt not kill'. Criminologists understand the main distinction between murder and killing to be that the former is committed with malice aforethought, rather than spontaneous.

Despite numerous murders committed by mentally ill individuals, the overwhelming majority of them are committed by individuals not insane at all. Rather, according to one forensic psychiatrist, 'their cost–benefit calculators' operate differently from others', meaning murder can be viewed as 'a deadly solution' to problems involving lust, greed, envy, fear, revenge, status or reputation.[2] But, when it comes to major felonies, the least likely to reoffend are murderers, who in most cases can be depended on to kill only once. Most murderers, and their victims, are male, a fact that remains 'consistent across cultures'. By some estimates more than 1 million Americans were murdered in the twentieth century, not including victims of warfare.[3] It is difficult to make any worldwide calculation due to less than reliable crime reporting in many countries. But wherever murder occurs, researchers have detected seasonal patterns that place the highest rates in the warmest months. Homicide rates are mostly static over time, but continue to vary by country and region. One thing that hasn't changed is that the United States continues to lead other industrial countries in its homicide rate.

From a global perspective, homicide laws vary widely across place and time. In Britain, to be found guilty of murder, intention needs to be proven. Manslaughter in the UK is a broad category that includes anything from accidental death to voluntary manslaughter, in which it can be proven that the killer was provoked. In Japan, the harshest penalties for murder are meted out to those who kill their direct descendants, while in Italy, murderers who killed to avenge their honour were until the early 1980s regarded as less dreadful than other types of killers according to the law. In contrast to the Western world, under Islamic law, murder is often treated as a civil infraction to be settled informally by the family of the victim. Retribution may be selected by the family, or financial compensation can be paid to them.[4]

Historians, anthropologists, writers and artists have all captured the darker impulses of our species. It was the ancient Greeks who first made the distinction between intentional and unintentional homicide. By 140 BC Rome had created special murder courts and except for the murder of parents (parricide), Roman laws demonstrated remarkable restraint by displaying leniency that would be regarded as excessive by some moral arbiters and death penalty advocates. In both ancient Athens and Rome murderers remained free until trial, allowing them the possibility of escaping to foreign lands.

Early references to serial murder activity in the historical record are hard to come by. One historian of serial homicide suggests that the first recorded case can be found in fourth-century Rome, where 170 'lethal women' were convicted of poisoning numerous male victims and then blaming their deaths on plague. In another Roman case the defendant Calpurnius Bestia was accused of murdering his wives by inserting poison into their vaginas during intercourse. And from fifth-century Yemen come tales of the wealthy Zu Shenatir, who reportedly lured boys to his home, like the Pied Piper of Hamlin, with promises of food and shelter, but instead treated them to rape and death. His ghoulish saga ended only when he was stabbed to death by one of his targets.[5]

Shakespeare's *Titus Andronicus* offers a lurid account of gang rape, ending with the young woman having her tongue cut out and hands chopped off in order to prevent her from testifying against her assailants. But researchers have gone back even further to try and explain the roots of violence in humankind. By some accounts, the origins of human violence can be found in the behaviour of our primate ancestors, the chimpanzees, which 'routinely commit acts of torture and mayhem as appalling as anything found in *Psychopathia Sexualis*'.[6] As serial murder chronicler Harold Schechter has pointed out, 'Not only do they prey upon vulnerable members of their own species, but their assaults are marked by gratuitous cruelty – tearing off pieces of skin, for example, twisting limbs until they break, or drinking a victim's blood.'[7]

Recent scholarship suggests that the scale of reported murder has diminished worldwide over the past 50 years. There is, however, one type of murder that often goes undetected and by most accounts has always been under-reported. One of the darkest figures of homicide is the crime of infanticide, an age-old practice by which mothers, mostly, kill their infants. Infanticide is committed in every class of people and culture. In the seventeenth and eighteenth centuries, French fathers had the legal recourse to decide whether their infants should live or die. In many cases it was unmarried women who decided they could not afford to raise children on their own. Infanticide was so common in England that in 1741 foundling homes were established to attempt to stem this form of murder. In other cultures infants were sacrificed for reasons ranging from population control and birth defects to being the wrong gender or to avoid social stigmatization. Children perished not only due to infanticide; many were victims of abuse and neglect. Others were hurt as an attack by one parent on the other, in revenge for some marital slight; this was portrayed some 2,000 years ago in Euripides' *Medea*, in which a vengeful Medea decides that the best way to hurt her husband, Jason (leader of the Argonauts), after he deserted her for greener pastures, is to kill their children. One is less likely to be harmed by a stranger than by a family member or acquaintance. By one account, three-quarters of all child abductions are committed by someone in the family or known to the child.[8] In 1992 FBI crime statistics showed that parents were responsible for 57 per cent of murders of children under the age of five, and that family friends or acquaintances killed 30 per cent. In contrast to the U.S., countries such as Israel, Britain, Canada and Australia have added infanticide as a category of murder – often defined as the killing of an infant by the mother in the first year of life.

Other types of homicide, including mass murders in peacetime and serial killing,[9] have increased in the modern era, but not to the extent one would imagine if one was to judge by the outpouring of movies, novels and scholarship based on serial killers. When it comes to murder or homicide, over the past 30 years most attention has been directed at serial killers and forms of mass murder. But serial killing attracts a disproportionate share of media coverage, particularly in the United States, where it represents only 1 to 2 per cent of murders. Serial killers appear in a number of incarnations: some are female, most are men and some kill in teams. They kill in hospitals and nursing homes, urban and rural areas, on the road or in other environs that they regard as their comfort zone. No continent or civilization is immune to this form of murder.

One criminologist has assembled a long-term historical database of nearly 400 serial killers, according to which 84 per cent were male, 20 per cent were black, and the average age when they committed their first murder 27.5 years.[10]

There is no reason to suppose that serial killers have not been around since before recorded history. What has probably most changed is the background of the perpetrators. One of the more convincing explanations posits that sexually motivated crime, as in the case of most serial killings, is a leisure activity requiring available time to develop and dwell on sex fantasies and having the freedom to act.[11] Before the industrial age most people were probably too occupied with fending for food and finding lodging, or surviving wars, revolts and plagues and did not have the luxury of time for fantasizing about sex. This perhaps accounts for the lower rate of serial homicide and sex crimes in the non-industrial developing world, where living standards are tenuous for the average inhabitant. Prior to the industrial age, Europe's two most chronicled sexual killers were aristocrats: the fifteenth-century French lord Gilles de Rais (Bluebeard), and the Hungarian countess Elizabeth Báthory (1560–1614), whose reputation for sadistic behaviour and sexual murder was not revealed until 1720, when a Jesuit scholar uncovered transcripts of an original official investigation. Their proclivities remained obscure for so long in part because both were protected by their membership of the aristocratic milieu and the fact they preyed on the most vulnerable.

In the Anglo-Saxon epic poem *Beowulf*, the 'monstrous character' of Grendel is portrayed as having been killing people for years. His description as 'crazed with evil anger' is a pathology that modern criminologists often detect in recent perpetrators of sexually motivated murder.[12] Until the mid-eighteenth century sex crime of any kind was virtually unknown (or at least underreported). Few specific cases are known before those of Jack the Ripper in Britain and America's first identifiable serial killer, H. H. Holmes, in the late Victorian era. The obvious question to ask here is why sexual and serial murder become more common in the modern era. Some suggest that these crimes have always been poorly reported or, more probably, were explained away by the creation of vampire and werewolf myths. The *Newgate Calendar* was a general title given to a number of publications in the late eighteenth century that were compilations of the records of executions at Newgate Prison, where the gallows were moved to (from Tyburn) in 1783. Many historians have combed the various editions of the *Calendar* over the years looking for details of convicted murderers and their crimes, seeking any that might have been sexually motivated or serial killers. Few have ever been found, leading some researchers to conclude (incorrectly) that perhaps this type of murder did not exist during that era. There are few other sources from this period from which to obtain detailed information about specific murders. During the so-called 'witch mania' of the late Middle Ages, a great many crimes were attributed to witches consorting with the Devil (as well as other supernatural beings). A number of cases collected by the author Montague Summers were regarded in their times as werewolf cases by courts in the sixteenth century. In any case there is a good chance that between the fifteenth and eighteenth centuries a great many sex offenders were probably punished as witches and vampires.

Another theory worth examining here relates to the increase in sex crime that accompanies rising population density, the expansion of the female workforce and certain types of sadistic pornography (in the vein of Marquis de Sade) in the West. Although empirical research has not yet proven a causal link between pornography and sex crimes, serial killers such as Ted Bundy have suggested in his case there was a link. So it is not out of the question that the rise of 'literature' featuring non-procreative sex, bondage and forced rape (and its increased accessibility) might be part of the equation.

By the nineteenth century, sex crime and serial homicide were no longer the purview of aristocrats as the other social classes enjoyed leisure time and the concomitant time to indulge in 'perverse' behaviour in greater numbers. Between the Victorian era and the interwar Depression of the 1920s and '30s a new form of criminality seemed to rear its ugly head. From Germany's Weimar Republic and Victorian England to America's Gilded Age, numerous cultures reported the antics of sexual and multiple murderers. Few elicited the sympathy or adulation of the practitioners of the previously chronicled bandit traditions. Indeed, by the Victorian era great social changes had turned the criminal into a dangerous outcast – a veritable danger to society.

Fairy Tales, Werewolves, Vampires and other Shape-shifters

It has been well documented that fairy tales can tell us much about 'real conditions in the world of those who told and those who heard the tales'.[13] The German brothers Jacob (1785–1863) and Wilhelm (1786–1859) Grimm have bequeathed to literature a collection of unforgettable fairy tales, made more so by their use of sex and violence as recurrent themes. They began collecting tales around 1806 – many connected to child abandonment and infanticide, which were widespread among the common poor of the time. As the scholar Maria Tatar has noted, 'In fairy tales, nearly every character – from the most hardened criminal to the Virgin Mary – is capable of cruel behaviour.' And so it is in real life, as demonstrated time and time again by mothers who kill their children, children who kill their parents and so forth. In one such Grimm tale, 'The Robber Bridegroom', a young woman watches as her husband-to-be and some of his cronies abduct a young girl and drag her into a building where they proceed to undress her, put her on a table and indulge their bloodlust by hacking apart her body and sprinkling the pieces with salt. The young bride becomes increasingly appalled when one of the accomplices decides to cut off the girl's finger in order to get a gold ring, which he accomplishes with one axe chop. The finger sails into her lap from whence he retrieves it and pops it in his mouth! Lest one believe this is a one-off, a number of fairy tales include themes of cannibalism, often based on stories of werewolves and witches. At the conclusion of the Second World War, these tales were considered so appalling that Allied occupiers of Germany attempted to ban *Grimms' Fairy Tales* from classrooms and even tried to get them withdrawn from general circulation, believing they 'came to be viewed as nourishers and reflectors of a cruel, perverse national mentality [of the Nazis]'.[14] In his introduction to his volume of folk tales the Italian writer Italo Calvino likewise stated that the 'continuous flow of blood' in the Grimms' brutal tales is not to be found in their Italian counterparts, which rarely dwell 'on the torment of the victim'.[15] However, the Grimms do not hold a monopoly on violent folk tales, since it has been oft-chronicled that they adapted some tales from those of other nations, even creating tamer versions of various French and Russian stories. In the end, it is a fool's errand to attempt to determine 'national rankings for the degree of violence and cruelty in fairy tales'.[16]

By the Middle Ages, witchcraft and lycanthropy (transformation of a man into a wolf) were closely associated. Witchcraft was included in a litany of crimes such as heresy and unnatural offences, which were traditionally accorded some of Europe's most brutal punishments. In fifteenth-century Scotland it meant being condemned to 'ane staik and wirreit', translated as 'burned at the stake and strangulation'.[17] European witch hunts followed a variety of patterns. Some regions experienced them every few years, others never. The most prodigious took place in

Germany between 1550 and 1650. These witch hunts took place during an era when Europe was riven by various wars of religion, leading to the burning at the stake of 368 suspected witches in Trier (1581–93), 250 in Fulda (1603–6) and 157 in Würzburg (1626–31). Other large witch persecutions took place in Scotland, Lorraine, Sweden and even Essex, England, in this era.

The formal legal framework for the witch hunts was contrived under the aegis of the Holy Roman Empire under the *Constitutio Criminalis Carolina*, or 'Carolina'. One of the most important legal codes of the sixteenth century, the Carolina was enacted by Emperor Charles v in July 1532.[18] It would form the foundation for the evolution of common German criminal law over the next 300 years. By law, defendants were required to declare themselves guilty or not. The function of judges was to extract confessions by legal means and substantiate the validity of the confessions through further inquiry. Confessions were legally extracted through torture, however, only when there was circumstantial evidence to lend specific grounds for suspicion. By most accounts, the elimination of trial by ordeal contributed to the use of 'judicial torture'. In many respects these legal procedures were derived from Roman law, which prescribed torture, mutilation and execution both for interrogation of unfree witnesses and as punishment for numerous offences.[19]

When Elizabeth i came to the English throne in 1558, witchcraft was still a statutory offence, as it would be until 1736. England killed its share of witch suspects, but never approached the scale of executions on the Continent. This might have had something to do with the charges mounted against them. England was distinct from the Continent since it tried accused witches for specific acts of malice against individuals, while on the Continent they were charged with entering into compacts with the Devil and of becoming agents of Satan on earth.[20] In England, typically, those charged with a first offence were given a year in prison, and the penalty for practising witchcraft 'to provoke unlawful love' was a stint in the pillory plus a year's imprisonment. A repeat offence meant life in prison and the forfeiture of all property. As one observer sagely put it, many more people were hanged for stealing sheep and cutting purses, and thus 'on a national scale, the impact of witchcraft on English life was probably not very great.'[21] However, estimates of witch executions throughout sixteenth-century Continental Europe have been estimated as as high as 100,000.[22]

Recent research has suggested that climatic change had a hand in the European witch hunts during the 'Little Ice Age', a period of cooling between the fourteenth and nineteenth centuries. It was especially severe in Europe between 1560 and 1660, a period that coincided with surges in European witch trials. During this period the climate was much cooler and stormier than usual, leading to 'a lethal mix of misfortunes' that included crop failures and cattle diseases. This was soon followed by famine, which only served to further create a climate of fear and distrust among the masses. According to the anthropologist and archaeologist Brian Fagan, author of *The Little Ice Age*, witchcraft accusations tended to increase in Europe during years of severe weather as people accused neighbours of creating bad weather.[23] It was therefore no coincidence that the height of witch accusations in France and England corresponded with the severe weather years of 1587–8. Between 1587 and 1593, 300 witches were burned at the stake in Toulouse, France, alone. In one small south German town, Ellwangen, 260 were executed in the year 1611–12.[24]

Noted for their ravenous appetites, wolves would also be linked to a sexual hunger. During the centuries of European witch persecutions, lycanthropy was regarded as merely another activity of witches, whose metaphysical powers allowed them to transform into wolves and range the countryside for victims. There are numerous broadsides from sixteenth- and seventeenth-century France portraying witches riding on not just broomsticks, but the backs of wolves.[25] The first accounts of werewolves date back to the Book of Daniel (4:15–33), in which King Nebuchadnezzar exhibits certain symptoms of werewolfism for seven years. According to Greek legend, King Lycaon of Arcadia was transformed into a wolf by Zeus for offending the God by serving him a meal of human flesh, his name thus giving rise to the term 'lycanthropy'. Over the millennia werewolves have appeared in the works of the Greek historian Herodotus as well as those by ancient Roman and Persian physicians.

There are numerous studies that suggest that ancient superstitions about werewolves, and fairy tales such as 'Little Red Riding Hood', were inspired by actual cases of mutilation murders committed with such bestiality it was thought it could only have been perpetrated by a wolf-man. One early case that seemed to define the werewolf–serial killer nexus was that of Gilles Garnier, a sixteenth-century French hermit who confessed to being a werewolf (probably after excruciating torture), what the French would have referred to as a *loup-garou*. Garnier admitted to cannibalizing and killing fourteen children and having acquired his 'powers' through some sort of witchcraft during a four-month rampage. Some accounts portray him devouring human flesh and baying at the moon in the village of Dole. According to court documents:

> It is proven that on a certain day, shortly after the feast of Saint Michael last . . . [Garnier] being in the form of a wolf, seized upon a vineyard a young girl, aged about ten or twelve years . . . where he slew and killed her both with his hands, seemingly paws, as with his teeth . . . he stripped her naked and not content with eating heartily of the flesh of her thighs and arms, he carried some of her flesh [home].[26]

More than 50 local residents swore they saw him transform into a werewolf. Garnier was rewarded for his dastardly deeds by being burned alive. Wolf attacks were not unknown in parts of France in the late sixteenth century and early seventeenth. It was in this curious environmental melange of predatory wolves, witchcraft and unexplained child murders that cases such as that of Garnier, executed in 1573, came to prominence. In fact, 30 years earlier a farmer confessed to similar crimes, claiming he was a werewolf 'whose pelt was inside-out'.[27]

A variety of interesting explanations have been posited for werewolf and other shape-shifting hysteria over the years. Some have diagnosed rabies symptoms, others lycanthropia, a mental illness in which the sufferer believes they have actually turned into a werewolf. One theory that has garnered much attention posits that witnesses to these supernatural acts were possibly victims of ergot poisoning, caused by a fungal parasite sometimes found in bread that produces hallucinations. Did individuals simply imagine they were seeing a werewolf, or for that matter witches and other representatives of the Devil? The only thing that is certain is that once bread was treated with safer modern processing techniques these outbreaks decreased, as did mass werewolf sightings.[28] For others it is simply a case of the vivid imaginations of ignorant peasant villagers living in an era and region of Europe that was a hotbed of werewolf and witch activity. By some accounts, 30,000 cases were reported in medieval France alone in less than a century (according to the sixteenth-century witch finder Henry Boguet).

Not all cultures regarded wolves as malevolent figures; typically this was the case in places where wolves were considered great predators, and where famine brought them into proximity with peasants – thus in legends the wolf becomes a beast of ill-repute.[29] Man has been at odds with wolves since each first evolved, leading to the virtual hunting to extinction of wolves in most of the world. It is no coincidence that the werewolf (from Old English *wer*, man) has been a mainstay of popular folklore for centuries in countries around the world. Spain had its *lob ombre*, Portugal *lob omen*, Germany the *Werwolf*, Italy the *lupo mannaro* and French-speaking nations, as previously noted, have been well aware of the *loup-garou*. What's more, countries with no history of having wolves have created parallel shape-shifting stories such as the were-tigers of India and were-leopards in Africa, as well as were-jackals and were-hyenas. Indeed, in some African tribes the leopard is regarded as a totem animal that is believed to guide spirits of the dead to their final rest. As late as the mid-twentieth century, the so-called 'Leopard Men' were a deadly cult that expressed their 'were-leopard' lust for human blood and flesh in West Africa for several centuries. In Nigeria and Sierra Leone, for example, there are accounts of flesh-eating during religious ceremonies. Initiates are expected to bring back bottles of their victims' blood and imbibe it in front of other members. Members mimicked the killing mechanics of leopards – slashing and mauling victims with steel claws and knives – as they made preparations for brewing a magical elixir from the victims' intestines, guaranteeing its users the ability to turn into leopards and possess superhuman powers. There was a particularly serious spate of Leopard Men killings after the First World War, with authorities executing a number of members. As late as 1948, 48 murders were attributed to them. However, once cult members succumbed to police bullets they proved to be nothing but human predators. In 1949, 73 were arrested and 39 hanged.[30]

There are only a handful of actual individuals who have been specifically identified with werewolf killings. No serial killing case illustrates the werewolf connection better than that of Peter Stubbe (also Stube, Stump or Stumpf, or Stubbe Peeter), the most detailed account of a purported werewolf's activities in the pre-modern era. His macabre crimes were collected and published in a pamphlet translated into English from Dutch in 1590, titled *A True discourse Declaring the damnable life And Death of one Stubbe Peeter, a most Wicked Sorcerer, who in the likenes of a Woolfe, committed many murders, continuing his divelish practice 25 yeeres, killing and devouring Men, Woomen, and Children*. Besides humans, he was accused of killing sheep, lambs, goats 'and other cattle'.[31] It goes on to describe how he achieved his wolf-man status through a pact made with the Devil. In this way the Devil bestowed on Stubbe a wolf-skin belt that he would wear in order to morph from man into animal.

Although his crimes strain credulity, during torture Stubbe admitted to multiple counts of adultery, rape, incest, murder and cannibalism. Neighbours bolstered the prosecution's case, reporting to have discovered body parts 'scattered up and down the fields'. In the pamphlet there are a number of illustrations depicting Stubbe as a wolf, mauling victims. In any case, he terrorized the German countryside for almost 25 years before being tortured, beheaded and burned.

Several years later, in May 1603, the fourteen-year-old Jean Grenier boasted to fellow goat herders that he could turn himself into a wolf on a whim, simply by donning a magic skin, a boast that would ultimately lead to his arrest and sensational trial. His case became the best-known of the few werewolf trials held in France during the early modern era, when beliefs and legends revolving around the transformation of humans into wolves were widespread in southwest France.[32] Unfortunately, having made his claims in an era when many residents actually believed werewolves existed, and where there had been cases of local children being attacked and killed by wolves, the teenager was given the death penalty. In some cases, after a dead body was found, suspected witches in the vicinity were rounded up and accused of being werewolves; in other cases local shepherds and beggars might be captured by wolf hunters who lost track of a killer wolf, such as in the 1598 case in which hunters pursuing a killer wolf lost track of it, but ran into Jacques Roulet. Roulet was a French beggar who became known as the 'Werewolf of Angers'. Following his capture he was condemned to death for a litany of crimes, including werewolfism and murder (after an appeal, he was instead placed in an asylum). The case of Peter Stubbe, who was executed in 1598, is similar, as he was caught and accused after walking out of the forest. Shown the rack, he confessed quite readily.[33]

Vampirism and the Genesis of the Dracula Myth

In the darkness of night an Iranian taxi driver dubbed the 'Tehran Vampire' held this city in the grasp of a singular reign of terror as 'he stalked, kidnapped, raped, stabbed and burned' nine women, including a mother and her pre-teen daughter, over a three-month period beginning in March 1997. He covered his tracks by burning the bodies and was caught only by serendipity, when his suspicious behaviour at a shopping mall led to a police complaint that led to the discovery of blood stains in his car and a subsequent confession and criminal conviction. In most parts of the world his actions would have merited a simple death sentence if not life in prison. Sentenced to death nine times, Iranian justice conjured up something different. In order to assure the public that the serial killer had indeed been caught, authorities ignored public policy and decided to punish him publicly in the neighbourhood where he cruised for victims. This was after he had been whipped by prison officials for two days as part of his 214-lash sentence. With 1,000 police cordoning off the area, he was taken to his cruising grounds and 'tied to a metal bed set up on the roof of a small brick shed, and whipped by one male relative of each of his victims wielding a thick leather belt, in full view of the spectators'. Finally he was led underneath a yellow crane from which a noose dangled, where it was then tightened around his neck and he was hanged.[34]

Actual cases of human vampirism are quite rare, but seem to have habitually occurred over the millennia. In one classic Italian case, Vincenzo Verzeni (1849–1918) was convicted of mutilating and drinking the blood of his victims, some of whom had their genitalia ripped from the body. The so-called 'vampire brigand' Gaetano Mammone found his victims in the eighteenth century, believing he could drink blood when his strength needed fortification, much in the way twenty-first-century men might seek a shot of testosterone when they begin to feel their youthful vigour deserting them. Mammone used two methods for sating his bloodlust: severing the artery and sucking blood from the victim while still alive, or cutting off the head, removing the brains and then making a cup from the skull to drink the blood.

If werewolf legends are most closely connected to those of witches, vampires find their parallel in ghost stories, since most are considered corpses, or the living dead, who rise out of their coffins to wreak havoc on the living by sucking their blood. By most accounts the werewolf legend presages the vampire by centuries. One of the better explorations into the vampire phenomenon links it to Europe's history of plagues and epidemics, particularly wasting diseases, which might have given rise to the supernatural fears and added strength to rumours of vampirism (and premature burial). There has been a long-held association between vampirism and disease, and it is easy to see why. Cholera, for example, debilitates its victims due to the loss of bodily fluids, causing weight loss and dehydration. Similarly, tuberculosis leads to extreme fatigue and weight loss – symptoms associated with vampire victims. Thus it should be no surprise that vampire 'epidemics' occurred during periods of epidemic disease. In other cases, victims of albinism and porphyria, both misunderstood into the modern era, especially in developing regions where folklore may still trump science, suffered from light sensitivity, hence the vampiric 'fear of light' myth. Porphyriacs have difficulty metabolizing iron and need to take it in some digestible form, perhaps as blood, to satisfy the craving. Garlic has long been recognized in Eastern Europe for its medicinal values in combating a range of ailments. But beyond its curative powers, villagers have used it as a 'spiritual talisman' to protect against vampires, who are alleged to hate the smell. Peasants in Eastern Europe have been known to protect their houses against evil spirits by placing garlic crosses on windowpanes, doorknobs and door locks, thus adding another element to the vampire legend.[35]

The vampire of folklore is found universally in pre-Christian times and in non-Christian countries, and survived long after the Church imposed itself on superstitious societies throughout the world. The basic vampire story developed in the sixteenth and seventeenth centuries most notably in the Balkan region, where monks and travellers transported stories home to other regions of Europe. Despite a number of variants in Eastern European languages the term 'vampire' did not enter the English lexicon until 1734. Looking beyond the Dracula genesis and the Slavic variant of this phenomenon (the *upir*, a vampiric being from the Ukraine and Russia that operates during daylight hours), similar examples of the undead appear throughout the world, including China, Indonesia and the Philippines.

The classic vampire exemplar was the legendary Count Dracula, brainchild of the English writer Bram Stoker. Inspired by Romanian history and folklore, there are a number of parallels between his fictional character and the medieval warlord Vlad 'the Impaler' Tepes (he was a prince, but never a count). Born in the fortress town of Sighişoara around 1430, the inspiration for the Dracula legend was the scion of Vlad II Dracul, the military governor of Transylvania and a member of the Order of the Dragon.[36] The word 'dracula' may be derived from the Romanian *drac*, devil, and *ul*, the definite article – which then brings up the question of why local peasants would have connected a 'devil' with a prince who was respected for his construction of numerous churches and monasteries. Perhaps it was used by enemies of the prince as a strategy of vilification, or he was indeed as evil as his reputation suggests. A number of philologists support the link between Dracul and 'the Dragon', especially considering that Vlad was a member of the Order of the Dragon.[37] Members of the Order of the Dragon wore black cloaks over a red inner garment, another inspiration for the sartorial elegance of the fictional Dracula, adapted by Stoker. In any case the son of Vlad Dracul was given the name Vlad Tepes, or 'Vlad the Impaler'. By some accounts the young Vlad showed signs of his future depredations when he developed a fascination for executions at an early age, enthralled by the marching of criminals from jail to the gallows.

Both the fictional Dracula and his purported inspiration ruled as Prince of Wallachia (where, by the way, he was never viewed as a vampire by the populace) three times during a 25-year period.[38] Other elements of Vlad's life gel nicely with the vampire mythology. As a military strategist, Tepes shunned the sun, favouring night-time raids. According to tradition, the only way to kill a vampire was with a stake through the heart and decapitation; similarly, impalement became Vlad's favourite method of execution.[39]

The Dracula legend needs to be assessed according to the standards of his life in the fifteenth century, a century that gave rise to a number of brutal contemporaries. The historical Dracula was most associated with the torture and mass killings of his opponents, not an uncommon method for maintaining power in this region. As witnessed throughout history, many political leaders met challenges to their authority as well as consolidating it through the mass execution of those seeking to usurp power. In 1442, Vlad Dracul was forced to send Vlad and his brother Radu to Constantinople to serve as hostages of the Turks. It was probably here that he became familiar with the Turkish method of impalement with stakes, later adopting it as his favourite method of punishment and utilizing it on an unprecedented scale. Dracula adopted the Turkish method of impalement in dealing with criminals and political enemies alike. Almost any crime, from lying and stealing to murder, could earn the culprit a public impalement in the town square. Not surprisingly, it followed that crime and political corruption diminished and commerce flourished. It must be remembered that most of the written sources that embellished the history of the real Dracula were based on propagandistic pamphlets spread by Germans thanks to the new invention of the printing press in the fifteenth century. Accounts, some verified, others not, report that impalement stakes were permanently prepared in courtyards, public squares and other venues. The stakes were carefully rounded and supposedly bathed in oil so that the entrails of victims should not be pierced, causing immediate fatal wounds. Impalements ranged from the buttocks upwards to impalement through the navel, stomach or chest.

Impalement as punishment dates back to Asian antiquity and was practised by the Turks and other Balkan rulers, including Vlad Tepes's cousin Stephen of Moldavia, who in 1473 reportedly impaled 2,300

Wallachian prisoners through the navel. However you look at it, there was a certain method to this madness, for after all, 'Terror, the order of the day, was used as a psychological device to frighten the impressionable Eastern mind.'[40] In a report to the Vatican detailing Tepes's crimes in 1464, some 40,000 of all ages and nationalities were reportedly massacred,

> some by breaking them under the wheels of carts; others, stripped of their clothes, were skinned alive up to their entrails; others placed upon stakes, or roasted on red hot coals placed under them; others punctured with stakes piercing their head, their breast, their buttocks and the middle of their entrails, with the stake emerging from their mouths.[41]

Released from Turkish captivity in 1456, Vlad Tepes returned to Wallachia and took over after the assassination of his father. Hardened by the past decade, he embarked on a path of cruelty that led to his prominence in the rogue's gallery of bloodthirsty despots. While tales of his cruelty abound, none exemplifies it better on a small scale than the occasion when visiting emissaries refused to remove their hats in Vlad's presence, according to custom. Vlad rewarded their hubris by nailing their hats to their heads (a method later adopted by Russia's Ivan the Terrible). But this was easily surpassed by Vlad's first major act as leader, when he arrested all disloyal high-class Russian nobles (boyars) and their families, impaling the older aristocrats on stakes.

Dracula's Romania was a place where folk tales provide insight into the place of violence in society. According to one, probably far-fetched, tale, any wife caught having an affair could be punished by her husband by 'having her sexual organs cut' before being 'skinned alive [and] exposed in skinless flesh in the public square, her skin hanging separately from a pole or placed in a table in the middle of the marketplace'. According to the same account, the use of this punishment was later expanded to punish unmarried women who had lost their virginity, and 'unchaste widows'. If this account is to be believed, even less serious infractions could result in the excision of a nipple and 'a red-hot iron stake shoved into her vagina so that it penetrated her entrails and emerged from her mouth'. The woman was then 'tied to a pole naked and left exposed there until the flesh fell from her body and bones detached from sockets'.[42]

A Brief History of Sexually Motivated and Serial Murder

It has become a goal of many researchers to uncover the lives and crimes of the world's earliest serial killers. Unfortunately, due to a paucity of records, inadequate investigation and forensic tools, and more importantly a lack of understanding of this complex phenomenon, a list of exemplars is woefully lacking from the years before the twentieth century. Any list of pre-modern serial killers is invariably stacked with the usual cast of suspects including Gilles de Rais, Vlad Tepes and Elizabeth Báthory, and a handful of others.[43] What distinguishes these early serial killers is the number of aristocratic killers in their ranks. There were no newspapers to chronicle the suspicious disappearances and bestial murders in the pre-industrial era; but this does not mean they did not occur. It would not be until the birth of the cheap tabloid papers in the nineteenth century that one would find widespread coverage of sex murders, such as those committed by Jack the Ripper or by H. H. Holmes. But, even if in the fifteenth century there was widespread printed coverage of these crimes, the few who were literate came from the aristocracy or the clergy and preferred to read about their peers rather than the common riff-raff.[44]

The study of serial killers has become a cottage industry among researchers and storytellers since the 1980s and shows no signs of slowing down, despite the fact that, at least in the United States, this crime has appeared to decline since the 1990s. As more and more researchers look for tangible evidence of the earliest serial murderers, they find themselves revisiting the abominable actions of a handful of identifiable suspects who have been tied to crimes disturbingly similar to those committed by modern serial killers.[45] The Roman emperor Caligula, for example, was subject to bouts of boredom, during one of which he perhaps came up with his famous utterance, 'would that [the Roman people] had but one neck, so that I might sever it.' In one instance, Caligula reportedly started laughing and, when he was asked what was so humorous, replied, 'I was thinking how one word from me would send all your heads rolling on that floor, cut off from your bodies.'[46]

It might seem counterintuitive from a modern perspective that the first serial killers probably came from the ranks of the elite. Whether dictator, despot, emperor or nobleman, they killed because they could get away with it. One of the closest parallels between serial killers of the current era and the past is that they have been able to go undetected for so long by preying on people deemed inconsequential – the poor, the weak and the disenfranchised. Prior to the advent of the urban world, community residents constantly kept tabs on each other; there were few secrets in small communities. All visitors and strangers were subject to scrutiny from the minute they arrived in town until the moment they moved on, thus it would have required 'superhuman cunning to lure, unobserved, a succession of victims into one's home or deserted place'.[47]

One of the stranger cases in the history of murder involved a rich nobleman, Gilles de Rais (1404–1440). The type of murders committed by De Rais would fall under the category of lust murders in modern parlance due to the reportedly 'voluptuous pleasure' he took in committing his outrages against young, mostly male children. As Marshal of France he was a companion-in-arms with Joan of Arc in the struggle to unite France under Charles VII in the fifteenth century. In his book *Crux Ansata: An Indictment of the Roman Catholic Church* (1943) the writer H. G. Wells wrote that 'there was no Monte Carlo for [De Rais] in those days and no turf', insinuating that if de Rais had lived in the twentieth century he would probably have squandered his fortune betting on horses or gambling, instead of turning to the dark side and finding his excitement in other places. Credited as the original 'Bluebeard', Gilles de Rais reportedly 'loved cruelty, mutilation and murder beyond all things';[48] he also happened to be one of the wealthiest and most cultivated men of his era. His reign of terror did not come to the attention of authorities until his victims numbered in the hundreds. First of all, it must be understood that when children between the ages of three and sixteen began disappearing in the neighbourhoods of his castles, it 'did not arouse the curiosity and suspense that would be aroused in our own day'.[49] His victims were drawn from the likes of beggars, prostitutes, the homeless, tramps and gypsies who, much like their modern-day counterparts, represented the 'wandering and uncherished class',[50] hence were unlikely to be missed nor draw the type of scrutiny that would be accorded disappearances among the more respected classes. Indeed, there were few alternatives for the medieval poor to escape poverty: they could enter the Church or, if vexing and charming, they might attract the notice of a lord or lady of the manor who could take them from their parents and train them as pages, as in the cases of Báthory and De Rais.[51] For De Rais, if victims were not available in this fashion, he could simply rely on a ready source of street children who flocked to his gates daily for alms, or snatch them off streets, at play or while tending livestock. Estimates put his victims at between

141 and 800 as murder became his 'avocation' in the last eight years of his life.

According to extracts from De Rais' judicial confession, he admitted under oath that

> he had stolen or caused to be stolen very many boys – the number he could not remember – that he had put these boys to death and caused them to be killed, and that with them he had committed crimes and sins . . . that he had killed these boys sometimes himself with his own hand [and with accomplices] . . . by the amputation of their heads from their bodies, using daggers, poignards and knives; others with sticks or other implements for striking, by beating them on the head with violent blows; others again by tying them with cords and fastening them to some door or iron work . . . in his own room that these might be strangled and languish . . . After their death he took delight in kissing, gazing intently at those who had the more beautifully formed heads, and in cruelly opening and causing to be opened their bodies that he might see their interior, and that frequently, while these boys were dying, he would sit on their stomachs and take pleasure in seeing them dying.[52]

De Rais was burned to death as his servants reportedly cheered him on, exhorting him to die as 'a strong valiant knight'.[53]

Linked to vampirism through her supposed predilection for bathing in human blood, Elizabeth Báthory was descended from one of the oldest noble houses of Hungary, with bloodlines that included knights and bishops, cardinals and a king. By most accounts her family had descended into alcoholism, murder, sadism and possibly Satanism as it reached its nadir in the mid-sixteenth century. Nonetheless, as one of the few women linked to the elitist ranks of early serial killers, Báthory's legend seems to grow with each retelling. Chroniclers of De Rais and Vlad Tepes are, like those investigating the story of Báthory, hindered by the unreliability of contemporary evidence. It is especially glaring when one comes to the original testimony of Báthory's trial, in which vampirism and her tastes for blood were never alluded to. In fact, after her secret trial and death in 1611, the particulars of her life and death had been forgotten.

Myths and folk tales of a blood-drinking female vampire circulating in the Transylvanian mountains were eventually picked up by authors such as Bram Stoker in the nineteenth century and given new life by Bram Stoker as he stumbled onto the stories surrounding the four-teenth-century Vlad the Impaler, who by some accounts was distantly related through marriage to Báthory. The crimes of Báthory vanished from the public record until 1720, when they were rediscovered by a Jesuit scholar named Laszlo Turoczy and recounted in a book on her crimes, published only in Latin. In 1983, while conducting research in Hungarian and Romanian archives for their book *In Search of Dracula*, authors Raymond T. McNally and Radu Florescu discovered the original court documents, which not surprisingly revealed that it was a myth that she bathed in blood, a product of local gossip. But this revelation did little to burnish her life. For years common villagers had been filing complaints with royal authorities about the disappearances of their daughters while in Báthory's employ. It was not uncommon for masters to beat their servants in the 1600s. As a member of the aristocracy she was protected until she began targeting young women from privileged backgrounds. Báthory explained in her trial testimony that she did not send back the bodies of aristocratic employees due to the fact that they committed suicide and had to be buried immediately in an unmarked grave on unconsecrated ground; likewise, fears of epidemic diseases precluded sending infected corpses back to their homes. Four of her servants were first brought in for questioning (read: torture) and interro-gation. Ultimately, it was revealed that they had witnessed the murders of dozens of girls. In the ensuing trial two female servants were sentenced to have their fingers torn off with hot pincers before being burned alive. Another male servant was decapitated and burned and the fourth was acquitted. Báthory was sentenced to life in prison in 1611 after thirteen witnesses came forward with depositions that she had a list of 650 victims. She died in prison just three years later in 1614.[54]

Most murders originate in bar-room quarrels, domestic squabbles or hot-headed, often drunken, moments. Unlike these common typolo-gies of murder, multiple and serial killings have always been much rarer and unlikely to be overlooked by commentators past and present. There is a substantial body of evidence that serial murder existed in earlier periods of history. Multiple and serial murders surely occurred in the early modern period, but few were sensational enough to garner the type of attention that would enter the historical record or the public mind. One case that did can be found in a 1675 pamphlet, 'The Bloody Innkeeper', chronicling an English murder case in which the remains of seven men and women were uncovered from the yard of an alehouse near Gloucester. This 'cheap lodging house' was run by a local couple, serving mostly commercial travellers who needed night-time lodging. Eventually, the couple had scraped together enough money to move into a larger house. After they vacated the premises, workers digging the foundations for a new blacksmith's shop found seven fully clothed bodies, with one still bearing a 'rusty knife embedded in his chest'.[55]

The story of 'The Bloody Innkeeper' is an engrossing early account and does seem to offer a template for future serial killing cases. But, like some other reports of such crimes prior to the nineteenth century, there are no court records. It seems too detailed a case to be entirely the stuff of legend and most probably is an embellished account of a related case or possibly even completely factual. This case of a 'killer couple' resonates with tales in contemporary times of serial killer couples (sometimes called 'teams') who take part in similar schemes, the only difference being there is typically a sexual component to most modern team cases. In the end it is relatively uncommon to find mass killings during peacetime in the legal records, and true crime accounts prior to the nineteenth century rarely mention serial homicide-type cases.[56]

One of the earliest documented sexual murders took place in the small town of Alton, England, in 1867. In July, Frederick Baker, a young solicitor's clerk enjoying leisure time from work, sidled up to an eight-year-old girl and convinced her to take a walk with him. The girl would later be found decapitated and cut into pieces in a field. Despite claims of innocence, the clerk's office diary spoke otherwise, noting: 'Killed a young girl today. It was fine and hot.'[57] Baker would be tried and executed. The fact is that if he had lived in a much larger city he might have been able to continue his murders in anonymity.

In the nineteenth century the middle and lower classes joined the elites in the ability to indulge their hobbies during leisure time. For some, this included sexual crime and serial murder, thus 'sex crime was no longer the prerogative of only aristocrats or demented vagrants.'[58] An 1889 story by Leo Tolstoy illustrates the sinister opportunities linked to the emergence of more leisure time in *The Kreutzer Sonata*, featuring Pozdnyshev, who kills his wife in a jealous rage. Pozdnyshev ultimately rationalized his actions, blaming them on cultural changes that came with the Industrial Revolution, particularly the fact that the rise in leisure time for increasing numbers of workers allowed them to spend more time contemplating non-procreative sex. Tolstoy's character, like contemporary researchers studying the increase in sexually motivated murder, recognized that until the modern era most individuals worked a routine that kept them physically occupied from sunrise to sunset merely to put food on the table, with sexual activity kept 'in its proper place – only for reproducing the human race'.[59] The commoner and the peasant lived on the slim margins of survival for most of history. Forced to devote all of their precious resources to subsistence in a time of war, plague and famine, there was little time for leisure fantasizing beyond where the next meal would come from.

Murder comes in many guises. The Germans invented the term *Lustmord*, referring to 'murder for pleasure', or joy murder. Some of the earliest cases can be found in the journal of a German executioner from the early seventeenth century. Franz Schmidt, the public executioner of Nuremberg from 1573 to 1617, recounted in his diary executing a Nicklauss Stuller for committing eight murders with two accomplices:

> First he shot a horse-soldier; secondly he cut open the pregnant woman alive, in which was a dead child; thirdly he again cut open a pregnant woman in whom was a female child; fourthly he once more cut open a pregnant woman in whom were two male children.

One of his accomplices said they had committed a great sin and would take the infants to be baptized, but the other accomplice said he would be priest and baptize them, so he took them by the legs and dashed them to the ground. Stuller was punished for his inhumanity by being drawn out on a sledge and his body 'torn thrice with red-hot tongs and executed on the wheel'.[60]

In another case the executioner recorded his execution in 1574 of Kloss Renckhart for three murders committed with a co-defendant. In the most egregious of these he shot a miller to death and then 'did violence [i.e. rape] to the miller's wife and the maid, obliged them to fry some eggs in fat and laid these on the dead miller's body, then forced the miller's wife to join in eating them'.[61] He too would be executed on the wheel. Germany became the scene of a number of 'lust murders' between the world wars, leading one murder historian to opine that the end of the First World War inaugurated 'the age of sex crime'.[62] Indeed, some of the twentieth century's most memorable cases of serial and sex crime took place in Germany during this era. The 1920s alone saw Karl Denke killing and cannibalizing victims; George Grossman savaging young girls and selling their bodies as meat; and Fritz Haarmann, the 'Butcher of Hanover' and killer of at least 24 victims.

Serial Murder in the Modern Era

By most accounts there has been a global rise in serial killer cases over the past century. Criminologists who have examined the waxing and waning of reported serial killings cases over time suggest there are not actually more killers but 'more potential victims', citing the increasing abundance of marginalized people including immigrants, prostitutes, the homeless, runaways, senior citizens and the urban poor. This theory resonates back to the nineteenth century, when thousands of impoverished urbanized women turned to prostitution to make ends meet. Between 1970 and 2000 almost three-quarters of the world's serial killings took place in the u.s., followed by 21 per cent in Europe.

Until relatively recently the Developing World accounted for only 3 per cent of the world's reported serial killings. Some observers suggest this is only because of poor crime reporting, news censorship and under-financed police systems more focused on political repression than common criminality. Moreover, these countries have huge populations of impoverished, underprivileged and most importantly 'unwanted' people – the victims most at risk to the depredations of these killers. Over the past several decades, serial killers in these areas have been among the most prolific in terms of victims. Compared to killers such as Pedro Alonso López, a native of Colombia who is estimated to have killed 300 girls in several countries before his capture in 1980, and Javed Iqbal, sentenced to death in a Pakistani court in 2000 for the deaths of more than 100 children, America's pantheon of serial killers featuring Ted Bundy and his ilk are mere amateurs. Over the past several decades South Africa (which today perhaps has characteristics of both First and Developing World status) has been plagued by a disturbingly high (and hard to explain) number of serial killers, with an estimated 35 operating at one time (in the year 2000, this was second to the u.s.). By some accounts, South Africa had the highest per capita arrest rate for multiple murderers. This can perhaps be explained by the fact that most South African multiple killers are caught in less than two months, while the global average sits at around two years.[63]

Men dominate the ranks of serial killings, with only about 7 to 16 per cent committed by women. Female perpetrators, referred to as 'quiet killers', are often characterized by their choice of poison as a weapon, their careful selection of victims and ability to avoid apprehension. Unless they are killing in tandem with a male, sexual activity is rarely involved.[64]

The crime of serial killing is not going away anytime soon; no other crime captures the imagination of the public to such an extent. Furthermore, as the world continues to modernize it is becoming clear this is a worldwide phenomenon. Researchers suggest that serial murders have increased universally since the 1960s. Due to better crime reporting it has been revealed that few countries have escaped this horror, with Poland, Germany, China, Nigeria, Russia, Italy and Sweden among the countries reporting a rise in serial killings over the past decades.

Children, it seems, have increasingly become victims of serial homicide in Developing World countries. Explanations for the rise of such 'super' serial killers as Luis Alfredo Garavito, who killed 140 children in Columbia and Ecuador between 1994 and 1999, have focused on the socioeconomic pressures placed on populations that cannot provide adequate shelter and safety. In one of the most sensational murder cases, the previously mentioned Pedro López, the 'Monster of the Andes', killed perhaps 350 children in Ecuador, Columbia and Peru in the 1980s. Due to the peculiarities of Colombian criminal law, he was released for good behaviour after only eighteen years behind bars. Charles Sobhraj was convicted in India in 1976 for killing at least eight victims in Turkey, Thailand, Nepal and India; the South African 'Station Strangler', Norman Afzal Simons, killed 21 children during an eight-year period in the 1980s. Andrei Chikatilo, aka the 'Butcher of Rostov' and the 'Red Ripper', confessed to killing 55 victims in Russia between 1978 and 1992, and Anatoly Onoprienko surpassed the 50 victim mark between 1989 and his capture in 1996.[65]

Muti Murders

Most forms of murder can be found across a broad spectrum of global societies over the millennia. However, there are some types linked to local cultural beliefs that are much rarer, such as in the case of South African *muti* murders. The Zulu word *muti* refers to medicine and 'implies the intentional gathering of body parts for use in traditional African medicine'.[66] In order to gather the requisite body parts, adherents must first murder someone, a type of homicide that eludes any meaningful attempt to place this crime within a criminological context. In recent years, researchers have begun to associate *muti* murders with individuals seeking wealth and prestige and who attempt to protect themselves during the commission of a crime or in its aftermath to elude authorities. There have also been cases in which religious leaders have used *muti* murders to try to enhance the size of their congregations: by obtaining certain bodily organs, the leader would gain the power to recruit more members.

According to some African belief systems, individuals are born with only a certain amount of good fortune, and those that exhibit more good luck than others are suspected of having utilized supernatural powers to get ahead. There are just so many ways to make your own luck, and one of these avenues is through strong medicine, or *muti*. This can be accomplished by collecting body parts to increase the power of a medicinal potion. The most powerful body parts are those taken from victims while they are still breathing, said to be able to make a criminal's goal of stealing an expensive item or robbing a bank successful. According to the criminologist Eric W. Hickey, there are four actors in a *muti* murder. Initially there is a client, who seeks certain advantages in life, such as money, power or protection, and has the money to hire a healer and collect the *muti* once it is concocted. By most accounts, this type of healer is considered outside the traditional healers in the community, as they are regarded more as witches than healers, due to their tendency to inflict suffering, which goes against the traditional healer's inclination to heal, help and offer benevolence. In any case, once the healer-witch enters the contract with the client, he embarks on deciding what herbs, roots and body parts are required and sets about finding the third player: the murderer. The healer instructs the killer on which body parts to accumulate, how to extract them from the body and which parts need to be removed while the victim is still alive. The murderer is compensated financially, unless they are already an apprentice to the healer/witch. Finally there are the victims, who range from infants to adults, males to females, strangers to relatives.

Cagey killers, in an attempt to avoid committing a serious crime, have been known to steal body parts from hospital or freshly dug graves. Elderly victims are avoided at all costs, since their 'life essence is waning and not powerful'. Like the ancient Romans, who attributed certain types of luck to amulets made from body parts such as the rabbit's foot, specific body parts are needed for specific *muti* endeavours. For example, breast fat is considered 'mother luck' and will help women draw customers to their place of business. Genitals of either sex are said to enhance virility and are in demand by the infertile. Eyes are used for potions intended to offer the power of prescience; the tongue to win the love of the opposite sex; and hands are sought by businessmen, since they are associated with beckoning potential customers and receiving money.[67]

As recently as 2009, one South African report indicated that 70 per cent of the people surveyed in South Africa and Mozambique believed human body parts make *muti* more effective.[68]

From Running Amok to Rampage and Spree Killing

The term 'to run amok', from the Malay word *amuk*,[69] denoting 'mad with uncontrollable rage', has become shorthand for spree and rampage killings. One psychiatrist describes this form of multicide as 'an irrational-acting individual who causes havoc'. This type of killing seems to have become more common over the past twenty years. While psychiatric literature classifies running amok as a 'culture-bound syndrome', due to its discovery more than 200 years ago in 'remote primitive island tribes, where culture was considered the predominant factor in its pathogenesis', it does not explain why it has increased in frequency among modern societies that have no geographic isolation.[70] The famed mariner Captain James Cook is generally credited as the first Westerner to observe this behaviour: in 1770 while on his first circumnavigation of the world he witnessed it among Malay tribesmen. Today we recognize, unfortunately with increasing regularity, the pathology of certain individuals who embark on homicidal (and often suicidal) killing sprees that come to an end only due to their own death. Cook's observations of one such action is a template for such behaviour: he noted how one individual, seemingly without cause, went on a frenzied killing spree, indiscriminately targeting people and animals in his rampage. According to Cook's interpretation, amok attacks consisted of an average of ten victims and ended only when the killer was stopped by other tribesmen, often by being killed. In later investigations researchers would note this behaviour among tribes in such far-flung locations as the Philippines, Laos, Papua New Guinea and Puerto Rico.[71]

No matter where and how it occurs, mass murder is a rare crime in peacetime. When it does take place at the workplace, in schools, the domestic environment and so forth, public commentators rush to make certain assumptions about a quickly changing world, but rarely mention how uncommon it is compared to other violent crimes. One of the best definitions of mass murder asserts that it must be 'a continuous incident or a series of closely linked incidents in which more than 5 are injured and at least 3 of whom die'.[72] One of the earliest recorded cases in the modern era took place in Mühlhausen, Germany, in 1913, when Ernst Wagner, or 'Wagner von Degerloch' (1874–1938), described as 'an admirable citizen, dignified somewhat quiet' and the best teacher in the village, killed nine people plus his wife and four children and wounded twelve more. He was institutionalized for his efforts and died in 1938. He joined the Nazi Party in 1929, and suffered from the delusion that he was the target of a vast Jewish conspiracy that included using one of his dramas to make the silent film *Ben Hur* without his permission and that another best-selling author had plagiarized his unpublished works.[73]

Over the past several decades similar examples of mass homicide have been labelled as either spree or mass killing. What distinguishes this form of multicide from mass murder is that its perpetrators are more likely to die – either by suicide or in a police shoot-out. These events occur randomly and are virtually never predicted. Although these types of killings are most common in the United States, no country or region has a monopoly on this behaviour. Spree killings are less common in nations with stricter gun control, such as Britain, but there are few other distinctions that can be made between countries that have them and those that do not. This is made quite clear by the list of places that have experienced such incidents, which includes Canada, Korea, Japan, Australia, France, Finland, Germany, New Zealand, Colombia, Sudan, the West Bank, Nepal and Norway. But even the strictest gun laws will not prevent this crime, as witnessed in Japan, China and Britain which, while having among the strictest gun laws in the world, have also experienced killing rampages by lone gunmen. In 1938, for example, 21-year-old Mutsuo Toi used a shotgun, a Japanese sword and an axe to kill 30 individuals, including his grandmother, before killing himself. This would be the world's worst spree killing until it was surpassed by Woo Bum-kon's rampage in South Korea in 1982 that took the lives of 56 people. In Britain, Michael Ryan murdered fourteen and wounded fifteen in 1987, and in 1996, Thomas Hamilton killed seventeen people and wounded more than a dozen others.[74]

According to one historian, 'even the most bizarre and apparently unmotivated murder is not without social meaning. Like every other form of human behavior, murder is patterned by the prevailing relationships ... that exist within a society.'[75] The ways human beings murder each other, as well as their reasons for doing it, tell us much about particular societies, and as the aforementioned historian James Given has demonstrated in his analysis of English medieval violence, every society 'has its own specific patterns of violent behavior'.[76] Due to the paucity of record keeping throughout most of the historical record, much of the information is anecdotal. Prior to the twentieth century dependable data regarding patterns of homicide and sex crime is woefully lacking, leaving it to historians to cast a wide net in the search for documentation. As world crime data collection continues to improve into the twenty-first century, so does our understanding of the crime of murder – its variations, cultural anomalies and explanations for regional crime patterns. In 2006 North America reported more cases of serial homicide than any other continent – perhaps up to 80 per cent of all serial killers in the twentieth century, mostly in the United States. Second only to North America is Europe, with the United Kingdom and Germany leading the pack. Until the lifting of the Iron Curtain, except for high-profile cases that lasted into the post-USSR era such as that of 'Red Ripper', most information on what was regarded as 'decadent Western-style crime' remained a state secret in the Soviet Union, as it does in China, North Korea and elsewhere today.[77]

8

Crime and Punishment in a Post-colonial World

O ver the past 600 hundred years a number of world powers established colonies in far-flung regions of the globe. The birth of what we now refer to as 'globalization' helped transport and transmit their philosophies on crime and punishment to their colonies, territories and protectorates. Naturally, as these societies made the transition to sovereign states in the twentieth century, the former colonial justice regimes had a huge bearing on how the new nations responded to criminal behaviours. The English, for example, introduced common-law traditions to parts of Africa, America, Australia, Asia, Canada and New Zealand; likewise, the Japanese imparted their practices to parts of the Pacific Rim, China and Korea. One legal expert observed that 'lawyers trained in Singapore can, without much difficulty, read and understand a statute or a judicial decision' from any common-law country.[1]

The same case can be made for civil legal scholars, following the Spanish and Portuguese introduction of criminal justice practices to Latin America. The same goes for the Dutch who left their imprint on the criminal justice systems of Indonesia, South Africa and colonial American New Amsterdam. In the process of introducing institutions of justice to their colonies, these systems had to be modified in order to meet the new conditions they found in each region. In the New World, for example, the English, French, Dutch and Spanish colonizers were forced to adapt their institutions in order to coexist with hundreds of sovereign Indian nations, the vast wilderness and, later, with slavery, after introducing it to various colonial realms. Indeed, the history of American criminal justice began with the transplantation of European traditions to the New World. The criminal codes and punishments in the American colonies initially resembled those of England, Holland,

AN EYE FOR AN EYE

Spain and France (depending on which of the thirteen colonies is being considered). In the process, three criminal justice systems emerged in English North America; one for black people, one for white people and one for Native peoples – all with their distinct written and unwritten codes of law and behaviour.[2] Like other former colonies, in order to understand the history of crime and punishment in the Americas it is necessary to appreciate not just the diversity of legal traditions, but the way they were adapted to meet new conditions and environments.

All the modern countries of the Americas share a colonial background, though their legacies differ depending on the colonizing countries, the length and extent of colonization, and the level of acceptance of the imposed order by indigenous populations. Countries such as Canada, the United States, Belize, Jamaica and Trinidad and Tobago, for example, still retain a mostly common-law system of justice, while civil legal traditions, introduced by the Spanish, Portuguese, French and Dutch continue to flourish in Central and South America as well as several Caribbean nations, albeit with a number of permutations.

Meant to be the 'war to end all wars', the denouement of the First World War was also a turning point in geopolitics. Following the Paris Peace Conference of 1919, the map of much of the world had been redrawn as the victorious Allies reconfigured national boundaries from Finland to Czechoslovakia, 'recognizing a bewildering array of new countries that emerged from the ruins of fragmented empires'.[3] The two world wars were instrumental in setting off a chain of events that would change not just the geopolitical world but the world of crime and punishment. The decline of European colonialism and imperialism in the twentieth century was followed by a transfer of power to nascent states scrambling to create their own systems of governance and crime control. This process was already under way as part of the colonial state-building process. Britain, for example, had already allowed its diverse colonies to take a syncretic approach, combining customary criminal laws with those of the common-law tradition. In fact, colonial peoples often 'adopted modified, transformed or superseded British law and institutions'.[4] Similarly, centralized states such as the Ottoman Empire, once home to a multitude of legal codes, had to make the transition to Turkish nationhood as the empire dissolved and its various Arab lands divided up mostly between the French and British. The end of the First World War had similar consequences for the remnants of the Austro-Hungarian Empire and Tsarist Russia.

The Civil Law Tradition in the Americas

In the sixteenth century, Spanish and Portuguese administrators introduced elements of the civil legal tradition to what is now Latin America.
Over the ensuing centuries most countries in this region developed
hybrid systems, amalgamating rudimentary aspects of indigenous tribal
law and features of European legal traditions. For example, until the
nineteenth century, Venezuela belonged to the Spanish Empire and was
under the sway of the civil (inquisitorial) model. Like some of its neighbours, in recent decades it has adopted the common-law adversarial
model (in 1999), signalling a paradigmatic shift in criminal justice
procedure.

Beginning with Cortés's subjugation of the Aztecs in 1521, the
indigenous population of pre-Conquest Mexico was incorporated
into the Spanish Empire. Spanish authorities had to contend with well-
established tribal laws and customs, but the lack of any strong native
legal tradition led to the Transatlantic extension of Spanish law.[5] Spanish
legal standards proved to be much more punitive, doling out whippings
equally to both genders, and hangings and mutilations for robberies,
with punishment usually predicated by caste and colour. In a similar
vein, the Portuguese colonized Brazil in the 1500s and introduced their
particular brand of justice to the Americas. Between 1603 and 1803
Brazil linked law and religion inextricably, making sins and moral lapses
equivalent to crimes. Their imported penal sanctions included the
European standbys of mutilation, branding, torture and execution, typically by hanging or burning.

In the aftermath of the conquest of Mexico, Spain dubbed its New
World empire 'New Spain'. At its zenith it included present-day Mexico,
Central America (except for Panama), most of the United States west
of the Mississippi River and the Floridas. The Spanish established a
Tribunal of the Acordada to dispense justice in the eighteenth century.
Its officials exercised authority over all crimes of robbery, physical
violence, illegal seizure of property or women, arson, the maintenance
of private prisons outside the larger urban centres, and strict control
over alcohol consumption. According to a 1735 ordinance, the minimum
sentence was 200 lashes and six years in galleys, or heavier; for Spaniards
it was six years' incarceration in a *presidio* prison; for mestizos, six years
in a workhouse and 200 lashes.[6]

Except for a handful of countries, most of Latin America achieved
self-government from colonialism between 1810 and 1825, leading to

the protracted development not just of state formation but the creation of new penal systems that eventually included experimentation with various penitentiary regimes. As early as 1816, Argentina had already established several houses of correction. But it took almost a century for any substantial progress to occur. In 1904 Buenos Aires adopted a model penal regime that would eventually earn the country the accolade of having 'one of Latin America's leading prison systems'.[7] Peru began searching for confinement alternatives shortly before its independence from Spain in 1821. Prior to that period, jails were typically situated on the bottom floors of municipal buildings, earning the moniker *infiernillos*, or 'little hells'. The following year the first prison bylaws were introduced which eliminated prison fees and inaugurated classification of prisoners by gender and age.

There had been a long-established use of the *presidio* prison by the Spanish. Typically situated near ports, *presidios*, where inmates worked at hard labour, were commonly used throughout the Spanish Empire and sometimes functioned as penal colonies. So the notion of incarceration was already familiar to penal reformers. Ultimately, *presidio* confinement became the most common penal sentence in New Spain.

Beginning in the first half of the nineteenth century, North American and European prison models were adopted (in Brazil, 1834 and Chile, 1843). Brazil was among the first Latin American countries to adopt the penitentiary. Rio de Janeiro's Casa de Correção, one of Latin America's most famed prisons, was completed in 1836. By some accounts it was 'the first institution of confinement in Latin America to be built following penological principles'. Prison architectural historian Norman Johnston has gone as far as calling it the 'last prison ever constructed influenced by English architectural models'.[8] But as so often happens, after an initial surge of enthusiasm the pursuit of the penitentiary lost momentum and the Brazilian states diverted prison facilities towards correcting the behaviour of disobedient slaves rather than conventional criminal behaviours. The fervour for reform was reignited in the 1850s after a commissioner sent to the United States to survey prison design came back endorsing the Pennsylvania solitary system.

In some cases it would take other Latin American countries another hundred years to construct penitentiaries, as in the cases of Colombia (1934) and Cuba (1939).[9] Peru borrowed elements of the *presidio*, which was more medieval fortress than modern prison, exemplified by the construction of Lima's Presidio de Casas-Matas. No matter which prison design was adopted, it predictably followed, as in other areas of the world, that these institutions would gradually sink into decay, with poor sanitation and few internal controls becoming the rule rather than the exception.

Heavily influenced by Spanish law and the French Napoleonic Code, Bolivia has been one of the least politically stable countries of Latin America, with 193 *coups d'état* between 1825 and 1991. It shares with other countries in this region a predilection for imprisoning that has left most prisons egregiously overcrowded and inhumane. For indigenous communities, far from the reach of the traditional judicial system and the police, it often falls to the community to deal with serious crimes such as the theft of agricultural and farm products. Community punishment in Bolivia is distinctive for its punishments ranging from mockery and intimidation to stoning, exile and even death.

The use of the death penalty in Latin America has been marked by an inconsistent process of abolition and reintroduction. In Bolivia in 1961 the death penalty was abolished and within ten years was reintroduced during a period of terrorism, kidnappings and crimes against the government and security apparatus. Any citizen who took up arms against the government, joined its enemies or collaborated with them in time of war faced the firing squad (Che Guevara would find this out the hard way). In 1981 the death penalty was extended to drug trafficking. By 1997 it was abolished for common crimes but retained for murder, especially parricide, unless the president commuted the sentence to 30 years' imprisonment. Despite all the wrangling over the death penalty, the last execution there took place in 1974.

Unlike Bolivia, Venezuela abolished the death penalty in 1863 and has not reinstituted it. However, in the 1990s, human rights activists compared modern-day police death squads that summarily targeted criminals as just another form of capital punishment, albeit without trial. Indeed, extra-legal lynchings have increased over the past decades in conjunction with rising crime rates. Chile abolished the death penalty in 1930 but reinstituted it between 1930 and 1991. Firing squads were the preferred method for those who killed family members, kidnapped or physically abused children, kidnapped adults resulting in their death, or the murder of law enforcement agents. In 2001, the death penalty was formally replaced by 40-year prison stints. Argentina carried out its last judicial execution in 1916, but the death penalty was not officially abolished there until 2008.

Common-law Traditions in the Caribbean

Considered a 'backwater of the Spanish Empire' in the 1600s, much of the Caribbean became part of the British West Indies colonies, after conquest in 1797. This region is distinct for the evolution of criminal justice systems initially organized around the slave trade. Some scholars trace the high rates of crime in modern Caribbean nations back to the influence of colonial slave culture, when systematic brutality became a basic trait of plantation society and its associated systems of slavery and indentured servitude. One expert on Trinidad has made the case that, 'crucial to the success of colonialism was the notion of racial inferiority and the separation and treatment of people based on the immutable fact of colour of skin or racial origin.'[10] However, the Caribbean colonial experience was also distinct from other colonial slave societies. For example, when European colonists arrived in Africa and Asia, they were able to force foreign social structures on already flourishing social and political structures. On the other hand, the Caribbean experience would witness a longer drama in which the indigenous population was almost wiped out and a completely new society was established under forced circumstances.

Penal development in Guyana illustrates the often complex evolution of justice systems. One of the few Caribbean countries that is not an island, it has a mixed legal system based on civil and common-law precedents. First settled by the Dutch in 1616, it followed a combination of civil law and Germanic traditions. In 1814 the colony was ceded back to Britain, but the Roman–Dutch system remained dominant until 1916, when the British common-law system became more influential due to its better flexibility and the legal protections it offered.

Despite gaining independence, a number of Caribbean nations are still affiliated with the British Commonwealth and have elected to retain common-law practices to a great extent. A number of smaller countries still retain a territorial or dependency status within the Commonwealth, including several Caribbean island nations. However, there have been numerous revisions of colonial criminal law. For example, Antigua and Barbuda, independent (within the British Commonwealth of Nations) since 1981, in contrast to most other common-law countries, established its age of criminal responsibility at just eight years old. Though its mother country has abolished similar punishments, Antigua and Barbuda continues to offer a wide range of punishments including imprisonment, fines, probation and parole. Corporal punishments such as whipping are supplementary to other punishments for crimes in which the offender is convicted of injuring a victim by means of a deadly instrument; being armed with an offensive weapon or instrument; robbing a person and using personal violence at the time or immediately after the crime is committed; or assaulting any person with the intent to rob that person (females are excluded from lashings).[11]

The Bahamas retain five categories of punishment, including the death penalty, fines, imprisonment, payment of costs, and combinations of the aforementioned. Statutorily, crimes that do not provide a specific punishment are punished by seven years' imprisonment for felonies and two years for misdemeanours. By some accounts more than one out of every 200 Bahamians is behind bars, the eighth-highest rate of imprisonment in the world. The use of the death penalty continues to be a source of acrimony and debate within the Commonwealth and contravenes British law. In the Bahamas it has been used for murder, treason and piracy, and has been mandatory in the case of first-degree murder since British rule ended in 1929 (at least 50 have been hanged). As it now stands, the debate over the death penalty and corporal punishment, punishments abolished in Britain, are still on the books in a number of its former Caribbean colonies. Belize, for instance, still has the death penalty. Despite high popular support for it, however, it has not been used since 1985. This is mainly due to the fact that Britain's Judicial Committee of the Privy Council (JCPC) has refused to permit the execution of people convicted of murder who had spent more than five years pursuing various appeal options. The issue of crime and punishment has roiled the entire English-speaking Caribbean since 1994, when the Privy Council of the United Kingdom, the final court for Britain's thirteen dependencies and former colonies in the region, ruled that prisoners who had been held more than five years on death row had been subjected to cruel and unusual punishment and their sentences should be commuted to life. This went a long way in undermining public confidence in the criminal justice system in Trinidad and Tobago.

The actions of the Privy Council some 3,000 miles away enraged Trinidad and Tobago's population of 1.3 million, 80 per cent of whom supported the death penalty, 'a form of justice long denied them by their former colonial masters'. Inhabitants called for swifter accounting on death row in the face of a growing violent crime wave. Similar sentiments were shared by other Caribbean countries still under the sway of the Privy Council. Execution has often been regarded as a quick fix for stemming violent crime waves, although the jury is still out as to whether it works or not. In a number of Caribbean nations during the 1990s, in the face of international condemnation, several countries tried to speed up the hanging of condemned criminals. In 1999, the Council surprised many observers by rejecting the appeal of men who had been sentenced to die for butchering a family of four with no apparent motive four years earlier. Surprisingly, the appeal was rejected on the grounds that the island's constitution required it to carry out the execution. Trinidad's two official hangmen received £50 each for their services. The bodies of the condemned were buried in unmarked and unconsecrated graves in the grounds of the main island prison, Golden Grove.[12] The execution in 1999 of Trinidadian drug kingpin Dole Chadee, along with eight gang members, after the reinstatement of the death penalty, ended a 'homicidal empire that stretched from Colombia to Europe and America'; in the aftermath of these executions the murder rate in Trinidad fell by 25 per cent.[13]

Besides the common-law elements, the post-colonial Caribbean has seen the influence of other legal traditions. In Grenada, where common law prevails, it has also been receptive to Hindu, Muslim and Indian laws, and laws that have increasingly targeted same-sex relations and abortion, both crimes punishable by ten years in prison, while flogging for sex crimes is not unknown.

The End of Empire in Africa

Before the introduction of Western penal practices some African societies were already utilizing various permutations of penal confinement. The smaller in scale the society, the less likely it was that these holding facilities were intended to be permanent. African prison historian Florence Bernault has demonstrated that in decentralized societies individuals were typically tied up or chained in public, while more centralized Western African states, much like their European counterparts at a similar stage of development, made use of permanent holding pens to confine suspects until they went on trial and were subsequently punished. Towards the conclusion of the nineteenth century the modern penitentiary was imposed by European colonizers in Africa on an unprecedented scale, almost as soon as each territory fell under colonial domination. By the end of the century the whole of sub-Saharan African had been partitioned into no less than 30 colonial territories, established by seven European countries (France, Britain, Germany, Italy, Portugal, Spain and Belgium). The impact of their justice systems insured that 'prison custody was adopted as the primary and referential sentence in all sub-Saharan colonies.'[14]

In most cases new crimes were added to the local statute books and pre-existing offences deemed not in tune with the modern era were banned. Traditional cultural behaviours such as adultery by men, incest and bigamy would no longer be countenanced by the European legal arbiters, grounded as they were in Christian moral precepts. These former behaviours became criminalized. At the same time, new economic crimes were created and public order laws were initiated that criminalized acts of rebellion against the colonial authorities. The new economic laws were introduced in some regions 'to protect European trading interests', as in the case of its prohibition against producing and selling indigenous alcoholic drinks, protecting the European liquor market in the colonies.[15]

When considering the spread of penal practices in Africa one must take into account the influential spread of Islam from North Africa to west and east Africa in the twelfth century, paralleling the assimilation of Islamic law and criminal justice practices. As a result, by the time of colonization and the creation of new countries a confusing synthesis of legal systems and customs was already practised. To make matters even more perplexing, colonizers created new political boundaries that took negligible account of the various and often competing ethnic groups that made up these new political entities. The British colonization of Nigeria exemplified this conundrum, when it allowed Islamic criminal law to supersede common law, only intruding into the legal process when it deemed the application of penal measures 'repugnant to natural justice'. This process of 'domesticating' Islamic law by making it conform to Western notions of criminal justice became a hallmark of the British colonial experience. The utilization of Islamic criminal code was not banned until 1960, commuting sentences from crucifixion, amputation or death by stoning to imprisonment. But until then, the Northern Nigerian emirates used the *haddi* lashing for moral offences, particularly for adultery and drinking alcohol. In 1920 the governor reported to the colonial secretary that native court flogging had recently averaged about 3,500 per year, and he was strongly of the view that the power to order corporal punishment should be restricted to the courts of the more highly politically organized areas of the north and west. When it came to criminal justice, European administrators attempted to ensure uniformity and consistency in the legal process by adapting European criminal laws and justice systems.[16] As a result, sub-Saharan Africa's modern penal systems are mostly based on colonial models.

Beginning in the 1570s, European imperialists and traders were already in the process of constructing coastal forts and garrisons replete with their own jails and holding facilities. Portuguese navigators got an early start, signing treaties with local rulers to establish military outposts and trading forts along the coastline. But no matter what treaties they signed and the impressive edifices they built, the fact was that until the nineteenth century, Europeans were not able to exercise much authority beyond their settlements. As the slave trade gathered force most confinement along the west coast of Africa was directed at constraining slaves in preparation for the Atlantic crossings to the Americas. In the 1570s Portuguese colonists introduced imprisonment to Angola, filling cells with criminals, slaves and banished prisoners from Portugal and Brazil. Portugal continued to banish prisoners to Angola into the 1930s as an alternative to execution.

The Germans introduced Rwanda to western punishment and imprisonment during its occupation in the late nineteenth century. When it ended in 1907, Rwanda adopted standardized rules for flogging and other exhibitory punishments. German and Belgian penal practices would influence several colonial regimes, but it was not until Belgian rule after the First World War that actual detention centres were constructed in Rwanda. Like the knout in medieval Russia, Belgian officials used a particular lashing instrument, the *chicote*, which was a whip made out of bull's or hippopotamus's nerves and was used by warders in the Belgian Congo until independence in 1959–60. The Belgians were frequent targets of criticism from the humanitarian and international communities for this brutal tactic. In 1906, blows were limited to 50 strokes, declining to twelve lashings in 1923, eight in 1933 and finally four strokes in 1951. The Belgians were not alone in this practice. Long enamoured with whipping as a part of the penal regime, British officials enforced their control over recalcitrant Africans with whippings, beatings and caning until the 1930s (except in Ghana), when these were replaced with cane beatings only.[17]

The French introduced its first penitentiary to Burkina Faso (formerly Upper Volta) in 1920. During that decade African and European prisoners were housed together, but this would come to an end in 1928 and would not continue until prisoner segregation was outlawed in 1946 at the end of colonial rule. The French also influenced the penal code of Madagascar and in 1840 colonial officials opened Senegal's first prisons.

Before the decade was out jails were being utilized to control common urban criminals and a floating population of itinerant Africans. Nonetheless, throughout the colonial period penal institutions remained substandard when they appeared at all and were utterly lacking as confinement facilities. Except for trading post jails few people would be confronted with imprisonment on any level.

No group suffered more in prisons than women, due in no small part to the fact that genders were not separated in African prisons until the 1920s (although this segregation was mandated by the French in the 1850s). Recent scholarship suggests postcolonial regimes have done little to improve the conditions for women. As one historian put it, 'today's female quarters do not differ significantly from colonial ones.'[18]

Florence Bernault is among the recent historians who suggest that the introduction of corporal punishment in Europe's African colonies was the transplantation of European traditions, except this time it would be 'African bodies' bearing 'the physical mark' of colonial rule. The reliance on physical punishment over imprisonment into the modern era was hardly in keeping with a modern disciplining agenda, in the Foucauldian sense of the term.[19] Flogging remained or was reintroduced as part of the penal regime long after the arrival of the penitentiary. Most colonial legislatures, superseding native courts, permitted physical punishment, but only against black prisoners.

After brief Portuguese dominance, the Dutch Cape Colony was established by the Dutch East India Company in 1652, introducing forms of execution common throughout its trading empire. The Dutch ruled its colony with an iron fist until it was officially taken over by the British in 1806.[20] During Dutch rule the flogging post was considered one of the milder instruments utilized to gain a confession. As one scholar has put it, 'if lynching is as American as cherry-pie, then flogging is as South African as biltong.'[21] When it came to pain, nothing was more convincing than the thumbscrew and the rack. One elaborate form of torture employed suspension from the ceiling by a pulley system. If this was not unpleasant enough, it became excruciating when weights of 50 pounds (22 kg) each were attached to both big toes before the suspension process began.

In the early years of the colony capital punishment was determined by status; typically, the lower the status the more prolonged the suffering. Drowning was one form of execution. Under the Dutch, most executions were accomplished publicly. Freemen were usually hanged, shot or strangled; slaves could expect a much more pernicious death. One slave who was convicted of two murders received among the harshest sentences possible. He was tied to a wheel and had his flesh pinched before being broken alive by eight blows of a club 'without the mercy stroke'. In another case, a prisoner was bound to a cross, then ten pieces of flesh were flayed from his body with red hot pincers 'at lengthy intervals, his right hand hacked and thrown into his face, his body quartered and dragged in portions throughout the town'.[22] According to the South African judge and author Albie Sachs, early court records suggest mutilating sanctions were softened over time, but only because 'the sight of deformed persons' missing tongues and ears proved 'too much for the gentler born inhabitants'. It was more a matter of concern for a European sense of decorum than benevolence towards African slaves that the target of corporal punishment shifted from the head and face to the back.[23]

Until the British took the reins of the South African colony, the death penalty included hanging, strangling (of women), breaking on the wheel or cross, which was sometimes accompanied (thankfully) with a *coup de grâce* of some form, such as decapitation, before being quartered or burned. As late as 1804 an arsonist was punished in this fashion.[24] However, the British were more lenient when it came to the death penalty, only allowing for hanging, with 'no degrees of severity'. During the early nineteenth century a wide variety of crimes were treated as capital offences, including a man who was hanged for sodomy in 1831. With rising crime in this era the death penalty was also pronounced for serious cases of housebreaking, arson, cattle killing, theft, incest, rape and attempted murder. However, the death penalty was soon used only for murder.

British justice has influenced Africa from Egypt to South Africa. The British penal regime in South Africa diverged from other African countries on several levels. The Cape Colony was distinct for aiming incarceration toward those who violated pass laws, rather than common criminals. Thus, the development of the penitentiary system was more closely linked to the progressive institutionalization of racial discrimination. Pass laws were introduced by South Africa settlers in the late nineteenth century to control the movement of native Africans in order to regulate the labour force. Those sent to prison were often sentenced to convict labour for diamond and gold mining companies. Between 1916 and 1986 the system of apartheid would see more than 17 million black people imprisoned for violating pass laws. But it would take another four years for apartheid to be abolished in the prison system as well.[25]

There is still a paucity of research focusing on the impact of colonial justice systems on customary African social control that existed prior to the European onslaught, but by most accounts, Africans primarily regarded crime as a threat to religious morality. Rather than fixating solely on retribution, their responses often turned to purification rituals intended to protect and strengthen the community. According to the criminologist Biko Agozino, when punishments were used they took a variety of forms: 'deviants were often subjected to informal sanctions such as gossip, ridicule or public humiliation', while property crimes, such as the theft of agricultural produce and livestock, were settled through 'restitutive compensations'. The arrival of European penal practices in West Africa would change all of this by introducing 'incarceration and de-Africanization of social control'.[26]

Prior to colonial control, sub-Saharan Africa comprised an assortment of ethnic communities representing different stages of historical development; some were 'highly organized semi-feudal kingdoms' while others were 'stateless village communities'.[27] Modern sub-Saharan Africa features a number of complex legal systems. Due to a long and varied colonial history, vestiges of British, French, Dutch and Portuguese justice are still part of the legal process. It cannot be overemphasized that these formal systems were forcibly imposed, superseding traditional and customary laws, which have sometimes been assimilated into the law. Thus, as colonies transitioned to independence they had a number of justice options to choose from, and as they reformed their justice systems this often included drawing on ancient cultural traditions as well as more formal modern ones.

Variations in pre-colonial legal traditions extended into punishment as well. In some states treason and espionage were considered so harmful that these infractions could be punished only by the death penalty. Once a suspected spy was taken into custody, he would be executed along with all close relatives as a warning to others who contemplated such activities. Witchcraft was also met with the death penalty. In order to maintain their standing in the village, relatives of suspected witches were expected to be the first to attack the witch, a measure by which they conveyed their disassociation with the crime and made clear they sanctioned death as a suitable penalty for the offence.[28]

There was a notable lack of property offences in many regions of Africa, no doubt due to the low level of development of private property and, in some cases, its total absence in some countries. Among the exceptions was the Kilimanjaro area, where property differentiation resulted in the killing of robbers caught in the act. By the time of German intervention in the late nineteenth century, there was a system of compensation or fines for common crimes among the Chaga people. The system worked like this: theft of livestock was compensated with twice the number of animals stolen; theft of honey out of a hive would cost the malefactor one bull and one goat; crippling someone's arm, leg or destroying an eye required two cows and two goats; wounding with a weapon, one bull and one goat; and striking with a fist, two goats. This system was popular among the kingdoms of the Haya, Nyamwezi, Hehe and Sukuma prior to the arrival of the Germans.[29]

What is often lost in the study of pre-colonial law in Africa is that it was meant to steer individuals towards correct behaviour, rather than creating criminals and new criminal offences, or as one expert put it: 'Its whole object is to maintain an equilibrium, and the penalties . . . are directed, not against specific infractions, but to the restoration of this equilibrium.'[30]

Considering the European–African nexus, there were hardly any prisons in either region until the late eighteenth century, leading one Africanist to suggest that 'Africa was not much out of step' with its counterparts in the Western world at this juncture.[31] British empire builders introduced the modern prison to Nigeria beginning in the 1860s, although there is some evidence that indigenous Yorubas used some type of confinement for debtors (along with banishment for other malefactors). From the early days of British rule, colonial settlers reported numerous instances of customary courts sentencing men and women to be beaten in public for a wide range of offences, leading one observer to comment: 'a whole armoury of sticks, rods, branches and lashes' were used at the behest of the native courts.[32]

By the end of the nineteenth century, prisoners in the Northern Protectorate of Nigeria were living in their own villages and reporting for work each morning; but by 1912 prisons were being maintained by native or British keepers throughout the country. Under the direction of Nigeria's first governor, Sir Frederick Lugard, between 1912 and 1930, a two-tiered system of prison administration saw prisons at the national level holding offenders convicted in British colonial courts, and native prisons operated and controlled by native authorities.[33]

By 1900, Nigeria's customary criminal laws were superseded by British courts that could impose only penalties specified in the colonial written legal code. This transition to British colonial law marked the decline of customary criminal law in Nigeria, with many former customs specifically outlawed by statute, including prohibitions on such traditional mainstays as mutilations and torture and trial by ordeal. Native courts that had once issued death sentences such as hanging, beheading, stoning, drowning, burying alive and killing by the identical methods of the killers now had to conduct executions in a more 'humane' manner. Although these traditions were still possible, by the time the British took over Nigeria most of the more bizarre methods had been done away with in favour of hanging or decapitation by sword. Corporal punishments were not limited until 1933 when restrictions were adopted that limited the weapons of punishment to rattan canes and single-tailed whips of prescribed dimensions. During that same decade public executions were abolished.[34] The British colonizers introduced the stocks in 1900 and, reflecting Islamic legal tradition, particularly in the north, the punishment of lashing was still inflicted publicly late in the twentieth century 'in an enclosed space to which the public has the right of access or can be admitted for the occasion'.[35] While corporal punishment remained a public spectacle, public executions were banned for the most part in the 1930s.

Prior to its French and British colonial interludes, punishment in Cameroon ranged from fines and shaming to corporal punishment and imprisonment. The Mandara Kingdom had reached its nadir in the nineteenth century, and according to one scholar had already developed a 'classical penal system'.[36] While complex, it also featured solitary confinement, starvation and physical brutality. Furthermore, there is evidence that by the early 1800s the Fulani Empire in northern Cameroon was utilizing prison and forced labour. Confinement was mostly relegated to basic thatched huts, where prisoners were held to the floor with ropes and controlled with primitive handcuffs or iron chains attached to stakes in the floor. In 1965, both Cameroon and Malawi (influenced by both British law and African customs) reinstituted public executions in the hope that its exhibitory nature would have a deterrent effect – a subject of much debate whenever the death penalty is discussed. Nigeria maintained imprisonment as its most severe punishment after the colonial era ended, and commonly used sanctions such as fines to collect revenue and compensate victims.

India and Southeast Asia

Some form of forced confinement has existed in South Asian history since at least the third century BC. Incapacitation continued to factor into the penal regime under subsequent Indus and Muslim regimes, but typically consisted of little more than a fortress dungeon put into use to detain rivals and rebels. Until the eighteenth century, incarceration remained an uncommon sanction, with fines and mutilations more commonly used. One scholar has suggested – and this would probably be true of other pre-colonial regimes – that they 'lacked the means to create a fully-fledged prison system'.[37] So, to begin with, the prison was not solely a colonial contribution; rather, its form and purpose evolved under colonial rule. In India, one of the biggest challenges to introducing a modern justice regime was creating a prison system that could handle the diversity of castes, races and religions, in matters of diet, dress and labour. Traditionally, imprisonment was considered insufficient punishment and hardly a deterrent to most Indians, unless it was supplemented with additional sanctions such as branding with a mark or transportation overseas – which Hindus especially dreaded as it violated a taboo against crossing the 'black water' and could entail one's loss of caste.[38]

From the beginning it was apparent that the British did not understand the complexities of Indian culture, featuring caste-related anomalies, as in the case of high-caste Brahmins, who were protected from facing such corporeal sanctions as flogging and execution, but were banished instead. Prior to the British, shaming, mutilation, hanging and confinement were all part of the penal continuum on the Indian subcontinent. During the British colonial era an extensive traffic in pan-imperial convicts across the empire impacted the development of punishment systems, particularly in South Asia, where the 'convict stream was most significant'. Perhaps as many as 80,000 convicts were transported overseas between 1787 and 1943. In order to differentiate between convicts, between 1789 and its abolition in 1849, convicts from Bengal and Madras who were sentenced to life sentences were recognizable by having their name tattooed on their forehead, along with their crime and date of sentence – a system called *godna* or *godena*. These marks had a dual purpose as a penal identification and surveillance strategy. Women were also marked this way, but unlike their male counterparts were exempt from flogging.[39]

Under the direction of the East India Company in the early nineteenth century, the colonial state sought to administer Hindu law to the Hindus and Islamic law to the Muslims, utilizing British law for the British and for company servants in India. During the nineteenth century, British criminal justice at home was distinguished from that of its many foreign colonies by the sheer number of criminal acts punishable by the death penalty. By contrast, India was influenced by the Islamic legal system of the former Mughal Empire, which was consistent with Hanafi law (like the Ottomans) and thus, compared to British law, recognized few capital crimes. Nonetheless, by the late eighteenth century the British (conveniently) found mutilation punishments beyond the pale, or as Rudolph Peters put it, seemed to 'value limbs more than lives, as they attached great(er) value to capital punishment as a deterrent'.[40] It followed that in both Egypt and the Ottoman Empire, fixed punishments of amputation and stoning became obsolete during the first half of the nineteenth century as the death penalty took more precedence in the penal regime.

Islamic scholars have suggested that the British 'transformed Islamic criminal law totally and beyond recognition' in regions such as Bengal.[41] As noted above, British expansion favoured penal systems that preferred inflicting the death penalty over corporal punishments and mutilations. During its colonization of Bengal, Britain introduced a law that mirrored its own 'bloody code' at home, mandating that any case of wilful homicide was a hanging offence. The British found Islamic law too nuanced and untimely, evidentiary rules too onerous and thus applied British standards in order to be sure punishment was meted out, even if evidence was less than circumstantial. The British were flabbergasted by the long-held Islamic tradition that allowed victims of crime and their heirs to accept a financial or other form of settlement in lieu of the maximum penalty, thus it was abolished.[42] This was accomplished in part in 1799 with the establishment of the office of public prosecutor, vested with the power to pursue punishment even if the victim and their heirs protested otherwise. The crime of rape exemplified some of the issues British meddling in the law precipitated. Under Islamic law, rape was rarely prosecuted, since a settlement was first reached in which the family of the victim withdrew charges if the perpetrator married her, a 'better strategy for salvaging family honour than a public trial where all the painful details of the case would be made public'.[43]

The legal systems of many Asian countries are still rooted in European colonialism as civil and common traditions came into conflict with local traditions, with the latter prevailing in the end. There was already quite a variety of penal sanctions in Southeast Asia prior to colonial rule. In Malay society the death penalty was used for a range of crimes, from treason and murder to the theft of royal property or adultery with the wife of a high-ranking member of society. Stealing from a monastery in Siam or highway robbery and arson in Burma were considered capital offences as well (as murder and treason). Execution protocol, as usual, depended on status. In some Malay communities the upper classes were executed with a thrust to the heart with traditional dagger, known as the *kris*. One European witness in the mid-nineteenth century recounted Siamese aristocrats being taken to a public spot and placed into some sort of sack before being beaten to death; commoners, on the other hand, were beheaded, a switch from the reverse Western tradition, where nobility could count on a swift death from the headsman and commoners endured a more prolonged death. The aforementioned European observer recounted how one perpetrator, who had violated the prohibition against melting down silver or golden idols stolen from a temple, was 'bound to a large pole and roasted alive over a slow fire'.[44] Other cruel forms of death included being impaled on a stake, dismembered while still breathing and being torn asunder by wild animals, such as in one case from late seventeenth-century Siam, where a Dutch observer witnessed an adulterer being trampled to death by an elephant. When it came to wild beasts, Southeast Asia offered a virtual arsenal of death-dealing animals that could be used in executions, including snakes, tigers, crocodiles and even buffaloes. Justice was meted out to thieves by amputating hands and limbs; at one time, low-scale theft was rewarded with severing the thief's fingertips. Counterfeiters faced various brutal punishments, which included some type of amputation and an array of cuts, increasing in severity depending on one's complicity in the counterfeiting enterprise. For example, whoever blew the bellows had the fingers from his right hand severed, while the individual that actually formed the fake coin had the entire right hand cut off. The most serious sanction was reserved for whoever impressed the royal stamp onto the coin; he would have his entire right arm chopped off. Branding on the cheeks for adultery and on the forehead for other crimes was common as well. Facial brands were often accompanied by a description of the crime tattooed across the chest, whether 'murder' or 'horse thief'. Serving time in Burmese jail during the 1820s, one British merchant learned that the practice of branding on the face did not just attest to 'their criminal character', but made escaping undetected virtually impossible.[45]

During the pre-colonial period some form of determinate (fixed) prison sentence was available, but conditions varied according to its costs and, unlike in the West, criminals in this region were being confined solely as a form of punishment, with little concern for reformation or rehabilitation. Most accounts suggest that prior to the colonial era prisons had little priority in the penal continuum. In most cases inmates were kept immobile in their crude jails and had to depend on the kindness of strangers for food. In most cases it was probably more convenient to select from other punishments and get the whole process over quickly, rather than relying on the human benevolence to survive a stint in jail. Potential prisoners probably preferred the alternatives of paying fines, being whipped or mutilated, or banished or even being executed to a stint in confinement, starving to death, bound to a wall in a wood hut and wondering where the next meal would come from. Nonetheless, imprisonment was probably an uncommon penalty, and was more common while prisoners were still being investigated, waiting for trial or having their physical punishments carried out. Ian Brown, an authority on Southeast Asian prison history, put it best, claiming prisons were unnecessary in the modern context during the pre-colonial period, since in many cases serious recidivists were often already marked with some type of recognizable facial or bodily brand, or if not that, had endured some type of amputation, in effect creating conditions where the perpetrator was actually 'confined without being in prison'.[46]

The British introduced common-law penal sanctions to Malaysia and Singapore. Both were granted independence from Britain in 1963, before separating into two separate nations in 1965. These countries are often heralded as among the world's safest countries – as well as the most punitive. This can be explained in part by the fact that for centuries secret societies were behind most crime, ranging from terrorism to torture and extortion. In order to suppress these groups, rigid judicial policies were adopted. Malaysia and Singapore follow the British model of law and jurisprudence, but use a more draconian system of punishments for what they consider serious crimes. Their drug-related penalties are among the strictest in the world, with the death penalty mandated for trafficking 30 grams (1 oz) of morphine. Possession of guns, drugs, pornography, gambling and public solicitation are all strictly dealt with. Less offensive crime can be punished by caning. All cases of vandalism, theft and robbery receive a mandatory caning with imprisonment. Firearms cases – whether selling or possessing them, or using them in a crime – are all capital offences.

English common-law practices came indirectly to Singapore, first exported from England to colonial India and thence to Singapore. Since independence Singapore has developed its own legal traditions and philosophy, which have become increasingly more punitive, leading one legal scholar to suggest that the country's 'crime control model has led to a significant dismantling of the traditional common-law and adversarial system'.[47] Among the punishments most associated with Singapore is caning, a tradition originally imported by the first British colonizers. Caning was in fact legal in the United States until ruled unconstitutional in 1948, and according to one expert, only Malaysia and Brunei use the cane as 'fiercely as Singapore'. Originally targeted at crimes of personal violence, there was a 'retributive logic'[48] to its use against crimes of violence, but in the 1960s caning was extended to non-personal violations such as illegal entry and vandalism. However, there is also an explanation for this extension, rooted in public security. Caning for graffiti and vandalism was introduced in 1966 by the Vandalism Act to suppress politically inspired graffiti that favoured the communist insurgency at that time, while the rising problem of foreign workers exacerbated the issue of the illegal entry of immigrants and the over-staying of their visas. Nonetheless, a strict protocol is followed in Singapore, in which the caning has to be performed by a trained officer. The process entails using a rattan rod to inflict blows which cut the skin, causing bleeding and intense pain, and often leaving permanent scars. What many critics find so reprehensible about this sanction is that it is directed at non-violent offences, especially vandalism and the possession of small amounts of drugs. It is not uncommon for it to lead to shock and fainting, therefore doctors are on standby to revive mis-creants to ensure they are still fit to endure the remainder of punishment. According to Singapore's Vandalism Act, the flogging can use 'no less than three strokes' and 'no more than eight' in cases of vandalism. The only exception to this limit is if it is a first conviction that involves use of 'pencil, crayon, chalk or other delible substance or thing', in which case the number of maximum strokes can be increased.[49]

If there was ever a caning sweepstake, the trophy would likely go to the former British colony of South Africa, where more than 1 million lashes were doled out on 30,000 young men between 1985 and 1995. In contrast to Singapore, the South African process is not meant to scar for life, with so-called 'juvenile cuts' meted out with a light cane and not exceeding seven strokes. Typically, the youth is ordered to lower or remove his underpants and lie down on a padded bench, where he is instructed to grab his legs and not let go. Beginning in 1977, with the passing of the Criminal Procedure Act 51, juveniles no longer received canings on bared bottoms, and the strokes were reduced in number from ten to seven. Unlike in Singapore, the caning ended as soon as the skin was broken. Adults, however, were not as lucky, since the old rules continued to apply for them.[50]

Like India and Southeast Asia, the rest of the Asian and Pacific regions tend to defy any overgeneralization, featuring flexible and syncretic systems of justice. Although civil and common-law procedures dominate (depending on the colonial precursors), in many parts of Asia, colonial legal systems operated in tandem with indigenous practices, creating a hybrid of combined customs. Britain introduced common law to India, Malaysia and Singapore and they remain heavily influenced by this tradition, while Dutch Indonesia is more impacted by the civil law tradition. However, other Asian countries such as Thailand and Japan never actually had external legal traditions forced upon them through the colonialization process and were inspired to adopt the civil legal system.

Asia and the Pacific are distinct from other regions for the high incidence of death sentences; by some estimates up to 85 per cent of the world's executions take place there. Again, this cannot be generalized, since many countries have the death penalty on the books but either do not use it or use it sparingly. Brunei, for example permits it, but it has not been applied since 1967; likewise in Laos, where alternatives include re-education without prison, imprisonment, and public criticism, either in court or without publicity. However, it still features in the penal processes of China, India, Japan, Mongolia, Singapore, Thailand and Vietnam.

Incarcerative sentences in Japan date back to the eighth century when, under the domination of China's Tang dynasty, penal sanctions of forced labour kept offenders busy on public works projects from one to three years. By the tenth century, corporal and capital punishment was being replaced by incarceration and in the 1700s penal servitude was reintroduced. One eighteenth-century observer suggested that Japanese prisons compared favourably with the American model of the 1790s. The rise of the Meiji regime from 1868 on paved the way for the abolition of corporal punishment in 1872 and the adoption of several model institutions.

The Former Ottoman Empire and the Modern Middle East

Once common throughout the Muslim world, by the nineteenth century it was rare to find a sovereign nation that utilized Islamic criminal law. It has only been in recent years that we find the revival of Islamic legal regimes in countries such as Iran, Pakistan, Sudan and the northern states of Nigeria. Muslim countries plagued by widespread apprehension of rising crime rates and Western moral corruption often welcomed the reintroduction of the Sharia as a panacea for cures from social evils and the return of virtuous society. Supporters of Islamic law time and again argued that the fear instilled by Sharia punishments was a deterrent to those aware of its propensity for severe and painful punishments such as whipping, amputations, lashings and stoning; its deterrence value is often supported by figures showing low crime rates in countries that adopt it when fixed and mandatory punishments are carried out.

The Pulitzer Prize-winning journalist Thomas L. Friedman is among those who blame the break-up of the Ottoman Empire and the machinations of the European powers after the First World War for much that has gone wrong in the modern Middle East, asserting, 'what we're actually dealing with in the Middle East today are the long delayed consequences of the end of the Ottoman Empire.' By the outbreak of the First World War, North African countries Morocco, Tunisia and Algeria were French colonies, while Italy controlled Libya and the British, Egypt. Following the war British and French colonialists divided up the former lands of the Ottomans as well, in the process imposing 'their own order on the diverse tribes, sects and religions that make up the Arab East'. As the French and English pulled out of the region they left their own hand-chosen leaders, who were often autocratic and ruled the diverse populations that once made up the former empire with 'iron fists'.[51]

At the peak of its power in the sixteenth and seventeenth centuries, the Ottoman Empire was a multinational empire that controlled vast swathes of southeast Europe, western Asia and northern Africa. As an Islamic state, its duration (1453–1922) and scale has seldom been rivalled in history. European travellers to the lands of the Turkish Empire reported a legal system with swift justice, one that compared quite favourably with European legal practices, which by contrast were often characterized by long, drawn-out and costly trials; others portrayed it as a cruel system of hasty executions and cruel punishments. Fines were heavily relied on and were often included along with floggings for certain crimes. Financial penalties were determined according to the number of cane strokes that were required – the more strokes by law, the larger the fine. For example, unless one is sentenced to hand amputation for stealing a purse or turban, a single judge, or *cadi*, 'shall chastise [him] and a fine of one acke shall be collected for [every] stroke'.[52]

Sharia punishment often depended on the interpretation, and for the Turks that meant the Hanafi legal theory, which in the case of homosexual acts imposes the death penalty only if committed by a habitual offender. Under this pathway a single judge applies justice, regularly imposing fixed penalties ranging from lashings to death. But, unlike some modern purveyors of the Sharia tradition, under the Ottomans amputation was rarely practised in the eighteenth century for theft. Likewise, stoning to death was extremely rare. One of the foremost experts on Ottoman justice found only one instance, which involved the killing of a woman in 1680 for having intimate relations with a Jew. The sentence was carried out at the Istanbul Hippodrome before Sultan Mehmed IV.[53]

European powers had been influencing penal codes in some Muslim lands since the beginning of the nineteenth century. For example, Western pressure convinced the Ottomans to end the death penalty for apostasy in 1844. But the dismantling of the Sharia courts would have to wait until 1924, when the foundation of the Turkish Republic under the modern reformer Kemal Ataturk abolished it, in step with his campaign of Westernization and secularization.

By the mid-nineteenth century, prisons were a regular feature in Ottoman provincial centres, each varying in size and salubrity. One observer in the 1850s recounted prison cells that were 'wretched, and filthy beyond conception, vermin of every description abounds, the flooring is of mud, quite bare and uncommonly damp, there is a sad want of ventilation and the atmosphere is tainted with all manner of disgusting and disagreeable odours'. Another Western observer described the Ottoman prison at Bagnio as 'a place that would kill an Englishman in a week', and still another opined of Alexandretta, 'if a prisoner was not liberated [from here] in 110 days death would liberate him'.[54]

The word *sijn* is Arabic for prison. In other parts of the Arab world, such as Egypt, some convict prisons are referred to by other terms. *Liman*, a derivation of the Turkish and Greek word for port, refers to a prison constructed at the Egyptian harbour at Alexandria. A *zindan*, from the Persian term for prison, refers to prison facilities constructed at Istanbul and Tunis.[55] According to Islamic scholars the prison played an insignificant role in indigenous Middle East penal traditions. Where it did emerge it was uncommon and was typically an adjunct to other forms of more primary punishment. And as in other regions of the world, one's social status determined whether one would be confined or not. As elsewhere, it was mostly used for pre-trial holding, to ensure one appeared in court for trial, to elicit testimony or to produce some type of penitence. The emergence of penal confinement often paralleled claims by Arab states to have made the transition to more modern societies.

Following the break-up of the Ottoman Empire after the First World War, modern prison reforms were implemented in former Turkish territories during subsequent French and British administrations. The creation of new states in the aftermath of the war included a widespread adoption of the prison with a parallel decline of traditional modes of punishment, or as one expert put it, from the nineteenth century on came the tacit 'acknowledgement that customary practices had become outdated'.[56] Indeed, the arrival of the prison in the Middle East during the last third of the nineteenth century would correspond with a transition to incarcerative sanctions from corporal, capital and financial ones.

The foundation for the modern Egyptian state can be traced in part to the rule of Muhammad Ali (*reg.* 1805–49), who also introduced the country's first modern penal code in 1829. Egypt was a semi-autonomous province of the Ottoman Empire under Muhammad Ali after he seized power from the French in 1805. As part of the new regime he abandoned a number of Ottoman punishments for a more limited repertoire of flogging, capital punishment and prison with forced labour. Subsequent administrations would eliminate corporal punishment from the penal code in 1861, as a transition was made from cruel and exhibitory sanctions to more measured forms of discipline, particularly confinement.

When it came to the incarceration of women, there was already a long tradition in the Middle East. As early as the eighteenth and nineteenth centuries special women's prisons were operating in parts of North Africa. Algeria, for example, converted an old hospital building called the 'Lazaret' for a range of female offenders and as early as 1851 was separating prisoners by gender. During the Ottoman period it was common practice to confine female prisoners in either the house of a religious leader or to marry them off to someone, where they would labour at domestic work.[57]

As the nineteenth century ended, imprisonment increasingly dominated Egypt's penal code. In the 1880s Egyptian penal code included a recidivist category of offender. Stricter prison sentences were mandated for repeat offenders, who were forced to wear distinctive black garb that earned them the moniker 'the Black Gang'. During the same period corporal punishment and the private use of the whip by landowners was prohibited. Capital punishment would decline as well, and by the first decade of the twentieth century it was being carried out privately in specially designed rooms behind prison walls. Most of the advancements in penal development took place intermittently, as various regimes adapted 'existing prison structures and administration'. By contrast, the French used Algerian prisons as part of its master plan to introduce direct rule to parts of North Africa as early as the 1830s. While prison terms were not fixed, apparently a prisoner's greatest challenge was 'being forgotten' somewhere in the deep recesses of some cell or dungeon. French Algeria had a larger European settler population than did Egypt. One expert declared its Lambèse prison, built in 1852, 'probably the first prison in the Middle East constructed according to latest contemporary European ideas'.[58] What was most insidious about this system was not just the separation of French and Arab prisoners, but the notion that Europeans were capable of learning a trade in prison, while Arabs were 'unsuited to anything other than striking the forge'. As for the partition of French and Arab inmates, it has been suggested that it was designed to protect Algerian natives from the contaminating influence of European vices.

The break-up of the Ottoman Empire in 1922 saw uncolonized states such as Turkey and Iran working towards modernizing, using European models as templates for their justice systems in the 1920s and 1930s. Likewise, after the British withdrew from Israel in 1948, the new country adopted British common law except for the old British stalwart of flogging as legal punishment, which was abolished. Elsewhere, the transition from Ottoman law to other systems was a mixed bag. In Saudi Arabia, for example, prior to 1932, serious crimes from murder and robbery to theft and tribal reprisal were relatively common. As the Saudi monarchy consolidated its power it helped suppress the rise of crime and public disorder by implementing Sharia throughout the country, decreasing crime significantly. Saudi Arabia, indeed, is one of the few modern Middle Eastern states that have been identified with 'an uninterrupted application of Islamic criminal law'. The state, for the most part, eschews involvement with substantive laws, but at times determines which parts of the Sharia are enforced. In furtherance of the goal of state direction, Saudi Arabia has codified, or modernized, parts of the Sharia that are applied in the courts. In order to catch up with the modern world of crime, new *tazir* offences were defined and introduced by criminal legislation, as in the case of counterfeiting, drug abuse and trafficking, bribery and cheque-related offences. When it comes to the most serious cases, those with fixed sentences – *hudud* offences – the state attempts to ensure sentences are not rashly pronounced. For example, between 1982 and 1983 almost 4,300 *tazir* sentences for theft were issued, resulting in only two amputations.[59]

Judicial fatwas demonstrate the pragmatism and occasional mutability of Islamic law. Fatwa No. 85, issued on 8 September 1981, exemplifies how rising crime in Saudi Arabia led the Board of the Senior Ulama to target the rise in urban violent crime, drug-related cases and the abduction of women and girls for sexual purposes. The fatwa expounded on the *hudud* law of banditry, allowing *qadis* more discretion in assigning fixed punishments for armed attacks in urban areas, and by now equating sexually motivated abduction with the stealing of property. Moreover, it stipulated that judges had the authority to choose punishments from a list that included banishment, cross-amputation (right hand and left foot), death, or death with crucifixion. As part of the multi-structured fatwa, drug-related crimes were placed under the category of 'spreading corruption on earth', mandating that a first offence was punishable with a draconian discretionary punishment, ranging from fines to imprisonment and flogging. A second offence could be punished with any penalty including death.[60]

Supporters of Saudi Arabia's punitive penal regime can take solace from the fact that it is considered a 'low-crime' nation, and are usually quick to point out how murder and theft rates by the late 1980s ranked the second-lowest among 25 countries listed by Interpol. Together with low sexual assault rates and drug offences, Sharia proponents point out that this was accomplished without exorbitant imprisonment rates as is so often the case in the Western world. As one scholar put it,

> Before the implementation of the Sharia, the Kingdom of Saudi Arabia was a theater of anarchy, confusion, instability and looting. It was a place where neither life nor property could be safe. When pilgrims came they used to bid their last farewell to their family thinking they might not return safely.[61]

After the Second World War, Arab nations gained independence either through diplomacy or through revolutionary struggle. The governments that emerged were overwhelmingly secular, although many were helmed by pan-Arab nationalists such as Egypt's Gamal Abdel Nasser. Most Arab countries seemed intent on modernizing at this point and looked forward to future economic prosperity and stability. Although Sharia courts still existed, they were relegated to secondary status in the secular Arab world. However, these regimes were often undone by repressive regimes, as the juxtaposition between wealth and poverty became untenable. In response, groups such as Egypt's Muslim Brotherhood (1929) emerged as opposition to secular regimes. Various opposition groups saw the reintroduction of Sharia law as a way of solving the nations' ills and a strategy for acquiring a modicum of self respect. But it would take the Islamic revolution in the non-Arabic country of Iran in 1979 to provide a model for revival movements and the reintroduction of the Sharia into the Muslim world. Except for a handful of Muslim countries, Europeans had a negligible impact on their legal systems, as exemplified by the justice systems of Saudi Arabia, Yemen and Qatar.

Mixed Penal Systems

Even the common-law countries such as Scotland and England, while sharing the same legal tradition, have various permutations, often predicated on local variations of law. Perhaps no common-law country exemplifies this issue more than Scotland's reverence for the 'not proven' verdict – an eighteenth-century tradition found nowhere else in the world. The murder case of twenty-year-old Amanda Duffy in the spring of 1992 best illustrates a system that allows jurors three verdict options when voting on sentencing: guilty, not guilty and *not proven*. Amanda Duffy was a sociable 'free spirit' who was found murdered, mutilated in such a way as to make her virtually unrecognizable. Press reports indicated she suffered horrific injuries that included having her nose and jaw broken, her face kicked, sharp objects dragged across her skin and so savaged sexually that as the details were provided in court 'one spectator vomited'.[62] A suspect was soon arrested and on trial; in fact, this former schoolmate was the last person to see her alive. This system is apparently very popular among defence attorneys since having two possible verdicts out of three puts them at a distinct advantage at trial. The case was far from airtight and in the end the suspect was acquitted, due in no small part to the protections granted the defendant by Scottish law. The community responded with rage, collecting 60,000 names on a petition in protest. As the events took on a life of their own, one reporter recalled the words of Sir Walter Scott, who once vilified 'the bastard verdict, illogically and wholly indefensible'. In any case, this verdict is rare, occurring in perhaps 5 per cent of murder cases. With a strong anti-England bias, the continued use of this verdict represents something else to pundits who regard it as Scotland's 'cultural reflex' to English law, with an understanding perhaps that 'if it was something the English did not have it must be good or worth keeping'. Others harked back to the old refrain, that it is 'better that nine guilty men go free than one innocent go to jail'. But in times of rising violent rising crime, support has dwindled at times for what many regard as a legal anachronism.[63]

It is the rare country whose legal system (or system of criminal law) is composed solely of the rudiments of a single legal tradition. Afghanistan, for example, currently employs a penal regime that combines vestiges of Islamic, civil, common and customary law (and at one time even socialist). Variations in legal systems often coincide with regime changes. In the aftermath of nationhood in the 1920s and 1930s the Hanafi School of jurisprudence was used by the state criminal justice system, while customary law was reserved for remediating dispute resolutions. In the mid-twentieth century strides towards modernizing state law was soon elevated in precedence over Islamic law. Following the Soviet coup and invasion in the late 1970s, Afghanistan adopted a Soviet-style judicial system. With the victory of the mujahedeen in 1989, the triumphant rebel groups reinstated Islamic law as the primary source of justice. Years of conflict and regime change left so many contradictory and confusing laws that by 2001 there were 2,400 separate laws, many obsolete or overlapping. Over the ensuing decade the emergence of the Taliban saw the implementation of a far-right patriarchal interpretation of Sharia law – the only source recognized during the Taliban era before 2001. This system was enforced with brutality and disregard for human rights. Since then, punishments have varied according to region and tribe, yet certain characteristics influence each of these cultures. For example, in most regions the penalty for murder ranges from paying fines to a victim's family to the death penalty. In some cases there is a form of restorative justice in which the victim's and perpetrator's families are bound together by having a woman from the perpetrator's family marry a son from the victim's family.

Once the Taliban took control of Afghanistan in the mid-1990s it attempted to re-establish order by enforcing a strict interpretation of the Islamic legal code. Its adaptation began with a list of sins that were to be handled by officials from the Ministry for the Prevention of Vice, focused on 'quelling' pleasurable activities such as kite-flying and listening to or making music. Women were forced to stay concealed under the hijab and chador; if seen in public or in a vehicle they could receive one to five days in jail. Men who dared to shave or trim their beards could expect a mandatory ten-day jail term. The use of mind-altering substances such as hashish, heroin and wine required between three and six months' confinement. In a matter of months the Taliban had transformed the country's urban and rural environments, banning any pictures in shops, hotels and public places. Dog and cock fights and usury were added to the list of prohibitions; those who dared to appear in public with 'Beatles-style hair' risked arrest and a quick shave.

Brunei Darussalam, a British protectorate from 1888 until independence in 1984, now uses a justice system that is a mix of Islamic, common and customary law. Common punishments include banishment from the country, caning, life in prison, fines and other forms of compensation. Unlike in most Western countries, however, life means life. Since 1988, caning has been a mandatory punishment for 42 different crimes. The maximum number of strokes for adults is 24, while for those under eighteen, it is eighteen. However, men and women over the age of 50 and those sentenced to the death penalty (when it was still in force) are exempt from caning. By most accounts, offenders prefer caning to long-term imprisonment. Caning is typically carried out in the presence of a doctor. Convicted rapists receive 30 years in prison and a caning, while a mandatory death sentence is used in certain drug trafficking cases, such as possession of more than 500 grams of cannabis. In any case, no one has been executed in Brunei since 1957. Similar to other mixed legal tradition countries, certain laws apply to specific groups. For example Sharia law is applied only to Muslims, who face punishment for crimes that violate Islamic laws, such as moral offences including adultery and alcohol consumption. Likewise, robbery is punished with hand amputation, as required by the Sharia; stoning for adultery, and so forth.

Continental Europe's civil law tradition influenced penal policies in some Islamic majority countries. Malaysia has a mixed system that combines features of customary, Islamic, common and civil legal traditions. Here Sharia law applied only to Muslims, and civil law to non-Muslims. This becomes clear when it comes to caning. Under civil law it cannot be used on non-Muslim females, males sentenced to death or those older than 50. Caning is typically reserved for cases when there is evidence of violence in a rape or robbery with weapons. Muslim women caned for adultery must receive lashings all at once unless they are certified medically unfit for the punishment. In accordance with Islamic customs women are whipped with no more than average force, meaning the executioners cannot lift his hand over his head to administer a stroke, thereby preventing the skin from being cut; what's more, the rod should be lifted upwards following the stroke, rather than being pulled (to lessen the stroke) – it may also be inflicted on any part of the person, except the face, head, stomach, chest and private parts. Another distinction is that only women are caned while sitting (males when standing). The Maldives also has a modified form of Sharia criminal law, but excludes excessive punishments such as amputations and stoning, and limits banishment to eight months up to two years. In such cases the prisoner is left to survive on an island with indigenous peoples and forced to earn subsistence money through hard labour. Banishment is the penalty for those who drink alcohol, engage in extramarital sex, theft, and eating in public during the Ramadan month.

Modification and Reintroduction of Islamic Law

Muslim states typically rely on the Sharia as a moral and spiritual guide, if not a legal one. Over the past century or so, the Sharia was reintroduced as law in a number of regions, including Saudi Arabia, the Gulf States, Iran, Iraq, Pakistan, Yemen and Mauritania. Parts of Nigeria and Sudan would reintroduce it as well. Other countries are still contemplating it, as in the cases of Bangladesh and Indonesia. Beginning with Libya in 1972, more than a half-dozen countries have promulgated new legislation to reintroduce Islamic criminal law. In many cases those that have re-introduced it in the wake of an Islamic revival have harshly applied Sharia law. For example, when it was reintroduced to Sudan in 1983, within its first two months a delegation, including an orthopaedic surgeon, had been dispatched to Saudi Arabia to learn the judicial and medical procedures for amputations that would be required under full implementation of the law.

Following a *coup d'état* led by Muammar al-Gaddafi, Libya stunned the world of criminal justice when it reintroduced Sharia legal provisions that included banning alcoholic beverages and other traditional penalties. Few observers could have predicted that this would inaugurate a new trend that saw other Muslim countries adopt Islamic penal code. Thus, Libya joined Saudi Arabia in reviving past punishments such as public amputations, as would other countries in the years that followed. Contrary to the notion that the influence of the modern world would relegate these punishments to the past, the opposite has occurred as some of the former colonies have replaced modern common and civil law practices with Sharia practices.

Under the mercurial leadership of powerful dictators there was a nuanced deviation from classical doctrine when it came to enforcing some laws. In Libya, this could mean that a bandit who had not stolen property or committed murder was imprisoned instead of being banished; likewise, a bandit who had killed during a robbery would be executed, but his body not publicly exposed. Criminal responsibility in Libya was mandated at eighteen, instead of the traditional puberty. Further, if the malefactor was an individual who had already been punished with amputation, he would not be sentenced to further amputations after committing another theft, but instead imprisoned until he repented, for at least three years. Moreover, the law required all judicial amputations to be carried out under anaesthesia by a surgeon. This would be exemplified by its first use in 2003, when four robbers were cross-amputated (left hand and right foot). Compared to other locales that would later introduce stoning for sexual and moral offences, in Libya unlawful sexual intercourse was limited to flogging.

Following in the footsteps of Libya, General Zia ul-Haq seized control of Pakistan in 1977, thanks to support among Islamists. In 1979 he adopted the Islamic penal code, but again put his own personal stamp on it. Multiple lashings and imprisonment were used for banditry, instead of exile. His brand of Islam was carefully controlled and dished out, eschewing mutilations and stoning, and even reducing the use of flogging. Iran, on the other hand, went in a different direction from Libya and Pakistan when it reintroduced Sharia law after the 1979 Islamic Revolution and in 1981 the revolutionary courts began doling out the first lapidation (stoning) sentences. In effect, Libya and Pakistan initially adopted the new penal regime as a symbolic move, but initially did not implement any drastic changes from what preceded it.

After the Iranian Revolution in 1979 and the implementation of a strict Sharia regime, the country has ratcheted up its penal sanctions. Human rights organizations have been among Iran's biggest detractors, citing its utilization of all forms of punishment except for 'the possible' application of crucifixion. According to Article 207 of the criminal code, a convict can be punished by being tied to a cross and left on it for three days before being released (dead or alive).[64] There are a number of accounts in which prisoners prior to execution have been subject to lapidation, judicial amputations and whippings. The Shiite punishment for theft has been established as the amputation of four fingers from the right hand. In 1986 Iranian judicial police demonstrated for the public, journalists, officials and prisoners a device they had designed specifically for this task.

Saudi Arabia had a long uninterrupted history of using Sharia law, and despite penal sanctions on the books requiring stoning and amputation, these punishments were not widely used prior to the 1979 revolution in Iran. Likewise, Sudanese tyrant Gaafar Nimeiry, who had taken control of the country in 1969, began to tack a more Islamic course in penal sanctions as part of an effort to secure the hardcore Islamic elements. As a result a new penal code was promulgated in 1984, which broadened the definitions of certain crimes by applying fixed punishment to offences other than traditional crimes and relaxing rules of evidence.[65]

Socialist Countries

Of all of the world's modern legal traditions, the socialist penal tradition is the newest and faces the most challenges to its very existence, due in no small part to the collapse of the Soviet Union and the few countries that still adhere to this system. It is daunting to uncover meaningful crime data from any of the current socialist countries; so much of what is known about the criminal justice systems of North Korea, Cuba, Vietnam and China is speculative at best. However, in some cases it is possible to observe vestiges of other legal traditions along with the socialist tradition. In Cuba, for example, there is a mixture of socialist and civil law. The Spanish colonial era left the island with deep civil traditions not unlike Continental Europe's. It should not be surprising that as a long-time colony of Spain, Cuba's penal system after the 1959 revolution combined civil and socialist legal traditions, offering a wide variety of criminal sanctions that included the death penalty and fines. Cuba shares with other socialist countries a propensity for locking people up, and has as one of the highest imprisonment rates in world, but still has substantially fewer prisoners per capita than the United States. In 2006, for example, Cuba imprisoned 457 per 100,000, compared to 738 per 100,000 in the u.s.[66]

North Korea's penal system is rooted in Confucian moral precepts and Marxist philosophy. In 1950 it adopted its current penal code with the purpose of suppressing 'class enemies' and educating its inhabitants 'in the spirit of socialist patriotism' and rehabilitating individuals who commit crimes based on capitalist influences. The secretive nature of the so-called 'Hermit Kingdom' has hampered any detailed analysis of its penal system.

China's answer to the Soviet gulag is a system known as *laogai*, an abbreviation denoting 'reform through labour', as forced labour is known in Communist parlance. Countries under the socialist legal tradition have traditionally used various forms of imprisonment to silence dissent and suppress opposition. In Republican China a new penal institution, the *fanxingyuan*, or 'place for self examination', was inaugurated by the Nationalists in 1928. These facilities were rather small in scope and designed to follow the model prisons curriculum aimed at denouncing 'the evils of communism', enabling offenders to 'become aware of the error of their ways, gain basic education and acquire vocational training'.[67]

Prior to the Chinese Civil War following the Second World War, the number of prisoners was relatively low, especially when contrasted to the millions who perished under the Communist terror that began in 1949. With Communist victory, penal philosophy followed along the lines of the prison reforms put into practice after 1911 and the birth of the republic. The Communist regime, like its precursor, viewed 'human beings as profoundly malleable and open to moral transformation'. Indeterminate sentencing and agricultural labour formed the backbone of the reform through labour system. The onus of guilt fell heaviest on suspected Nationalist collaborators, who were branded criminals following the proclamation of the People's Republic of China on 1 October 1949. Some accounts place the number of people interned in labour camps at 4 to 6 million.[68] Soviet advisers influenced the shaping of China's penal system in the 1950s. But the Soviet prison population would remain much higher than that of the Chinese. Unlike the Stalinist regime, Mao Zedong actually intended to reform 'every' inmate. As one expert put it, in the Soviet gulag prisoners 'were left with their own thoughts' with 'a heavy emphasis placed on remoulding every aspect of a prisoner's morals, ideas and habits, ultimately leading to the birth of a "new man"'. By contrast, the Chinese version was less concerned with creating 'new men' and more focused on 're-education through labor'. This allowed the legal system to be bypassed and local governments to remove undesirable elements without any limit placed on the lengths of their sentences.[69]

Torture was widespread in Chinese labour camps during Mao's lifetime. One of the signature punishments was called 'hanging a chicken by the feet', which went something like this: an inmate's wrists were bound behind his back, supporting the full weight of the body when suspended from the rafters of a building, arms being pulled out of the shoulder sockets. Most accounts suggest conditions improved somewhat after the demise of Mao, but there was little diminishment in the inmate regime that included physical punishments, meagre nutrition and deplorable hygienic conditions. Apparently in modern day labour camps indeterminate sentences still prevail, as inmates serve up to three years for re-education through labour by a simple administrative sentence, which can be renewed for up to ten years.

Since the post-socialist transition in central Eastern Europe, the punishment regime has seen a number of changes, most notably in the diminished use of imprisonment. Between 1989 and 1990 the countries of Bulgaria, the Czech Republic, Slovakia, Hungary, Poland and Romania reduced their prison populations greatly by granting general amnesties to prisoners formerly held for mostly political reasons. By contrast a number of newly free countries witnessed rising fear of anarchy and crime, leading to increased punitive sanctions and seeing jails filled again. Between 1990 and 1994 the imprisonment rate of the Czech Republic doubled, as it did in Hungary, Slovakia and Croatia.

Summary

It has been well documented how numerous modern legal systems are inextricably linked to pre-colonial and colonial roots. Sometimes this has been an advantage, at other times detrimental. In 2013, Bangladesh, a country that retains much of Britain's legal code as a legacy of its colonial past, witnessed perhaps the 'deadliest disaster in the history of the garment industry'. More than 1,100 workers perished in the collapse of a garment factory. But it seems unlikely that anyone will be held accountable. This is probably not so surprising in a country in which the legal system, influenced by the colonial past, is still predisposed towards controlling the population and protecting what many see as the remnants of the old colonialist power structure. By most accounts, despite a chorus of voices in favour of the modernization of the machinery of justice, in Bangladesh and elsewhere justice still favours the wealthy elite, which in this case happens to include the garment factory owners.[70]

As new justice traditions are assimilated into and adopted by distant societies it is a given that as these new ideas cross national borders and cultures they will have to be modified to the special conditions, what one penal historian terms a process of 'inculturation', where the 'local appropriation of global ideas' are adopted in a variety of equally incompatible environments, ranging from the French *bagne* in Vietnam to cellular confinement in China and concentration camps in South Africa.[71] Wherever colonial regimes have influenced foreign penal regimes, the introduction of confinement has occupied a central position in the new punishment hierarchy. The prison played an important role in European societies beginning in the sixteenth century. Over the following centuries, the sanction of incarceration or forced detention has spread across the globe and has taken its place next to fines, probation, community service and the death penalty as a major criminal sanction.

Countries with different legal traditions, political ideologies and cultural backgrounds have replaced a variety of pre-existing modes of punishment with custodial sentences.[72] In the Americas, for example, colonial expansion created more heterogeneous populations. The more diversity increased the more difficult it became to achieve some type of consensual understanding. As a result, there are many instances in which customary laws and indigenous legal mechanisms coexist within national legal systems, such as in the cases of Bolivia, the British Virgin Islands, the United States and so forth. The same holds true in most of the post-colonial world.

In the modern era little expenditure was devoted to prison systems prior to the 1960s and 1970s, when the parallel increase in crime and incarceration required new rehabilitation and reformation regimes. In many Western societies, incarceration weighs heaviest on minorities and indigenous peoples, such is the case in Australia where it was reported in 1993 that the aboriginal population was 'the most imprisoned ethnic group in the world'. Only 2 per cent of the country's population, they made up 20 per cent of the prison population.

During a timespan measured in centuries, various 'cultures of confinement' developed around the world. Confinement of course comes in many guises and is part of a penal continuum ranging from probation and community service to the death penalty. A number of early societies had already developed rudimentary carceral institutions prior to colonial control. As for other colonial institutions, what developed after the implementation of new penal regimes was often a syncretic version of what was intended by the colonizers, leading one authority to note that the prison, 'like all institutions was never simply imposed or copied, but was reinvented and transformed by a host of local factors, its successes being dependent on its flexibility'.[73]

9

Crime and Punishment in the Twenty-first Century

I t was the twenty-first-century version of the bank robbery. Fittingly, these hi-tech robbers 'never wore masks, threatened a teller, or set foot in a vault'. In this case, individuals from more than two dozen countries acting in concert pulled off two precision operations that netted the thieves $45 million from ATMs in just a matter of hours. Unlike the prototypical bank robber, who robs banks to feed a drug habit, these were technologically adept computer experts, capable of manipulating financial information with just a few key strokes (however, they still needed the street criminals to go out and loot the cash machines).[1]

In the second decade of the twenty-first century, criminal justice systems around the world are striving to keep pace with the new technologies utilized by criminals. Criminals have always been at the forefront at locating opportunities for profit as soon as a new technology first appears on the scene. Virtually every new technology has created 'a new crime alongside it'. Since the advent of the optical telegraph in 1794 and its electrical ancestor a half-century later, criminals have managed to keep abreast of the latest innovations. In 1888, one Chicago policeman lamented: 'It is a well-known fact that no other section of the population avail them more readily and speedily of the latest triumphs of science than the criminal class.' As far back as the 1830s, stock market information was already transmitted by optical telegraphs in France. Soon after, several French bankers bribed telegraph operators 'to introduce deliberate but recognizable errors into the transmission of stock market information'.[2]

Prior to the invention of the telegraph – which the British author Tom Standage termed the 'Victorian Internet' – communication and the transfer of information could only travel as fast as a horse, ship or train could take it. The arrival of the telegraph removed most distance barriers, offering criminally inclined schemers an 'information imbalance'. Nothing exemplified this better than modern horse racing, where the result of the race is known at the racetrack as soon as it is declared. Almost from the very beginning, rules were implemented prohibiting this type of information from being relayed by telegraph, but 'criminals tended to be one step ahead of rule makers'.

There continues to be a remarkable continuity between many of the crimes that are committed online and their counterparts in the pre-digital era. Although tools are different, the intent, goals and motivations remain the same. For example, in former times it was common for merchants in certain immigrant communities to pay protection to gangs under threat of harm or business disruption; today this is happening to many e-businesses if a ransom is not paid (DOS: denial of service). Bank robbers still rob banks and security vans, a dangerous and foolhardy avocation; others have found it safer to hack into a bank's computer system and transfer money using electronic payments systems. Long a serious felony, modern-day counterfeiters produce fake currency by manipulating scanners, printers and toner ink to create more passable counterfeit bills.

Medical advances, such as anti-organ rejection drugs, and the clandestine nature of the Internet have helped precipitate an underground organ market in many parts of the world, illegally transferring human organs from poor countries to rich ones. In the Balkans, the black-market trade in organs has led penal systems to create statutes directed specifically at this crime. In Serbia, where unemployment rates were in the 20 per cent range in 2013, there are reportedly thousands willing to sell organs legally. Since it is now punishable at home with a ten-year prison sentence, many reportedly try to sell body parts in neighbouring Kosovo and Bulgaria. One potential donor admitted that he 'will sell my kidney, my liver, or do anything necessary to survive'.[3] The global shortage of organs has insured that there will always be desperate individuals willing to sell organs and traffickers who would exploit their economic misery and poverty, especially when there are individuals willing to pay $40,000 for a kidney.

Although modern crime and punishment is marked by the added virtual realm of cyberspace, there are still regions of the developing world where age-old criminality continues. One of the oldest exemplars of transnational criminality, piracy, continues to plague far corners of the globe, typically in regions with weak central governments. Like many forms of crime, piracy remains a seasonal crime, with raids typically waning 'between the end of May and late September when the southwest monsoon lashes the Arabian Sea'. Piracy peaked in the years 2009–11, and more recently a sharp decline has been reported. According to the International Maritime Bureau, which tracks shipping crime, there were only 71 reports of boarding attempts in 2012, compared to 236 in 2011 and 219 cases in 2010.[4] Piracy dropped to a seven-year low in 2013. By most accounts this has been due to such factors as better international policing and information sharing, the imprisonment of captured pirates, together with the presence of armed guards aboard cargo ships and an international naval armada that carries out onshore raids in Somalia has put a major dent in that regional problem. Despite launching a record number of attacks in 2011 – 176 – they were able to steal only 25 ships – attesting to the effectiveness of the new defence regime. Prior to equipping ships with these countermeasures, fences and water cannons fell short. One observer has noted that as of November 2012, 'pirates never successfully hijacked a ship that had armed guards'.[5]

Penal officials are also going back to their earlier statute books to reform modern penal sanctions or to adapt old strategies to a new age. Like seventeenth-century Puritans dishing out scarlet letters, some American communities are placing pictures of men caught soliciting prostitutes on billboards and even on radio shows. Some would argue that this type of exhibitory punishment gives the community a sense of empowerment in an age where defendants can usually 'buy their way out' of the justice system by paying a fine in court or performing community service. In a country not known for alternatives to imprisonment, policymakers in the United States are reaching back to the colonial past, experimenting with various forms of shaming punishment. Although there is no empirical evidence that shaming affects criminal behaviours, in one town in New Mexico, bad cheque writers were featured on a large public marquee, while in Arizona, prisoners were taped during their bookings at the Maricopa Jail and posted on the Internet for viewing. One popular programme in Kansas City, Missouri, the shame-based 'John TV', features photographs of individuals arrested in prostitution stings. One Texas judge earned a reputation for his imaginative punishments, such as requiring a convicted wife abuser to apologize to his wife in front of City Hall. In another case a drunken driver was instructed to pace back and forth in front of a bar wearing a sign that read, 'I killed two people while driving drunk'.[6]

Shaming has been used by societies around the world into the modern era. The Amish and some Native American tribes use a form called 'shunning'. As recently as the late nineteenth century, rural communities in parts of western Europe utilized a host of rituals that combined shaming and punishment. In England, they were known as 'rough music', in Germany *Katzenmusik*, to the French it was *charivari*, and the Russian's *samosud*. Most were designed to enforce community values, with some limited to humiliation and corporal reprimand, and sometimes fatal violence.[7]

The loathsome practice of persecuting witches still haunts the outskirts of the modern world. But it was little more than 60 years ago that the British Parliament revoked and replaced the Witchcraft Act of 1735 with the 1951 Fraudulent Mediums Act. The initial law was targeted at those who conspired to cheat and defraud, although it conjures up much more sinister images. In the case of *Rex v. Duncan* (1944) Helen Duncan was sentenced to a nine-month term in prison (reduced to six months) for violating the Witchcraft Act, which stated, 'If any person shall pretend to exercise or use any kind of witchcraft, sorcery, enchantment, or conjuration, or undertake to tell fortunes, every person so offending shall suffer imprisonment by the space of one whole year without bail.' What's more, 'On market day the convicted shall stand openly on the pillory, by the space of one hour.' The trial of 'Hellish Nell' was patently ludicrous, with even the defendant grinning during the proceedings. Ultimately the charges, that she had duped the public with her spiritualistic claims, that she could 'manifest spirits of the dead' for a fee, led in 1951 to a slightly less improbable law against fraudulent mediums and her subsequent short stint in jail.[8]

Until the late nineteenth century Russian peasants 'routinely killed suspected witches and sorcerers', even burning some at the stake.[9] As recently as 1971, legislation was passed in New Guinea that criminalized sorcery and recognized the accusation of sorcery as a defence in murder cases. In the current century there are still parts of the world that are less forgiving in cases of purported witchcraft and sorcery. In February 2013, New Guinea police arrested two suspects for the grisly murder of a woman, who was tortured and burned alive in front of hundreds of spectators including children. The twenty-year-old mother had been accused of committing witchcraft before she was 'stripped, tortured with a hot iron rod, doused in gasoline and set alight on a pile of car tires and trash'. The spectators even blocked police and firefighters from intervening. The accusation surfaced after a six-year-old child died in hospital and his mother and uncle blamed it on the victim.[10] Throughout history, vigilante violence and the crime of witchcraft have been closely linked. One historian has suggested that vigilante justice, no matter where it is directed, is a reflection of a population that questions the prevalent disorder of a state and its lack of control. Following the afore-mentioned New Guinea attack the United Nations attempted to convince the country to revoke its controversial sorcery law. The February case was just the latest vigilante attack resulting in the death of accused sorcerers. In July 2012, police arrested 29 members of a 'witch hunting gang' who were accused of murdering and cannibalizing suspected sorcerers. Harking back to the witch trials in colonial Salem, the best-documented witchcraft trials in American history, police investigators discovered that 'women, particularly widows and those with no family members to protect them, were disproportionately affected' by the violence.[11]

Even western Europe has witnessed witchcraft-related crime in the twenty-first century. In 2009 Spanish police arrested 23 suspected mem-bers of a human-trafficking ring accused of forcing Nigerian women into prostitution by threatening them with voodoo curses. The authorities were alerted when a Nigerian woman in Seville claimed she was a victim, noting that traffickers enticed victims with promises of a better life in Europe. They solidified this by promising to take them to a voodoo priest before leaving Nigeria. Once smuggled into Spain the women were ordered to pay back added debts by working as prostitutes; other-wise they would succumb to the wrath of voodoo spirits. One Nigerian journalist explained that this was a common practice, noting that a voodoo priest made them swear they would not reveal the identities of the traffickers. The priest took pieces of fingernails or hair as part of the ritual and the women were told they would contract a fatal disease such as smallpox if they did not hold up their end of the bargain.[12]

Ancient Crimes and Penalties in a Modern World

Voodoo, witchcraft, banishment, shaming, blasphemy, heresy, adultery and even the death penalty seem like vestiges of a more brutal and primi-tive past, signs of less advanced and more superstitious cultures, yet they persist into the modern era. Pre-industrial societies have long used banishment as a way to purify communities, by eliminating malefactors who endangered residents and angered deities against the community if not removed like a cancer. By most accounts imprisonment and the death penalty are only the latest incarnations of banishment, with the latter a permanent form. In the United States, there are still dozens of sovereign Native American nations with their own justice systems that supersede federal law on several levels. It is not uncommon for there to be conflict between federal and Native law, just as there is between state and federal law over such issues as abortion, marijuana and gay marriage. One 1995 case brought this into clear focus, after two young Tlingit men were sentenced to imprisonment for the brutal robbery of a pizza deliveryman just north of Seattle, Washington, stealing pizza and a beeper and fracturing his skull with a baseball bat. When tribal elders interceded on their behalf, a compromise was reached in which the two perpetrators, who were cousins, would pay the victim compensation and then accept banishment to separate uninhabited islands in Alaska. Relatives of the perpetrators came up with $5,000 in cash for the victim, as well as a new house that the now permanently injured victim could navigate, having suffered lasting damage to his eyesight and hearing. The agreement was not without native assimilationist detractors who supported the modern criminal justice system and traditionalists within the tribe who saw banishment and restitution as crucial to the victim and the offender, what is now considered 'restorative justice'. Everything looked good on paper. The boys would be delivered to separate islands 1,000 miles to the north, where they would be expected to serve a banishment of between three and a half to five and a half years, equipped with only small hand tools. The teenagers had 'supposedly' spent almost eight months foraging for berries and kindling and edible shellfish to sustain them. But from the very start there were tribal members who questioned the veracity of this 'traditional form of punishment'. Ultimately, tribal leaders, elders and scholars, after more investigation and research, determined that this was not really a tribal penalty, and so the experiment failed, especially once local residents reported sightings of the boys back in town doing what teenagers do.[13]

Modern representatives of the industrialized world continue to grapple with crime issues once thought to have been consigned to an earlier age. For example, in June 2004 the Church of England moved to reintroduce heresy trials in an attempt to discipline members of the clergy who were beginning to 'stray from the straight and narrow over church doctrine and ritual'. What proved especially worrisome to Anglican leaders were priests who recognized 'the sanctity of gay marriage'. A move was afoot to defrock priests who condoned same-sex marriage or acknowledged that other religions besides Christianity could lead to salvation. Although the last heresy trial of this nature took place in the 1860s, support for a separate system for tribunals to deal with adulterous priests was discussed, although 'for more than a century it was almost impossible to prosecute clergy for heresy.'[14] Likewise, one would have expected the crime of adultery to been consigned to the waste bin of history, but in the United States it is still a crime in the statute books of 24 states. Usually treated as a misdemeanour, some regard it as a felony, although it is rarely pursued. By most accounts it typically only comes up in divorce and custody cases, and no one ever goes to jail for it. According to one sage, this is 'another example of American exceptionalism', where in nearly the entire rest of the world adultery is not covered by the criminal code.[15]

In less Judaeo-Christian parts of the world, issues of religious justice once thought resolved are still a matter of much debate among justice officials. Consider a recent blasphemy case in Pakistan, where on 21 September 2012 a mostly Muslim mob of anti-Hindus, led by a cleric, ransacked a Hindu temple, breaking statues of Hindu deities, shredding a copy of the Hindu scripture *Bhavagad Gita*, and carrying off decorative gold ornaments. Pakistani blasphemy laws regard this as a capital offence (or at least warranting life imprisonment). Typically, these laws are used against Hindus and Christians. What was notable on this occasion was that these laws might be used to punish Muslims, rather than members of a minority faith.[16] In another recent case a Christian girl was accused of burning a copy of the Quran in Pakistan, committing a serious crime of blasphemy, forcing her and her family to flee to Canada just steps ahead of the authorities in March 2013. The Muslim cleric who led the actions was later accused of fabricating evidence and the young girl was acquitted; even though this case was thrown out of court, people accused of blasphemy in Pakistan are often subject to extra-legal vigilante justice, hence her continued self-banishment from her homeland.

In at least 78 countries, the majority in the Muslim world, Africa and developing nations, homosexual sex is still treated as a crime, in many cases punishable by long prison stints and even death. While laws and attitudes have shifted throughout many Western countries, the attitudes of other countries show little chance of shifting anytime soon. But attitudes do change. Homosexuality was first decriminalized in Britain in 1967, and it was not until 2003 that the U.S. Supreme Court struck down the sodomy laws of fourteen states. One sign of generational change is the growth of gay marriage, first legalized in the Netherlands in 2000. Now seventeen countries, including Argentina, South Africa and parts of the United States and Mexico, recognize it. Most pundits suggest the changing attitudes are part of a generational shift in which younger people are maturing in a more tolerant world. On the other hand, while most churches still regard gay sex as a sin, in the u.s. there have been surveys demonstrating that changes of attitude are a reflection of churches losing some of their clout, with an estimated twice as many Americans holding no religious affiliation as just twenty years ago.[17]

Since a law against same-sex relations in Uganda was first proposed in 2009, public opinion there has become increasingly anti-gay, forcing many homosexuals to live in constant fear. In 2014 a vast majority of Ugandans believed that homosexuality should not be accepted. But there was a glimmer of hope when, in August 2014, the Constitutional Court of Uganda declared the recent Anti-Homosexuality Act 'null and void' (the Act was signed by President Yoweri Museveni in February 2014; at the time of writing, the Ugandan parliament is said to intend to mount an appeal against its overturning). While some observers were somewhat optimistic at this turn of events, most were more realistic – a position well expressed by one aid worker, who commented: 'You can overrule the law, but you can't overrule the mind.'[18]

There are various explanations for the vitriol directed at same-sex relationships, with most hingeing on powerful religious lobbies and traditions. In countries and regions such as Mauritania, southern Somalia, Sudan and northern Nigeria, where Sharia reigns supreme as an arbiter of law, homosexual acts are treated as capital crimes. However, in Uganda the evangelical Christian lobby has displayed a powerful impact on state politics as well, with 'traditionalists, religious leaders and politicians' at the forefront of the campaign. In fact some gay rights supporters have gone as far as suggesting that 'American evangelicals' have played a key role in pushing the anti-gay agenda in Uganda.[19] Nigeria has also joined the campaign against homosexuality, passing the Same Sex Marriage Prohibition Act in 2014, criminalizing homosexual clubs, associations and organizations, with penalties of up to fourteen years behind bars, effectively making it a criminal act for gay people to even hold a meeting. Like Uganda, homosexuality has been illegal in Nigeria since British colonial rule. While not as harsh as Uganda's, Nigeria's law also reflects a highly religious and conservative society that views anything but heterosexuality as deviant behaviour. In any case, Uganda and Nigeria are just the latest to join a trend that some view as perhaps a backlash to Western pressure to decriminalize homosexual behaviour. According to one rumour, the u.s. government paid activists $20 million to promote same-sex marriage in Nigeria.[20] Ultimately, the criminalizing of same-sex relations flies in the face of growing acceptance in Europe and the United States. Perhaps, before judging less developed countries in such matters, critics should look at where the U.S. and other Western countries stood on this issue at a similar stage in development.

Murder, She Wrote

The crime of homicide, or murder, is often used as the gold standard for judging the amount of crime and violence in a society. If that is true, what is one to make of what seems to be an international cycle of mass murder? The litany of names and places has been ingrained in the public consciousness, creating its own form of murder lexicon, as familiar to many modern citizens as the newest movie, books and sports stars. The Aurora, Colorado, cinema massacre that left twelve dead and 58 injured; the Virginia Tech shooting and rampage that resulted in 32 deaths in 2007. Observers are not surprised when it occurs in America, a country awash with guns, where two-thirds of all murders and more than half of its suicides are committed with guns. While America is indeed plagued by too many mass shootings, they are rare compared to other forms of murder in the U.S. and elsewhere. The United States has no monopoly on mass killings in schools, either. For example, more than a decade before America's Sandy Hook Elementary School mass shooting in December 2012 that left 26 children and adults dead, 43-year-old Thomas Hamilton shot dead a teacher and sixteen kindergarten students in Dunblane, Scotland, in 1996. Five years later, Mamoru Takuma stabbed eight primary school children to death and wounded seventeen others at a school in Osaka, Japan.

Today, homicide is the number-three killer of men in Latin America; but it ranks only twentieth worldwide. In the U.S. it is the 21st cause of death in men and 57th in western Europe.[21] Americans are 'four more times likely to be murdered' than their British peers, 'almost six times more likely than in Germany, and 13 times more likely than in Japan'.[22] When the average lifespans are computed among industrialized societies the United States life expectancy for men (75.6) is seventeenth among the seventeen countries used in the survey. Recent research has suggested that this is due to the number of violent deaths, more than any other wealthy nation. Not only does America have the highest rate of firearms ownership (89:100) among its peer countries, it also has a larger uninsured population than comparable economies, meaning less access to primary care. Besides more violent deaths, many of them due to the widespread possession of firearms and the habit of keeping them at home, the U.S.

also has higher rates of drug-related deaths, infant mortality and AIDS in comparison to Japan, Canada, Australia and western Europe. With six violent deaths per 100,000 residents, the closest analogue among its peers is Finland with two per 100,000.[23]

Demonstrating the often fluctuating nature of crime, some countries, such as Brazil, long identified with high modern murder rates, are now seeing declines. Brazil, for example, has been long stereotyped by the image of the 'teenage gunman wearing flip flops' by such international film sensations such as *City of God*. In the early twenty-first century Brazil had the fourth-highest murder rate among the most populous countries, following Venezuela, Russia and Colombia. However, between 2000 and 2008 Brazil's murder rate declined from more than 40 per 100,000 to almost 20 per 100,000. Murder further declined from a high of 64 per 100,000 in the mid-1990s to 39 in 2007. Nowhere has the decline been felt more than São Paulo's poor suburb of Jardim Ângela, once regarded as 'the world's most violent neighbourhood'.[24] Things had become so bad that the suburb created that country's first community police force. Its murder rate plunged from 112 per 100,000 in the 1990s to 33 per 100,000 in 2006. Like the widely heralded crime drop in the U.S. in the 1990s there is still much debate as to what is behind it. Among the most cited causes is tighter gun control. An amnesty and gun buy-back programme saw close to 500,000 guns taken off the streets. Changes in policing have also played a role. At one point in the 1990s, killings by Brazilian police accounted for one-fifth of all violent deaths in the country. Police have got better at solving murders and using computer profiling to locate patterns and to act preventively. The third factor is demographics. The 1990s saw a 'bulge' in the proportion of 19–24-year-olds in the population, which coincided with a rise in youth crime. Between 2000 and 2006 the proportion declined slightly. Other trends have reinforced changes: closing bars earlier, declining use of crack cocaine, and the fact that the nation's preeminent criminal gang, Primeiro Comando da Capital, has 'acquired a temporary monopoly of criminal thuggery, reducing the need to kill rivals'.

Like other crime trends, murder rates are often cyclical. For example, Mexico had one of Latin America's lowest murder rates as recently as 2007, experiencing 9 per 100,000, on a par with the American South, and no higher than Brazil. The Yucatan was as safe as Finland, and amid the ongoing cartel-related carnage in Mexico, murders began to subside in 2012.[25] It appears that levels of violence have dropped along the Mexican–U.S. border and in some cases dropped dramatically.

Once dubbed 'Murder City', Ciudad Juárez, west of Tijuana, had fewer homicides in October 2012 than did Chicago.[26]

While murder rates are waning in some regions, they continue to spin out of control in parts of Latin America. By 2008, Venezuela's murder rates had tripled since 1999, when the late president Hugo Chávez took office. With 13,000 (reported) murders in a population of 27 million, its murder rate of 48 per 100,000 was second only to El Salvador.[27] According to the United Nations, '8 of the world's 10 most violent countries are in Latin America and the Caribbean'. With a murder rate 80 times that of western Europe, Honduras had the highest homicide rate in the world until recently. Much of the problem can be traced back to the battle over billions of dollars of drug profits over the past 30 years. With little or no success in the so-called 'drug war,' countries in this region are considering what was once thought heretical – either ending drug prohibition or decriminalizing possession of certain drugs. In the words of Colombian president Juan Manuel Santos in 2011, 'If [taking away trafficking profits] means legalizing, and the world thinks that is the solution, I will welcome it.' Drugs and violence have plagued countries of Central America; Mexico and the Dominican Republic have lent their voices to the rising chorus demanding changes to drug laws, leading some countries in the region to explore alternatives and take a softer approach towards drug use by focusing more on treatment and education programmes. Brazil, most recently, now allows those caught with small amounts of drugs to do community work rather than jail time.[28]

Capital Punishment

Fewer and fewer countries are utilizing capital punishment in the twenty-first century. Even death penalty stalwart China has made concerted efforts towards using it less. The director of Human Rights Watch suggested in 2008 that the United States had become 'a global pariah' for its continued support for the death penalty, asserting at that time that the u.s. was the world's fourth-leading executioner, following China, Iran and Saudi Arabia. At the time of writing, since the return of the American death penalty in 1977, more than 1,385 prisoners have been hanged, shot, gassed, electrocuted or lethally injected. According to one historian, 'among affluent democracies, the death penalty, like the u.s. homicide and incarceration rates marks an American exception.'[29] However, one of the unexpected trends in American criminal justice was the diminished number of death sentences doled out since 2009. In 2008, 111 were sentenced to death, the lowest number since the reinstatement of the death penalty in 1976. By most accounts when juries have the option of life without parole in all death penalty states, jurors and judges are more willing to avoid the death penalty.

The trend of dwindling executions in America can be traced to a number of factors, including the increasing number of exonerations of falsely accused individuals. In 2013 alone 87 people were exonerated for crimes they did not commit, a record number. Many of the false convictions had been initiated by law enforcement or were the result of police and prosecutorial cooperation. The governor of Washington state announced in February 2014 that no executions would take place while he was in office, the third Democratic governor to do so over the last few years. By 2014 death sentences and executions had plummeted by more than 60 per cent from their zenith in the 1990s.[30] Other considerations have contributed to the decline as well, especially concerns about violating the Eighth Amendment, which protects against cruel and unusual punishment. Pressure from abolition groups has stopped most suppliers from making the traditional 'death cocktail' for lethal injections. Its u.s. manufacturer no longer makes it. Active death rows have been forced to improvise, leading to drawn-out executions, such as the 25 minutes it took to carry out an execution in Ohio in January 2014, using a combination of drugs never used before. The inmate's lawyer attempted to block his execution, claiming that this experimental method could lead to a 'medical phenomenon known as air hunger and cause him to suffer "agony and terror" while struggling to catch his breath'.[31] The death penalty was once more under fire in July 2014, when it took 1 hour and 57 minutes to put to death Joseph R. Wood III, a convicted killer, in Arizona by lethal injection. Designed to take about fifteen minutes, this drawn-out affair has fuelled the debate over the types and sources of drugs used in executions, and led to a temporary halting of executions in Arizona. Witnesses to Wood's execution testified that he gasped hundreds of times for air, comparing his breathing to the working of a 'piston' as his 'mouth opened, the chest rose, [and] the stomach convulsed'.[32]

For a number of years Singapore was considered the 'capital of capital punishment', with execution rates estimated to be double that of China and 24 times that of Texas, America's leading death penalty state.[33] When the country's chief executioner retired in 2006 at age 75, he admitted to having hanged about 1,000 men, which by his estimate came out to about two men a month for 50 years. He was awarded the accolade 'world's fastest hangman' for his ability to carry out seven executions in 90 minutes. His busiest day, he remembered, was sometime in 1964, when he 'hanged eighteen men before lunch'. In Singapore a conviction for homicide or drug possession with intent to traffic in low amounts of heroin (15 g / 0.5 oz), cocaine (30 g / 1 oz), methamphetamine (250 g / 9 oz) or cannabis (500 grams / 18 oz) result in mandatory death sentences. But since 2004, Singapore has seen a drop in executions, from an average of 66 per year in the mid-1990s to an average of just five since 2004, due in no small part to the fact that prosecutors are now allowed discretion in charging defendants for cases of possession. Since there is a certain threshold that needs to be met to get the death penalty, prosecutors will often seek to avoid this by having defendants charged for the possession of cocaine, heroin, methamphetamine and cannabis in amounts just under the death penalty limit – what court observers have alluded to as '14.99 charges'. This pragmatic doling out of death sentences in some ways resembles nineteenth-century England, where juries had a penchant for assigning fictitious values to stolen goods to downgrade a capital offence (theft of an object worth 12 pence or more) to petty larceny (under 12 pence) to spare a defendant from the gallows. Unlike in neighbouring Asian nations Japan and Taiwan, last meals and visits with the condemned are permitted in some cases in Singapore. However, supporters are still barred from attending the execution.[34]

China has publicly declared its intent to reform the process of capital punishment, particularly after several embarrassing cases of errant executions of innocent parties, including a man executed for killing his wife, who showed up quite alive several years after his death. This case supposedly kick-started a reform effort summed up best by its motto, 'kill fewer, kill carefully'.[35] The previous regime made this almost impossible with some capital cases finishing in less than one hour. What also obviated against any type of compassion when it came to homicide was the fact that Chinese law does not have distinct first-, second-, or third-degree gradations of murder. In 2011, human rights activists were encouraged when China dropped the death penalty for twelve non-violent crimes and for offenders older than 75 years. This was the first time since 1979 that there had been a reduction in the number capital crimes. Critics have argued that this is mostly for show, since the crimes that were dropped were typically forging invoices to avoid paying taxes, smuggling cultural relics out of the country and such like – crimes that rarely elicited the death penalty. Moreover, there were still more than 40 capital crimes on the books.

Perhaps 90 per cent of the world's executions occur in Asia, but few share data, therefore it is unknown for certain the number of executions in such countries as China, Vietnam and North Korea. Occasionally news leaks out chronicling public executions, such as in the 2013 case of North Korea, where 10,000 residents were apparently forced to watch the firing-squad executions of 80 people, who had committed such offences as watching South Korean entertainment videos or owning a Bible. These reports are often based on 'unidentified sources' such as North Korean defectors.[36] But anecdotal evidence is often the only source available to researchers scrutinizing death penalty issues in closed countries.

In stark contrast to the aforementioned 'Hermit Kingdom', most of the countries of South Asia have given up on the death penalty, despite countries such as India hosting 400 prisoners on its death row. India's Supreme Court ruled in 1980 that the death penalty should be used only in the 'rarest of rare cases', and with fewer than 50 executed since Independence in 1947 this is how it has stood. The hanging of the surviving terrorist from the 2012 Mumbai attacks that left 166 dead and hundreds injured was the first execution in India since 2004. India, along with Pakistan and other nations, voted against the UN General Assembly resolution on 12 November 2012 calling for a ban on capital punishment. In fact a number of nations have scrapped their informal moratoriums on executions. Pakistan hanged a soldier for murder on 15 November 2012, its first execution in four years. Executions were rare in Afghanistan following the fall of the Taliban in 2001, but on two days in November 2012, fourteen convicts were hanged.[37]

Meanwhile, countries such as Sri Lanka were having a hard time replacing their hangmen. After an advertisement for an executioner, 178 responded, as 369 prisoners on death row languished, hoping for a failed job search. The cast of potential executioners included a man with one eye, retired soldiers, rickshaw drivers, labourers and a student. The one woman was turned down for being potentially 'too emotional'. Ten were eliminated because they were either too old or too young. The only essential requirement was a basic school education and once the dust had cleared two new hangmen were hired to replace one who had retired and another who had been promoted to another position. The first problem was training them since no one had been hanged in Sri Lanka in three decades.[38]

India has had better luck with its hangmen. According to an interview with an executioner in Lucknow, Uttar Pradesh, he had taken over the job from his father in 1965 and had conducted 40 executions, but none in twenty years. This was mostly a result of the previously cited 1983 Indian Supreme Court order that reserved capital punishment for only extraordinary cases. It was evident from the interview that the executioner took pride in his work, nonetheless, admitting to guarantees of 'as quick and painless a death as possible', adding, 'he drops dead, not even alive when he drops, this is my specialty'. He added that he hoped his son would not enter the family business.[39]

In Africa, Swaziland was among the countries in the late twentieth century 'in urgent need of a "hangperson"', or looking for 'an able-bodied man or woman who has what it takes' to clear out the crowded death row at Matsapha Central Prison. In 1998 it had been fifteen years since the last execution. The justice minister reported that he would gladly welcome a female executioner, commenting, 'I advise them to try their luck'. One of the biggest hurdles in finding an executioner anywhere is the stigma that comes with the occupation, in which 'no one wants to get close to you'. Others suggest 'it's a lonely job', and 'you have no friends'.[40]

The Instruments of Death and Justice

A convicted two-time killer, who had murdered a Salt Lake City lawyer during a botched court escape attempt in 1985, he sat on death row for almost 25 years before his execution took place. He was allowed to choose the method of his own demise. He told the judge: 'I would like the firing squad, please.' The convicted killer was now front and centre with his selected killers, sitting in a chair, a hood covering his head. Witnesses described the execution: 'death was not instant', 'the procedure seemed surgical and sanitized – no visible spilling of blood', while another described the six different restraints that attached the convict to a specially designed chair, fitted with anchors and a tin tray beneath the chair to collect any blood that might escape. On 18 June 2010 five marksmen fired four bullets (one had a blank, as required by law, in case one was afflicted with conscience) from .30-30-caliber rifles at targets over his heart. He was dead just two minutes after a prison spokesman informed the media room that the death warrant had been served. This took place in Utah in 2010, only the second time the firing squad had been used since the return of the death penalty in 1976. A firing squad execution in twenty-first-century America was considered unimaginable to many, but the truth is that, according to Amnesty International, the u.s. became part of a select group of nations that included China, Libya, Syria, Yemen and Vietnam that used the firing squad in 2010. Vietnam would end the firing squad in favour of lethal injection only one day before the aforementioned Utah execution of Ronnie Lee Gardner.[41]

An overwhelming majority of prisoners executed in the United States over the past 35 years have been lethally injected, the first on 7 December 1982: Charles Brooks was executed with a lethal concoction of sodium thiopental (an anaesthetic), pancuronium bromide (a muscle relaxant) and potassium chloride (to stop the heart). In recent years death penalty opponents have successfully lobbied the few companies that supply these drugs to stop providing them. Since 2012 Texas has been forced to use a single drug, pentobarbital, for executions. In July 2012, the state of Missouri announced that it also had a shortage of the drugs required for lethal executions. Many state statutes offer death row inmates a choice of two options. In Missouri it is lethal injection and the gas chamber. According to that state's attorney general, returning the gas chamber might be the only solution.[42] When the gas chamber was first used in Nevada in February 1924, it was touted, like other innovations that preceded it, as a more humane method, killing fast and painlessly 'without the horror' of the noose and electric chair.[43] Eleven states would eventually adopt this method and, between 1924 and 1999, almost 600 would die in this manner.

However, by many accounts the gas chamber was not actually an improvement at all. One San Quentin Prison physician found hanging to be 'simpler, quicker and far more humane'. Another physician who attended executions there claimed that

> the idea that cyanide kills immediately is hooey. These men suffered as their lungs no longer absorbed oxygen and they struggled to breathe. They died of internal suffocation against which they had to fight and from which must have suffered.[44]

In surely one of the more macabre stories about San Quentin's gas chamber, a convict named Alfred Wells, serving time for burglary, helped put together and install the first gas chamber at the prison, afterwards exclaiming: 'That's the closest I ever want to come to the gas chamber.'[45] Little could he imagine that just five years later he would take his last breath in it after participating in a triple murder. The gas chamber never caught on in the United States, at least compared to hanging, the electric chair and lethal injection. One of the issues was the fear of contamination from the poison gas. Others suggest that its association with the Nazi death camps created a backlash against it. In any case the last execution by this method took place in Arizona in 1999.

In 2002, Thailand made the transition from bullets to lethal injection. Until 1934, prisoners were flogged with 90 lashes and then tied to a cross on the ground, attached with the back to it and arms outstretched, before being beheaded. While Christians have searched for significance for death on the cross in this manner, the executioner was more circumspect, suggesting that the cross was 'simply the best shape for the job', since 'a man's weight can be spread out across it and it is the perfect shape for taking someone's limp weight after they have been shot' or beheaded.[46] Three men were initially used in the beheading process, with one expected to try and distract the prisoner by making a sudden loud noise, while another struck off the head, and the third was available just in case he was needed.

The last Thai executioner described the former execution room, where he personally executed 55 men and women with gunshots: 'Just past the kitchen is the wooden diamond shaped gazebo where prisoners are brought before their execution. A table is usually set up with flowers and incense to calm the condemned.' Then the condemned is finally taken into a room that 'looks more like a white wooden shed with a large front porch'. A sign overlooking the porch translates into English as 'the place to end all sorrow'.[47]

Thailand's last official executioner witnessed his first execution in 1972. The process worked to a meticulous timetable that began with the inmate receiving his last meal at 5 a.m., and the execution taking place two hours later. It was an execution process used nowhere else in the modern world: the inmate was blindfolded and secured to a wooden cross, with his back to the gun, 'his arms were brought over the arms of the cross and tied together, as if in prayer, behind the horizontal beam'. According to tradition he was also secured in two other places – around the torso and stomach – 'and pulled astride a bar that struck out from the cross forcing him to hug the cross between his knees. His ankles were chained together so the cross was now completely supporting him . . . there was a square white cloth on the screen (separating him from the gun and pulled across) with a concentric circle pinned on it which denoted the prisoner's heart.'[48] According to the executioner, the gun looked 'like a sewing machine'. He then fired his Bergmann gun into the back of the heart. He remembered on one occasion that before the execution was completed an officer asked the prisoner if he would come to him in his dreams 'and give him [winning] lottery numbers', conforming to a Thai belief that when someone dies they can visit in dreams and pass on useful lotto numbers. Recounting his last execution, he used eight bullets, although fifteen are permitted and five are probably about right. Subsequent to his retirement Thailand's last executioner entered the priesthood.[49]

As recently as 2001, more than half of all nations had the death penalty on the books, as did 38 of the 50 U.S. states. In 2012 five more states dropped the death penalty, including Connecticut, where the death penalty dated back to the seventeenth century, when witches were executed. In recent years it has been seldom used. Between 1973 and 2007, of the state's 4,686 murders, only 66 resulted in capital convictions and only nine in actual death (the last time in 2005). With the rise in death row exonerations due to advances in DNA technology, fewer American states are using this punishment, especially if actual life imprisonment is an alternative.

At the same time that the world has seen a diminished use of the death penalty, a number of countries have also changed their traditional methods of execution. Explanations range from expediency to geopolitics and pressure groups; but as times have changed so have the methods. Historically, Communist China has favoured a bullet to the back of the head. By most estimates it routinely executes more people each year than the rest of the death penalty countries combined. Historians have demonstrated how over the centuries China has preferred public executions, the 'more cruel, the better'. One law professor suggests that the country has perhaps turned the corner, noting how 'civilization has evolved and its time we abandon, or at least severely limit' its use.[50] Nationwide crackdowns have typically followed crime waves and resultant fears that the social order is under siege. Police are under pressure to solve crimes quickly, often using torture to gain confessions. A case that exemplifies the relationship between tortured confessions and executions was that of a twenty-year-old who was convicted of a rape that someone else later confessed to. When his parents came to visit their son, guards told them to stop wasting their time bringing soap and toothbrushes because their son had already been executed.[51] According to Hunan Province newspapers, police solved 3,000 cases in two days in April 2001. Sichuan Province reported 6,704 solved in just six days that same month, including murders, robberies and bombings. This wave of arrests was followed by a wave of executions, often carried out within an hour of sentence confirmation. Crimes such as bribery, tax fraud, stealing diesel fuel and drug trafficking, which would have received light sentences in the West, were considered capital crimes in China.

By most accounts China has experienced three waves of executions since the Communist Revolution. The first occurred shortly after 1949, and saw perhaps 5 million put to death. The second began in 1996, and was backed by broad popular support despite the likelihood of false confessions. Some executions were carried out publicly, such as one in Hubei Province where more than 5,000 people witnessed the sentencing of thirteen and the execution of eight immediately afterwards on 25 June 1996.[52] Harking back to more medieval times, those condemned to death were paraded through villages and towns on the beds of open trucks, before being taken to the execution grounds just outside town. The trucks were often trailed by legions of onlookers eager to watch the prisoners' final moments. Similar to Japan and several other death penalty countries, the condemned are not allowed to see family members before death and families often only hear of the execution after it has been carried out when they are notified that they can collect ashes. Until recently, prisoners were ordered to kneel before being shot in the back of the head at point-blank range. Any way you look at it, a gunshot is the cheapest punishment. According to one authority, each execution costs about $87, including the transportation, cremation, bullets and death notices, with the ages of offenders ranging from eighteen to 87.[53] In some cases guards have reportedly asked prisoners to open their mouths so the bullet can pass out of the mouth and leave the face intact.[54] While information is still unclear, there are increasing reports that medical staff have been involved in the removal of organs, rushing them to nearby facilities for transplant operations.

Beginning in 2004, China introduced mobile execution chambers as part of a push to phase out shooting and firing squads in favour of lethal injections. Critics assert that lethal injection is employed because it leaves the body intact and facilitates the illegal organ trade. It was not until 2005 that the country's vice minister of health admitted that the majority of organs for transplants came from dispatched prisoners. Unlike any other country that uses lethal injection today, China metes out executions in specially equipped death vans which travel from town to town. According to the designer of the death van, the transition from bullets to needles is a sign that China 'promotes human rights now'.[55]

One of the first to die in this fashion was Zhang Shiqiang, convicted of a double murder and rape; he earned the moniker the 'nine-fingered devil', the result of his father having cut off one of his fingers for stealing when he was thirteen years old. In order to guarantee that executions are carried out legally they are recorded and played live for local police authorities. Some proponents of the mobile death vans suggest that this process ensures that the execution occurs closer to communities where the law was broken and has more deterrence value than carrying it out far away. What's more, poor communities lack the funds to construct their own facilities.

As the 2008 Olympics loomed on the horizon, China implemented a number of death penalty reforms that included restoring the review of all capital cases by the Supreme People's Court, a move that Chinese legal experts suggested could result in up to a 30 per cent decrease in executions. As of 2008, China maintained the death penalty for 68 offences including non-violent ones such as the 2007 cases of a State Food and Drug Administrator executed for taking bribes and an official who swindled investors out of about $300 million. That same year came word that new regulations prohibited trading organs and live organ transplants from those aged under eighteen. Unmentioned, it has to be assumed this did not affect the condemned on death rows. Later in the year came word that medical officers had agreed not to transplant organs from prisoners or others in custody except into immediate family members.[56]

In early 2012 China announced plans to end the practice of prisoner organ removal after executions over the next three to five years, although no mention was made of the ethical issues involved. The announcement was instead couched in terms of medical issues, citing worries about high rates of fungal and bacterial infections in organs taken from prisoners. Some observers have suggested that this might explain why long-term survival rates of organ recipients in China are consistently lower than others. One of the biggest challenges to legitimate organ donation in China is the cultural prohibition against being buried without one's organs intact.[57] In August 2013 came word that the prohibition against prisoner organ 'donation' would come into effect in November, since this practice 'tarnished China's image'. If China's figures are correct, organ removal had already declined by 10 per cent during the first six months of 2013.

In the twenty-first century it appears that the unavailability of professional hangmen and headsmen has forced several countries to alter their forms of capital punishment. Nowhere was this more apparent than in Saudi Arabia, where after centuries of beheadings the firing squad was considered as an alternative death penalty, in no small part due to 'the scarcity of swordsmen and their unavailability in a number of regions'. Over the past two years, 75 decapitations by sword have taken place – the only country in the world to conduct such executions in public. In March 2013, the firing squad was used for the first time on seven men convicted of theft, looting and armed robbery.[58]

During the first decade of the twenty-first century Japan sentenced 112 criminals to death, executing 46 of them at seven secret execution sites by 2009. The main gallows is located in Tokyo, where the condemned will find rather Spartan trappings that consist of a trapdoor, a Buddha statue and a ring for the noose. Inmates are not informed until the last minute that their time is up (in order to 'prevent panic among inmates'), just enough time to clean their cells, receive last rites and perhaps write a last letter. Once sentenced to death, there is little chance of a pardon, and inmates can remain on Death Row for 40 years, although six is average. Their sentences are served in solitary confinement in cells of 50 square feet (4.5 square metres) and it is not uncommon for prisoners to be old and infirm or mentally ill by the time they mount the gallows. Inmates are allowed to leave only to bathe and exercise. Relatives can visit, friends cannot; prisoners can have a chess set, but must play alone. What is most striking is that with a murder rate perhaps one-fifth of that of the United States, Japan's execution rate is somewhat comparable per capita; in 2007 Japan executed nine and the United States 42. Despite the rarity of its use in the industrialized world, in 2010, 86 per cent supported it.[59]

Rape

The crime of rape has garnered international headlines and condemnation throughout 2012 and 2013 after several high-profile rapes in Asia and Africa. But views and laws continue to vary widely over its definition. In some countries sex with a minor is automatically considered rape, in others not. Laws and perceptions vary widely according to culture and countries and over time. More recently, WikiLeaks founder Julian Assange (an Australian), who won asylum from Ecuador, claimed that his alleged behaviour might have been 'really sordid and bad sexual etiquette', but his sexual conduct would not have merited a rape charge in Latin America. Jacob Zuma, the polygamous president of South

Africa claimed his first sexual conquest was a rape, stating his belief that 'you cannot just leave a woman if she is ready'. After his acquittal at a rape trial in 2006 he had the gall to tell the judge that to deny a woman sex would be 'tantamount to rape'.[60]

There is an average of 232 rapes reported to police in the United States every day, where there is still no nationwide definition of rape. According to the federal penal code, rape refers to aggravated sexual abuse, but it is defined state by state, according to such provisions as whether force must have been used or not. English common law defines rape as 'non-consensual penetration of any of three orifices by a penis'.

Sharia law makes rape especially hard to prove since it cannot be proven without a confession from the actual rapist or by four witnesses. In countries such as Somalia and Bangladesh it is not uncommon for rape victims to be punished for engaging in illegal sex, by lashing or stoning. One recent account claims perhaps three-quarters of women in jails in Pakistan are rape victims.

India's caste system has contributed to a stark disparity in the way justice is meted out depending on a person's class status. In September 2012, for example, eight men raped a sixteen-year-old low-caste girl and warned her they would kill her if she reported it. As a member of the Dalit caste, once better known as the Untouchables, her status traditionally would have prevented her from speaking out, especially in a village system dominated by high-caste individuals. What made this assault even more jarring was that the men had all taken videos on their mobile phones and shared them with local men. When her father was alerted to this he committed suicide by drinking pesticides. His fellow Dalit community responded with demands for justice.

It was not long after the aforementioned rape that a higher-caste victim, a young physiotherapy student, suffered gang rape and murder in New Delhi, drawing world attention. In India its savagery provoked outrage and for many became a symbol of the mistreatment of women in a country where rape is common and convictions are low. In this case five men were charged with the attack (the sixth was a juvenile) that left the woman dead after clinging to life for two weeks. The men, who had been out drinking, picked up the woman and a male friend and attacked them with an iron rod; she died from internal injuries. In one 2010 survey more than two-thirds of women questioned in New Delhi claimed to have been sexually harassed in the previous year, although less than 1 per cent actually reported it. Some surveys have suggested that India has one of the highest rates of sexual violence in the world.

In order to counter this phenomenon new fast-track courts were set up in the aftermath of the attack, specifically to handle crimes against women.[61]

One would have expected great strides in punishing rapists in India after the spate of high-profile cases. But in 2014 India was once more the target of human rights groups after a young woman in West Bengal was gang raped at the direction of village elders, who did this to punish her for her intention to marry a man from another village.[62] Despite growing awareness of the rape problem in India, in rural villages councils are common and often direct the enforcement of strict codes of behaviour. Like many communities around the world playing catch-up with the modern century, rural villages such as those in India are often stifled by age-old traditions and cling to their medieval roots which are more influential than modern law.

In February 2013, a young South African woman lay dying among the detritus of a construction site. 'Her bowels spilling from her abdomen', she was able to whisper the name of the individual who had assaulted her to medics desperately trying to save her life. The following day a 22-year-old suspect was arrested and the case produced national outrage, symptomatic of the rampant sexual violence plaguing South Africa. This case would force the same type of soul searching energizing women's movements in India, Egypt and Brazil, especially after charges were dropped for insufficient evidence. With some 64,000 sexual assault cases reported each year, South Africa has 'one of the highest rates of non-partner rape in the world'. Together with a deficient criminal justice system, poor police investigation and less than a 10 per cent conviction rate, it is little wonder that one survey found that 25 per cent of South African men admitted to raping someone, with almost half stating they had done this more than once. Researchers suggest that part of the problem is a history and culture that is deeply patriarchal and devalues crimes against women. Almost twenty years after apartheid, South African law enforcement is still making the transition from security force to a modern police force, one that will take rape as seriously as it did domestic security matters during the apartheid era.[63]

Other recent cases in majority Muslim countries have demonstrated a certain amount of flexibility and pragmatism when it comes to cases of rape. More often than not these changes in law favour the perpetrator, rather than the victim. However, one ruling that went against this trend took place in Morocco, when the country's parliament voted in 2014 to unanimously amend the law that had previously allowed men convicted of statutory rape to evade punishment if they agreed to marry their under-age victims. This ruling followed the 2012 rape of a sixteen-year-old girl, who was then forced by her own family to marry the attacker who had raped her at knifepoint. According to Article 475, if the individual did not marry the victim, he would serve several years behind bars and pay a small fine. However, with the change in law, the exoneration in this article would be withdrawn and the punishments remain in force. The Justice Ministry followed this ruling by promising to seek harsher penalties for rape, while others pushed to criminalize a variety of behaviours against women, and to eschew the stigmatization of births out of wedlock.[64]

Towing the more traditional line, that usually advocated against women's rights, in January 2014 Afghanistan's parliament approved changes to the nation's criminal code that would prevent relatives of alleged abusers from testifying against them. What makes this change so alarming is the fact that most violent crimes against women in this region were witnessed *only* by relatives. As of March 2014 President Karzai had not signed his final approval, as Western human rights groups urged him to veto the prospective legislation. This amendment was just one small part of almost 100 pages of new criminal code, better known as Article 26. The law itself does not specify women or mention domestic violence, but since the movement of women is restricted they are typically in the company of family members. According to legal experts, the approval of this bill would prevent a woman from testifying against a male relative, such as an uncle, who had raped her. Likewise, if a mother observed the beating of her daughter by other family members, she could not testify. In any case, it once more reminds students of crime and punishment that legal systems, past and present, have been used to set back the rights of women.[65]

Imprisonment

As sanctions go, imprisonment continues to dominate penal regimes in most of the world. There are still parts of the world that use Soviet-style gulag systems, but none more so than North Korea, which modelled its prison camps on this design, adding several home-grown features. GULAG is a Russian acronym for 'Chief Administration of Corrective Labour Camps'. Established under Joseph Stalin in 1929, 'gulag' became shorthand for a vast system of slave labour camps and the repressive coordination of arrests, interrogations, transportation and obliteration of family units that kept the camps flourishing.[66] By most accounts the camps did not end at once but were redesigned in the last decades of the Soviet Union to punish a 'new generation' of criminals that also included political activists. In 1987 Mikhail Gorbachev directed the dissolution of these camps. Although this system has been dismantled in Siberia, it continues to flourish in North Korea. As hundreds of Koreans flee the north to South Korea they bring tales of harrowing brutality and of a regime that often works prisoners to death. By some accounts there is so little food to eat that inmates are forced to subsist on rats and snakes, others conjure up tales reminiscent of the twentieth-century Chinese famines that saw starving villagers picking through animal dung for a few grains of corn. Due to a 1972 edict by its leader Kim Il-sung, 'up to three generations' must be punished in order to wipe out the seed of class enemies. This was accomplished by incarcerating entire families for 'guilt by association'.[67]

North Korea's gulag system, what human rights activists call 'The Hidden Gulag', comprises specialized prisons for different levels of offenders. For example the Kyo-Hwa-So prison, which translates to 'a place to make a good person through education', is designed for political and criminal offenders, who work at hard labour. A number of them are released early due to serious illness. This serves two functions; it lowers the numbers of deaths under detention and saves the prison the money it would cost to send home bodies to families. According to the testimony of an unidentified prisoner, known as #12, he was among 15,000 inmates in the 1990s working at hard labour as copper miners, loggers and furniture makers. Prisoners worked from 5 a.m. to 5 p.m., with most serving between one and fifteen years at this camp. Punishments included reduced rations, extended sentences and detention in tiny (5 feet by 5 feet) punishment cells, where it was almost impossible to stand up or lie down and inmates were forced to subsist on one-quarter rations for days on end. Prisoners are executed for attempting to escape, being caught while escaping, committing crimes while on sick leave, or committing capital crimes in other regions and brought to the camp for execution. Prisoners sleep head to toe on wooden floors in groups of 50 to 100, with no opportunity to bathe or change clothing. Death rates are not surprisingly quite high. Another former prisoner recounted being forced to sit in the front row to witness the execution of his parents and having one of his fingers cut off at the knuckle for committing an accidental mistake at a textile factory. Other prisoners were punished in the 1990s with water torture, hanging by the wrists, sleep deprivation, beatings, forced abortions and even the murder of infant children. Forced abortion and infanticide were targeted at inmates who were forcibly repatriated from China while pregnant, with the mind-set that North Korea 'should not have to feed the children of foreign fathers'.[68] In 2014 a United Nations Special Commission produced the most authoritative indictment of North Korea's detention system, accusing the government of crimes against humanity including murder, enslavement, torture, rape, forced abortions and persecution on religious, racial and political grounds. Furthermore, the document asserted that 'the gravity, scale and nature of these violations reveal a state that does not have any parallel in the contemporary world.'

During the 1950s Mao Zedong directed the overhauling of China's labour camp system to quickly neutralize his political opposition. This system, predicated on re-education through hard labour, has since grown to a sprawling system of 350 camps with more than 100,000 prisoners. These camps, known as *laojiao*, enable police to detain individuals in a prison environment without trial for up to four years. In the words of one observer, these camps are among the 'most anachronistic elements of the country's creaky system of law and order'.[69] By 2008 it was estimated that the number of inmates in the 350 *laojiao* had grown to at least 160,000. It should be remembered this is just one part of China's correctional system, with the difference being that the inmates of other institutions have been winnowed through the judicial process, while the *laojiao* residents were usually exempt from the legal process. Among the residents of these camps are the usual enemies of communism – prostitutes, political dissidents, petitioners, drug addicts, Christians and members of banned spiritual groups such as Falun Gong.

Since the end of the Soviet Union, Russia and the fourteen other nations that emerged from the collapse have been playing catch-up when it comes to modernizing their prison regimes. Some 1,500 miles (2,500 km) northeast of Moscow is penal colony #76 in Lozva. When President Boris Yeltsin banned the death penalty in 1999, its 277 death row inmates had their sentences commuted to life. In 2000, journalists were granted rare interviews with the lifers, several of whom reported that they would rather be shot than live in their current conditions. This penal colony was one of only two special facilities where death row inmates had been transferred. The other is on an island in Vologda, 300 miles north of Moscow. Formerly, during the execution regime a special unit would drag shackled prisoners out of their cells and then deliver one shot to the back of the neck. The transition has been similar to

Lozva, with some inmates also requesting executions to put them out of their misery. It is easy to understand why. Each cell is 12 feet by 12 feet (4 by 4 metres). Meant to house two, it now houses six. Garbed in grey and black striped uniforms, prisoners' daily routine mainly consisted of sitting on metal bunk beds and basically staring into the ether. A naked light bulb is kept on 24 hours a day. The cells are barren of any natural light and no running water is available, except for when they wash every ten days. They are allowed out of their cells for 90 minutes each day. Lozva in particular offers a hellish existence. Constructed on the site of a Soviet gulag colony used for logging, its isolation compounds the deprivation. Forty hours by train from Moscow, winters there last almost nine months, with temperatures sometimes falling to -45 degrees. Although inmates are allowed two four-hour visits a year, most family and friends cannot afford to make the exorbitant trip to see them.[70]

After years of economic depression, Russia's prison conditions continued to decline. Plagued by poor diet and medical treatment, tuberculosis reached epidemic proportions in 1999, affecting an estimated 100,000 prisoners.[71] There is a bit of irony here, in that when the great prison reformer John Howard visited Russia almost two centuries earlier he contracted typhus, known then as 'gaol fever' while visiting Russian prisons. In the twenty-first century it is rare to find a prison system that is *not* characterized by overcrowding, poor sanitation and other intolerable conditions. One wonders what John Howard would have to say about these conditions, but at best he would suggest that little attention is devoted to rehabilitation and reform and thus would not be surprised by high rates of recidivism among prison inmates.

As much of Europe is plagued by austerity measures, particularly in the southern countries, one unexpected result of the downturn in national economies is that some prisoners prefer staying locked up where they can be assured of free rent and enough food to subsist on. What's more, the deteriorating conditions in the free world have had unintended consequences for prison employees, such as in Portugal, where guards are forced to supply their own toilet paper at work. Petty crime rates have skyrocketed with the downward spiral of the Portuguese economy, leaving many citizens unable to pay traffic fines, ending up in jail and increasing the prison population. Budget cuts have eliminated free shampoo and detergent, creating an underground economy where guards can overcharge prisoners for such essential items.[72]

Japan, on the other hand, has low incarceration and recidivism rates. For example, it imprisons 55 per 100,000, compared to 149 per 100,000 in the UK, and 716 per 100,000 in the U.S. However, the Japanese system is among the most draconian of industrialized countries, with a regime that prohibits talking except during breaks, leaving prisoners no choice but to work as unpaid labour. Following a series of high-profile murders in the late 1990s, this low-crime country saw an escalation in the fear of crime. Like the United States, this was fostered by saturation media coverage of grisly mass murders, which in fact were not part of a general trend. Japanese society, like its Western counterparts, has reacted to rising crime fears with what one criminologist refers to as 'penal populism', in which the criminal justice system turns more punitive with the support of the country's population. Thus, recent changes in Japanese criminal code increased the upper limits in punishment for certain crimes (fifteen years to twenty; twenty years to thirty). What's more, the age-old bogeyman, fear of juvenile predation, has led to such penalties as life imprisonment and the death penalty for certain crimes.[73]

The Japanese correctional system has been criticized for its secrecy and reliance on solitary confinement. In Chiba Prison more than two-thirds of inmates are serving time for deaths caused by murder, manslaughter and arson; half of its inmates are serving life sentences. The inmate population at Chiba averages around 50 years of age, with many in the midst of terms that have effectively prevented them from having ever held a mobile phone or used a credit card. Conjugal visits are not allowed. Daily routines consist of making shoes and furniture in vast workshops. By most accounts escapes and riots are rare, as are drugs and contraband. The high guard-to-prisoner ratio (1:4) together with a punitive system of rules may have achieved a remarkable order in terms of correctional management, but human rights groups claim this has been 'achieved at a very high cost' in terms of mental deterioration among some of the inmates, particularly those of Western origin.[74]

Like Japan, most of the countries of Scandinavia are homogeneous in population. But in sharp contrast, Scandinavian countries offer a far less punitive system of corrections, one that has evolved over the centuries. Countries such as Denmark, for instance, have implemented numerous reforms since the 1880s including the abolition of the death penalty and corporal punishment, as well as imprisonment at hard labour. In recent decades lenient imprisonment has become the most common form of incarceration, operated on a foundation of humane treatment. Penal policy includes imposing when possible the shortest sentences available, including sentences to open prisons. However, if prisoners in these facilities violate prison protocol they know a more punitive environment awaits them with a transfer to a closed facility. With rehabilitation the number one jail, 85 per cent of prison sanctions are forms of lenient imprisonment for property offences and drunk-driving. In the end most criminal sanctions in Denmark include fines and suspended sentences, sometimes in combination with probation, lenient imprisonment, restitution, and day fines according to income.

Finland has perhaps the fewest prisons in Europe. As a relatively classless culture, it lacks the economic and social disparities that plague other countries. Just 30 years earlier, Finland had a rigid penal system with one of the highest rates of imprisonment on the Continent, more akin to its neighbour Russia than the rest of western Europe. However, the Finnish experience has demonstrated what can be achieved through rethinking penal policies and accepting input from academics and other penal specialists. Modern facilities are open prisons, where 'walls and fences have been removed in favor of unobtrusive camera surveillance and electronic alert networks.' The traditional sounds of the prison lock-up have traded the clanking of heavy metal doors and medieval cells for living conditions that resemble college dormitories. Here guards and their charges address each other by their given names and inmates are allowed home leaves and four-day visits with family members in special houses.[75]

When it comes to per capita imprisonment rates no country in the world can match the United States over the past several decades. As 2010 dawned it had the world's highest per capita incarceration rate. Containing only 5 per cent of the world's population, the u.s. housed close to 25 per cent of the world's 'reported' prisoners. The rate worked out to 756 per 100,000, almost five times the world's average (125 per 100,000).[76] One of the most perplexing aspects of America's so-called 'war on crime' is that while the total prison population has continued to grow over the past twenty years, the overall crime rate in the United States has been declining. While longer prison terms and more prisoners probably have contributed to the crime drop, much of the prison increase has been driven by other factors, such as the penal policies supported by the electorate and the criminal justice system.

Critics of gulag-style prison regimes in North Korea, China and elsewhere find it easy to knock their penal practices. What is less seldom mentioned is that American prisons continue to isolate prisoners in super-maximum structures for up to 23 hours per day, with only an hour's release from their 6-by-9-foot cells for solitary exercise in a restricted area. Journalist David Brooks, alluding to Aleksandr

Solzhenitsyn's magisterial work on the Russian gulag system, recently described this American phenomenon as 'the Archipelago of Pain'.[77] More than 150 years after Charles Dickens wrote his screed on the horrors of solitary confinement at Philadelphia's Eastern State Penitentiary, the practice continues. Prisoners might not be racked and pinioned, or even pilloried and shamed, but observers from the Enlightenment to Michel Foucault have noted the propensity of solitary confinement to produce what some have called 'social pain'. There are a number of good reasons for ghettoizing violent and disorderly prisoners, but most studies have found that this form of punishment is more likely to cause suicides, acute psychosis and is a strong predictor for future violence when and if the inmate gets out. There are signs that several states are beginning to come to grips with this reality. In 2014 Colorado announced it would no longer send inmates with severe mental illness into solitary confinement, and in New York officials have finalized plans to introduce new guidelines that will limit how long isolation can be permitted.[78]

Between 1985 and 1991 the United States Congress passed twenty new mandatory sentencing laws that took much of the sentencing discretion out of the hands of judges. In 1993, the refrain 'three strikes and you're out', a phrase coined in Washington state after voters approved a ballot measure requiring life sentences without the possibility of parole for third-time serious felony offenders, became the rallying cry for get-tough politicians. Subsequently, more than a dozen states followed suit with similar laws. Three-strikes sentencing policy originated in California in the early 1980s, after the abduction and murder of young Polly Klaas by a career criminal who had been in and out of prison most of his life. This crime resonated throughout the country, after Polly was taken from her bedroom and brutally murdered, leading one legal historian to assert that this crime 'was a powerful stimulus to some draconian pieces of legislation'.[79] In the second decade of the twenty-first century a number of new trends have contributed to the slowing of American incarceration rates, most importantly, the diminished reliance on mandatory minimum sentences and the softening of harsh drug convictions.

Inventing Justice

Over the past few years there has been a recrudescence of draconian punishment among various extremist religious groups. Islamic scholars have asserted that many of the punishments and crimes punished by the Taliban in Afghanistan and Pakistan (as well as other groups in the Islamic world) have no correlation with the Quran and Sharia law. Indeed, the militant extremism extolled by al-Qaeda-affiliated supporters contrasts sharply with the more moderate version of Islam that had until recently prevailed in Timbuktu, Mali; that is, until the crackdown by Islamists in this country the size of Afghanistan. Lapidation for adultery was among the new sanctions introduced by the Islamists, exemplified by the case of a couple stoned to death after being first forced to dig 'a hole the size of a man', then to kneel inside the hole as villagers looked on. In another case a woman was caught in the company of an unrelated man and given 95 lashes (severe even by Islamic standards). The young lady was first taken to the public market on 4 January 2013, where her crime and punishment were pronounced to the spectators, and then the flogging began, 'with a switch made from the branch of a tree. He hit her so hard and for so long that at one point she wasn't sure if the veil had fallen off. She could feel the blood seeping through.' Once the beating stopped she was warned that the next time she would be executed.[80]

With the Islamic takeover of northern Mali in 2012 came one of the harshest examples of Sharia law. Perhaps one villager put it best when he commented, 'these people who have come among us have imposed their justice', adding, 'it comes from nowhere.'[81] By the end of the year there were more than a dozen cases of amputation. In one case an individual was accused of the attempted theft of firearms. He was subsequently tied down to a chair, his right arm strapped to an armrest with a rubber tube. A physician administered a sedative injection and then the arrestee's own brother, who also happened to be the police chief, took a knife used to kill sheep and carried out the sentence (an almost half-hour process in which the purported thief passed out), noting he had 'no choice but to practice the justice of God'.[82] In another theft case, prisoners were forced to watch one of their own sit in a chair with his arms strapped tightly to it. The jailer proceeded to trace a circle around his forearm and then sawed of his hand in three minutes that must have seemed like a lifetime to the poor miscreant. By forcing the public to watch, these episodes were designed to provoke fear among north Mali's mostly Islamic population. In other cases, thieves have had their feet amputated and public lashings with camel-hair whips or tree branches have been bestowed on those caught smoking or listening to music on the radio. They were more pragmatic when it came to mobile phones: these were allowed, as long as the ringtones were Quranic in tone, otherwise a flogging would be warranted.

What was most troubling about this new round of punishments was the lack of trials. Extremists were free to bring suspects to a public square they renamed Place de Shariah, where they amputated limbs in full view of the community, such as in the case where the purported thief was laid out on the ground with his arms and legs tied down, and then his right hand and forearm were amputated with a knife, causing the 39-year-old to pass out from the pain.[83]

Like other extremists, Taliban members are quite pragmatic when it comes to implementing punishment. Crime is often determined according to the eye of the beholder. For most Afghans the return of the Taliban has been like pre-9/11 déjà vu, as they travelled through towns and villages beating people for smoking cigars, listening to music and chewing tobacco. Reminiscent of the 1990s, morality police garbed in black from head to toe enforce codes banning television, kite flying, cutting beards and showing female flesh. According to a number of reports from 2012, one 28-year-old had his hands tied behind his back and was given 70 lashes to his back for 'failing to grow his beard long enough'. If caught at Taliban checkpoints with photos or music on mobile phones, one could be detained, fined and even beaten. Even wearing a collared shirt was considered the mark of an infidel and was worth up to fifteen lashes to the palm of the hand. Punishments ranged from fifteen lashes for wearing a shirt collar and 30 lashes for chewing tobacco and smoking cigarettes to 70 for failing to grow one's beard long enough.[84]

Searching for Alternatives to Incarceration

In the United States, the world leader in locking people up, the search for alternatives to prison sentences began almost 170 years ago when John Augustus helped establish probation sentences in 1841. Today it is the most common penal sentence in the United States. By the 1980s, judges were relying on the standard options of probation and incarceration. But prison overcrowding became such an issue during that era's 'get-tough war on crime' that a number of other alternative sanctions were incorporated, including home confinement, boot camps, intensive supervision parole and probation, and a handful of others. But these did little to reduce rising recidivism rates and overcrowding.

The world's penal systems are constantly developing as they respond to crime in a rapidly changing world. In some cases that means revisiting earlier eras of crime and punishment for inspiration and on some occasions alternatives can be found in the historical record if one looks deeply enough. Among the more popular alternatives is a process known as 'restorative justice'. While the practice of restorative justice might seem like a recent development to the uninformed, its roots date back centuries (albeit under different nomenclature). The modern incarnation of this process is grounded in traditions that date back to antiquity. One leading scholar alludes to the ancient Arab, Greek and Roman societies that 'accepted a restorative approach even to homicide'. Indeed, he was so bold as to assert that 'restorative justice has been the dominant model of criminal justice throughout most of human history for perhaps all the world's peoples.'[85]

In America, restorative justice dates back to Native American cultures and the colonial era. Others suggest it dates back even further, to customs and religions of the ancient world, where communities played pivotal roles in the healing and retributive process following the commission of a crime. In many traditional cultures new ways of managing conflict were met by 'a ritualized process' involving members of the community and families from both sides of the conflict. This has been adapted to modern penal sanctions by involving both parties in the aftermath of a crime, representing both the victim and the perpetrator. Until fairly recently a typical trial in the United States would end up in a plea bargain in which the victim had virtually no input. What's more, the perpetrator's accountability to the victim or the community is rarely addressed. According to one researcher the implementation of restorative justice programmes 'offers a new paradigm for structuring relationships among crime victims, offenders and communities' and 'hopefully some type of "victim–offender reconciliation"'.[86]

There is still a lack of consensus as to the specific definition of restorative justice. More than a decade ago a survey found that it 'emerged in various guises with different names', including an alternative process for resolving disputes, alternative sanctioning options, or a 'distinctly different, new model of criminal justice organized around principles of restoration to victims, offenders, and the communities in which they live'. It has rightfully taken its place beside a number of novel incarcerative strategies including diversion from formal court processes and meetings between victim and offender at any stage of the criminal process.[87]

Canada has been credited with introducing the first modern restorative justice project in Ontario in 1975. Due to skyrocketing crime rates in North America and elsewhere in the late 1970s and early 1980s various justice systems were willing to try anything and by the 1990s there were more than one thousand restorative justice programmes across North America.[88] Its emergence was a response to the long-held tradition of leaving the victim out of the justice process. By the end of the twentieth century this concept became more prominent in Europe, stressing a maximum involvement in the justice process on the part of the victim, offender and the community, finally giving victims of crime an active role in the criminal justice process. But critics are wary of its future success, particularly in America, arguing that if the offender does not want to cooperate or if the community is not supportive it renders the discussion moot. Others are convinced that there are dangers in giving this process priority over the time-tested ones of deterrence and incapacitation. However, by the twenty-first century, victim–offender mediation programmes, restitution and community service were the most common types of restorative justice programmes in use in the United States. Restorative justice has found its strongest advocates among those seeking a less punitive justice system, while others favour its emphasis on victim empowerment and the financial savings associated with economical use of punishment.

Despite a plethora of sentencing alternatives, imprisonment still reigns supreme in much of the world. The United States, for example, with 5 per cent of the world's population, accounts for 25 per cent of the world's prison population. Egregious examples of the penal regime can be found in most regions. In August 2013, it was revealed that the Texas Department of Corrections was paying $750,000 to rent six climate-controlled barns for a pig-farming programme, while at the same time inmates faced extreme heat in mostly non-air-conditioned prison cells. Fourteen deaths were blamed on the heat, which averaged 120 degrees in some prisons that summer. It affected not just the prisoners, but the officers hired to patrol the prisons. One union representative for the correctional officers lamented, no doubt tongue-in-cheek, that the prison system 'has made the decision that protecting its bacon is more important than protecting human lives'.[89]

In Northern California, the Pelican Bay 'supermax' facility continues (as do other supermax prisons) to use solitary confinement. Thousands of inmates spend up to twenty years living in one-person 8-by-10-foot cells. They are allowed about an hour per day for recreation, spent, often still shackled, in a cement enclosure not much bigger than their cells. A 2011 United Nations report described this practice as tantamount to torture, asserting that solitary confinement should be limited to no more than fifteen days. By stark contrast, the average term of confinement in a supermax facility in California is almost seven years.[90]

Supermaximum prisons, better known as 'supermax', were developed to house the most violent and dangerous inmates in America after a spate of violence in the 1970s and early '80s by inmates across the nation led to the deaths of dozens of correctional officers. Among the supermax's best-known features is the leaving of prisoners isolated in their cells, on 24/7 lockdown, thus making communal dining rooms and exercise yards redundant. Supermax architecture also prevents an inmate from seeing another, unless they are forced to share a cell due to lack of space. By most accounts, these prisons appear to actually make inmates more violent, the dangerous impact of which may be seen and felt once the inmate is released from prison into public life. Heaven knows what Quaker prison reformer John Howard or Charles Dickens, who so boldly challenged the Pennsylvania solitary system in 1842, would have to say about the state of the American prison system today.

Epilogue

White-collar financial crime has become the signature crime of the twenty-first century (thus far), particularly in the developed parts of the world. Financial crimes such as fraud date back to at least the fourth century BC and ancient Egyptians counted fraud and tax evasion as serious offences. Counterfeiters were clipping or duplicating products of the royal mint more than 2,000 years ago. In his book on mass counterfeiting, John K. Cooley chronicled how European colonists defrauded America's native cultures using counterfeit wampum (shells and beads used as currency by Native Americans) to purchase everything from foodstuffs to precious metals.[91] But this is just a footnote to the amount of forgery that took place before the American Civil War, when the country did not have a single national currency, and an estimated one-third to one-half of the nation's money was probably illegal.[92] America's counterfeiting penalties were mild in contrast to Newtonian England's, but virtually all countries have created severe penal sanctions for this form of financial crime.

China takes a hard-line approach towards financial crimes. In recent years real estate developers, small business owners, political figures and CEOs of large corporations have landed on death rows, and many have been executed (unless they have political connections). In some cases the guilty are given execution with a two-year reprieve. If one toes the line of good behaviour during this period they can have their sentence converted to life in prison. In November 2009, Zhang Yujun and Geng Jinping were executed for selling more than 3 million gallons of contaminated milk powder, killing six children and sickening 300,000. Their crime was adding the industrial product melamine to milk in order to give it the illusion of possessing higher protein content then it did. That same year a beauty parlour operator was executed for illegally raising $100 million from investors which she diverted to her luxurious lifestyle.[93] Although China ended the death penalty in 2011 for thirteen economic crimes, including tax fraud and various forms of smuggling, it still executes an unknown number of white-collar criminals today.

China was not the first to take a hard line towards financial crimes. According to Hammurabi's Code, anyone violating a financial contract 'shall be put to death as a thief'. One of the oldest financial crimes is usury, also known as loansharking and shylocking (in homage to the money lending antagonist of Shakespeare's *Merchant of Venice*).[94] In fourteenth-century Catalonia a banker was executed after he was unable to pay his depositors. And in Renaissance Florence anyone found cheating clients was liable for torture, which according to Rule 70 included being punished on the rack 'or other corrective instruments'.[95]

The world's nations continue to play catch-up with the world of economic crime. This is especially true when it comes to money-laundering, which allows criminals to instantly transfer millions of dollars through computers and other high tech devices. In 1986 the United States became the first country to pass a law against it. In order to understand why it took so long, it must be understood that this criminality was a low priority until the multi-billion-dollar cocaine trade of the 1970s and '80s put it on the government radar.

No country is more identified with a single type of financial crime than Nigeria and the advance fee fraud, better known as 419 Fraud (after the statute number). It is rather perplexing that a developing country should be the epicentre of this sophisticated fraud, but one observer has suggested that this scam is the result of conditions in which 'normal paths of opportunity are closed to all but the well-connected'.[96]

Lately there has been a push in the United States to go 'medieval' on a parade of mammoth fraudsters such as Bernard Madoff, perpetrator of one history's greatest financial crimes. Politicians have joined the bandwagon to ratchet up sanctions on Wall Street fraudsters. While many observers suggest adopting Chinese sanctions to stop the pillaging of the banking system, others are probably on firmer ground suggesting that it would be more effective to reform the financial system to prevent bankers and Wall Street hustlers from ruining it. While increasing fines and prison terms have been viewed as a panacea, in reality it is a challenge to prosecute these often complicated crimes with multiple violations. However, substantial penalties have been imposed for financial fraud, as in the case of Madoff, who received 150 years for his $60 billion fraud and will probably die in prison.

In the twenty-first century so much has changed in the realm of crime and punishment. Yet so much has stayed the same. Poor people, minorities and other disenfranchised people still bear the brunt of punitive penal sanctions wherever they are found. A nation of indigenous peoples, descendants of slaves and immigrants from all over the world, the United States is among the world's most diverse countries. Yet, there is such juxtaposition between wealth and poverty or as former president George W. Bush famously put it, between the 'have-nots' and the 'have-mores'. At the end of the first decade of the twenty-first century there were more African Americans under correctional control, including prisons, jails, on probation or parole, 'than were enslaved in 1850'.[97]

In countries with rampant inequality and historic caste barriers, such as India, elected leaders are reluctant to confront upper-class Jats, who often pull the strings in rural regions of Haryana, still regarded as 'one of India's most entrenched bastions of feudal patriarchy'. Low-caste Dalit women, therefore, can expect little from the criminal justice system when they are sexually assaulted, and in some cases are blamed for their own complicity – the age-old 'blame-the-victim' premise in a region with 861 females for every 1,000 males, and the 'most skewed gender ratio in India' due to a longstanding social preference for sons and the aborting of female foetuses.[98]

In Singapore, visitors arriving by air must fill out a disembarkation form that warns in large red letters: 'DEATH FOR DRUG TRAFFICKERS UNDER SINGAPORE LAW'. Yet when one investigates further, one finds the criminal justice system works clandestinely and is too often 'biased against the weak and impoverished'. Not unlike the last days of the Bloody Code of late eighteenth-century and early nineteenth-century England, once some type of prosecutorial discretion is allowed, the justice system becomes better disposed towards those found guilty of capital offences. In England, what separated petty from grand larceny was 1 shilling, the difference between hanging and a fine. Prosecutors in Singapore have found a way around the death penalty as well, with the previously mentioned '14.99 charges', which allow them to charge indigent prisoners for the possession of drugs just under the amount that require mandatory capital punishment.[99]

Prohibitions of certain behaviours have existed longer than the printed word. It often depends on which culture you belong to as to what this behaviour consists of. There are no universals when it comes to criminal behaviour. Nowhere is this clearer than in the case of prohibition against certain mind-altering substances. However, governments are now beginning to take new approaches on several fronts, particularly on the so-called 'war on drugs'. The United Nations estimates that more than $300 billion flows untaxed into the hands of criminals each year. What is even more troubling is the amount of violent crime that often appears in tandem with the drug trade. Seven of the world's most homicide-ridden nations parallel the cocaine traffic route between the Andes of South America and markets in the United States and Europe. The only regions one can find that would compare to the number of murders in such countries as Honduras are located in war zones. Despite a 'United Nations led fantasy event' in 1998 that was hoped would lead to a 'drug-free world', the world's consumption of cocaine and cannabis has risen 50 per cent since then, and opiates have more than tripled.[100] If anyone is winning the war on drugs it is the cartels and gangs that sell them. Recently, there have been signs that some countries are beginning to fight back by rethinking alternatives to penal sanctions and giving legalization and decriminalization strategies a chance. Mexico and Uruguay are among the Latin American countries that are discussing the potential for such legal modifications. In the United States, where marijuana was criminalized by the federal government in 1937, over the past few years fifteen states have decriminalized cannabis possession, treating it along the lines of a traffic infraction, and in 2014 Colorado became the first state to legalize marijuana use. However, these are just battles, rather than wars won. Decriminalization falls well short of legalization, but it would be a start in the political battle to replace the stigma and fear of criminal punishment with alternatives such as fines and community service.

One prohibition long associated with Islamic law is against drinking alcohol, a ban that has been challenged on some levels by scholars. A number of historians believe alcohol originated in the Middle East, the term itself perhaps from the Arabic *al-kohl*, an eyeliner concocted by mixing distilled ethanol and antimony salts; in time similar substances, without the powder, were used to create popular beverages. These drinks have been identified as part of the fuel that drove debauched nights in the courts of caliphates and were later enshrined in the *khamriyaat* – odes to wine – written by the eighth-century poet Abu Nuwas.[101] This is considered fanciful in a number of modern Muslim countries. It is unknown when some Islamic scholars determined that drinking alcohol was sinful. But in the 1970s the emergence of political Islam in Iran and Pakistan led some countries to ban it. Punishment can be severe, with 80 lashes in Iran. Islamist parties from Indonesia to Tunisia continue to debate restrictions on alcohol. Nonetheless, all prohibition has accomplished, like drug laws, has been to push it out of sight behind closed doors. During Prohibition in America it was easy to find alcoholic drinks in virtually every community, albeit often inferior and dangerous home-made concoctions. Likewise, black markets flourish wherever alcohol is banned in the Arab world, with one Pakistani admitting 'drinks can be ordered to the door quicker than pizza'.[102]

Despite the various prohibitions, some surveys suggest that over the past decade drinking has been on the rise in countries dominated by Muslims. While the global increase averaged about 30 per cent, in the Middle East the estimate was 72 per cent, and as one *Economist* reporter noted, it is 'unlikely to be accounted for by non-Muslims and foreigners alone'. Unfortunately open debate is often muted, while in private some scholars argue that as long as the alcohol is not made with dates or grapes, substances specifically mentioned in the Quran, it is permissible. As it stands, despite the shifting governments of the Middle East, countries such as Turkey, Lebanon and Egypt (so far) have legalized alcohol, while it is still illegal in Pakistan, Iran and Saudi Arabia. No matter its standing, many choose to abstain from its use as part of a backlash against the decadence of the Western world, which they associate with sinful lifestyles.

One of the biggest challenges in writing a global history of crime and punishment is the very definition of crime, since it conjures up so many different images, all depending on the time period, the culture and the legal tradition of the moment. In order to pursue this topic it is necessary to define criminal behaviour in terms in which contemporaries saw it, while making it recognizable to the modern reader. Estimates of crime rates from earlier periods of history are mostly speculative. While there are numerous accounts chronicling crime and punishment in countries with long written traditions, such as western Europe, in other areas the written record is sparse, therefore forcing researchers to consult other sources, such as anthropology, folklore and oral traditions passed down from generation to generation. What we can surmise is that between the late Middle Ages and the twentieth century European countries experienced a ten- to fiftyfold decline in murder rates. Some historians attributed this to the 'consolidation of a patchwork of feudal territories into large kingdoms with centralized authority'.[103] As noted previously, the subsequent Enlightenment set the scene for the first organized movements towards abolishing socially sanctioned forms of violence such as slavery, duelling, judicial torture, cruelty to animals and sadistic punishments. On the other hand there are regions of the world that only experienced the Enlightenment and later the Industrial Revolution second hand if at all, thus the history of crime and punishment across the millennia remains an inconsistent chronicle of experimentation, borrowing and adaptation, often dependent on time, place and history. The global history of crime and punishment remains a work in progress.

REFERENCES

Introduction

1 Itamar Eichner, 'Israelis Enjoying Life in Swedish Prison', www.ynetnews.com, 12 June 2006.
2 Karl Menninger, MD, *Whatever Became of Sin?* (New York, 1973), p. 50.
3 James Buchanan Given, *Society and Homicide in Thirteenth-century England* (Stanford, CA, 1977).
4 See for example Norbert Elias, *The Civilizing Process*, trans. E. Jephcott (Oxford, 1978); Steven Pinker, *The Better Angles of Our Nature: Why Violence has Declined* (New York, 2011); Manuel Eisner, 'Long-term Historical Trends in Violent Crime', *Crime and Justice: A Review of Research*, xxx (2003), pp. 83–142.
5 Paula S. Fass, *Kidnapped: Child Abduction in America* (New York, 1997), p. 10. The term 'kidnapper' came from the word 'thief' and, according to the *Oxford English Dictionary*, was a combination of the slang for child ('kid') and seize ('nap') dating back to 1682.
6 Pieter Spierenburg, *A History of Murder: Personal Violence in Europe from the Middle Ages to the Present* (Cambridge, 2010), p. 1.
7 Roger Lane, *Murder in America: A History* (Columbus, OH, 1997), pp. 1–5.

I
Crime and Punishment: In the Beginning

1 Jean Guiliane and Jean Zammit, *Origins of War: Violence in Prehistory* (Oxford, 2005), p. 231. See also Ian Armit, 'Violence and Society in the Deep Human Past,' *British Journal of Criminology*, LI (2011), pp. 499–517.
2 Ronald Hutton, *Pagan Britain* (New Haven, CT, 2014).
3 Karin Sanders, *Bodies in the Bog and the Archeological Imagination* (Chicago, IL, 2009), p. 4.
4 Ibid.
5 R. S. Rattray, *Ashanti Law and Constitution* (London, 1911), pp. 232–3.
6 Ibid., p. 292.
7 Ibid., pp. 372–5.
8 To avoid mutilation or bleeding during strangulation, the leather thong or bare hands were used. When it came to bludgeoning, high ranking victims were battered to death with the tusk of an elephant or some type of pestle, in Rattray, *Ashanti Law*, p. 375.
9 Ibid., p. 376.

10 Jacques Barzun, *From Dawn to Decadence: 500 Years of Western Cultural Life, 1500 to the Present* (New York, 2001), p. 762.

11 Robert H. Lowie, *Primitive Society* (New York, 1920), p. 401.

12 Ibid., p. 416.

13 Karin Bullard, '"Blood Money" could Free American', *Houston Chronicle*, 5 March 2011, p. A14.

14 Lowie, *Primitive Society*, pp. 413–14.

15 Jo Tuckman, 'Vengeance Allowed to Flourish', *Houston Chronicle*, 30 June 2002, p. 24A.

16 Reed Lindsay, 'Bolivia's Aymara Taking Justice into Own Hands', *Houston Chronicle*, 26 September 2004, p. A30.

17 By most accounts it had been taken to Susa by later Elamite conquerors, where it was found in 1901. Today it resides in the Louvre in Paris.

18 Marc Van De Mierop, *King Hammurabi of Babylon: A Biography* (Malden, MA, 2005), p. 99.

19 Although 'corn' as we know it was discovered in the Americas, the term pre-dates colonialism and is used as shorthand for 'grain' or any grain of cereal grass that is a locally grown primary crop.

20 Frances F. Berdan, 'Crime and Control in Aztec Society', in *Organised Crime in Antiquity*, ed. Keith Hopwood (Swansea, 2009), pp. 255–70.

21 Alan Milner, *The Nigerian Penal System* (London, 1972).

22 Lowie, *Primitive Law*, pp. 402–3.

23 'Divorce', in *Encyclopaedia Judaica*, 2nd edn, vol. v, ed. Fred Skolnick and Michael Berenbaum (Farmington Hills, MI, 2007), p. 710; see also Ruth 3:9.

24 Israel Drapkin, *Crime and Punishment in the Ancient World* (Lexington, MA, 1989), p. 32.

25 Victor H. Matthews and Don C. Benjamin, *Social World of Ancient Israel, 1250–587 BCE* (Peabody, MA, 1993), pp. 11–12.

26 Pew Global Attitudes Project, 2009, 'Pakistani Public Opinion: Growing Concerns about Extremism, Continuing Discontent in the United States', at http://pewglobal.org.

27 'Saudis Defensive as Swords Swing, Heads Roll', *Houston Chronicle*, 25 April 2000.

28 Drapkin, *Crime and Punishment*, p. 37.

29 Joyce Tydlesley, *Judgement of the Pharaoh: Crime and Punishment in Ancient Egypt* (London, 2002).

30 Ibid., p. 65.

31 Ibid., p. 72.

32 Ibid.

33 In Pierre Montet, *Everyday Life in Egypt in the Days of Ramses the Great* (New York, 1958), p. 269, the author suggests that rather than being impaled on the stake, victims were merely tied to a stake and left to die.

34 *The Strange Cases of Magistrate Pao: Chinese Tales of Crime and Detection*, trans. Leon Comber (Rutland, VT, 1964).

35 Nick Fisher, '"Workshops of Villains": Was there Much Organised Crime in Classical Athens?', in *Organised Crime in Antiquity*, ed. Hopwood, pp. 53–96.

36 *Plutarch's Lives (The Lives of the Noble Grecians and Romans)*, vol. I, trans. Arthur Hugh Clough (New York, 1992), p. 117.

37 Demosthenes, quoted in Douglas M. MacDowell, *Athenian Homicide Law in the Age of the Orators* (Manchester, 1999), p. 8.

38 Ibid., p. 113.

39 Ibid.

40 Herbert A. Johnson, Nancy Travis Wolfe and Mark Jones, *History of Criminal Justice*, 3rd edn (Cincinnati, OH, 2003).

41 John K. Cooley, *Currency Wars: How Forged Money is the New Weapon of Mass Destruction* (New York, 2008), pp. 56–62; the title of this subsection is taken from the chapter of the same name in Cooley's book, p. 55.

42 J. Thorsten Sellin, *Slavery and the Penal System* (New York, 1976), p. 1; Orlando Patterson, *Slavery and Social Death: A Comparative Study* (Cambridge, MA, 1982).

43 M. I. Finley, *Ancient Slavery and Modern Ideology* (New York, 1980), pp. 67–8.

44 Patterson, *Slavery and Social Death*, p. 128.

45 The 200,000-square-foot Criminal Justice Center, at Sam Houston State University in Huntsville, Texas, was built using prisoner labour in the 1970s.

46 Israeli Defense Forces during the intifadas used a similar tactic in the 1990s, bulldozing the family homes of Palestinian suicide bombers and others in retaliation for terrorist attacks.

47 Norman Johnston, *Forms of Constraint: A History of Prison Architecture* (Urbana, IL, 2000), pp. 5–6.

48 This site is now open to the public, the author having visited there recently.

49 Sumeria was part of Babylonia, the southern half of ancient Mesopotamia; while Assyria was in the north.

50 Drapkin, *Crime and Punishment*, p. 31

51 Martin Hengel, *Crucifixion* (Philadelphia, PA, 1978), pp. 22–3; Lewis Lyons, *The History of Punishment* (London, 2003), p. 162.

2

The Rise of Legal Traditions

1 The six that disappeared were Egyptian, Mesopotamian, Hebrew, Greek, Celtic and Ecclesiastical. Hebrew law, Wigmore argued, was replaced by Roman rule by the second century AD, and functioned mostly as local custom and as ceremonial and moral rules.

2 Ian Gibson, *English Vice: Beating, Sex and Shame in Victorian England and After* (London, 1978).

3 Alejando Reyes, 'Rough Justice: A Caning in Singapore Stirs up a Fierce Debate about Crime and Punishment', *Asiaweek*, 25 May 1994, at www.corpun.com.

4 Richard A. Bauman, *Crime and Punishment in Ancient Rome* (London, 1996), p. 18.

5 O. F. Robinson, *The Criminal Law of Ancient Rome* (London, 1995), p. 43.

6 Naphtali Lewis and Meyer Reinhold, eds, *Roman Civilization, Source Book II: Empire* (New York, 1966), pp. 548–9.

7 Bauman, *Crime and Punishment*, p. 18

8 Lucius Annaeus Seneca, *De ira*, in *Moral Essays*, vol. 1, trans. John W. Basore (Cambridge, MA, 1928).

9 Steven Pinker, *The Better Angels of Our Nature: Why Violence has Declined* (New York, 2011), p. 14, suggests that this method was brought back to Europe from

Persia by Alexander the Great, where it would find popularity in the Mediterranean world.

10 Ibid., p. 14.

11 'A Death in Jerusalem', *Time*, 18 January 1971, pp. 64–5; Brad Lemley, 'Israeli Anthropologist is a Cross-examiner', *LA Times*, 25 December 1985, pp. 10–11.

12 Suetonius, *The Twelve Caesars*, trans. Robert Graves (New York, 1979), p. 167.

13 Ibid., p. 169.

14 Robinson, *The Criminal Law of Ancient Rome*, p. 72.

15 Bauman, *Crime and Punishment*, p. 32.

16 Ibid., p. 68.

17 Sadakat Kadri, *The Trial: A History from Socrates to O. J. Simpson* (New York, 2006), p. 13.

18 Harold J. Berman, *Law and Revolution: The Formation of the Western Legal Tradition* (Cambridge, MA, 1983).

19 Katherine Fischer Drew, trans., *Laws of the Salian Franks* (Philadelphia, PA, 1991), p. 3.

20 'The Salic Law', from *Select Historical Documents of the Middle Ages*, ed. and trans. Ernest Flagg Henderson (London, 1892), pp. 176–83.

21 Frederick Pollock and Frederic W. Maitland, *The History of English Law: Before the Time of Edward I* (Cambridge, 1978), vol. II, p. 26.

22 Ibid., p. 451.

23 Ibid., p. 452.

24 Barbara Holland, *Gentlemen's Blood: A History of Dueling From Swords at Dawn to Pistols at Dusk* (London, 2003), pp. 9–11.

25 Judith Romney Wegner, 'Islamic and Talmudic Jurisprudence: The Four Roots of Islamic Law and Their Talmudic Counterparts', in *The American Journal of Legal History*, XXVI (1982), pp. 25–71.

26 M. Abu-Zahra, *Crime and Punishment in Islamic Jurisprudence* (Cairo, 1950), p. 23.

27 David A. Jones, *Crime and Criminal Responsibility* (Chicago, IL, 1978), p. 3.

28 Jeffrey Gettleman, 'As an Enemy Retreats, Clans Carve Up Somalia', *New York Times*, 10 September 2011, p. A1.

29 There is no imprisonment, thus the man can go back to work and care for his family.

30 Bernard Lewis, ed., *Islam: From the Prophet Muhammad to the Capture of Constantinople* (New York, 1974), vol. II, p. 39.

31 'Saudi Court Sentences Female Driver to 10 Lashes', *USA Today*, 28 September 2011, p. 7A.

32 The victim, Ameneh Bahrami, would chronicle her ordeal in her book *Eye for an Eye*, published in Germany (Bahrami, *Auge um Auge*, Munich, 2012). Despite the best efforts of doctors they were not able to save her sight.

33 Thomas Erdbrink, 'Acid-blinding Punishment Postponed by Iran Officials', *Houston Chronicle*, 15 May 2011, p. A21.

34 Charles T. Powers. 'Sudanese Gather to Watch Islamic Justice', *LA Times*, 12 May 1984, p. 6.

35 James C. McKinley, 'Islamic Movement's Niche: Bringing Order to Somalia's Chaos', *New York Times*, 23 August 1996, www.nytimes.com.

36 Rod Nordland, 'Broadcast of Afghanistan Stoning Video Rekindles Outcry', *Houston Chronicle*, 2 February 2011, p. A5.

37 'Execution by Taliban: Crushed Under Wall', *New York Times*, 16 January 1999.
38 John F. Burns, 'Execution Punctuates Taliban Rule', *New York Times*, 19 December 1996.
39 Todd Pitman, 'Stoning Sentence Overturned in Nigeria', *Boston Globe*, 26 September 2003.
40 Robert F. Worth, 'Crime (Sex) and Punishment (Stoning)', *New York Times*, 22 August 2010, pp. 1, 4.
41 Thomas Erdbrink, 'Mercy and Social Media Slow the Noose in Iran', *New York Times*, 9 March 2014, pp. 1, 4.
42 Robert Van Gulik, *Celebrated Cases of Judge Dee* (New York, 1976), pp. xviii–xix.
43 Derk Bodde and Clarence Morris, *Law in Imperial China* (Cambridge, MA, 1967), pp. 76–80, 102–12.
44 Joseph Kahn, 'Deep Flaws, and Little Justice, in China's Court System', *New York Times*, 21 September 2005, pp. A1, A12.
45 Hong Lu and Terance D. Miethe, *China's Death Penalty: History, Law, and Contemporary Practices* (New York, 2007), pp. 33–4.
46 Jack Weatherford, *Genghis Khan and the Making of the Modern World* (New York, 2004), p. 68.
47 Philip L. Reichel, *Comparative Criminal Justice Systems: A Topical Approach* (Upper Saddle River, NJ, 2005).

3
Crime in a Changing Landscape: From Feudalism to the City and the State

1 The term feudal, an adjective, was first coined in the seventeenth century, but was not used in a political context or as a noun, as in 'feudalism', until the nineteenth. Since the 1970s there has been a debate by historians over whether feudalism should be removed from the scholarly discussion altogether. See, for example, Elizabeth Brown, 'The Tyranny of a Construct: Feudalism and Historians of Medieval Europe', *American Historical Review*, LXXIX/4 (October 1974), and Susan Reynolds, *Fiefs and Vassals: The Medieval Evidence Reinterpreted* (New York, 1994).
2 Church law was held in its own ecclesiastical courts, where justice was administered in cases involving clerics, church buildings, sex offences and family law.
3 Jacques Barzun, *From Dawn to Decadence: 500 Years of Western Cultural Life, 1500 to the Present* (New York, 2001), pp. 225–6.
4 Sean McGlynn, *By Sword and Fire: Cruelty and Atrocity in Medieval Warfare* (London, 2009), p. 5.
5 François-Louis Ganshof, *Feudalism* (London, 1977).
6 Marc Bloch, *Feudal Society* (Chicago, IL, 1961), pp. 147–60.
7 Joseph B. Strayer and Rushton Coulborn, 'The Idea of Feudalism', in *Feudalism in History*, ed. R. Coulbourn (Princeton, NJ, 1956), p. 4.
8 Quoted in Brian Fagan, *Little Ice Age: How Climate Made History, 1300–1850* (New York, 2001), pp. 18–19.
9 Quoted in J. Thorsten Sellin, *Slavery and the Penal System* (New York, 1976), p. 39.
10 Likewise, under Islamic law it was rare for someone to be seriously punished for stealing just enough victuals for sustenance.

11 Frederick Pollock and Frederic W. Maitland, eds, *The History of English Law: Before the Time of Edward I*, 2nd edn (Cambridge, 1978), p. 498.

12 John Bellamy, *Crime and Public Order in England in the Later Middle Ages* (London, 1978), p. 37.

13 Ibid.; when the author visited Havana, Cuba, in 1999 it was impossible to miss the rampant prostitution wherever one ventured. Later that year the government reacted by forcibly removing prostitutes, shaving their heads and putting them to work in rural cane fields.

14 Trevor Dean, *Crime in Medieval Europe, 1200–1550* (Harlow, 2001).

15 Ibid., pp. 131–2.

16 Pollock and Maitland, eds, *The History of English Law*, p. 500.

17 Alfred Marks, *Tyburn Tree: Its History and Annals* (London, 1908), p. 31.

18 Pollock and Maitland, eds, *The History of English Law*, p. 500.

19 James Reston, Jr, *The Last Apocalypse: Europe at the Year 1000 AD* (New York, 1999), p. 50.

20 Pollock and Maitland, eds, *The History of English Law*, p. 478.

21 Sadakat Kadri, *The Trial: A History from Socrates to O. J. Simpson* (London, 2006), p. 34.

22 Norman Johnston, *Forms of Constraint: A History of Prison Architecture* (Urbana, IL, 2000), p. 7.

23 Edward M. Peters, 'Prison before the Prison: The Ancient and Medieval Worlds', in *Oxford History of the Prison: The Practice of Punishment in Western Society*, ed. Norval Morris and David J. Rothman (New York, 1995), pp. 29–30.

24 Johnston, *Forms of Constraint*, p. 7

25 Pierre François Souyri, *The World Turned Upside Down: Medieval Japanese Society*, trans. Käthe Roth (New York, 2001).

26 John S. Critchley, *Feudalism* (London, 1978), p. 35.

27 Christopher Ross, *Mishima's Sword: Travels in Search of a Samurai Legend* (Cambridge, MA, 2006), p. 144.

28 Souyri, *The World Turned Upside Down*, p. 2.

29 Ibid., p. 59.

30 Herman Ooms, *Tokugawa Ideology: Early Constructs, 1570–1680* (Princeton, NJ, 1985), p. 147.

31 Richard H. Mitchell, *Janus-faced Justice: Political Criminals in Imperial Japan* (Honolulu, HI, 1992), p. 1.

32 Brian E. McKnight, *Law and Order in Sung China* (Cambridge, 1992), p. 40.

33 Timothy Brook, Jérôme Bourgon and Gregory Blue, *Death by a Thousand Cuts* (Cambridge, MA, 2008), p. 11.

34 Ibid.

35 James Legge, trans., *Li Chi: Book of Rites*, vol. I (New Hyde Park, NY, 1967), p. 288.

36 McKnight, *Law and Order in Sung China*, p. 451.

37 Brook, Bourgon and Blue, *Death by a Thousand Cuts*, p. 11.

38 McKnight, *Law and Order in Sung China*, p. 454.

39 T. T. Meadows, 'Description of an Execution at Canton', *Journal of the Royal Asiatic Society*, 15 (1856), p. 55.

40 Norman Thomas, *The Honoured Society: The Sicilian Mafia Observed* (Melksham, Wiltshire, 1991), p. 53.

41 Letizia Paoli, *Mafia Brotherhoods: Organized Crime, Italian Style* (New York, 2003), p. 173.

42 Antonio Nicaso and Marcel Danesi, *Made Men: Mafia Culture and the Power of Symbols, Rituals, and Myth* (Lanham, MD, 2013), p. 120.

43 Ibid., p. 17.

44 Jerome Blum, *Lord and Peasant in Russia: From the Ninth to the Nineteenth Century* (Princeton, NJ, 1972), p. 3.

45 Ibid., p. 440.

46 Ibid., p. 267.

47 Adam Olearius, *The Travels of Olearius in 17th-century Russia*, trans. Samuel H. Baron (Stanford, CA, 1967), pp. 134–5.

48 Ibid., pp. 140–41.

49 Blum, *Lord and Peasant in Russia*, p. 437.

50 Ibid., p. 438.

51 Ibid.

52 Ibid., p. 430.

53 Ana Siljak, *Angel of Vengeance: The 'Girl Assassin', The Governor of St Petersburg, and Russia's Revolutionary World* (New York, 2008), pp. 92–3.

54 Stephen P. Frank, 'Popular Justice, Community and Culture among the Russian Peasantry, 1870–1900', *Russian Review*, XLVI/3 (July 1987), pp. 239–65.

55 Similar to the *samosud* of rural Russia, *charivari*, a ritual form of local shaming, was used throughout Europe and parts of North America throughout the nineteenth century. It was variously referred to as *Haberfeldtreiben*, *Katzenmusiken*, *Schnurren*, skimmingtons, shivarees and rough music. The difference was that unlike the *samosud*, *charivari* was used only on members of the community. See Frank, 'Popular Justice, Community and Culture', p. 244.

56 Ibid.

57 Cathy Frierson, 'Crime and Punishment in the Russian Village: Rural Concepts of Criminality at the End of the Nineteenth Century', *Slavic Review*, XLVI/1 (Spring 1987), pp. 55–69 (quote p. 55).

58 Quoted ibid., p. 55; see Sidney Post Simpson and Julius Stone, *Law and Society in Evolution* (St Paul, MN, 1948), p. 3.

59 Frank, 'Popular Justice, Community and Culture', p. 259.

60 Grigori Golosov, 'Kushchevskaya: Crime and Punishment in a Russian Village', www.opendemocracy.net, 10 December 2010.

61 Ibid.; Nona Shahnarzarian, 'Violence, Politics, and Ethnicity in the "Russian Riviera"', *PONAS Eurasia*, Policy Memo No. 191 (September 2011), pp. 1–5; 'A Good Treaty: The Kushchevskaya Massacre and the Putin Era', www.agoodtreaty.com, 8 December 2010.

62 'A Good Treaty'.

63 Norman F. Cantor, *In the Wake of the Plague: The Black Death and the World it Made* (New York, 2002), p. 214.

64 Ibid., p. 203.

65 Sellin, *Slavery and the Penal System*, p. 43.

4
The Transformation of Punishment and the Rise of the Penitentiary

1 Bastille comes from the Old French *bastide*, which alluded to a fortress in the medieval period.
2 Joy Cameron, *Prisons and Punishment in Scotland from the Middle Ages to the Present* (Edinburgh, 1983).
3 Cesare Beccaria, *On Crimes and Punishment*, trans. and introd. by Henry Paolucci (Indianapolis, IN, 1963).
4 Michel Foucault, *Discipline and Punish: The Birth of the Prison*, trans. Alan Sheridan (New York, 1977), pp. 3–4.
5 Pieter Spierenburg, 'The Body and the State: Early Modern Europe', in *The Oxford History of the Prison*, ed. Norval Morris and David J. Rothman (New York, 1995), p. 49, pp. 49–77.
6 Pieter Spierenburg, *The Broken Spell: A Cultural and Anthropological History of Preindustrial Europe* (New Brunswick, NJ, and London, 1991), pp. 1–13; Richard J. Evans, *Rituals of Retribution: Capital Punishment in Germany, 1600–1987* (London, 1997), p. 14.
7 Florence Bernault, 'The Shadow of Rule: Colonial Power and Modern Punishment in Africa', in *Cultures of Confinement: A History of the Prison in Africa, Asia and Latin America*, ed. Frank Dikötter and Ian Brown (Ithaca, NY, 2007), pp. 78–9.
8 Alan Macfarlane, *The Justice and the Mare's Ale* (Oxford, 1981), p. 1
9 Quoted ibid., p. 2. See also Adam Smith, *An Inquiry into the Nature and Causes of the Wealth of Nations*, 5th edn (Chicago, IL, 1976), p. 433.
10 Lord Macaulay, *The History of England from the Accession of James the Second*, vol. v (Philadelphia, PA, 1848), pp. 213–14; Macfarlane, *The Justice and the Mare's Ale*, p. 3.
11 Lawrence Stone, *The Crisis of the Aristocracy, 1558–1641* (Oxford, 1967), p. 93; Macfarlane, *The Justice and the Mare's Ale*, p. 16.
12 Cameron, *Prisons and Punishment in Scotland*, pp. 10–11.
13 There were six Wardens of the Marches, three on either side of the border. One scholar described the wardens as 'a mixture of soldier, judge, lawyer, fighting-man, diplomat, politician, rough rider, detective, administrator, and intelligence agent.' George MacDonald Fraser, *The Steel Bonnets: The Story of the Anglo-Scottish Border Reivers* (Pleasantville, NY, 2001), pp. 128–9.
14 Ibid., p. 150, n. 1.
15 Vanessa McMahon, *Murder in Shakespeare's England* (London, 2004).
16 Austin Lane Poole, *From Domesday Book to Magna Carta, 1087–1216* (New York, 1986), p. 415.
17 Quoted in Thomas Levenson, *Newton and the Counterfeiter: The Unknown Detective Career of the World's Greatest Scientist* (Boston, MA, 2009); Lord Macauley, *History of England*, vol. v, p. 2566.
18 Alan M. Stahl, 'Coin and Punishment in Medieval Venice', in *Law and the Illicit in Medieval Europe*, ed. Ruth Mazo Karras, Joel Kaye and E. Ann Matter (Philadelphia, PA, 2008), pp. 162–79, p. 170.
19 Robert Massie, *Peter the Great: His Life and World* (New York, 1980), p. 261.
20 Levenson, *Newton and the Counterfeiter*, p. 133.

21 Ibid., p. 155.

22 Ibid., p. 163.

23 Quoted in Richard J. Evans, *Rituals of Retribution: Capital Punishment in Germany, 1600–1987* (London, 1996), pp. 27–8, reprinted in C. Hindley, ed., *The Old Book Collector's Miscellany*, vol. III (London, 1873).

24 Hindley, *The Old Book Collector's Miscellany*, pp. 11–12, n. 1.

25 Ibid.

26 Ibid.

27 John Fosberry, *Criminal Justice through the Ages: From Divine Judgment to Modern German Legislation* (Rothenburg, 1981).

28 Evans, *Rituals of Retribution*, p. 30.

29 Mike Jay, *The Unfortunate Colonel Despard: The Tragic Story of the Last Man to be Hung, Drawn and Quartered* (New York, 2005), p. 13.

30 John Bellamy, *Crime and Public Order in England in the Later Middle Ages* (London, 1973), p. 186.

31 'Guillotine', *Harper's New Monthly Magazine*, 266, July 1872, pp. 186–7.

32 Spierenburg, 'The Body and the State', pp. 49–77.

33 McMahon, *Murder in Shakespeare's England*, p. xvi.

34 Frank McLynn, *Crime and Punishment in Eighteenth-century England* (London, 1989), p. xi.

35 Ibid., p. xii.

36 Ibid., p. xiii.

37 Ibid., p. 277.

38 Stephen Coote, *Samuel Pepys: A Life* (New York, 2001), p. 71.

39 Ruth Pike, *Penal Servitude in Early Modern Spain* (Madison, WI, 1983), p. 3.

40 Ibid., pp. 3–4.

41 Ibid., p. 15.

42 In earlier years it was reported that since prisoners in detention had to purchase food or have it delivered (otherwise they would starve to death), it was not uncommon for prisoners to ask to be transferred to galley service where they could count on meals provided by the King.

43 According to Pike, *Penal Servitude in Early Modern Spain*, *presidios* (from the Latin *praesidium*, meaning 'a garrison or fort surrounded by protective walls', p. 41, were equivalent to forts, surrounded by protective walls, arguing that this sanction developed from the medieval tradition of using forts and castles as custodial edifices.

44 Pike, *Penal Servitude in Early Modern Spain*, p. 150.

45 Colin M. MacLachlan, *Criminal Justice in Eighteenth Century Mexico: A Study of the Tribunal of the Acordada* (Berkeley, CA, 1974), p. 29.

46 McLynn, *Crime and Punishment*, p. 285.

47 John Hirst, 'The Australian Experience: The Convict Colony', in *Oxford History of the Prison*, ed. Morris and Rothman, pp. 235–65.

48 Robert Hughes, *The Fatal Shore: The Epic of Australia's Founding* (New York, 1987).

49 Ibid.

50 Benson Bobrick, *East of the Sun: The Epic Conquest and Tragic History of Siberia* (New York, 1992), p. 281.

51 George Kennan, *Siberia and the Exile System* (Chicago, IL, 1958), p. 23.

52 Bobrick, *East of the Sun*, pp. 271–2.

53 Ibid., p. 273.

54 Quoted in Ana Siljak, *Angel of Vengeance: The 'Girl Assassin': The Governor of St Petersburg, and Russia's Revolutionary World* (New York, 2008), p. 181.

55 Peter Kropotkin, *In Russian and French Prison* (London, 1887), p. 167.

56 Satadru Sen, *Disciplining Punishment: Colonialism and Convict Society in the Andaman Islands* (New York, 2000).

57 Norman Longmate, *The Workhouse* (New York, 1974).

58 Miriam Allen DeFord, *Stone Walls: Prisons from Fetters to Furloughs* (Philadelphia, PA, 1962).

59 Chris Ryder, *Inside the Maze: The Untold Story of the Northern Ireland Prison Service* (London, 2000); Anthony Babington, *The English Bastille: A History of Newgate Gaol and Prison Conditions in Britain, 1188–1902* (New York, 1971).

60 David J. Rothman, *The Discovery of the Asylum: Social Order and Disorder in the New Republic* (Boston, MA, 1971); Harry E. Barnes, *The Evolution of Penology in Pennsylvania* (Montclair, NJ, 1968).

61 Norman Johnston, *Eastern State Penitentiary: A Crucible of Good Intentions* (Philadelphia, PA, 1994).

62 Charles Dickens, *American Notes: A Journey* (New York, 1985).

63 He would also die there in 1790, after contracting typhus probably after visiting various jails.

64 D. L. Howard, *John Howard: Prison Reformer* (New York, 1958), p. 91.

65 Ibid., p. 93.

66 Massey, *Peter the Great*, p. 259.

67 Ibid., p. 260.

68 John Perry, *The State of Russia under the Present Tsar* (London, 1716), quoted in Massey, *Peter the Great*, p. 260.

69 Ibid., p. 261.

70 Elyse Semerdjian, *Off the Straight Path: Illicit Sex, Law and Community in Ottoman Aleppo* (Syracuse, NY, 2008), p. 29.

71 Rudolph Peters, *Crime and Punishment in Islamic Law: Theory and Practice from the Sixteenth to the Twenty-first Century* (Cambridge, 2005), p. 69.

72 *Zina* crimes usually consisted of sexual intercourse between unmarried people, fornication and concubinage.

73 Semerdjian, *Off the Straight Path*, p. 158.

74 Ibid., pp. 129–30.

75 Ibid., p. 160.

76 Peters, *Crime and Punishment in Islamic Law*, p. 98.

77 Ibid.

78 Ibid., pp. 100–101.

79 Quoted in Carl F. Petry, 'The Politics of Insult: The Mamluk Sultanate's Response to Criminal Affronts', *Mamluk Studies Review*, xv (2001), pp. 87–115, quote p. 89.

80 Ibid., p. 89.

81 Ibid., p. 94

82 Huang Liu-Hung, *A Complete Book Concerning Happiness and Benevolence: A Manual for Local Magistrates in Seventeenth-century China* (Tucson, AZ, 1984), p. 273.

83 Ibid.; extra-heavy bamboo paddles were only occasionally used to suppress bullying and 'corrupt yamen underlings'. This device was known as the 'dragon-whisker slab' for its very heavy polished surface with rough fibres sticking out.

84 Ibid., p. 277.

85 Ibid., p. 454.

86 Ibid., p. 349.

87 *Ta Tsing Leu Lee; Being the Fundamental Laws, and a Selection from the Supplementary Statutes, of the Penal Code of China*, trans. George Thomas Staunton (London, 1810), p. 313.

88 Alain Peyrefitte, *The Collision of Two Civilizations: The British Expedition to China, 1792–4* (London, 1993), p. 412.

89 Ibid.

90 Norman Johnston, *Forms of Constraint: A History of Prison Architecture* (Urbana, IL, 2000), p. 5.

91 Ibid.

92 Frank Dikötter, 'The Promise of Repentance: The Prison in Modern China', in *Cultures of Confinement*, ed. Dikötter and Brown, pp. 269–303.

93 Spierenburg, 'The Body and the State', p. 52.

5
Highwaymen, Bandits, Brigands and Bushrangers: Bands of Thieves and Early Organized Criminality

1 Even if one was 'inlawed', or had a sentence of death lifted, property and goods that had been forfeited would not be necessarily recovered.

2 Anonymous, *The Lives and Exploits of the Most Celebrated Robbers and Banditti of All Countries* (Philadelphia, PA, 1860), pp. 19–21.

3 George MacDonald Fraser, *The Steel Bonnets: The Story of the Anglo-Scottish Border Reivers* (Pleasantville, NY, 2001), p. 5.

4 Eric Hobsbawm, *Social Bandits and Primitive Rebels* (Glencoe, IL, 1960). This was originally published as *Primitive Rebels: Studies in Archaic Forms of Social Movements in the 19th and 20th Centuries* (Manchester, 1959).

5 Richard White, 'Outlaw Gangs of the Middle Border: American Social Bandits', *Western Historical Quarterly*, XII (1981), pp. 387–408.

6 Eric Hobsbawm, *Bandits* (New York, 1969), p. 17.

7 Ibid.

8 *Tao* meaning 'robbery' or 'taking openly' and *tsei*, 'pillaging', which in the parlance of the day indicated weapons were used. The quotation is from Brian E. McKnight, *Law and Order in Sung China* (Cambridge, 1992), pp. 85–6.

9 Quoted ibid., p. 93.

10 Huang Liu-Hung, *A Complete Book Concerning Happiness and Benevolence: A Manual for Local Magistrates in Seventeenth-century China* (Tucson, AZ, 1984). This book was first published in 1699 as a manual for local administrators as well as legal and fiscal advisers.

11 Quoted in William Wayne Farris, *Japan's Medieval Population: Famine, Fertility, and Warfare in a Transformative Age* (Honolulu, HI, 2006), p. 57.

12 Pierre François Souyri, *The World Turned Upside Down: Medieval Japanese Society* (New York, 2001), pp. 106–7.

13 Ibid.

14 Peter B. E. Hill, *The Japanese Mafia: Yakuza, Law, and the State* (New York, 2003), p. 97.

15 D.Crummey, ed., *Banditry, Rebellion and Social Protest in Africa* (London, 1986).

16 Peter Gastrow, *Organized Crime in South Africa*, iss Monograph Series, 28, Institute for Security Studies, South Africa (August 1998).

17 Henry John May and Iain Hamilton, *The Foster Gang* (London, 1966).

18 Gastrow, *Organized Crime in South Africa*.

19 John Bellamy, *Crime and Public Order in England in the Later Middle Ages* (London, 1973), pp. 71, 84.

20 Ibid., p. 42.

21 Arty Ash and Julius E. Day, *Immortal Turpin: A Well-documented Biography of the Greatest 'Gentleman of the Road'* (London, 1948), p. 127.

22 Peter Newark, *The Crimson Book of Highwaymen* (London, 1979), pp. 21–2.

23 Ibid., p. 28.

24 Frank McLynn, *Crime and Punishment in Eighteenth-century England* (London, 1989), pp. 24–5.

25 Horace Bleakley, *The Hangmen of England* (London, 1929), p. 47.

26 Born in 1584, Mary Frith dressed as a man and carried a sword as she visited local taverns and joined the inner circle of the London underworld. She received her moniker for her ability to cut the strings of leather purses that were used to carry valuables in the sixteenth century. Having been branded on the hands four times as a thief, she somewhat miraculously lived until 1659.

27 María Antonia López-Burgos, *Travelling through a Land of Bandits: British Travellers in Andalusia, 1809–1893* (Malaga, 2002).

28 During this period's wars of independence much of the population was armed and French authorities never quite managed to disarm the populace.

29 Stephen Wilson, 'Banditry in Corsica: the Eighteenth to Twentieth Centuries', in *Organised Crime in Europe*, ed. Cyrille Fijnaut and Letizia Paoli (Dordrecht, 2004), p. 150.

30 Ibid., p. 165.

31 Katrin Lange, '"Many a Lord is Guilty, Indeed for Many a Poor Man's Dishonest Deed": Gangs of Robbers in Early Modern Germany', in *Organised Crime in Europe*, ed. Fijnaut and Paoli, pp. 109–49, quote p. 109.

32 Florike Egmond, 'Multiple Underworlds in the Dutch Republic of the Seventeenth and Eighteenth Centuries', in *Organised Crime in Europe*, ed. Fijnaut and Paoli, pp. 77–107.

33 Hobsbawm, *Bandits*, p. 31.

34 Lange, '"Many a Lord is Guilty"', pp. 118–19.

35 Ibid.

36 Stephen Tatum, *Inventing Billy the Kid: Visions of the Outlaw in America, 1881–1981* (Albuquerque, nm, 1985).

37 Richard Maxwell Brown, *No Duty to Retreat* (Norman, ok, 1994), p. 44.

38 Ibid., pp. 44–6; see also Alan Trachtenberg, *The Incorporation of America: Culture and Society in the Gilded Age* (New York, 1982).

39 White, 'Outlaw Gangs of the Middle Border', p. 394.

40 For the best account of the Depression-era bandit gangs see Bryan Burroughs, *Public Enemies: America's Greatest Crime Wave and the Birth of the FBI, 1933–1934* (New York, 2004). Two excellent biographies on social bandits from these two eras are Michael Wallis, *Pretty Boy: The Life and Times of Charles Arthur Floyd* (New York, 1992), and T. J. Stiles, *Jesse James: The Last Rebel of the Civil War* (New York, 2002).

41 John Boessenecker, *Gold Dust and Gunsmoke: Tales of Gold Rush Outlaws, Gunfighters, Lawmen, and Vigilantes* (New York, 1999), pp. 75, 133.

42 Ibid.

43 Horace Bell, *Reminiscences of a Ranger: Early Times in Southern California* (Norman, OK, 1999), p. 99. Bell had been a mounted ranger before trying his hand as an attorney and journalist.

44 Remi Nadeau, *The Real Joaquin Murieta: Robin Hood Hero or Gold Rush Gangster* (Corona del Mar, CA, 1974), pp. 145–6.

45 Paul Vanderwood, *Disorder and Mexican Development* (Wilmington, DE, 1992), p. 9.

46 Ibid., p. 12.

47 Ibid., p. 14; Billy Jaynes Chandler, *The Bandit King: Lampião of Brazil* (College Station, TX, 1978).

48 Dacoity refers to crimes committed by five or more individuals who gather to commit such crimes as extortion or theft by the use or threat of force. The term 'dacoit' is of Hindi derivation, from *daka parna* (to plunder) or *dakna* (to shout). Kanjars were nomadic, small-time operators who lived on the lucre from their robberies. They mostly targeted villages in British territory and never reached the prominence of other forms of Indian banditry.

48 Quoted in Mike Dash, *Thug: The True Story of India's Murderous Cult* (London, 2005), p. 20.

50 Ibid., p. 21.

51 J.D.P. Jatar and M. Z. Khan, *The Problem of Dacoity in Bundelkhand and the Chambal Valley* (New Delhi, 1980), p. 4.

52 Quoted ibid., p. 32.

53 George Bruce, *The Stranglers: The Cult of Thuggee and its Overthrow in British India* (New York, 1968).

54 Jatar and Khan, *The Problem of Dacoity*, p. 33.

55 Philip Meadows Taylor, *Confessions of a Thug* (Oxford, 1998).

56 Dash, *Thug*. The term 'thug', properly spelled 'thag' and sounding like 't'ug', dates back to ancient Sanskrit. It refers to concealing or covering, and literally means 'robber' or 'cheat'. In the twelfth century it was shorthand for swindler, rogue and deceiver.

57 See Taylor, *Confessions of a Thug*, for an excellent introduction by Patrick Brantlinger.

58 Dash, *Thug*, p. 228.

59 Kevin Rushby, *Children of Kali* (New York, 2002).

60 Ibid., p. 8.

61 Dash, *Thug*, p. xi.

62 Taylor, *Confessions of a Thug*.

63 Jatar and Khan, *The Problem of Dacoity*, p. 1; E. Kitts, *Serious Crime in an Indian Province* (Byculla, 1889).

64 Jatar and Khan, *The Problem of Dacoity*, p. 5.
65 Roy Moxham, *Outlaw: India's Bandit Queen and Me* (London, 2010), p. 4.
66 Robert Hughes, *The Fatal Shore: The Epic of Australia's Founding* (New York, 1987), p. 203.
67 Michael Sturm, *Vice in a Vicious Society: Crime and Convicts in Mid-nineteenth-century New South Wales* (St Lucia, Queensland, 1983).

6
Prohibitions, Pirates, Slave Traders, Drug Smugglers and the
Internationalization of Criminality

1 Quoted in Fred D. Pasley, *Muscling In* (New York, 1931), p. 258.
2 F. G. Madsen, *Transnational Organized Crime* (London, 2009). See also Mitchel P. Roth, 'Historical Overview of Transnational Crime', in *Handbook of Transnational Crime and Justice*, ed. Philip Reichel and Jay Albanese (Los Angeles, 2013), pp. 5–22.
3 Paul Lunde, *Organized Crime: An Inside Guide to the World's Most Successful Industry* (New York, 2004), p. 17.
4 Axel Klein, *Drugs and the World* (London, 2008), p. 15.
5 Ibid., p. 16.
6 Quoted in Steven B. Karch, *A Brief History of Cocaine* (Boca Raton, FL, 1998), p. 1.
7 Iain Gately, *Tobacco: A Cultural History of How an Exotic Plant Seduced Civilization* (New York, 2001), p. 3.
8 Ibid., pp. 85–6.
9 Ibid., p. 36.
10 Ibid., p. 43.
11 Quoted ibid., p. 50.
12 Ibid., p. 66.
13 Ibid.
14 Ibid., p. 86.
15 Jack Beeching, *The Chinese Opium Wars* (New York, 1976), pp. 76–7.
16 Barbara Hodgson, *Opium: A Portrait of the Heavenly Demon* (San Francisco, CA, 1999), p. 41.
17 In the late 1920s the notorious but brilliant Arnold Rothstein moved into the international narcotics trade and was soon sending representatives to Europe and Asia to purchase opium for the American market. Heroin, cocaine and morphine were still available from legitimate pharmaceutical companies in Europe, making it an important cog in the international traffic in narcotics.
18 Jill Jonnes, *Hep-cats, Narcs, and Pipe Dreams: A History of America's Romance with Illegal Drugs* (Baltimore, MD, 1999), p. 95.
19 Jeffrey Gettleman, 'What Tho. Jefferson Knew About Pirates', *New York Times*, 12 April 2009, p. WK4; Mike Mazzetti, 'Navy's Standoff with Pirates Shows U.S. Power has Limits', *New York Times*, 10 April 2009, p. A15.
20 N. Lewis and M. Reinhold, *Roman Civilization, Sourcebook I: The Republic* (New York, 1966), pp. 32–45.
21 C. H. Karraker, *Piracy was a Business* (Rindge, NH, 1953).
22 Quoted in P. Gosse, *The History of Piracy* (New York, 1932), p. 317.
23 Marcus Rediker, *Villains of All Nations: Atlantic Pirates in the Golden Age* (Boston,

MA, 2004), p. 83; John L. Anderson, 'Piracy and World History: An Economic Perspective on Maritime Predation', in *Bandits at Sea: A Pirate Reader*, ed. C. R. Pennell (New York, 2001), p. 82.

24 W. Blackstone, *Commentaries on the Laws of England of Public Wrongs* (Boston, MA, 1962).

25 Candice Millard, 'Pirates of the Caribbean: The Rise and Fall of Captain Morgan, Blackbeard and Other Swashbuckling Rogues', *New York Times Book Review*, 3 June 2007, p. 28.

26 David Cordingly, ed., *Pirates: Terror on the High Seas, from the Caribbean to the South China Sea* (North Dighton, MA, 2006), p. 7.

27 David Cordingly, *Under the Black Flag: The Romance and Reality of Life among Pirates* (New York, 1996) pp. 223–4.

28 Tar was usually on hand for executions along the docks since it was a popular preservative for protecting wooden hulls against the elements.

29 Cordingly, *Under the Black Flag*, 1996.

30 Jennifer Marx, 'Brethren of the Coast', in *Pirates*, ed. Cordingly, p. 123.

31 Angus Konstam, *Blackbeard: America's Most Notorious Pirate* (Hoboken, NJ, 2006), pp. 271–2.

32 Jennifer G. Marx, 'The Golden Age of Piracy', in *Pirates*, ed. Cordingly, pp. 100–123; 105–6.

33 Richard Zacks, *The Pirate Hunter: The True Story of Captain Kidd* (New York, 2002), p. 265.

34 Ibid

35 Ibid., pp. 38–57, quote p. 44–5.

36 Dian H. Murray, 'Chinese Pirates', in *Pirates*, ed. Cordingly, p. 214.

37 Alan L. Karras, *Smuggling: Contraband and Corruption in World History* (Lanham, MD, 2010), p. 20.

38 Ibid., p. 19.

39 Steven Pinker, *The Better Angels of Our Nature: Why Violence has Declined* (New York, 2011), p. 153; Pinker notes that the word 'slave' is rooted in the term 'Slav', which testifies to the fact that during the Middle Ages it was common to capture and enslave Slavic peoples.

40 Nayan Chanda, *Bound Together: How Traders, Preachers, Adventurers, and Warriors Shaped Globalization* (New Haven, CT, 2007), p. 215.

41 Pinker, *The Better Angels of Our Nature*, p. 153.

42 C. Martin Wilbur, *Slavery in China during the Former Han Dynasty, 206 BC–AD 25* (New York, 1967), p. 73.

43 Adam Hochschild, *Bury the Chains: Prophets and Rebels in the Fight to Free an Empire's Slaves* (New York, 2005), p. 293.

44 In *Slave Patrols: Law and Violence in Virginia and the Carolinas* (Cambridge, MA, 2001), Sally E. Hadden makes a strong case that these patrols should be considered as some of the first real advances in American policing. Over time they would be authorized to enforce laws against black literacy, trade and gambling as well.

45 Karen Farrington, *Dark Justice: A History of Punishment and Torture* (New York, 1996), p. 18.

46 Hochschild, *Bury the Chains*, p. 2.

47 Ibid.

48 Ibid., quote p. 2.

49 Nina Siegal, 'Recalling a Dark Secret of the Slave Trade, Buried in the Deep', *New York Times*, 1 July 2013, p. C3; James Walvin, *The Zong: A Massacre, The Law and the End of Slavery* (New Haven, CT, 2011).

50 David Eltis, 'The Abolition of the Slave Trade: Suppression', in Essays, http://abolition.nypl.org, accessed 6 September 2013.

51 Robin Law, 'Abolition and Imperialism: International Law and the British Suppression of the Atlantic Slave Trade', in *Abolitionism and Imperialism in Britain, Africa, and the Atlantic*, ed. Derek R. Peterson (Athens, OH, 2010), p. 165.

52 Pinker, *The Better Angels of Our Nature*, p. 157.

53 Peter Andreas and Ethan Nadelmann, *Policing the Globe: Criminalization and Crime Control in International Relations* (New York, 2006), p. 33.

54 C. Winick and P. M. Kinsie, *The Lively Commerce: Prostitution in the United States* (Chicago, IL, 1971), p. 269.

55 Pinker, *The Better Angels of Our Nature*, pp. 157–8.

56 Ibid., p. 157.

57 Julia Glotz, 'Fake Vodka and Basmati Rice Seized in UK Food Fraud Crackdown', *The Grocer*, 14 February 2014.

58 'Food Crime: A la Cartel', *The Economist*, 15 March 2014, p. 55.

59 The word 'tariff' offers mute testimony to the fact that trade had been internationalized centuries ago. Almost twelve centuries ago the Moors founded the town of Tarifa on the Spanish coast near Gibraltar. Here they inaugurated a system that revolutionized commercial trade. It was here that a predatory band of pirates established their headquarters from which they sailed out to stop merchant ships, demanding fixed tributes according to the scale of the merchandise they carried. Those who reluctantly paid what to them seemed to be simple extortion money soon attached the term 'tariff' in association with the Tarifa connection. This idea would be adapted by the governments of Europe who would establish a tariff system for imported goods well before the colonial New World era.

60 Neville Williams, *Contraband Cargoes: Seven Centuries of Smuggling* (Hamden, CT, 1961).

61 Andreas and Nadelmann, *Policing the Globe*, p. 22.

62 Ibid., p. 31.

7
The Face of Modern Murder

1 David M. Buss, *The Murderer Next Door: Why the Mind is Designed to Kill* (New York, 2005), pp. 9–10.

2 Ibid., p. 15.

3 Ibid., pp. 22–3.

4 Kimberly Davies, *Murder Book: Examining Homicide* (Upper Saddle River, NJ, 2008), p. 7.

5 Michael Newton, *The Encyclopedia of Serial Killers* (New York, 2006), p. 116.

6 Harold Schechter, *The Serial Killer Files: The Who, What, Where, How, and Why of the World's Most Terrifying Murders* (New York, 2013), p. 122. Peter Vronsky, *Serial Killers: The Method and Madness of Monsters* (New York, 2004), p. 61.

Richard von Krafft-Ebbing, *Pscychopathia Sexualis: With Special Reference to the Antipathic Sexual Instinct* (New York, 1965). The Austrian psychiatrist's name has since become synonymous with unnatural sexual urges. Working in Berlin's court system he dealt with a number of bizarre sexual crimes, including serial murder, which he called '*Lustmord*'.

7 Schechter, *The Serial Killer Files*, p. 122. See also Richard Wrangham and Dale Peterson, *Demonic Males: Apes and the Origins of Human Violence* (New York, 1996).

8 Davies, *Murder Book*, p. 164; Benjamin Radford, 'Child Abductions by Strangers Very Rare', http://news. discovery.com, 14 May 2013.

9 Of the various forms of multiple murder, or multicide, the best known is serial murder, which in the United States peaked in the 1990s. By definition, a serial killer murders three or more individuals in separate events, with cooling off periods between each victim that can last from days to years. Though the origin of the term is still debated, 'serial killer' entered the criminal lexicon in the 1980s. FBI agent Robert Ressler is among those credited with using the term. However, there is evidence it was used as early as the 1960s and 1970s in Europe. See Robert Ressler and Thomas Schachtman, *Whoever Fights Monsters: My Twenty Years Tracking Serial Killers for the FBI* (New York, 1993).

10 Eric W. Hickey, *Serial Murderers and their Victims* (Belmont, CA, 2010).

11 Vronsky, *Serial Killers*, p. 43.

12 Ibid., p. 45.

13 Maria Tatar, *The Hard Facts of Grimms' Fairy Tales* (Princeton, NJ, 2003), p. 50.

14 Ibid., p. 185.

15 Italo Calvino, *Italian Folktales: Selected and Retold by Italo Calvino* (New York, 1980), p. xxix.

16 Tatar, *The Hard Facts*, p. 190.

17 Joy Cameron, *Prisons and Punishment in Scotland from the Middle Ages to the Present* (Edinburgh, 1983), p. 11.

18 The Holy Roman Empire was not a state in the modern sense of the word – it had no civil service, standing army or regular income from taxation, but had enough influence to ensure the Carolina of 1532 was used as the basis of criminal law throughout its lands.

19 Patrick Geary, 'Judicial Violence and Torture in the Carolingian Empire', in *Law and the Illicit in Medieval Europe*, ed. Ruth Mazo Karras, Joel Kaye and E. Ann Matter (Philadelphia, PA, 2008), pp. 79–88.

20 Gamini Salgado, *The Elizabethan Underworld* (Gloucester, 1984), p. 89.

21 Ibid.

22 John Hale, *The Civilization of Europe in the Renaissance* (New York, 1994), p. 447.

23 Brian Fagan, *The Little Ice Age: How Climate Made History, 1300–1850* (New York, 2001), p. 91.

24 Hale, *The Civilization of Europe*, p. 448.

25 Catherine Orenstein, *Little Red Riding Hood Uncloaked: Sex, Morality, and the Evolution of a Fairy Tale* (New York, 2002), p. 95.

26 R.E.L. Masters and Eduard Lea, *Sex Crimes in History: Evolving Concepts of Sadism, Lust-Murder, and Necrophilia – from Ancient to Modern Times* (New York, 1964), p. 58.

27 Orenstein, *Little Red Riding Hood Uncloaked*, p. 97.

28 Mary K. Matossian, *Poisons of the Past: Molds, Epidemics and History* (New Haven, CT, 1989), pp. 11–12.

29 Orenstein, *Little Red Riding Hood Uncloaked*, p. 94.

30 Brad Steiger, *The Werewolf Book: The Encyclopedia of Shape-shifting Beings* (Canton, MI, 2011), pp. 171–2.

31 Orenstein, *Little Red Riding Hood Uncloaked*, pp. 87–9.

32 Caroline Oates, 'The Trial of a Teenage Werewolf, Bordeaux, 1603', in *Criminal Justice History: An International Annual*, IX, ed. Louis A. Knafla (London, 1988), pp. 1–29.

33 Ibid.

34 '"Vampire" of Tehran Flogged, then Hanged for Rape-slaying Spree', *Houston Chronicle*, 14 August 1997, p. 30A.

35 Radu Florescu and Raymond T. McNally, *Dracula: A Biography of Vlad the Impaler, 1431–1476* (New York, 1973), p. 170.

36 This semi-military and religious order was created in Rome in 1387 to further Catholic interests and crusades.

37 Florescu and McNally, *Dracula*, pp. 9–11.

38 Paul Barber, *Vampires, Burial, and Death: Folklore and Reality* (New Haven, CT, 1988), p. 2.

39 Trow, *Vlad the Impaler*, p. 3.

40 Florescu and McNally, *Dracula*, p. 78.

41 Raymond T. McNally and Radu Florescu, *In Search of Dracula* (New York, 1972), p. 114.

42 Manuela Dunn Mascetti, *Vampire: The Complete Guide to the World of the Undead* (New York, 1994), p. 143.

43 See for example, Eric W. Hickey, *Serial Murderers and their Victims* (Belmont, CA, 2010), pp. 319–21.

44 David Lester, *Serial Killers: The Insatiable Passion* (Philadelphia, PA, 1995), p. 125.

45 Steven A. Egger, *The Killers Among Us: An Examination of Serial Murder and its Investigation* (Upper Saddle River, NJ, 2002), p. 21.

46 Philip Beaufroy Barry, *Twenty Human Monsters: In Purple and in Rags from Caligula to Landru, AD 12–1922* (Philadelphia, PA, 1930), pp. 29–30.

47 Pieter Spierenburg, *A History of Murder: Personal Violence in Europe from the Middle Ages to the Present* (Cambridge, 2010), p. 196.

48 Barry, *Twenty Human Monsters*, p. 44.

49 Ibid., p. 48.

50 Ibid.

51 Leonard Wolf, *Bluebeard: The Life and Crime of Gilles de Rais* (New York, 1980), pp. 136–7.

52 A. L. Vincent and Clare Binns, *Gilles de Rais: The Original Bluebeard* (London, 1926), pp. 203–4.

53 Ibid., p. 187.

54 Peter Vronsky, *Female Serial Killers: How and Why Women Become Monsters* (New York, 2007).

55 Bernard Capp, 'Serial Killers in 17th-century England', *History Today*, XLVI (1996), pp. 21–6.

56 Vanessa McMahon, *Murder in Shakespeare's England* (London, 2004), pp. 225–6.

57 Vronsky, *Serial Killers*, p. 57.

58 Ibid.
59 Colin Wilson, *The History of Murder* (Edison, NJ, 2004), p. 410. Wilson notes that Tolstoy's 'perceptive analysis' work was written a year after the murders of Jack the Ripper.
60 Albrecht Keller, ed., *Hangman's Diary: Being the Journal of Master Franz Schmidt, Public Executioner of Nuremberg, 1571–1617* (London, 1929), pp. 112–13.
61 Ibid., p. 110.
62 Colin Wilson, 'Introduction', *Monsters of Weimer* (London, 1999), p. 5.
63 Vronsky, *Serial Killers*, p. 36.
64 Michael D. Kelleher and C. L. Kelleher, *Murder Most Rare: The Female Serial Killer* (Westport, CT, 1998), pp. 8–9.
65 Egger, *The Killers Among Us*, p. 71.
66 Hickey, *Serial Murderers and their Victims*, pp. 346–7.
67 Ibid.
68 Tshwarelo eseng Mogakane, 'Muti Killings Up Ahead of 2010?', 6 March 2010, *African Eye*, available at www.news24.com. Researchers interviewed 139 people, including social workers, nurses, fishermen, teachers and even radio presenters.
69 *Amok* originated from the Malay word *mengamuk*, which, roughly defined, means 'to make a furious and desperate charge'. See A. A. Hempel et al., 'Cross-cultural Review of Sudden Mass Assault by a Single Individual in the Oriental and Occidental Cultures', *Journal of Forensic Sciences*, XLV (2000), pp. 582–8.
70 Manuel L. Saint Martin, 'Running Amok: A Modern Perspective on a Culture-bound Syndrome', *Primary Care Companion Journal of Clinical Psychiatry*, 1 (1999), pp. 66–70, at www.ncbi.nlm.nih.gov.
71 Ibid.
72 Christopher H. Cantor, Paul E. Mullen and Philip A. Alpers, 'Mass Homicide: The Civil Massacre', *Journal of American Academy of Psychiatry and the Law*, 1 (2000), pp. 55–63.
73 Graham Chester, *Berserk!: Motiveless Random Massacres* (London, 1993), p. 5.
74 Al Cimino, *Spree Killers* (London, 2010).
75 James Buchanan Given, *Society and Homicide in Thirteenth-century England* (Stanford, CA, 1977), p. 1.
76 Ibid.
77 The author has made attempts to research serial homicide in China while teaching at a major police college there periodically over the past four years. However, faculty members were unable to come up with any figures on serial murder or other forms of multicide – still state secrets.

8
Crime and Punishment in a Post-colonial World

1 Michael Hor, 'Singapore's Innovations to Due Process', *Criminal Law Forum*, XII (2001), pp. 25–40.
2 Roger Lane, *Murder in America: A History* (Columbus, OH, 1997).
3 Adam Hochschild, *To End All Wars: A Story of Loyalty and Rebellion, 1914–1918* (New York, 2011), p. 355.
4 Barry Godrey and Graeme Dunstall, eds, *Crime and Empire, 1840–1940: Criminal Justice in Local and Global Context* (Cullompton, Devon, 2005).

5 Colin M. MacLachlan, *Criminal Justice in Eighteenth Century Mexico: A Study of the Tribunal of the Acordada* (Berkeley, CA, 1974), p. 28.

6 Ibid., p. 69.

7 Ricardo D. Salvatore and Carlos Aguirre, eds, *The Birth of the Penitentiary in Latin America: Essays on Criminology, Prison Reform, and Social Control, 1830–1940* (Austin, TX, 1996), p. 9.

8 Marcos Luiz Bretas, 'What the Eyes Can't See: Stories from Rio de Janeiro's Prisons', in *Birth of the Penitentiary*, ed. Salvatore and Aguirre, pp. 101–22.

9 Salvatore and Aguirre, eds, *Birth of the Penitentiary*, p. 9.

10 David Vincent Tropman, *Crime in Trinidad: Conflict and Control in a Plantation Society,* (Knoxville, TN, 1986), p. 138.

11 H. M. Kritzer, *Legal Systems of the World: A Political and Cultural Encyclopedia* (Santa Barbara, CA, 2002).

12 James Langton, 'Trinidad Welcomes Return of the Hangman', *Sunday Telegraph*, 30 May 1999, p. 28.

13 Larry Rohter, 'In the Caribbean, Support Growing for the Death Penalty', *New York Times International*, 4 October 1998, p. 10; Langton, 'Trinidad Welcomes Return of the Hangman', p. 28.

14 Florence Bernault, 'The Shadow of Rule: Colonial Power and Modern Punishment in Africa', in *Cultures of Confinement: A History of the Prison in Africa, Asia, and Latin America*, ed. Frank Dikötter and Ian Brown (Ithaca, NY, 2007), pp. 55–94.

15 Justin Willis, 'Thieves, Drunkards and Vagrants: Defining Crime in Colonial Mombasa, 1902–32', *in Policing the Empire: Government, Authority and control, 1830–1940*, ed. David M. Anderson and David Killingray (New York, 1991), pp. 219–35.

16 Bankole A. Cole, 'Postcolonial Systems', in *Policing across the World: Issues for the Twenty-first Century*, ed. Roy I. Mawby (New York, 1999), pp. 88–108.

17 Ibid.

18 Dior Konate, 'Ultimate Exclusion: Imprisoned Women in Senegal', in *A History of Prison and Confinement in Africa*, ed. Florence Bernault (Portsmouth, NH, 2003), pp. 155–64.

19 Bernault, 'The Shadow of Rule', pp. 55–94.

20 The British also ruled the colony briefly from 1795 to 1802.

21 Albie Sachs, *Justice in South Africa* (Berkeley, CA, 1973), p. 58. Biltong is a type of cured meat that originated in South Africa.

22 Ibid., p. 26.

23 Ibid., p. 27.

24 Ibid., p. 26.

25 Mitchel P. Roth, *Prisons and Prison Systems: A Global Encyclopedia* (Westport, CT, 2006), pp. 247–8.

26 Biko Agozino, 'Crime Criminology and Post-colonial Theory: Criminological Reflections on West Africa', in *Transnational and Comparative Criminology*, ed. James Sheptycki and Ali Wardak (London, 2005), pp. 117–34.

27 Leonard P. Shaidi, 'Traditional, Colonial and Present-day Administration of Criminal Justice', in *Criminology in Africa*, ed. Tibamanya mwene Mushanga (Rome, 1992), pp. 1–20.

28 Ibid., p. 2.

29 Ibid., p. 3.
30 Ibid.
31 Agozino, 'Crime Criminology and Post-colonial Theory', p. 126.
32 Alan Milner, *The Nigerian Penal System* (London, 1972), p. 297.
33 T. Asuni, 'Corrections in Nigeria', in *International Corrections*, ed. Robert J. Wicks and H.H.A. Cooper (Lexington, MA, 1979), pp. 163–81; Bernault, ed., *A History of Prison and Confinement in Africa*.
34 Bernault, ed., *A History of Prison and Confinement in Africa*, p. 23.
35 Ibid., p. 71.
36 Thierno Bah, 'Captivity and Incarceration in Nineteenth Century West Africa', in *A History of Prison and Confinement in Africa*, ed. Bernault, pp. 69–77.
37 David Arnold, 'India: The Contested Prison', in *Cultures of Confinement*, ed. Dikötter and Brown, pp. 147–84.
38 Ibid., p. 151.
39 Clare Anderson, 'Sepoys, Servants and Settlers: Convict Transportation in the Indian Ocean, 1787–1945', in *Cultures of Confinement*, ed. Dikötter and Brown, pp. 185–220.
40 Rudolph Peters, *Crime and Punishment in Islamic Law: Theory and Practice from the Sixteenth to the Twenty-first Century* (Cambridge 2005), p. 108.
41 Ibid., p. 118.
42 Ibid., p. 112.
43 Ibid., p. 114.
44 Ian Brown, 'South East Asia: Reform and the Colonial Prison', in *Cultures of Confinement*, ed. Dikötter and Brown, pp. 221–68.
45 Ibid., pp. 225–6.
46 Ibid., p. 227.
47 Hor, 'Singapore's Innovations to Due Process'.
48 Ibid. By some accounts the belief in 'the deterrent effect of harsh punishment is based more on what [one Senior Minister] experienced during the Japanese occupation of Singapore' during the Second World War than any empirical evidence.
49 Firouzeh Bahrampour, 'The Caning of Michael Fay: Can Singapore's Punishment Withstand the Scrutiny of International Law?', *American University International Law Review*, x (1995), pp. 1075–108.
50 'Judicial Corporal Punishment in South Africa: Section 3', www.corpun.com/jcpza2.htm, accessed 25 August 2014.
51 Thomas L. Friedman, 'Syria Scorecard', *New York Times*, 23 June 2013, p. 11.
52 Quoted in Peters, *Crime and Punishment in Islamic Law*, p. 74.
53 Ibid.
54 Quoted in Anthony Gorman, 'Regulation, Reform and Resistance in the Middle Eastern Prison', in *Cultures of Confinement*, ed. Dikötter and Brown, pp. 95–146.
55 Ibid.
56 Ibid., p. 142.
57 Ibid., p. 106.
58 Ibid., p. 117.
59 Peters, *Crime and Punishment in Islamic Law*, p. 150.
60 Ibid., pp. 151–2.
61 Quoted in Ali Wardak, 'Crime and Social Control in Saudi Arabia', in

Transnational and Comparative Criminology, ed. James Sheptycki and Ali Wardak (London, 2005), pp. 91–116.

62 Dick Polman, '"Not Proven" Verdict in Woman's Murder Sparks Scottish Rage', *Houston Chronicle*, 24 June 1993.

63 Ibid.

64 Peters, *Crime and Punishment in Islamic Law*, p. 162.

65 Ibid., p. 164.

66 Raymond Michalowski, 'Cuba', in *Crime and Punishment Around the World*, ed. Janet Stamatel and Hung-en Sung (Santa Barbara, CA, 2006), pp. 117–27.

67 Frank Dikötter, 'The Promise of Repentance: The Prison in Modern China', in *Cultures of Confinement*, ed. Dikötter and Brown, p. 295.

68 Ibid., p. 298.

69 Ibid., p. 299.

70 'In Bangladesh, Accountability Difficult', *Houston Chronicle*, 30 June 2013, p. A26.

71 Dikötter and Brown, eds, *Cultures of Confinement*, p. 6.

72 Pieter Spierenburg, *The Prison Experience: Disciplinary Institutions and their Inmates in Early Modern Europe* (New Brunswick, NJ, 1991); Dikötter and Brown, eds, *Cultures of Confinement*.

73 Dikötter and Brown, eds, *Cultures of Confinement*, p. 1.

9
Crime and Punishment in the Twenty-first Century

1 Marc Santora, 'In Hours, Thieves Took $45 Million in ATM Scheme', *New York Times*, 10 May 2013, pp. A1, A23.

2 Tom Standage, *The Victorian Internet: The Remarkable Story of the Telegraph and the Nineteenth Century's On-line Pioneers* (New York, 1999), p. 105.

3 Dan Bilefsky, 'Black Market for Body Parts Spreads among the Poor in Europe', *New York Times*, 29 June 2012, p. A8.

4 'Hung, Drawn and Quartered', *The Economist*, 10 November 2012, p. 62.

5 'Party Seems Over for Somali Pirates', *Houston Chronicle*, 26 September 2012, p. A11; Ben West, 'The Expensive, Diminishing Threat of Somali Piracy', *Stratfor Security Weekly*, 8 November 2012.

6 Dean E. Murphy, 'Justice as a Morality Play that Ends with Shame', *New York Times*, 3 June 2001.

7 'Justice With Our Own Hands: Lynching, Poverty, Witchcraft and the State in Mozambique', in *Globalizing Lynching History: Vigilantism and Extralegal Punishment from an International Perspective*, ed. Manfred Berg and Simon Wendt (New York, 2011), pp. 225–41.

8 Nina Shandler, *The Strange Case of Hellish Nell: The Story of Helen Duncan and the Witch Trial of World War II* (Cambridge, MA, 2006), p. 101.

9 Manfred Berg and Simon Wendt, 'Lynching from an International Perspective', in *Globalizing Lynching History*, ed. Berg and Wendt, pp. 1–18.

10 '2 Charged in Killing of Witch', *Houston Chronicle*, 19 February 2013, p. A6; 'UN Calls for End to Vigilante Violence, Use of Sorcery Law', *Houston Chronicle*, 9 February 2013; 'Papua New Guinea: PM Says he Wants to Repeal Sorcery Law', *New York Times*, 13 April 2013, p. A10.

11 'UN Calls for End to Vigilante Violence', p. A16.

12 Victoria Burnett, 'Spain Links Voodoo to Prostitution', *Houston Chronicle*, 23 May 2009, p. A25.

13 Louis Sahagun, 'Banishment Tests Not Only Criminals but their Tribe as Well', *New York Times*, 21 June 1995, p. A5; John Balzar, 'Two Teenagers are Banished to Islands', *Houston Chronicle*, 16 July 1994; Karen Alexander, 'Banishment Talks Sought – Judge Fears the Plan is Faltering', *Seattle Times*, 2 August 1995.

14 Ruth Gledhill, 'An Age-old Controversy', *The Times*, 22 June 2004, p. 3; 'Church to Hold Heresy Trials', *The Times*, 22 June 2004, p. 3.

15 Ethan Bronner, 'Adultery, an Ancient Crime that Remains on Many Books', *New York Times*, 15 November 2012, p. A12.

16 'Charges of Blasphemy', *Houston Chronicle*, 1 October 2012, p. A8.

17 'To Have and to Hold', *The Economist*, 17 November 2012, pp. 57–8.

18 Corrine Chin, 'Why Ugandan Gays who Fled to Kenya Still Feel they are in Danger', *Huffington Post*, 17 August 2014, www.huffingtonpost.com.

19 Nicholas Kulish, 'Ugandan President Says he will Sign Tough Antigay Measure', *New York Times*, 16 February 2014, p. 12.

20 'Nigeria's New Anti-gay Law Condemned by U.S. and Britain', *Houston Chronicle*, 14 January 2014, p. A7; 'Dozens Arrested for Being Gay in Northern Nigeria', *Houston Chronicle*, 15 January 2014, p. A12.

21 'Study: People Living Longer, but Often Sicker', *Houston Chronicle*, 14 December 2012, p. A10.

22 'Colorado's Dark Night', *The Economist*, 28 July 2012, p. 12.

23 'Violence Plays Big Role in Shorter U.S. Life Span', *Houston Chronicle*, 10 January 2013, p. A4.

24 'Not as Violent as You Thought', *The Economist*, 23 August 2008, p. 31.

25 'Once More to the Gallows', *The Economist*, 24 November 2012, p. 8.

26 'Mexicans Feeling Safer as Murders Dip', *Houston Chronicle*, 4 November 2012, p. A22.

27 'Look for the Silver Lining', *The Economist*, 19 July 2008, p. 47.

28 'Burn-out and Battle Fatigue', *The Economist*, 17 March 2012, pp. 43–4.

29 Jill Lepore, 'Rap Sheet: Why is American History so Murderous', *The New Yorker*, 9 November 2009, p. 79.

30 Ian Lovett, 'Executions are Suspended by Governor in Washington', *New York Times*, 12 February 2014, p. A12.

31 'Execution Nears 25 Minutes with New Drug Combo', *Houston Chronicle*, 17 January 2014, p. A6.

32 Fernanda Santos and John Schwartz, 'A Prolonged Execution in Arizona Leads to Temporary Halt', *New York Times*, 25 July 2014.

33 In June 2013 Texas put to death the 500th inmate since the return of the death penalty in 1976.

34 David T. Johnson, 'The Jolly Hangman, the Jailed Journalist, and the Decline of Singapore's Death Penalty', *Asian Journal of Criminology*, VIII (2013), pp. 41–9.

35 Mark Magnier, 'China's High Court to Review Death Sentences', *Los Angeles Times*, 1 November 2006, p. A5.

36 '80 People Reportedly Executed', *Houston Chronicle*, 12 November 2013.

37 'Once More to the Gallows', p. 45.

38 'Hanging About', *The Economist*, 6 October 2012, p. 48.

39 'An Executioner's Tale', *The Economist*, 11 February 2012, p. 43.
40 Dean E. Murphy, 'In Search of an Executioner – and Answers to Violence', *Houston Chronicle*, 15 March 1998, pp. A3, A16.
41 Andrew Buncombe, 'World Opinion Condemns U.S. for a "Savage" Execution', *The Independent*, 19 June 2010, p. 2; David Usborne, 'Debussy, Four Bullets, a Dozen Balloons: A Utah Firing Squad Does its Job', *The Independent*, 19 June 2010, pp. 2–3.
42 'State May Bring Back Gas Chamber for Executions', *Houston Chronicle*, 4 July 2013, p. A12.
43 Scott Christianson, *The Last Gasp: The Rise and Fall of the American Gas Chamber* (Berkeley, CA, 2010).
44 Quoted ibid., p. 121.
45 Ibid., p. 120.
46 Chavoret Jaruboon and Nicola Pierce, *The Last Executioner: Memoirs of Thailand's Last Prison Executioner* (Dunboyne, County Meath, 2006), p. 170.
47 Ibid., p. 85.
48 Ibid., p. 105.
49 Ibid., p. 115.
50 Andrew Jacobs, 'China Limits the Crimes Punishable By Death', *New York Times*, 30 July 2009.
51 Mark Magnier, 'Concerns Over Executions in China', *Los Angeles Times*, p. A1.
52 Craig S. Smith, 'Chinese Fight Crime with Torture and Execution', *New York Times*, 9 September 2001.
53 Magnier, 'Concerns over executions in China', p. A1.
54 'China Makes Ultimate Punishment Mobile', *USA Today*, 15 June 2006.
55 Ibid.
56 Amnesty International, *Issues and Facts: Stop Executions, China's Choice* (February 2008).
57 Keith Bradsher, 'China Moves to Stop Transplant of Organs after Executions', *New York Times*, 23 March 2012.
58 'Firing Squads May Take Place of Beheadings', *Houston Chronicle*, 11 March 2013, p. A9; 'Firing Squads Used for First Time', *Houston Chronicle*, 14 March 2013, p. 7.
59 Hiroko Tabuchi, 'Japan Gives Journalists a Tour of its Execution Chambers', *New York Times International*, 28 August 2010, p. A7.
60 'Crime and Clarity', *The Economist*, 1 September 2012, pp. 59–60.
61 Heather Timmons, Niharika Mandhana and Sruthi Gottpati, 'Six Accused in Rape Case in India are Charged with Murder', *New York Times*, 30 December 2012, p. 8; Gardiner Harris, 'Charges Filed Against 5 over Rape in New Delhi', *New York Times*, 4 January 2013.
62 Gardiner Harris and Hari Kumar, 'Village Council in India Accused of Ordering Rape', *New York Times*, 24 January 2014, p. A10.
63 Lydia Polgreen, 'Dropped Charges in Deadly Rape Provoke Fury in South Africa, and Pessimism', *New York Times*, 9 June 2012, pp. 6, 10.
64 Aida Alami, 'A Loophole for Rapists is Eliminated in Morocco', *New York Times*, 24 January 2014, p. A10.
65 'Activists Blast New Law on Domestic Abuse', *Houston Chronicle*, 12 February 2014.

66 Anne Applebaum, *Gulag: A History* (New York, 2003).

67 'Another Reprieve', *The Economist*, 21 April 2012, pp. 55–6.

68 David Hawk, *The Hidden Gulag*, 2nd edn (Washington, DC, 2012), pp. 148–53.

69 'Long Overdue', *The Economist*, 12 January 2013, p. 40; 'Beijing Overhauling Labor Camp System', *Houston Chronicle*, 8 January 2013.

70 Mark Franchetti, 'Living Hell of Russia's Death Row, *Sunday Times*, 6 August 2000, p. 26.

71 Andrew Kramer, 'Drug-resistant TB Grows in Russian Prison System', *Houston Chronicle*, 25 April 1999, p. 26A.

72 Raphael Minder, 'Crowding and Austerity Strain Portugal's Prisons', *New York Times*, 27 November 2012.

73 Dag Leonardsen, *Crime in Japan: Paradise Lost?* (New York, 2010), p. 123.

74 'Eastern Porridge', *The Economist*, 23 February 2013, p. 40.

75 Warren Hoge, 'Finland's Kindly Justice Keeps Jail Population Low', *International Herald Tribune*, 3 March 2003, p. 3.

76 Jim Webb, 'Why We Must Fix Our Prisons', *Parade*, 29 March 2009, pp. 4–5.

77 David Brooks, 'The Archipelago of Pain', *New York Times*, 7 March 2014, p. A21.

78 Ibid.

79 Lawrence M. Friedman, *American Law in the 20th Century* (New Haven, CT, 2002), p. 591.

80 'Forbidden Love in Mali: A Brutal Tale', *Houston Chronicle*, 10 February 2013.

81 Adam Nossiter, 'Harsh Justice is on the Rise in North Mali', *New York Times*, 28 December 2012.

82 Ibid.

83 'For Amputee, Islamic Radicals' Legacy Lingers', *Houston Chronicle*, 16 December 2013.

84 Mike Amoore, 'Lash and Burn: Taliban Vice Squads Returning to the Fray', *Sunday Times*, 24 June 2012.

85 John Braithwaite, *Restorative Justice and Responsive Regulation* (Oxford, 2002), pp. 3–5.

86 Richard Delgado, 'Goodbye to Hammurabi: Analyzing the Atavistic Appeal of Restorative Justice', *Stanford Law Review*, LII (2000), pp. 751–75;

87 Theo Gavrielides, 'Restorative Justice – The Perplexing Concept: Conceptual Fault-lines and Power Battles within the Restorative Justice Movement', *Criminology and Criminal Justice*, VIII (2008), pp. 165–83.

88 Mark S. Umbreit and Jean Greenwood, 'National Survey of Victim–Offender Mediation Programs in the United States', *Mediation Quarterly*, XVI (1999), pp. 235–51.

89 'Pig Barns Cooled as Inmates, Staff Sweat', *Houston Chronicle*, 18 August 2013.

90 Jesse Wegman, 'Climbing Out of the Hole', *New York Times*, 21 July 2013.

91 John K. Cooley, *Currency Wars: How Forged Money is the New Weapon of Mass Destruction* (New York, 2008).

92 Stephen Mihm, A *Nation of Counterfeiters: Capitalists, Con Men, and the Making of the United States* (Cambridge, 2007).

93 Mamta Badkar, '22 Chinese People who were Handed the Death Sentence for White Collar Crime', *Business Insider*, 15 July 2013.

94 Loansharking remained a mainstay for American crime syndicates after

Prohibition ended in 1933. Illegal money lending remains a multi-billion-dollar industry, allowing drug dealers and persons with bad credit to obtain illegal loans, paying extortionate interest rates higher than the maximum allowed by law.

95 Jason Zweig, 'Should Crimes of Capital Get Capital Punishment'?, *Wall Street Journal*, 27 July 2012; G. Geoffrey Booth and Sanders S. Chang, 'Domestic Exchange Rate Determination in Early Renaissance Florence', *Journal of Empirical Finance* (2008), pp. 131–44.

96 George Packer, 'The Megacity: Decoding the Chaos of Lagos', *New Yorker*, 13 November 2006, p. 72.

97 Michelle Alexander, *The New Jim Crow: Mass Incarceration in the Age of Colorblindness* (New York, 2012).

98 Jim Yardley, 'A Village Rape Shatters a Family, and India's Traditional Silence', *New York Times*, 28 October 2012.

99 David T. Johnson, 'The Jolly Hangman, the Jailed Journalist, and the Decline of Singapore's Death Penalty', *Asian Criminology* (2013), p. 55.

100 'Towards a Ceasefire', *The Economist*, 23 February 2013, pp. 57–9.

101 'Tipsy Taboo', *The Economist*, 16 August 2012, p. 55.

102 Ibid.

103 Steven Pinker, *The Better Angels of Our Nature: Why Violence has Declined* (New York, 2011).

SELECT BIBLIOGRAPHY

Abu-Zahra, M., *Crime and Punishment in Islamic Jurisprudence* (Cairo, 1950)

Alexander, M., *The New Jim Crow: Mass Incarceration in the Age of Colorblindness* (New York, 2012)

Andreas, Peter, and Ethan Nadelmann, *Policing the Globe: Criminalization and Crime Control in International Relations* (New York, 2006)

Applebaum, Anne, *Gulag: A History* (New York, 2003)

Ash, Arty, and Julius E. Day, *Immortal Turpin: A Well-documented Biography of the Greatest 'Gentleman of the Road'* (London, 1948)

Bauman, Richard A., *Crime and Punishment in Ancient Rome* (London, 1996)

Beccaria, Cesare, *On Crimes and Punishments* [1764], trans. Henry Paolucci (Indianapolis, IN, 1963)

Bellamy, John, *Crime and Public Order in England in the Later Middle Ages* (London, 1973)

Berg, M., and S. Wendt, eds, *Globalizing Lynching History: Vigilantism and Extralegal Punishment from an International Perspective* (New York, 2011)

Bernault, Florence, ed., *A History of Prison and Confinement in Africa* (Portsmouth, NH, 2003)

Bloch, Marc, *Feudal Society* (Chicago, IL, 1961)

Blum, Jerome, *Lord and Peasant in Russia: From the Ninth to the Nineteenth Century* (Princeton, NJ, 1972)

Bodde, Derk, and Clarence Morris, *Law in Imperial China* (Cambridge, MA, 1967)

Brackett, John K., *Criminal Justice and Crime in Late Renaissance Florence, 1537–1609* (Cambridge, 1992)

Brook, Timothy; Jérôme Bourgon and Gregory Blue, *Death by a Thousand Cuts* (Cambridge, MA, 2008)

Brown, Richard Maxwell, *No Duty to Retreat* (Norman, OK, 1994)

Burroughs, Bryan, *Public Enemies: America's Greatest Crime Wave and the Birth of the FBI, 1933–1934* (New York, 2004)

Cameron, Joy, *Prisons and Punishments in Scotland from the Middle Ages to the Present* (Edinburgh, 1983)

Chandler, Billy Jaynes, *The Bandit King: Lampião of Brazil* (College Station, TX, 1978)

Christianson, Scott, *With Liberty for Some: 500 Years of Imprisonment in America* (Boston, MA, 1998)

Cordingly, David, ed., *Pirates: Terror on the High Seas from the Caribbean to the South China Sea* (North Dighton, MA, 2006)

Coulbourn, R., ed., *Feudalism in History* (Princeton, NJ, 1956)

Crummey, Donald., ed., *Banditry, Rebellion and Social Protest in Africa* (London, 1986)

Dean, Trevor, *Crime in Medieval Europe, 1200–1550* (Harlow, 2001)

DeFord, Miriam Allen, *Stone Walls: Prisons from Fetter to Furloughs* (Philadelphia, PA, 1962)

Dikötter, Frank, *Crime, Punishment, and the Prison in Modern China, 1895–1949* (New York, 2002)

——, and Ian Brown, eds, *Cultures of Confinement: A History of the Prison in Africa, Asia, and Latin America* (Ithaca, NY, 2007)

Drapkin, Israel, *Crime and Punishment in the Ancient World* (Lexington, MA, 1989)

Drew, Katherine Fischer, *Laws of the Salian Franks* (Philadelphia, PA, 1991)

Egmond, Florike, *Underworlds: Organised Crime in the Netherlands, 1650–1800* (Cambridge, 1993)

Elias, Norbert, *The Civilizing Process* (New York, 1982)

Evans, Richard J., *Rituals of Retribution: Capital Punishment in Germany, 1600–1987* (London, 1996)

Guilaine, Jean, and Jean Zammit, *The Origins of War: Violence in Prehistory* (Oxford, 2005)

Farris, William Wayne, *Japan's Medieval Population: Famine, Fertility, and Warfare in a Transformative Age* (Honolulu, HI, 2006)

Fijnaut, Cyrille, and Letizia Paoli, eds, *Organised Crime in Europe* (Dordrecht, 2004)

Foucault, Michel, *Discipline and Punish: The Birth of the Prison*, trans. Alan Sheridan (New York, 1977)

Friedman, Lawrence M., *Crime and Punishment in American History* (New York, 1993)

Frierson, Cathy, 'Crime and Punishment in the Russian Village: Rural Concepts of Criminality at the End of the Nineteenth Century, *Slavic Review*, XLVI (1987), pp. 55–69

Gately, Iain, *Tobacco: A Cultural History of How an Exotic Plant Seduced Civilization* (New York, 2001)

Gibson, Ian, *English Vice: Beating, Sex and Shame in Victorian England and After* (London, 1978)

Given, James Buchanan, *Society and Homicide in Thirteenth-century England* (Stanford, CA, 1977)

Hanawalt, Barbara A., *Crime and Conflict in English Communities, 1300–1348* (Cambridge, MA, 1979)

——, *'Of Good and Ill Repute': Gender and Social Control in Medieval England* (New York, 1998)

Hawk, David, *The Hidden Gulag* (Washington, DC, 2012)

Hengel, Martin, *Crucifixion* (Philadelphia, PA, 1978)

Hinckeldey, Christoph, *Criminal Justice through the Ages: From Divine Judgment to Modern German Legislation*, trans. John Fosberry (Rothenburg, 1981)

Hobsbawm, Eric, *Social Bandits and Primitive Rebels* (Glencoe, IL, 1960)

Hopwood, Keith, ed., *Organised Crime in Antiquity* (Swansea, 2009)

Howard, D. L., *John Howard: Prison Reformer* (New York, 1958)

Huang Liu-Hung, *A Complete Book Concerning Happiness and Benevolence: A Manual for Local Magistrates in Seventeenth-century China* [1699], trans. Djang Chu (Tucson, AZ, 1984)

Hughes, Robert, *The Fatal Shore: The Epic of Australia's Founding* (New York, 1987)

Ignatieff, Michael, *A Just Measure of Pain: The Penitentiary in the Industrial Revolution, 1750–1850* (New York, 1978)

Jaruboon, Chavoret, and Nicola Pierce, *The Last Executioner: Memoirs of Thailand's Last Prison Executioner* (Dunboyne, County Meath, 2006)

Jatar, D. P., and M. Z. Khan, *The Problem of Dacoity in Bundelkhand and the Chambal Valley* (New Delhi, 1980)

Jay, Mike, *The Unfortunate Colonel Despard: The Tragic Story of the Last Man Condemned to be Hung, Drawn and Quartered* (New York, 2005)

Johnson, David T., 'The Jolly Hangman, the Jailed Journalist, and the Decline of Singapore's Death Penalty', *Asia Journal of Criminology*, VIII (2013), pp. 41–9

Johnston, Norman, *Eastern State Penitentiary: A Crucible of Good Intentions* (Philadelphia, PA, 1994)

——, *Forms of Constraint: A History of Prison Architecture* (Urbana, IL, 2000)

Kadri, Sadakat, *The Trial: A History from Socrates to O. J. Simpson* (New York, 2006)

Karch, S. B., *A Brief History of Cocaine* (Boca Raton, FL, 1998)

Karras, Alan L., *Smuggling: Contraband and Corruption in World History* (Lanham, MD, 2010)

Karras, R. M., J. Kaye and E. A. Matter, eds, *Law and the Illicit in Medieval Europe* (Philadelphia, PA, 2008)

Keller, A., ed., *Hangman's Diary: Being the Journal of Master Franz Schmidt, Public Executioner of Nuremberg, 1571–1617*, trans. C. Calvert and A. W. Gruner (London, 1928)

Kennan, George, *Siberia and the Exile System* (Chicago, IL, 1958)

Kropotkin, Peter, *In Russian and French Prisons* (London, 1887)

Leonardsen, D., *Crime in Japan: Paradise Lost?* (New York, 2010)

Levenson, Thomas, *Newton and the Counterfeiter: The Unknown Detective Career of the World's Greatest Scientist* (Boston, MA, 2009)

Li Chi: Book of Rites, trans. James Legge (New York, 1967)

López-Burgos, María Antonia, *Travelling through a Land of Bandits: British Travellers in Andalusia, 1809–1893* (Malaga, 2002)

MacDowell, Douglas. M., *Athenian Homicide Law in the Age of the Orators* (Manchester, 1999)

Macfarlane, Alan, *The Justice and the Mare's Ale* (Oxford, 1981)

McKnight, Brian E., *Law and Order in Sung China* (Cambridge, 1992)

MacLachlan, Colin M., *Criminal Justice in Eighteenth-century Mexico: A Study of the Tribunal of the Accordada* (Berkeley, CA, 1974)

McLynn, Frank, *Crime and Punishment in Eighteenth-century England* (London, 1989)

McMahon, Vanessa, *Murder in Shakespeare's England* (London, 2004)

Masters, R.E.L., and E. Lea, *Sex Crimes in History: Evolving Concepts of Sadism, Lust-Murder, and Necrophilia – from Ancient to Modern Times* (New York, 1964)

Morris, Norval, and David J. Rothman, eds, *The Oxford History of the Prison: The Practice of Punishment in Western Society* (New York, 1995)

Moxham, Roy, *Outlaw: India's Bandit Queen and Me* (London, 2010)

Ooms, H., *Tokugawa Ideology: Early Constructs, 1570–1680* (Princeton, NJ, 1985)

Peters, Rudolph, *Crime and Punishment in Islamic Law: Theory and Practice from the Sixteenth to the Twenty-first Century* (Cambridge, 2005)

Pike, Ruth, *Penal Servitude in Early Modern Spain* (Madison, WI, 1983)

Pinker, Steven, *The Better Angels of Our Nature: Why Violence has Declined* (New York, 2011)

Pollock, F., and F. W. Maitland, *The History of English Law: Before the Time of Edward I* (Cambridge, 1978)

Rediker, Marcus, *Villains of All Nations: Atlantic Pirates in the Golden Age* (Boston, MA, 2004)

Reid, John Philip, *A Law of Blood: The Primitive Law of the Cherokee Nations* (New York, 1970)

Robinson, O. F., *The Criminal Law of Ancient Rome* (London, 1995)

Roper, Lyndal, *Witch Craze: Terror and Fantasy in Baroque Germany* (New Haven, CT, 2004)

Roth, Randolph, *American Homicide* (Cambridge, MA, 2009)

Rothman, David J., *The Discovery of the Asylum: Social Order and Disorder in the New Republic* (Boston, MA, 1971)

Rushby, Kevin, *Children of Kali* (New York, 2002)

Salgado, Gamini, *The Elizabethan Underworld* (Gloucester, 1984)

Salvatore, Ricardo D., and Carlos Aguirre, eds, *The Birth of the Penitentiary in Latin America: Essays on Criminology, Prison Reform, and Social Control, 1830–1940* (Austin, TX, 1996)

Sansom, George, *A History of Japan, 1334–1615* (Tokyo, 1963)

Schreiber, Mark, *The Dark Side: Infamous Japanese Crimes and Criminals* (Tokyo, 2001)

Sellin, J. Thorsten, *Slavery and the Penal System* (New York, 1976)

Semerdjian, Elyse, *Off the Straight Path: Illicit Sex, Law and Community in Ottoman Aleppo* (Syracuse, NY, 2008)

Sen, Satadru, *Disciplining Punishment: Colonialism and Convict Society in the Andaman Islands* (New York, 2000)

Shaw, A.G.L., *Convicts and the Colonies: A Study of Penal Transportation from Great Britain and Ireland to Australia and Other Parts of the British Empire* (London, 1966)

Souyri, Pierre François, *The World Turned Upside Down: Medieval Japanese Society*, trans. Käthe Roth (New York, 2001)

Spierenburg, Pieter, *The Broken Spell: A Cultural and Anthropological History of Preindustrial Europe* (New Brunswick, NJ, and London, 1991)

——, *The Prison Experience: Disciplinary Institutions and their Inmates in Early Modern Europe* (New Brunswick, NJ, 1991)

——, *A History of Murder: Personal Violence in Europe from the Middle Ages to the Present* (Cambridge, 2010)

Sturm, M., *Vice in a Vicious Society: Crime and Convicts in Mid-nineteenth-century New South Wales* (St Lucia, Queensland, 1983)

Tatar, Maria, *The Hard Facts of Grimms' Fairy Tales* (Princeton, NJ, 2003)

Taylor, Philip Meadows, *Confessions of a Thug* (Oxford, 1998)

Trow, M. J., *Vlad the Impaler: In Search of the Real Dracula* (London, 2006)

Tydlesley, Joyce, *Judgement of the Pharaoh: Crime and Punishment in Ancient Egypt* (London, 2002)

Vincent, A. L., and C. Binns, *Gilles de Rais: The Original Bluebeard* (London, 1926)

Vronsky, P., *Female Serial Killers: How and Why Women Become Monsters* (New York, 2007)

——, *Serial Killers: The Method and Madness of Monsters* (New York, 2004)

Weatherford, Jack, *Genghis Kahn and the Making of the Modern World* (New York, 2004)

Wilson, Colin, *Monsters of Weimar* (London, 1999)
Wolf, Leonard, *Bluebeard: The Life and Crimes of Gilles de Rais* (New York, 1980)
Wu, Hongda Harry, *Laogai: The Chinese Gulag* (Boulder, co, 1992)

ACKNOWLEDGEMENTS

No author writes a book alone. Every work of scholarship is built on the backs of those who have devoted their lives to sharing their knowledge and research with those who would follow in their tracks, and I owe a debt of gratitude to the generations of scholars who have helped make this book possible. I especially want to thank Michael Leaman, publisher at Reaktion Books, for bringing this project to me several years ago. A global history of crime and punishment you say? Who would be foolish enough to bite that one off? Well, I did, and now realize why this project has never been attempted before – but I gave it my best. I would like to thank the reviewers for providing timely and helpful advice and suggestions for making this a better manuscript. My 89-year-old cousin-several-times-removed, Ida Goldapple, formerly of the Old Vic, allowed me to trespass in her computer room to work on my page proofs in August 2014 despite the fact I always left her computer on when I finished each evening. Finally, I would never have completed this book without the constant support of my wife, Ines Papandrea, and children, Eric and Rusty. I am sure Ines hopes she will now hear no more about crucifixion, beheadings and amputations – that is, at least for the short term.

INDEX